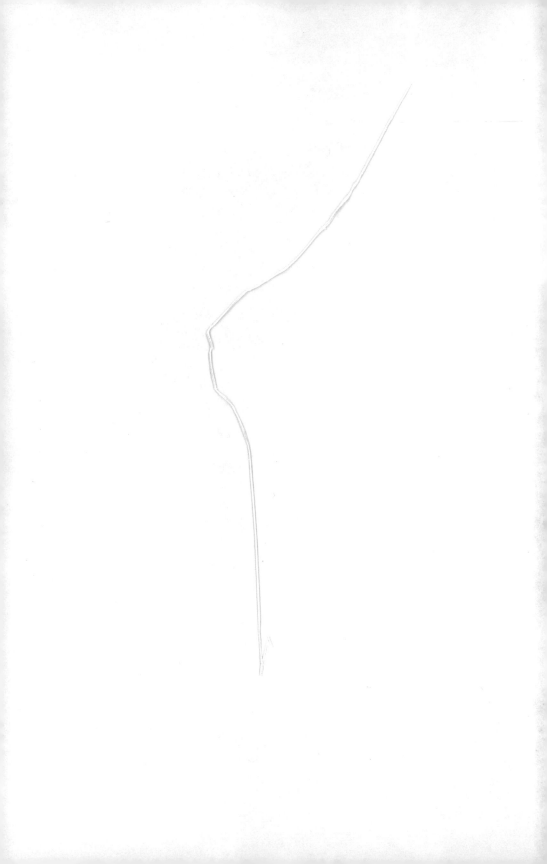

AMERICAN WOMEN PHILOSOPHERS 1650-1930

Six Exemplary Thinkers

AMERICAN WOMEN PHILOSOPHERS 1650-1930

Six Exemplary Thinkers

Edited by

Therese Boos Dykeman

The Edwin Mellen Press
Lewiston/Queenston/Lampeter

Library of Congress Cataloging-in-Publication Data

American women philosophers : 1650-1930 : six exemplary thinkers /
  edited by Therese Boos Dykeman.
     p.   cm.
    Includes bibliographical references and index.
    ISBN 0-7734-9266-6
    1. Philosophy, American. 2. Women philosophers--United States.
I. Dykeman, Therese Boos.
B850.A44 1993
191'.082--dc20   93-9573
                                                                  CIP

A CIP catalog record for this book
is available from the British Library.

The Edwin Mellen Press   The Edwin Mellen Press
Box 450   Box 67
Lewiston, New York   Queenston, Ontario
USA 14092   CANADA L0S 1L0

Edwin Mellen Press, Ltd.
Lampeter, Dyfed, Wales
UNITED KINGDOM SA48 7DY

Printed in the United States of America

To my mother and grandmothers
who did not have access to
the works of these women

Alvina Marek Boos
Alvina Bakula Marek
Theresa Bruning Boos

Philosophy
Tell me not that she is silent,
Tell me not that she is dead.

Julia R. Anagnos
Philosophiae Quaester
1895

The Philosopher, who would wish to mingle
the joys of friendship...complains that the sex
are destitute of every idea.

William Alexander, M.D.
**The History of Women
from   Earliest Antiquity to
the Present Time**, 1732.

Contents

Foreword

This book is designed to introduce colleagues and students to the study of American women philosophers. It is a beginning--one that I hope will stimulate further research and investigation by the whole philosophical community: students, teachers, and other inquirers. It may be that a number of women who have contributed even greater accomplishments to philosophy in America from colonial times to the beginnings of the twentieth century have not been included in this anthology. Perhaps the texts of such philosophers will one day be brought to the light for careful exposition and analysis. Ongoing research promises that discoveries of women philosophers will arise from today's growing concern for the recovery of the intellectual labor of American women.

The heritage of philosophy has deprived women one generation after another. The serious consequences are that not having known or read or digested women's words along with those of Jonathan Edwards, Thomas Jefferson, Abraham Lincoln and John Dewey, no assimilation into the vocabulary of allusion has been allowed to take place, and unnecessary ignorance has been perpetuated. The loss in the silence of these mentors--who spoke so eloquently--is a loss forever to those generations already gone. The loss in the study of philosophy to the utilitarianism of Jeremy Bentham without Frances Wright, to American ethical theory without Anne Bradstreet, to American political theory without Judith Sargent Murray and Mercy Otis Warren, to aesthetics without Ednah Dow Cheney, to the "classical American" philosophy of William James and Josiah Royce without Mary Whiton Calkins--is unredeemable for the past. But now, with this anthology and with works like it, the legacy of deprivation will come to an end. The example of these women's lives, their courage to speak, and the intelligence of what they had to say, will be available to succeeding generations. Our philosophical tradition can be made whole by the contributions of American women, and this is the aim of my book.

This is not a history book, even as it presents exemplars: from the Puritan Age, with Anne Bradstreet; from the Age of the American Revolution, with Mercy Otis Warren; from the American Age of Reason, with Judith Sargent Murray; from the Jacksonian Age, with Frances Wright; from the time of the Civil War, with Ednah Dow Cheney; and from then to the end of World War I, with Mary Whiton Calkins. This work barely discusses how each of these women portrays and defines the historical characterizations of the standard interpretation of her period in our history. The intention here is to invite reflection and investigation among students, teachers and inquirers.

This is not a complete survey of the schools of American philosophy, although examples of Cambridge Neoplatonism in the colonies with Anne Bradstreet; the British Empiricism of Locke, Berkeley and Hume at the time of the War for Independence with Mercy Otis Warren; the European Enlightenment of the late Eighteenth Century with Judith Sargent Murray; Bentham's newly developing utilitarianism with Frances Wright; the apex of American Transcendentalism with Ednah Dow Cheney; and American Idealism represented by Mary Whiton Calkins are all present. However, so much is not present: the American pietism of Benjamin Franklin and Thomas Jefferson, the empiricism of Calvinists like Jonathan Edwards, the midwestern Platonism of Hiram K. Jones and Thomas More Johnson, the accomplishments of William Torrey Harris and the St. Louis Hegelians, the evolution of consciousness with Chauncey Wright and John Fiske, the birth of American pragmatism with C.S. Pierce and William James. These traditions each have women philosophers. Surely a full anthology of American philosophy would contain selections of contributions to each important philosophical school by American women. Once again this work invites the philosophical community to make such investigations, to recover and discover the philosophical treasures that would make a more complete anthology possible.

Nevertheless, to study this volume will deepen your understanding of the forces, often hitherto unnoticed, which have formed American culture and civilization, and which continue to do so today. These treasures of America are allowed to speak for themselves for the most part, even as they are introduced, in biographies, bibliographies and suggestive interpretation by this book. The women chosen are thought to be representative rather than inclusive.

Bibliographies of each philosopher, with selected secondary literature, are present at the end of the individual chapters. Anne Bradstreet is the only philosopher in this volume of whom independent and definitive bibliographical studies have been published. The bibliographies of primary sources published in this book on Mercy Otis Warren, Judith Sargent Murray, Francis Wright, Ednah Dow Cheney, and Mary Whiton Calkins are the most complete presently available in print. Each of these women deserves a bibliography like the comprehensive **Anne Bradstreet: A Reference Guide** compiled by Raymond F. Dolle.

Acknowledgements

King J. Dykeman, author of the section on Mary Whiton Calkins, contributed to the formulation of this entire text. He contributed especially to the sections on Anne Bradstreet and Mercy Otis Warren. More important was his enthusiasm for the project and his encouragement to my sometimes flagging soul. The Center for Independent Study at Yale Station in New Haven has been supportive of this project in a variety of ways. The librarians at Yale and Fairfield University, too, have lent their time, energy and expertise. Also, for substantial assistance, I would like to thank Michael Cioffi of Fairfield University. I am grateful to these people, for without their efforts, this book could never have been written.

Illustrations

Anne Bradstreet p. 15
Mercy Otis Warren p. 61
Judith Sargent Murray p. 107
Frances Wright p. 189
Ednah Dow Cheney p. 261
Mary Whiton Calkins p. 329

Sources for works included here:

Anne Bradstreet: "Meditations Divine and Moral," **The Works of Anne Bradstreet in Prose and Verse** edited by John Harvard Ellis, Charleston: Cutter, 1867.

Mercy Otis Warren: **Observations on the New Constitution, and on the Federal and State Conventions** by a Columbian Patriot, Boston: 1788.

Judith Sargent Murray: "Equality of the Sexes," **Massachusetts Magazine,** 1790 (April:132-35, March:223-26). "Observations on Female Abilities," **The Gleaner**: A Miscellaneous Production, Vol.III, Boston: I. Thomas and E.T. Andrews, 1798:188-224.

Frances Wright: "Nature of Knowledge" and "Free Inquiry," **Course of Popular Lectures,** New York: Office of Free Enquirer, 1829:4-20, 21-37.

Ednah Dow Cheney: "Art," **Gleanings in the Fields of Art**, Boston: Lee and Shepard, 1881:9-32. "Reign of Women," **Reminiscences of Ednah Dow Cheney**, Boston: Lee and Shepard, 1902:223-236.

Mary Whiton Calkins: "The Just Man," **The Good Man and the Good: Introduction to Ethics**, New York: Macmillan, 1921:119-140. "Self and Soul," **Philosophical Review** 17(January 1908:272-280).

1

Introduction

She could not hold back a spirit all aflame.

Gravestone epitaph for
Marie le Jars de Gournay
1565-1645.

Hence it comes that in after times the reader of history finds no more record of our names throughout a long period than a ship leaves traces of her course through the waves...

Anna Maria van Schurman
1607-1678.

Histories are writ by them; they recount each other's great exploits

Mary Astell
1666-1731.

Twentieth century women philosophers exist. Women teach philosophy, write philosophy, attend conferences on philosophy and some enjoy world-wide fame as important philosophers.[1] Did these women evolve from the rib of men's philosophy? Did they spring full blown from a Jove's philosophical thinking? It would seem, as current scholarship suggests, that present day women philosophers are continuing rather than beginning the work of women philosophers, and that there is, indeed, a tradition of philosophy by women within and without the traditional history of philosophy.

The question is, where are these deepest workings of women's minds, their philosophical roots? The search for these roots, taken on by the curious scholar,

1

century after century, has culminated each time, with little more than a compilation of names from Aspasia forward, and that record, always incomplete.[2] The lists confirm the exhilarating notion of the existence of women writers, artists, thinkers, but the verifiable evidence is in their works, many of which are still interred or irretrievably lost. Hence, the task to find and make available more works of women's minds continues, though serious effort is simultaneously being given to those works already at hand.

Many of the current debates in femininst studies in philosophy and political science are not explictly treated in this text. This text seeks to address a wider audience, and it aims to present the women philosophers and their works in the milieu of traditional modern philosophy. The problem is that while controversies deepen, many women's texts remain unavailable. "Standpoint" theory, i.e. the view of history from a feminist perspective, and feminist postmodernism and post-structuralism continue to focus on male philosophical works and traditional texts in modern philosophy which exclude many important works by women.

Thus this book presents an opportunity for contemporary feminists to reflect on the texts of philosophy written by American women authors. Perhaps their investigation will reveal, for example, that Frances Wright's philosophy adumbrates the very features Nancy Hartsock believes a new theory of power might offer.[3] To ensure that efforts of this kind are possible, previously unavailable works such as that of Frances Wright are presented here not with any current theory in mind but rather in light of the tradition of modern philosophy.

Here the student of philosophy is offered whole philosophical works when that choice was possible, and also, when possible, works which present feminist claims. (This "feminist" philosophy presents an American tradition in itself that is integral to the philosophical canon.[4]) Such work affords textual proof that a philosophical tradition of American women from the seventeenth to the twentieth century does indeed exist. My hope is that once studied in accord with recent scholarship, this philosophical tradition will in succeeding decades make possible a more complete and a better history of American philosophy.

When I began, the project of seeking textual evidence for a woman's philosophical tradition in the United States from the seventeenth century forward appeared feasible. It did not seem possible that there had been no American women who could accomplish a serious, sustained, systematic idea. Was it possible, that because education for women was put off in this country for two centuries, that women had produced no history, no tradition, no contributions in philosophy? Perhaps, there were women omitted from the lists of philosophers, or women considered as poets, historians, or idealists who were philosophers as well but not claimed as such; or, perhaps there were those women documented as philosophers in their time but through neglect were excluded from the acknowledged philosophical tradition. My discovery was that all three probabilities were, in fact, true.

Women's Philosophy Made Visible

It happened that because women's philosophic seeds were sown through the centuries on the hard ground of disbelief, disbelief in women and what they had to say, the fruit of these seeds appear invisible, preserving "woman philosopher," until well into the twentieth century, an oxymoron. How? Seventeenth century Anne Bradstreet recognized as a poet has never before been acknowledged as a moral philosopher. Mercy Otis Warren, eventually noted as an historian, has never before been noted as political philosopher. Her younger eighteenth century compatriot, Judith Sargent Murray regarded, but not seriously, as an essayist and feminist, has never before been accepted as a feminist philosopher. Frances Wright, endorsed as radical and pioneer, has never before been authenticated as philosophical innovator. Nineteenth century Ednah Dow Cheney's transcendentalism has been minimalized, her theories of aesthetics and feminism totally neglected. Lastly, turn of the century Mary Whiton Calkin's once widely published work has been buried with her bones, despite the fact that Calkins while professor at Wellesley reigned as president of both the American Philosophical Association and the American Psychological Association.

It was some time into the search, that I began to see the unacknowledged tradition of philosophy by American women. This did not occur until I began to reread and re-examine recognized works obscured by labels: "unimportant," "third-rate," "idealist," or by categories: "essayist," "historian," and "poet" for myself and to discover new works by obscure women, that I found testimony of a

3

tradition not only of philosophy but of philosophy with particular concerns for these American women philosophers.

The very word "philosophy" historically implies "male philosophy," i.e. philosophy written by, carried forward by, taught by, studied by and therefore existing only from the point of view of male experience. So no philosophy was ever categorized as "masculin-ist." However, the lack of women representation has been noted throughout much of history, and when the issue was also the focus, categorized as "femin-ist" philosophy.

Perhaps the reader will find this discussion about what was taken for granted redundant. But having accepted with varying degrees of consciousness, the partial male tradition as the whole, the majority of students of philosophy still have not been made aware of or have disregarded the feminist arguments through the centuries. Nevertheless, arguments have been made. But having to make these arguments has been a burden for women philosophers who have oftentimes been compelled to address the issue of feminist philosophy in addition to their work on other philosophical issues.

Now, such effort is evident in the formation of newer organizations within the American philosophical community, namely, the Society of Women In Philosophy and the more recently formed (1987) Society for the Study of Women Philosophers, and in the founding of journals such as **Feminist Studies**, **Hypatia**, **Signs**, **Nous**, **Journal of the History of Ideas**, **Radical Philosophy**, **Resources for Feminist Research.**

The modern tradition presented here demonstrates original contributions to the philosophical disciplines of epistemology, metaphysics, and ethics as well as to feminist philosophy. Although Anne Bradstreet and Mercy Otis Warren barely developed their feminist philosophy, they put forward an understanding of women's importance in their various writings. They made the unfair treatment of women as women sharply evident, and as it affected their own political and intellectual lives and work, poignant. Judith Sargent Murray developed her theory of how women are in fact equal to men, and should therefore be allowed the same opportunities to participate in life's offerings. That women should be educated becomes a philosophical concern, educated for this life and the next: this life to participate in the fullness of their humanity, this life to be fully citizens of the state,

4

this life to be fully their own sex. Once it is established that women should be allowed education, it must next be established that they should exercise rights as wives, citizens, and persons, i.e. rights in relation to others and rights in relation to themselves.

Feminist philosophy is inevitably linked to the cultural milieu of the times. Mercy Otis Warren hoped for a full participation in public life through liberty for women. Judith Sargent Murray's philosophy integrates the preoccupation with the spiritual and the political changes brought about by the Revolutionary War. Frances Wright's philosophy revolts against male dominated religious revivalism and looks to the requirements and opportunities of U.S. constitutional government for progress for women. Ednah Dow Cheney rethinks the idea of a single-sex god, and from that all human endeavors, arts and sciences. Mary Whiton Calkins challenges the harsh masculine individualism of an industrial capitalism.

The issue of language is an evolving concern of feminist philosophy. The reader will note the masculinity of language protruding in these philosophers. A particular word or a conception of god as male and female followed by a masculine pronoun reference will appear awkward in our feminist-conscious time. Whole works on the problem of neutral-gender language did not appear until the last half of the twentieth century when study in linguistics, psycho-linguistics, semiotics, new rhetorics as well as feminist philosophy resurged (note footnote 1 for current examples).

It is understandable that I have included introductions to the works presented here. But why so much biography and bibliography? The obvious reason is that many of these women are little known if known at all. The less obvious reason is that with biographies of women problems arise which are directly related to their work and the reception of that work. One such problem was identified above, the unique philosophical anonymity of earlier women philosophers. The life experiences of women provoke questions about influence and criteria. What have women as independent scholars outside the intellectual milieu brought to philosophy? What has the off-center or marginal reality of their lives, lives which admit to no governing power in universities, or boardrooms, or political institutions, nor even in churches or chambers of commerce meant to their philosophical insights? If, "power is the ability to take one's place in whatever

5

discourse is essential to action and the right to have one's part matter" [5], how is it that they have participated in the dynamism of the thinking of their day? How must it have affected their thinking to have written, to have published, to have in fact made a difference, and yet be compelled to expect the waiting oblivion of a world designed in the word and image of but half the human race? Have their contributions to the philosophical tradition been negligible?

Like the argument familiar to the women of this text, "women should not be educated, therefore I do not accept women because they are not educated," it is "begging the question" to say "we place women's lives in the aisle, therefore we do not accept their lives because they are in the aisle." In fact, the concept of a lived past is centered more accurately by incorporating these "peripheral" lives. Knowledge of the inventiveness and courage in the marginality of these philosopher's lives as well as of their unclaimed philosophical work is profitable.

By presenting both these women's lives and their works, I hope to bring these philosophers into the philosophical dialogue, and by doing so make the dialogue more complete. The table around which serious dialogue has been taking place, has in the past been set with chairs for men only. So, this book attempts to create space at the feast of ideas for those women who in my understanding of the past were crowded out.

Two misconceptions linger about women's philosophy. Being classified as visionaries or mystics does not necessarily preclude women from being philosophers, nor does the number of them prove women more intuitive and less logical. At times when women were not allowed to have opinions, "receiving the word" from a divine source provided a camouflaged method for publicly giving an opinion. Although none of these visionary philosophers are included in this work, they are a significant part of women's philosophical tradition from ancient and medieval to contemporary times. Some of their influences are evident in the works presented here. [6]

Secondly, although women philosophers were influenced by male philosophers and were, like many philosophers, aligned with schools of philosophy, this does not mean that they were male-philosopher clones, made in the procrustean bed of men's thought, but were, rather, scholars receiving from and contributing to the philosophical tradition, century by century. The possibility remains that an "enlarged" tradition of ethics and other philosophical disciplines has existed, unrecognized and devalued as the women themselves have been. And it may be that once an historical compilation of women's philosophical work has been studied, the meaning of a "pre-feminist world" of thought will be noted as one that is evolutionary. [7]

A History of Philosophical Influences

The predominant philosophical tradition and school of which English speaking American women in the seventeenth century were a part, withstanding their gender restriction and their colonial perspective, was dominated by the cross fire of Sir Walter Raleigh, Sir Philip Sidney and Lord Francis Bacon whose arguments, explications and quarrels were carried on in America through the tracts and pamphlets of the time. These publications were available to every well taught nonconformist woman. Bernard Bailyn has found over four hundred of these pamphlets in America and has published two volumes of them. "The pamphlets include all sorts of writings--treatises on political theory, essays on history, political arguments, sermons, correspondence, poems--and they display all sorts of literary devices." [8]

By the end of the seventeenth century the effects of the doctrines of early deism (Lord Edward Herbert - 1583-1648 [**Truth**, 1624]), the mathematical structure and operation of the physical world (Galileo, 1564-1642 [**Two Chief World Systems**, 1632] and Descartes, 1596-1650 [**Meditations**, 1641]), the materialism of Thomas Hobbes (1588-1679) with the Cambridge Platonist response to Hobbes, were all a part of the American philosophical, political, and religious controversy. Anne Bradstreet's work reflects most of this tradition and names many of these philosophers directly.

In the eighteenth century the natural philosophy of Robert Boyle and Sir Issac Newton prevailed in English speaking America. The epistemological and political theory of John Locke was greatly respected. David Hume with his skepticism and Voltaire with his free thought, were rejected by most through the power of George Berkeley, Francis Hutcheson and Edmund Burke. These male philosophers are directly addressed in the poetry as well as the prose of Mercy Otis Warren. Judith Sargent Murray responded to many of these men and directly to

7

the work of Marie de Gournay, Catherine Macauley and Mary Wollstonecraft. From Aspasia of Miletus through Anna Maria van Schurman--to Dorothy Schlosser, Germany's first woman Ph.D.--to her own work, Judith Sargent Murray traced a tradition established through the insights and influence of each of these intellectually powerful women.

By the end of the eighteenth century, the American political thought of Benjamin Franklin, Ethan Allen, Thomas Jefferson, John Taylor, and the American religious philosophy of Jonathan Edwards and his detractors became an independent and prevalent native intellectual force. With the philosophical, political and religious thought of Anne Bradstreet, Mercy Otis Warren and Judith Sargent Murray totally eclipsed, a male-only joint Anglo-American influence began that still greatly influences our social, moral and political lives.

With the pure reason of Immanuel Kant, the romance of Jean Jacques Rousseau, and the poetry of Wordsworth, a new transcendence emerged. Many have maintained that this emergence became the first truly American philosophy: Transcendentalism. Not until Margaret Fuller translated Kant and Ednah Dow Cheney translated Goethe, were Ralph Waldo Emerson and Bronson Alcott acquainted with these as original sources. Hitherto Emerson and Alcott were restricted to interpretations like those of James Marsh's introduction to Coleridge. Emanuel Swedenborg's work brought some sense of Hindu and oriental culture, and a pale mysticism to many of the men and women Transcendentalists.

In the American academic community of the nineteenth century, English philosophy was still primary. Transcendentalism was considered dilettantish. William Paley was taught in almost all colleges as the moralist. Friedrich Schleirermacher gained attention in the seminaries. Thomas Reid and the Scottish common sense defense against Hume was widespread.

At the halfway mark of the nineteenth century came the beginnings of the new science. In America many theories of evolution developed, all finding wider and wider discussion, until Charles Darwin, with his "survival of the fittest" popularizer, Herbert Spenser, overcame them all. G.W.F. Hegel, especially through William Torrey Harris's **Journal of Speculative Philosophy** opened up alternatives to the growing American interest in Adam Smith, James Mill, William Hamilton, and Utilitarianism. Abolition, suffrage and anarchist theories, all

8

brought pamphleteering and journalistic opportunities to women philosophers, just as they had done in the pre-revolutionary days. Francis Wright much earlier (1825), had introduced utilitarian theory, but among the literati, it had gone unnoted. American Pragmatism with Chauncey Wright, C.S. Peirce, and William James, along with the Absolute Pragmatism of Josiah Royce came together in the Absolute Idealism of Mary Whiton Calkins. Calkins was denied the Harvard Ph.D. that she earned, but professional philosophers acknowledged her as both a philosopher and a scientist by election to the Presidency of the American Philosophical Association and the American Psychological Association during the first quarter of the twentieth century.

Within the second quarter of the twentieth century, British analytic philosophy and the beginnings of phenomonolgy and existentialism, eclipsed English language forms of idealism and traditional American philosophy and rendered silent the work of Mary Whiton Calkins. The wide expansion of graduate education and foreword progress of women has brought about what growth there has since been in this generation of contemporary American women philosophers in all schools, systems and academic organizations.

Rather than write a book tracing all these influences and arguing this overview, I intend to present introductions and inductive instances of representative work by American women philosophers from colonial times to the beginning of the twentieth century. Anne Bradstreet, living in the situation of a pioneering pilgrim woman, acknowledged as the first great lyric and narrative poet of America, wrote a work in ethics that defies the usual interpretation of American puritanism and all the sociological pronouncements of a need for sophisticated leisure to develop new and effective ethical theory. Mercy Otis Warren represents the development of original and singular doctrines of American freedom and economic rights in her poetry, in her plays, in her history, in her anti-federalist pamphlet and in all her philosophical observations. Judith Sargent Murray presents the earliest sophisticated and articulate whole feminist philosophy in America. Yet her three volumes of essays have never been reprinted, books of her handwritten letters, essays and poems have not yet been transcribed, and her name is practically unknown in America. Francis Wright precedes J. S. Mill's developments in utilitarian theory; she argues against the male dominant understanding of the greatest pleasure for the greatest number, and maintains that a new and representative understanding of reality can come only from those on the outside, without a commitment to the present inequalities. Mary Whiton Calkins joins the professional male philosophers of her time, and joins the predominant American philosophy of her time, and still gains no more than a temporary acceptance of her ideas.

Whether it be in ethics, political philosophy, feminist philosophy, utilitarianism, or idealism; whether it be in the pilgrim circumstances, or the revolutionary war experience, or in the nineteenth century meliorism, or the early twentieth century idealism, America's women philosophers are forgotten. But in these women, these texts and these disciplines is found a demonstration of the power and the riches, and as well, the eclipse of American philosophy by women.

Endnotes

---

[1] Nearly a third of the philosophers listed in Ethel Kersey's **Women Philosophers** are twentieth century ranging from the European phenomenologist Edith Stein to the American logician/ aesthetician Suzanne K. Langer. Women professors of philosophy and those with membership in such organizations as the Society for the Advancement of American Philosophy and the American Philosophical Association are given extensive listing in Caroline Whitbeck's **A Directory of Women in Philosophy 1979/80**. French psycho- linguists Julia Kristeva and Luce Iragaray are being recognized as philosophers. Philosophy books by women are proliferating in the 1990's, for example: Nancy J. Holland's **Is Women's Philosophy Possible**, 1990, Andrea Nye's **Words of Power: A History of Logic**, 1990, Claudia Card's **Feminist Ethics**, 1991, Lorraine Code **What Can She Know**, 1991.

[2] Examples of books listing women scholars have appeared periodically in the 17th, 18th and 19th centuries: **Wonders of the Female World, or A General History of Women**...Printed for T. Malthus at the Sun in the Poultrey, 1683; **Her and His, or the Feminine Gender more worthy than the Masculine...** Printed for J. Norris, 1683; Gilles Menage's 1690 **History of Women Philosophers**; William Alexander's 1732 **History of Women from Earliest Antiquity** and Lydia Maria Child's 1835 **Brief History of the Condition of Women in Various Ages and Nations**.

[3] Nancy Hartsock's "Foucault on Power: A Theory for Women?"in **Feminism/Postmodernism** (Linda J. Nicholson, ed. New York: Routledge, 1990:157-75) suggests five features a new theory of power would include (1) reconstitution of "ourselves as subjects as well as objects of history" (2) "on an epistemological base that indicated that knowledge is possible" (3) recognizing "our practical daily activity" (4) while recognizing "the difficluty of creating alternatives" (5) all of which leads to engagement, a call "for change and participation in altering power relations." Harstock rejects Richard Rorty's stance of ignoring power relations and Foucault's stance of resisting them, insisting that present theories need transforming.

[4] "Nearly every single philosopher over the first two thousand years of western philosophy thought about the identity of women in relation to man...thus the concept of women has been a fundamental area of philosophical research since the sixth century B.C."(Allen, Sr. Prudence. **The Concept of Woman**. Montreal: Eden,1985:1).

[5] Carolyn Heilbrun in **Writing a Woman's Life** (New York: W.W. Norton, 1988:8) articulates the outcome of re-investigating the chronicling of women's lives and demonstrates the resulting changes taking place in the writing of biography.

[6] Mary Ellen Waithe lists many mystics with philosophic merit in her history of women philosophers: Beatrice of Nazareth, Hildegard of Bingen, Hadewych of Antwerp, Julian of Norwich, Mechtild of Magdeburg, Teresa of Avila and more. **History of Women Philosophers** Volume 2/500-1600, Dordrecht, The Netherlands: Kluwer, 1989.

[7] Alison M. Jaggar in "Feminist Ethics: Some Projects and Problems" **From the Center: A Newsletter** (Fall 1990) articulates the current circumstances of "feminist ethics."

[8] Bernard Bailyn. **The Ideological Origins of the American Revolution**. Cambridge, Harvard Press, 1971, v-vi.

Bibliography

Allen, Sr. Prudence. **The Concept of Women.** Montreal: Eden, 1985.

Alexander, William. **History of Women from Earliest Antiquity to the Present Time.** London: C. Dilly, 1732.

Bailyn, Bernard. **The Ideological Origins of the American Revolution.** Cambridge: Harvard UP, 1971.

Card, Claudia, ed. **Feminist Ethics.** Lawrence: University of Kansas, 1991.

Child, Lydia Maria. **Brief History of the Condition of Women in Various Ages and Nations** (1835) New York: C.S. Francis, 1845.

Code, Lorraine. **What Can She Know.** Ithaca: Cornell UP, 1991.

Hartsock, Nancy. "Foucault on Power: A Theory for Women?" in **Feminism/Postmodernism.** Linda J. Nicholson, ed. New York: Routledge, 1990.

Heilbrun, Carolyn. **Writing a Woman's Life.** New York: W.W. Norton, 1988.

Her and His, or the Feminine Gender More Worthy Than the Masculine, London: J Norris, 1683.

Holland, Nancy J. **Is Women's Philosophy Possible?** Savage, MD: Rowman and Littlefield, 1990.

Jagger, Alison M. "Feminist Ethics: Some Projects and Problems," **From the Center: A Newsletter** [Center for Values and Social Policy, University of Colorado at Boulder] (Fall 1990) n.p.

Kersey, Ethel M. **Women Philosophers: A Biocritical Source.** Westport, Ct.: Greenwood , 1989.

Mènage, Gilles. **History of Women Philosophers** (1690-92) trans. Beatrice H. Zedler, Lanham, MD: University Press of America, 1984.

Nicholson, Linda J., ed. **Feminism/Postmodernism.** New York: Routledge, 1990.

Nye, Andrea. **Words of Power: A History of Logic.** New York: Routledge, 1990.

Waithe, Mary Ellen. **History of Women Philosophers.** (Vol I (1986), Vol II (1989), Vol III (1991) Dordrecht, The Netherlands: Kluwer.

Whitbeck, Caroline. **A Directory of Women in Philosophy 1979-80.** Bowling Green, Ohio: Philosophy Document Center, 1980.

Wonders of the Female World, Or a General History of Women, London: T. Malthus, 1683.

Anne Bradstreet, A fanciful portrait
An Account of Anne Bradstreet The Puritan Poetess, 1898
(Colonel Luther Caldwell, ed. Boston: Damrell and Upham)

Chronology

Anne Bradstreet 1612/13 - 1672

1612/13	Born to Dorothy and Thomas Dudley in Northamptonshire, England;
1617	Began education living at Earl of Lincoln's; attendance with brother's tutor.
1628	Marries Simon Bradstreet.
1630	Arrives in Massachusetts Bay Colony, settles in Charlestown.
1631	Moves to Newton (later called Cambridge).
1632	Almost dies, first preserved poem.
1633	Son Samuel born.
1635	Daughter Dorothy born; died 1686. Move to Agawam (later called Ipswich).
1638	Daughter Sarah born.
1640	Son Simon born.
1641 - 1646	First drafts of all the formal narrative poems.
1642	Daughter Hannah born. A number of personal lyric poems.
1643	December, her mother, Dorothy Dudley dies, writes "An Epitaph..."
1645	Daughter Mercy born.
1647	Move to another wilderness community, Merrimac (later called Andover).
1648	Son Dudley born.
1650	**The Tenth Muse** published in London.

1652	Son John born.
1653	July, her father dies, writes "To the memory of..."
1666	House burns and with it final draft of "The Four Monarchyes."
1672	September 16, dies in her home in Andover.

2

Anne Dudley Bradstreet

1612/13-1672

Anne Dudley Bradstreet is increasingly becoming known as one of the greatest writers of the English language. "Anne Bradstreet was the first resident poet of English-speaking North America, and also the first significant woman poet of England. (White vii)." Her poetry now is receiving greater scrutiny and higher praise than ever before. Here is a poet raised and writing in what historians and literary scholars have seen as the most unlikely circumstances for creative literary accomplishment: the ferocious struggle for survival in a harsh land, conflict with a uncultivated people, disastrously cold winters, infectious epidemics, and disastrous fires. Yet filled with a grateful attitude, and a deep sensitivity, she produced spontaneous, humor filled, pathos rendering, beautiful lyric poetry. Equally well, and sometimes with the same flourish of irony and fun, Anne wrote excellent formal narrative and historical poems. In all her writing she sets forth argumentative structures that move her readers to new understandings of the goodness of life.

The acknowledgement of such accomplishment, however, had to wait for over 200 years. Her work, as **The Tenth Muse Lately Sprung up in America** (1650) and its expanded second edition as **Several Poems Compiled with Great Variety of Wit and Learning, Full of Delight** by "a Gentlewomen in New-England" (1678) saw only one 18th century publication (Boston, 1758). There was the appearance of a couple of poems in early 19th century anthologies (**Specimens of British Poetess**, London, 1827; and **Specimens of American**

19

Poetry, Boston, 1827). John Harvard Ellis in 1867 produced the first complete and carefully documented edition of **The Works of Anne Bradstreet in Prose and Verse**, presenting for the first time her prose writing. The additional texts in this edition came from a manuscript book, most of which is in her handwriting, and which she had given to her son, Simon Bradstreet. From that time the growth of critical examination and the representation of her poetry can be easily traced in Raymond F. Dolle, **Anne Bradstreet, A Reference Guide** (Boston 1990). This superb bibliography tells the story of the deepening appreciation of Anne Bradstreet as a great poet. For the eighteenth, the nineteenth and most of the twentieth century her poetry was thought to be inferior. In 1930 Samuel Morrison wrote in his **Master Builders of the Bay Colony** it is "curious fact that the historians (and critics) of American literature, most of them New Englanders, rated Anne Bradstreet with an almost offensive condescension" (331). It is the intent of this anthology to introduce the study of Anne Dudley Bradstreet as America's first moral philosopher.

Anne Dudley was born to Thomas Dudley and Dorothy York Dudley in 1612 or 1613 in Northamptonshire, East Anglia, England. During her childhood, Thomas Dudley was a steward and friend of the Earl of Lincoln. The library of the Earl and the encouragement of her father created an unusual intellectual opportunity for the precocious Anne. Her "education probably began in 1617, when she was four years old, and continued in one form or another until she married in 1628" (White 60). Anne joined her brother in his tutorial studies for Cambridge. The extent of her knowledge and its character is so varied and so wide that it bursts the probability of a mere eleven years. Because her father had America's outstanding library, there is ample evidence that Anne read much more than any of the Pilgrim Puritans are supposed to have read. We know of her especially high regard for Sir Walter Raleigh's **History of the World**, 1614. There are references to Helkiah Cooke's **Description of the Body of Man**, 1615, much of the work of Sir Philip Sidney, the histories of John Speed, William Camden, William Pemble, Richard Knolles, Archbishop Ussher, all of which were published during the first quarter of the 17th century. Many other works are also evidenced in her poetry: Robert Burton's **Anatomy of Melancholy**, John Smith's **General History of Virginia, New England and the Summer Isles**. Her prose,

"Meditations, Divine and Moral," shows the direct or at least indirect influence of the style and content of Francis Bacon's **Essays** and **Novum Organum**. It has been powerfully argued that Shakespeare as well as Guillaume DuBartes were transplanted into the American tradition by Anne Bradstreet's works (Galinsky, 1959). Her allusions to Plutarch occur in the second edition and not the first edition of "The Four Monarchies," which tells that some of her education in the classics, like so many of ours today, didn't take place until later in her life.

> Among the few English women writers before her none displayed so encyclopedic mind and in the seventeenth century only the Duchess of Newcastle, who soon followed her into print, seems to have possessed the same kind of intellectual avidity (White 60).

Simon Bradstreet, a younger friend of Thomas Dudley, was also a protégé of the Earl of Lincoln. Anne married Simon two years before the **Arbella** set sail for the Massachusetts Bay colony. Eleven ships made up the fleet that carried 700 colonists to include the leading stockholders in the venture, Issac Johnson and his wife the Lady Arbella. They arrived between June 12 and July 6, 1630. By December, 100 people had returned with the ships, and 200 had died, to include Isaac Johnson and Lady Arbella.

In the Spring of 1631 the Dudley's and the Bradstreets moved from their small cramped quarters in Charlestown to the well planned and pleasant Newtown later called Cambridge. After about four years Anne, with her husband and two children and her father's family, moved to the frontier town Agawam later called Ipswich. Ten years later Anne and her immediate family, now numbering six children, moved to yet another wilderness community, Merrimac, later called Andover. This was to be Anne's home until her death in 1672. The original Merrimac family house burned to the ground on July 10, 1666 destroying her papers including her last draft of "The Roman Monarchy" of the then never to be completed narrative "The Four Monarchies." So, the manuscripts we have, and the emendations to her previously published poems, had to have been done or redone during the last six years of her life. White maintains that the settled years in Ipswich, 1642-1647, were the "period of Anne Bradstreet's greatest literary activity" (199). However, some of her most personal, most reflective and presently most critically acclaimed poems were written in Andover. It is amazing that a seventeenth century puritan women transplanted through three different pioneering homesteads should also have the power, the presence of mind, the creative energy and the work discipline to produce great lyric reflection on the poignancy of human life that still quicken the sensitivities of so many twentieth century readers.

In 1650 the formal works of Anne Bradstreet were published in London under the title: **The Tenth Muse Lately Sprung up in America**. The first sixty eight pages of this work are made up of what Anne called the "four times four" poems, and what scholars call "the quaternions," Anne's formal name for the four.[1] After a dedicatory poem to her father and a prologue to the reader, the first, "The Four Elements," is the metaphysical foundations of all the rest, Here four sisters contest: Fire, Earth, Air and Water, and in this contention everything has its being. In the second, "Of the Four Humors of Man's Constitution," another four women, the daughters of the elements, cause the character of all humankind: argumentative Choler, desirous Sanguinity, proud Melancholy, and mild Flegme, pleading for unity. "The Four Ages of Man" present the grandchildren of the womanly elements: childhood, "son unto flegm, grandchild to water;" youth from blood, air and sanguinary; the manly from fire by way of choler; and old age from earth and "heavy melancholy." The last "The Four Seasons of the Year," re-presents and unifies, in accordance with Flegme's request, the previous three: spring as air, blood and "man in his minority;" summer as "fire, choler and middle age;" autumn as "old, cold, dry Age and Earth" and then the "cold, moist young flegmy winter." Full circle have we come in four expository poems with the womanly as cause and symbol for it all, so much so, that John Harvard Ellis has eloquently argued that the four are really "four parts of one entire poem (xli). With all the classic allusions, zodiac references, allegorical and figurative devices,[2] these poems typify Anne Bradstreet not only as "the child of the Renaissance" (White, 184) as seen therein by Elizabeth Wade White, but every bit as much the feminist of the gender-based argument of Sandra M. Gilbert and Susan Guber in **The Norton Anthology of Literature by Women** (58-61)[3]. The sixteen separate allegorical figures that make up the principals in the presentation of elements, humors and their offspring in human beings as well as in the seasons, all correspond to the division of nature as fundamentally female. This fundamental character of reality as feminine is foundational to an understanding of her work.

In her unfinished "The Four Monarchies" the high Elizabethan style continues and is punctuated with outstanding praise for women: queens and warriors. This poem takes up more than half of the whole volume. In the first monarchial tradition, the Assyrian, the forty two years of the Babylonian foundress Queen Semiramis are portrayed as "both (the) shame and glory of her Sex" (71). However, the so-called shame part is most likely merely the slander the Greeks cast upon "her name and fame" (72). Among the sixteen kingdoms discussed in this section of the poem, only the reigns of Sardanapalas and Nebuchadnezzer get more lines than this powerful Queen Semiramis.

In the second monarchy, the Persian, the famed founder Cyrus, who married the daughter of Darius, reigned through one son, and then "The male line, of great Cyrus now had end, / The Female to many ages did extend (96)." The famous campaign of Xerxes is joined by the "Brave Artemisia, Halicarnassus Queen." with a magnificent fleet "But hers she kept still separate from the rest / For to command alone she jud'd was best" (104).

The third monarchy, the Greek, begins with the reign of Alexander in the "112 Olimpiad," and ends with "fair Cleopatra" in Egypt. Anne Bradstreet calls attention to many of the most famous women of this time: "Great Sisigambis," the mother of Darius, who with her daughters, gave glory to the character of Alexander because of the way he treated them after their capture. Upon Sisigambis' death, Alexander mourned and Darius prayed to the gods that they bestow dignity on Alexander. Thalestris, the Queen of the Amazons, although thought a mythic character by Anne Bradstreet, still gives honor to the story of Alexander by the mere claim of the tellers that she too "brought her traine to Alexander (143)" as he conquered the world. Statira, the wife of Alexander, and Roxana, who Bradstreet makes the second wife of Alexander and mother of his son, are with Alexander's sister, Cleopatra, all prominent in the power struggle following his death. Phisa, the uniter of her father, Craterus, and her husband, Antipater, against the rebellious Greeks, and the queens and commanders like Eurydice, Cyna, Ceria, all of these women found their ultimate downfall by the cruel and first among them: Olimpias, the mother of Alexander and the supporter of the assassins of his father, Philip, "this most cruel Queen,/ whose fury yet unparalled hath been" (172). This Queen-mother reappears in the poem more than any other character. As an antidote to these cruel struggles of history the story of Statonice is told: how this wonderful young women is married to the aged Seleucus, King of Syria, whose son falls passionately in love with her. But the kind and wise father gives over his bride to save his son from such a devastating love (179). Anne then names quickly, characterizing them by rhetorical apostrophe, all the rest of the Greek rulers up to Cleopatra, who as the last of this race was not captured nor murdered and "'Twas not death nor danger she did dread,/ But some disgrace in triumph to be led" (184). As Anne Bradstreet brings this first version of the poem to its conclusion she characterizes each of the four monarchies: the Assyrian, is a golden lion; the Persian, is a silver bear; the Greek, is a brass leopard with four wings, and the unwritten Roman monarchy, is an iron ram; but "All trembling stand before the powerful Lamb" (185).

The Roman monarchy, was partially presented in the first edition of **The Tenth Muse**, and according to "An Apology" in the second edition almost completed before the fire on July 10, 1666. What we have of Rome begins with the Romulus story and ends four pages later with Tarquinius "the last King of the Romans" (190). According to Anne Bradstreet, Rome has its foundation in the "vestal Rhea" who brought Romulus to the world without the fatherhood of Mars, as is most commonly alleged. Rather it was Aemulus disguised in Mars-like armor who thus took his niece by surprise and brought about Rome the "Mistress of the world in each respect" (187). The taking of the Sabine women is glossed over in this poem. Numa, a Sabine and the second king, was beloved of the goddess Aegeria, and through her the founder of Roman religious worship. Servius Tullius also owed his kingdom to the power of a woman. Tullius, the son of a female slave to Queen Tanquil, was seen by the queen to have special powers as he was to give to Rome a new constitution. Through her influence he became king, and he was protected from assassination by her machinations. The end of the monarchy as such was brought about through the rape of chaste Lucretia. The rape brought her spouse to such anger that he expelled the Tarquins. Thus "the government they change, a new one bring,/ And people swear ne'er to accept of King" (190).

With that report of a woman's effect, the "The Four Monarchies" comes to a close. The power, the bravery, and the wisdom of women is a constant theme in this narrative of the four ancient times. Nowhere in the growing literature on Anne Bradstreet do we have a critical analysis of this poem that treats the remarkable use of women in the formation of the four pre-christian traditions. Certainly, such research would be wonder-filled.

The Tenth Muse continues this centering on female protagonists with a "Dialogue between Old England and New; Concerning their Present Troubles, Anno 1642" (192). Here is a frank and intellectually equal discussion of a family crises between a mother and her adult daughter. Elizabeth Wade White's explication of this poem is excellent. With White, I find the poem "essentially feminine," "dramatic," but, unlike her, I find it nowhere "pedantic," and, again, with her, surely the best "literary expression of the emotional relationship between the wartorn parent country and its colonial offspring" (159-172).

Over the last ten years some remarkable feminine-centered research and criticism has focused on the elegies we are about to discuss (see: Tim Sweet, 1988; Ivy Schweitzer, 1988; Wendy Martin, 1984: Ritamarie Sargent, 1984; Cheryl Walker, 1982; and Lyle Koehler, 1980 for examples).

"The Elegy on Sir Philip Sidney," (203) in both its exuberant early version, as well as in its more sedate second edition version, represents her kinsman, in its first sentence, as courage and philosophy, Mars and Minerva, arms and art. The poem continues in the next ten lines to characterize Sidney, through the nine muses, as the best in lyric poetry, music, history, eloquence, logic, rhetoric, tragedy, comedy, and epic poetry. This "refiner of our British tongue," fills his texts with valor, justice, morality, friendship, warm hospitality and piety. And all of this is before an early death at thirty two years old.

The next poem is also an elegy, this time "In Honor of DuBartes, 1641" (206). Guillaume Du Bartes (1544-1590) a French poet whose most famous work was translated in 1621 as **DuBartes His Divine Weeks and Works** by Joshua Sylvester and became a most influential work to Sidney, Spenser, Milton, Dryden as well as Bradstreet. Nonetheless in our times he is more famous as an influence on each of these poets rather than as a poet himself. This poem contains a lovely reminiscence on an Elizabethan childhood which starts: "My muse unto a child I may compare, / Who sees the riches of some famous Fair, / He feeds his eyes, but understanding lacks / To comprehend the worth of all those knacks" (207).

"Queen Elizabeth of Happy Memory" (210) is an elegiac defense of the regal pre-eminence of the feminine. For Anne Bradstreet, Queen Elizabeth should have put forever to rest the chauvinism that appears at the beginning of **The Tenth Muse**:

> She has wip'd off the aspersion of her sex,
> that Women lack the wisdom to play the rex.
>   *   *   *
> But can you doctors now this point dispute,
> She is argument enough to make you mute.
>   *   *   *
> Since time was time, and man unmanly man,
> Come show me such a Phoenix if you can?
> Was ever a people better ruled than hers?
> Was ever a land more happy freed from stirrs?
> Did ever wealth in England more abound?
>   *   *   *
> Had ever a Prince such counsellours as she?
> Herself Minerva caus'd them so to be.
>   *   *   *
> Let such as say our sex is void of reason,
> Know is slander now, but once was treason.

Lest the reader argue that Elizabeth is just a unique accident, throughout the poem Bradstreet brings up the accomplishments of other queens: the powerful founding queen of Babylon, Semiramis, the fierce queen of the Massagetae, Tomris, who killed Cyrus in battle in 529 B.C., Dido who was the first foundress of Carthage, the proud and clever Cleopatra, and Zenobia the potent Empress of the East. "Now say, have women worth? or have they none? " (214)

The next to last poem in **The Tenth Muse**, "David's Lamentation for Saul and Jonathan" (215), is sometimes seen as a mere restatement of the Geneva Bible version of II Samuel, Chapter I, verses 19-17. Looking, however, at Elizabeth Wade White's careful explication of the poem as the shocked response of a loyal Puritan to the judicial murder of the anointed king and all of the long dreadful carnage that that civil war had brought to so many that Anne had personally known, gives the poem the force and compassion of an elegy not only for Charles I, but a lament for all the English speaking peoples of the world.

The last poem "The Vanity of All Worldy Things" (233) is not only the commonly accepted statement of her character and religious conviction, but more so her profound philosophical reflection on the **summum bonum** as she asks "where is it then?" After examining the answers traditionally given by the philosophers and having found them lacking, she asks:

> If not in honor, beauty, age, nor treasure,
> Nor yet in learning, wisdome, youth nor pleasure,
> Where shall I climb, found, seek search or find
>   * * *
> But where and what it is, from heaven's declared,
> It brings to honour, which shall ne're decay,
> It stores with wealth which time can't wear away.

It is to reflections on the nature, the power and the glory of that revelation to which so much of her later and more personal prose and poetry is directed.

The Tenth Muse makes Anne Bradstreet the perfect beginning for this anthology. After many years of neglect or patronizing attention, Bradstreet has gained respect as a genius, yet many still give her such credit only for her poems published after her death. But more and more the formal poetry of Anne Bradstreet is gaining critical praise. Nevertheless, her ethics is seen as "the devotional legacy for her children" (White 298), a means to understand her religious faith and troubles (Westbrook, 1988), the spiritual expression of her voyage on the **Arbella** (Wharton 1983), "some of the best prose of her generation" (Hutchinson, 29), but never as America's first moral philosophy. When Cicero and Seneca, in imitation of Aristotle's **Nicomachean Ethics**, address long and short works in morality to their children - we take such work as philosophy not devotional. However, when Anne Bradstreet writes seventy-seven "beautifully worded" (Hutchinson, 29) aphorisms, in a voice very much in accord with Carol Gilligan's conception of morality (**In a Different Voice**), it is not called moral philosophy.

In view of the feminist perspective developed by America's first published woman and in accordance with the originating intention of this anthology, it is fitting and proper that the first text we will study is **Meditations, Divine and**

Moral, with the hope that Anne Bradstreet will be increasingly and ceaselessly become known as America's first great moral philosopher.

Endnotes

[1] Page citations are from the second edition, **Several Poems,** published in Boston in 1678 containing the author's correction and some unpublished pieces. This text is presently available in John Harvard Ellis's superb **The Works of Anne Bradstreet**, Gloucester, 1962.

[2] See especially Ann Stanford, 1974, pp. 29-51. Anne Hildebrand, EAL 1973, pp. 117-125 or the same title in Cowell & Stanford, 1983, 137-149. White, 185-189; 44-45, 208-215; 215-219. Piercy, 1965, pp. 41-46; 55-56.

[3] Rosamond Rosenmeier notes in her **Anne Bradstreet Revisited** that Bathsua Makin a contemporary of Bradstreet's and author of **An Essay to Revive the Antient Education of Gentlewomen** (1673) disclaims the plea of Cornelius Agrippa's **A Treatise of the Nobilitie and Excellence of Womankynde** for the preeminence of women. She lists Bradstreet with other women poets as proof for why women should be educated. But Rosemeier makes the point that unlike Makin, who adopts a male persona, Bradstreet adopts the "personas of women: sisters, daughters, wives and mothers" (12).

Introduction to
Meditations Divine and Moral

Prominent among Anne Bradstreet's posthumous papers, written in her own hand, addressed to her "dear son Simon Bradstreet," and "avoiding encroaching on other conceptions," is a work entitled **Meditations, Divine and Moral**. This work, contains a two page preface and seventy-four aphorisms. It was not wholly presented to the public until over two hundred years after it was written.

Even before its first full publication, it was receiving high critical acclaim whenever Anne Bradstreet's works were fully studied. In 1844 William Budington published extracts from her manuscripts in the **Congregational Visitor** and maintained that the writing in the meditations was much better than her poetry and could "be read with as much profit as ever, and perhaps with greater pleasure. (1 [January] 5-9). Again, in 1845, William Budington wrote that her "truly wise and pious meditations ...evince not only a thoughtful experience of life, but also a tender and chasten spirit of piety (116)."

When John Harvard Ellis did set forth the first complete and definitive edition of her works, he maintained:

> The "Meditations" display much more ability, much greater cultivation of mind, and a deeper thoughtfulness than most of her other works (1867, lxi).

Moses Coit Tyler in his 1878 **A History of American Literature** also thought her **Meditations** contained "the best example of her strength of thought and of her felicity in condensed and pungent expression (290)." In 1887, Charles F. Richardson, reflecting the whole of the nineteenth and early twentieth century opinion, found her poetry "a pitiable indication of. ..literary poverty," but the **Meditations** "of decided merit, easily surpassing the most ambitious of her labored productions in verse (2: 7-8.)." In 1891 in the first book length biography and study of Anne Bradstreet, Helen S. Campbell finds the **Meditations** "the best testimony to her real ability (280)." Charles Eliot Norton in his Introduction to **The Poems of Mrs. Anne Bradstreet**, 1896, after putting down her verse, says her **Meditations** "have remarkable sweetness and sensitivity, and express a confidence in the mercies of God, which it was seldom given to the tenderhearted in those days to attain (xxx)." In 1916 William Cairns in his **A History of American Literature** finds that the **Meditations** "are really superior to her poetical work (50)." So that all during the years that Anne Bradstreet's poetry was receiving such harsh evaluation, the **Meditations** was considered the height of her artistic accomplishments.

Even as her poetry star rose, the same critics that accomplished this feat, continued to praise the **Meditations**. Josephine Perry in her **Studies in Literary Types in 17th Century America**, after commenting on and quoting Cotton Mather, Samuel Williard and others claims:

> The best example of the meditative paragraph are those of Anne Bradstreet's "Meditations Divine and Moral." They are more compact, more unified , more impersonal, more epigrammatic, more like the Baconian or didactic essay than any of those just quoted (1939, 152).

George Frisbie Whicher in his essay in **Alas, All's Vanity, or A Leaf from the First American Edition of "Several Poems,"** in 1942 affirms that in:

> ..the juxtaposition of profoundly serious thought and homely household metaphor..one may find in her prose "Meditations" more than one passage that might be described as inchoate Emily Dickinson (1942, 27-28).

And Elizabeth Wade White, with a little less enthusiasm, finds:

> But the "Meditations" are well worth reading today. They reflect a keen, occasionally even ironic, sense of values, and also give some direct glimpses of a way of life that was spare, sturdy, and always, of necessity, practical (1971, 344).

At the end of the 50's, however, "Her prose meditations are as good as her poetry, exhibiting wit, skillful conciseness, pungent phrasing, and practical philosophy (Fuess, 1959, 47)." By the mid 60's, although her prose well expresses her dissatisfaction with narrow Puritan doctrines, her poetry sought answers to the ultimate questions and found solace (Leonard, 1965). And over the last ten years, for the most part, her poetry has become more highly praised than her prose (See Dolle, 1990).

Given such an extensive history of comment and criticism, it is meaningfully strange that no one has suggested that like Bacon, or Seneca, or Aristotle, who is reputed to have addressed the Nicomachean Ethics to his son Nicomachies just as Anne Bradstreet addressed the **Meditations** to her son Simon, this is moral philosophy and that Anne Bradstreet is a moral philosopher with an important and original doctrinal contribution. It is and she is.

Moral philosophers deal with the problems of attitude, decision, supreme value, and action. For Abelard, only our attitudes or desires fall under the requirements of free moral responsibility, and even these are not totally in our control. For when a starving man walks through an apple orchard, rich with ripened fruit, he cannot control his desire, and maybe not even his actions, but he can wish that he did not covet the property of another man. For John Stuart Mill the correct decision about moral justice is required, even when the accomplishment of the action is impossible. For example, the subjugation of women, in the 19th century was impossible to overcome, but the decision that it should be changed is morally required. For Kant, morality is not a matter of human action and experience at all. If no man can or ever has accomplished a truly moral action, nevertheless, morality is a matter of a universal command for all rational creatures. The categorical imperative is pure morality even if no rational creature can ever operate so purely. But for most American philosophers action is the center of morality. For John Dewey morality is conduct in a moral situation that is, in a situation where the actor has control of the manipulation of concrete and specific details within an environment. Morality is always practical and never pure. And as with Dewey so it is with his fellow American philosopher, Anne Bradstreet.

Moral philosophers are also distinguished by their methods of treating these problems. Francis Bacon, Benedict de Spinoza, Friedrich Nietzsche and Ludwig Wittgenstein all use the quick didactic or aphoristic essay. The object of these aphorisms is to direct attitudes, decisions, values or actions, by sudden but compelling insight.

For example in Bacon:

> He that hath a wife and children hath given hostages to fortune; for they are impediments to great enterprizes either to virtue or to mischief. Certainly the best works, and the greatest merit for the public have proceeded from the unmarried or childless men; which both in affection and means have married and endowed the public. (**Essays**, 8)

> The stage is more beholding to Love, than the life of man. For as to the stage life is ever matter of comedies, and now and then of tragedies; but in life it doth much mischief; sometime like a syren, sometimes like a fury. (**Essay**, 10)

> And certain it is, that the light a man reciéveth by counsel from another, is drier and purer than that which cometh from his own understanding and judgment; which is ever infused and drenched in his affections and customs. So there is as much difference between the counsel that a friend giveth, and that a man giveth himself as there is between the counsel of a friend and of a flatter. (**Essay**, 27).

For example in Spinoza:

> There is no rational life, therefore, without intelligence and things are good only in so far as they assist man to enjoy the life of the mind which is determined by intelligence. Those things alone on the other hand we call evil which hinder man from perfecting his reason and enjoying a rational life. (App of **Ethics** -IV, V).

> The love of a harlot, that is to say, the lust of sexual intercourse, which arises from mere external form, and absolutely all love which recognizes any other cause than the freedom of the mind, easily passes into hatred unless, which is worse, it becomes a species of delirium, and thereby discord is cherished rather than concord. (App of **E-IV**, XIX).

> There is a false appearance of piety and religion in dejection; and although dejection is the opposite of pride, the humble dejected man is very near akin to the proud. (App of **E-IV**, XXII).

For example in Nietzsche:

The sleep of virtue. When virtue has slept, she will get up more refreshed. [Human All To Human (83)]

Why beggars still live. The greatest giver of alms is cowardice. [The Wanderer and His Shadow (240)]

One becomes moral -- not because one is moral. Submission to morality can be slavish and vain or selfish or resigned or obtusely enthusiastic or thoughtless or an act of desperation, like submission to a prince: in itself it is nothing moral. [The Dawn (97)]

Whoever praises him as a god of love does not have a high enough opinion of love itself. Did this god not want to be a judge too? But the lover loves beyond reward and retribution. [Thus Spake Zarathustra (4th Part)]

For example in Wittgenstein:

Everything that can be thought at all can be thought clearly. Everything that can be said can be said clearly. (Tractatus, 4.116)

The limits of my language means the limits of my world. (Trac, 5.6).

It is clear that ethics cannot be expressed. Ethics is transcendental. (Ethics and aesthetics are one.) (Trac, 6.421).

The world of those who are happy is quite another from that of those who are unhappy. (Trac, 6.43).

As contrasted with Anne Bradstreet:

There is no object that we see, no action that we do, no good that we enjoy, no evil that we feel or fear, but we may make some spiritual advantage of all; and he that makes such improvement is wise as well as pious. (1).

Authority without wisdom is like a heavy axe without an edge: fitter to bruise than polish. (12).

Few men are so humble as not to be proud of their abilities, and nothing will abase them more than this: what hast thou but what

33

thou hast received? Come give an account of thy stewardship.
(17).

An aching head requires a soft pillow, and a drooping heart a strong
support. (25)

God hath by his providence so ordered that no one country hath all
the commodities within itself, but it wants another shall supply that
there may be a mutual commerce through the world. As it is with
countries so it is with men; there was never yet any one man that
had all excellences, let his parts natural and acquired, spiritual and
moral, be never so large, yet he stands in need of something which
another man hath (perhaps meaner than himself) which shows us
perfection is not below, as also that God will have us beholden one
to another. (77).

Here is the same pithy turning, quick argument that teaches, challenges and
changes our attitudes, decisions, values and actions. But a peculiarity and
substance distinguishes Bradstreet from the others.

Francis Bacon appeals to the standard of history. We see, upon ready
reflection, that Alexander the Great, Jesus, Queen Elizabeth I, Thomas Jefferson
were unmarried yet married to their work. And, in subsequent reflection, that
those who have created the greatest works in general have ignored or slighted their
spouses and children and fastened on their mission. Spinoza sees the life of true
goodness in the life of the mind -- only the wise are truly virtuous. All others do
what they do out of ignorance or good fortune, and thus not from morality but
from coincidence. Nietzsche wants us to go beyond morality - beyond any kind of
submission, to sheer creative force - to the full, pure, free will to power. Ludwig
Wittgenstein thinks that morality is a not a compilation of language, mere word
systems, but thoughts or feelings that are divorced from and outside of philosophy
and univocal language.

Anne Bradstreet rejects each of these philosophies and maintains that
morality and religion deal with the spiritual opportunities for action we have as a
community. Ethics is not a matter of individual thoughts (Wittgenstein) nor power
(Nietzsche) nor intelligence (Spinoza), nor individual greatness (Bacon). Morality
is judged in terms of a community of action, each individual contributing what each

34

especially has in accordance with the concrete needs of that chosen community. Anne Bradstreet's entire adult life took place in just such community efforts: whether fighting Indians, or expelling religious heretics - it was always a matter of the community.

These are my hypotheses, that the feminine is central to all Anne Bradstreet's work, and that she is an original and powerful philosopher of ethics. Now let me direct you to the reading of the complete **Meditations, Divine and Moral** for the test of such claims. Of the seventy-seven aphoristic essays forty-five are divine meditations, thirty-two moral meditations, four are divine teachings about morals, and four are moral teachings about the divine. Fifty-two are proportional analogical arguments, "given this and this, you see this and this." Five are forms of enthymematic argument, one of the premises of the argument is assumed or the conclusion is unspecified, but clear. Thirteen are explications of scriptural texts or Christian doctrines. All are philosophical, pithy and convincing.

Meditations Divine and Moral

FOR MY DEAR SON SIMON
BRADSTREET

Parents perpetuate their lives in their posterity and their manners; in their imitation children do naturally rather follow the failings than the virtues of their predecessors, but I am persuaded better things of you. You once desired me to leave something for you in writing that you might look upon, when you should see me no more; I could think of nothing more fit for you nor of more ease to myself than these short meditations following. Such as they are, I bequeath to you; small legacies are accepted by true friends, much more by dutiful children. I have avoided encroaching upon others' conceptions because I would leave you nothing but mine own, though in value they fall short of all in this kind; yet I presume they will be better prized by you for the author's sake. The Lord bless you with grace here and crown you with glory hereafter, that I may meet you with rejoicing at that great day of appearing, which is the continual prayer of

your affectionate mother,

A. B.

March 20, 1664

MEDITATIONS DIVINE
AND MORAL

1

There is no object that we see, no action that we do, no good that we enjoy, no evil that we feel or fear, but we may make some spiritual advantage of all; and he that makes such improvement is wise as well as pious.

2

Many can speak well, but few can do well. We are better scholars in the theory than the practic part, but he is a true Christian that is a proficient in both.

3

Youth is the time of getting, middle age of improving and old age of spending; a negligent youth is usually attended by an ignorant middle age, and both by an empty old age. He that hath nothing to feed on but vanity and lies must needs lie down in the bed of sorrow.

4

A ship that bears much sail and little or no ballast is easily overset, and that man whose head hath great abilities and his heart little or no grace is in danger of foundering.

5

It is reported of the peacock that, priding himself in his gay feathers, he ruffles them up, but spying his black feet, he soon lets fall his plumes; so he that glories in his gifts and adornings should look upon his corruptions, and that will damp his high thoughts.

6

The finest bread hath the least bran, the purest honey the least wax, and the sincerest Christian the least self-love.

7

The hireling that labours all the day comforts himself that when night comes he shall both take his rest and receive his reward; the painful Christian that hath wrought hard in God's vineyard and hath born the heat and drought of the day, when he perceives his sun apace to decline and the shadows of his evening to be stretched out, lifts up his head with joy, knowing his refreshing is at hand.

8

Downy beds make drowsy persons, but hard lodging keeps the eyes open; a prosperous state makes a secure Christian, but adversity makes him consider.

9

Sweet words are like honey: a little may refresh, but too much gluts the stomach.

10

Diverse children have their different natures: some are like flesh which nothing but salt will keep from putrefaction, some again like tender fruits that are best preserved with sugar. Those parents are wise that can fit their nurture according to their nature.

11

That town which thousands of enemies without hath not been able to take hath been delivered up by one traitor within, and that man which all the temptations of Satan without could not hurt hath been foiled by one lust within.

12

Authority without wisdom is like a heavy axe without an edge: fitter to bruise than polish.

13

The reason why Christians are so loath to exchange this world for a better is because they have more sense than faith: they see what they enjoy; they do but hope for that which is to come.

14

If we had no winter, the spring would not be so pleasant; if we did not sometimes taste of adversity, prosperity would not be so welcome.

15

A low man can go upright under that door where a taller is glad to stoop; so a man of weak faith and mean abilities may undergo a cross more patiently than he that excels him both in gifts and graces.

16

That house which is not often swept makes the cleanly inhabitant soon loath it, and that heart which is not continually purifying itself is no fit temple for the spirit of God to dwell in.

17

Few men are so humble as not to be proud of their abilities, and nothing will abase them more than this: what hast thou, but what thou hast received? Come, give an account of thy stewardship.

18

He that will undertake to climb up a steep mountain with a great burden on his back will find it a wearisome if not an impossible task; so he that thinks to mount to heaven clogged with the cares and riches of this life, 'tis no wonder if he faint by the way.

19

Corn, till it have past through the mill and been ground to powder, is not fit for bread. God so deals with his servants: he grinds them with grief and pain till they turn to dust, and then are they fit manchet for his mansion.

20

God hath suitable comforts and supports for His children according to their several conditions. If He will make His face to shine upon them, He then makes them lie down in green pastures and leads them besides the still waters. If they stick in deep mire and clay, and all His waves and billows go over their heads, He then leads them to the rock which is higher than they.

21

He that walks among briars and thorns will be very careful where he sets his foot, and he that passes through the wilderness of this world had need ponder all his steps.

22

Want of prudence as well as piety hath brought men into great inconveniences, but he that is well stored with both seldom is so ensnared.

23

The skillful fisher hath his several baits for several fish, but there is a hook under all; Satan, that great Angler, hath his sundry baits for sundry tempers of men, which they all catch greedily at, but few perceives the hook till it be too late.

24

There is no new thing under the sun: there is nothing that can be said or done, but either that or something like it hath been both done and said before.

25

An aching head requires a soft pillow, and a drooping heart a strong support.

26

A sore finger may disquiet the whole body, but an ulcer within destroys it; so an enemy without may disturb a commonwealth, but dissentions within overthrow it.

27

It is a pleasant thing to behold the light, but sore eyes are not able to look upon it; the pure in heart shall see God, but the defiled in conscience shall rather choose to be buried under rocks and mountains than to behold the presence of the Lamb.

28

Wisdom with an inheritance is good, but wisdom without an inheritance is better than an inheritance without wisdom.

29

Lightning doth usually precede thunder, and storms rain, and strokes do not often fall till after threatening.

30

Yellow leaves argue want of sap and gray hairs want of moisture; so dry and sapless performances are symptoms of little spiritual vigor.

31

Iron, till it be thoroughly heat, is uncapable to be wrought; so God sees good to cast some men into the furnace of affliction and then beats them on His anvil into what frame he pleases.

32

Ambitious men are like hops that never rest climbing so long as they have anything to stay upon, but take away their props, and they are of all the most dejected.

33

Much labour wearies the body, and many thoughts oppress the mind; man aims at profit by the one and content in the other, but often misses of both and finds nothing but vanity and vexation of spirit.

34

Dim eyes are the concomitants of old age, and shortsightedness in those that are eyes of a republic fortells a declining state.

35

We read in Scriptures of three sorts of arrows: the arrow of an enemy, the arrow of pestilence, and the arrow of a slanderous tongue. The two first kill the body, the last the good name; the two former leave a man when he is once dead, but the last mangles him in his grave.

36

Sore labourers have hard hands and old sinners have brawny consciences.

37

Wickedness comes to its height by degrees. He that dares say of a less sin "Is it not a little one?" will ere long say of a greater, "Tush, God regards it not."

38

Some children are hardly weaned; although the teat be rubbed with wormwood or mustard, they will either wipe it off, or else suck down sweet and bitter together. So is it with some Christians: let God embitter all the sweets of this life, that so they might feed upon more substantial food, yet they are so childishly sottish that they are still hugging and sucking these empty breasts that God is forced to hedge up their way with thorns or lay affliction on their loins that so they might shake hands with the world, before it bid them farewell.

39

A prudent mother will not cloth her little child with a long and cumbersome garment; she easily forsees what events it is like to produce, at the best, but falls and bruises or perhaps somewhat worse. Much more will the allwise God proportion His dispensations according to the stature and strength of the person He bestows them on. Large endowments of honour, wealth, or a healthful body would quite overthrow some weak Christian; therefore God cuts their garments short to keep them in such a trim that they might run the ways of His commandment.

40

The spring is a lively emblem of the resurrection: after a long winter we see the leafless trees and dry stocks (at the approach of the sun) to resume their former vigor and beauty in a more ample manner than what they lost in the autumn; so shall it be at that great day after a long vacation, when the Sun of righteousness shall appear; those dry bones shall arise in far more glory than that which they lost at their creation, and in this transcends the spring that their leaf shall never fail nor their sap decline.

41

A wise father will not lay a burden on a child of seven years old which he knows is enough for one of twice his strength; much less will our heavenly Father (who knows our mold) lay such afflictions upon his weak children as would crush them to the dust, but according to the strength he will proportion the load. As God hath His little children, so He hath His strong men, such as are come to a full stature in Christ, and many times He imposes weighty burdens on their shoulders, and yet they go upright under them, but it matters not whether the load be more or less if God afford His help.

42

"I have seen an end of all perfection" said the royal prophet, but he never said, "I have seen an end of all sinning." What he did say may be easily said by many, but what he did not say cannot truly be uttered by any.

43

Fire hath its force abated by water, not by wind, and anger must be allayed by cold words and not by blustering threats.

44

A sharp appetite and a thorough concoction is a sign of a healthful body; so a quick reception and a deliberate cogitation argues a sound mind.

45

We often see stones hang with drops not from any innate moisture, but from a thick air about them; so may we sometime see marble-hearted sinners seem full of contrition, but it is not from any dew of grace within but from some black clouds that impends them, which produces these sweating effects.

46

The words of the wise, saith Solomon,.are as nails and as goads, both used for contrary ends; the one holds fast, the other puts forward. Such should be the precepts of the wise masters of assemblies to their hearers, not only to bid them hold fast the form of sound doctrine, but also so to run that they might obtain.

47

A shadow in the parching sun and a shelter in a blustering storm are of all seasons the most welcome; so a faithful friend in time of adversity is of all other most comfortable.

48

There is nothing admits of more admiration than God's various dispensation of His gifts among the sons of men, betwixt whom He hath put so vast a disproportion that they scarcely seem made of the same lump or sprung out of the loins of one Adam, some set in the highest dignity that mortality is capable of, and some again so base that they are viler than the earth, some so wise and learned that they seem like angels among men, and some again so ignorant and sottish that they are more like beasts than men, some pious saints, some incarnate devils, some exceeding beautiful, and some extremely deformed, some so strong and healthful that their bones are full of marrow and their breasts of milk, and some again so weak and feeble that while they live they are accounted among the dead; and no other reason can be given of all this but so it pleased Him whose will is the perfect rule of righteousness.

49

The treasures of this world may well be compared to husks, for they have no kernel in them, and they that feed upon them may soon stuff their throats, but cannot fill their bellies. They may be choked by them, but cannot be satisfied with them.

50

Sometimes the sun is only shadowed by a cloud that we cannot see his luster although we may walk by his light, but when he is set, we are in darkness till he arise again. So God doth sometime veil His face but for a moment that we cannot behold the light of His countenance as at some other time, yet He affords so much light as may direct our way, that we may go forwards to the city of habitation, but when He seems to set and be quite gone out of sight, then must we needs walk in darkness and see no light; yet then must we trust in the Lord and stay upon our God, and when the morning (which is the appointed time) is come, the Sun of righteousness will arise with healing in His wings.

51

The eyes and the ears are the inlets or doors of the soul, through which innumerable objects enter; yet is not that spacious room filled, neither doth it ever say it is enough, but like the daughters of the horseleach, cries, "Give, give"; and which is most strange, the more it receives, the more empty it finds itself and sees an impossibility ever to be filled but by Him in whom all fullness dwells.

52

Had not the wisest of men taught us this lesson that all is vanity and vexation of spirit, yet our own experience would soon have spelled it out, for what do we obtain of all these things, but it is with labour and vexation? When we enjoy them it is vanity and vexation, and if we loose them, then they are less than vanity and more than vexation, so that we have good cause often to repeat that sentence: vanity of vanities, vanity of vanities, all is vanity.

53

He that is to sail into a far country, although the ship, cabin, and provision be all convenient and comfortable for him, yet he hath no desire to make that his place of residence, but longs to put in at that port where his business lies. A Christian is sailing through this world unto his heavenly country, and here he hath many conveniences and comforts, but he must beware of desiring to make this the place of his abode, lest he meet with such tossings that may cause him to long for shore before he sees land. We must, therefore, be here as strangers and pilgrims, that we may plainly declare that we seek a city above and wait all the days of our appointed time till our change shall come.

54

He that never felt what it was to be sick or wounded doth not much care for the company of the physician or surgeon, but if he perceive a malady that threatens him with death, he will gladly entertain him whom he slighted before; so he that never felt the sickness of sin, nor the wounds of a guilt conscience cares not how far he keeps from him that hath skill to cure it, but when he finds his diseases to disrest him, and that he must needs perish if he have no remedy, will unfeignedly bid him welcome that brings a plaster for his sore or a cordial for his fainting.

55

We read of ten lepers that were cleansed but of one that returned thanks; we are more ready to receive mercies than we are to acknowledge them. Men can use great importunity when they are in distresses and show great ingratitude after their successes, but he that ordereth his conversation aright will glorify him that heard him in the day of his trouble.

56

The remembrance of former deliverances is a great support in present distresses. "He that delivered me," saith David, "from the paw of the lion and the paw of the bear will deliver me from this uncircumcised Philistine," and "He that hath delivered me," saith Paul, "will deliver me." God is the same yesterday, today, and forever; we are the same that stand in need of Him, today as well as yesterday, and so shall forever.

57

Great receipts call for great returns; the more that any man is intrusted withal, the larger his accounts stands upon God's score. It therefore behoves every man so to improve his talents that when his great Master shall call him to reckoning, He may receive His own with advantage.

58

Sin and shame ever go together - He that would be freed from the last must be sure to shun the company of the first.

59

God doth many times both reward and punish for one and the same action, as we see in Jehu; he is rewarded with a kingdom to the fourth generation for taking vengeance on the house of Ahab; and "Yet a little while," saith God, "and I will avenge the blood of Jezreel upon the house of Jehu." He was rewarded for the matter, and yet punished for the manner, which should warn him that doth any special service for God to fix his eye on the command and not on his own ends, lest he meet with Jehu's reward, which will end in punishment.

60

He that would be content with a mean condition must not cast his eye upon one that is in a far better estate than himself, but let him look upon him that is lower than he is, and if he see, that such a one bears poverty comfortably, it will help to quiet him, but if that will not do, let him look on his own unworthiness and that will make him say with Jacob: I am less than the least of Thy mercies.

61

Corn is produced with much labour (as the husbandman well knows), and some land asks much more pains than some other doth to be brought into tilth; yet all must be ploughed and harrowed. Some children (like sour land) are of so tough and morose a disposition that the plough of correction must make long furrows on their back and the harrow of discipline go often over them before they be fit soil to sow the seed of morality much less of grace in them. But when by prudent nurture they are brought into a fit capacity, let the seed of good instruction and exhortation be sown in the spring of their youth, and a plentiful crop may be expected in the harvest of their years.

62

As a man is called the little world, so his heart may be called the little
commonwealth; his more fixed and resolved thoughts are like to inhabitants, his
slight and flitting thoughts are like passengers that travel to and fro continually;
here is also the great court of justice erected, which is alway kept by conscience,
who is both accuser, excuser, witness, and judge, whom no bribes can pervert
nor flattery cause to favour, but as he finds the evidence, so he absolves or
condemns; yea, so absolute is this court of judicature that there is no appeal
from it, no not to the court of heaven itself, for if our conscience condemn us,
He also who is greater than our conscience will do it much more, but he that
would have boldness to go to the throne of grace to be accepted there must be
sure to carry a certificate from the court of conscience that he stands right there.

63

He that would keep a pure heart and lead a blameless life must set himself alway
in the awful presence of God. The consideration of His all-seeing eye will be a
bridle to restrain from evil and spur to quicken on to good duties. We certainly
dream of some remoteness betwixt God and us, or else we should not so often
fail in our whole course of life as we do, but he that with David sets the Lord
alway in his sight will not sin against Him.

64

We see in orchards some trees so fruitful that the weight of their burden is the
breaking of their limbs, some again are but meanly loaden, and some have
nothing to show but leaves only, and some among them are dry stock; so is it in
the church, which is God's orchard; there are some eminent Christians that are so
frequent in good duties that many times, the weight thereof impairs both their
bodies and estates, and there are some (and they sincere ones, too) who have not
attained to that fruitfulness, although they aim at perfection, and again there are

others that have nothing to commend them but only a gay profession, and these are but leavie Christians which are in as much danger of being cut down as the dry stock, for both cumber the ground.

65

We see in the firmament there is but one sun among a multitude of stars and those stars also to differ much one from the other in regard of bigness and brightness, yet all receive their light from that one sun; so is it in the church both militant and triumphant: there is but one Christ, who is the sun of righteousness, in the midst of an unnumerable company of saints and angels; those saints have their degrees, even in this life: some are stars of the first magnitude, and some of a less degree, and others (and they indeed the most in number) but small and obscure, yet all receive their luster (be it more or less) from that glorious sun that enlightens all in all, and if some of them shine so bright while they move on earth, how transcendently splendid shall they be when they are fixt in their heavenly spheres!

66

Men that have walked very extravagantly and at last bethink themselves of turning to God, the first thing which they eye is how to reform their ways rather than to beg forgiveness for their sins. Nature looks more at a compensation than at a pardon, but he that will not come for mercy without money and without price, but bring his filthy rags to barter for it, shall meet with miserable disappointment, going away empty bearing the reproach of his pride and folly.

67

All the works and doings of God are wonderful, but none more awful than His
great work of election and reprobation; when we consider how many good
parents have had bad children, and again how many bad parents have had pious
children, it should make us adore the sovereignty of God, who will not be tied to
time nor place, nor yet to persons, but takes and chooses, when and where and
whom He pleases; it should also teach the children of godly parents to walk with
fear and trembling. lest they through unbelief fall short of a promise; it may also
be a support to such as have or had wicked parents, that if they abide not in
unbelief, God is able to gaff them in. The upshot of all should make us with the
apostle to admire the justice and mercy of God and say how unsearchable are
His ways and His footsteps past finding out.

68

The gifts that God bestows on the sons of men are not only abused but most
commonly employed for a clean contrary end than that which they were given
for, as health, wealth, and honour, which might be so many steps to draw men to
God in consideration of His bounty towards them, but have driven them the
further from Him that they are ready to say: we are lords, we will come no more
at Thee. If outward blessings be not as wings to help us mount upwards, they
will certainly prove clogs and weights that will pull us lower downward.

69

All the comforts of this life may be compared to the gourd of Jonah, that
notwithstanding we take great delight for a season in them and find their shadow
very comfortable, yet there is some worm or other, of discontent, of fear, or grief
that lies at the root, which in great part withers the pleasure which else we should

take in them, and well it is that we perceive a decay in their greenness, for were earthly comforts permanent, who would look for heavenly?

70

All men are truly said to be tenants at will, and it may as truly be said that all have a lease of their lives, some longer, some shorter, as it pleases our great Landlord to let. All have their bounds set, over which they cannot pass, and till the expiration of that time, no dangers, no sickness, no pains, nor troubles shall put a period to our days. The certainty that that time will come, together with the uncertainty, how, where, and when, should make us so to number our days as to apply our hearts to wisdom, that when we are put out of these houses of clay we may be sure of an everlasting habitation that fades not away.

71

All weak and diseased bodies have hourly mementos of their mortality, but the soundest of men, have likewise their nightly monitor by the emblem of death, which is their sleep (for so is death often called), and not only their death, but their grave is lively represented before their eyes by beholding their bed, the morning may mind them of the resurrection, and the sun approaching of the appearing of the Sun of righteousness, at whose coming they shall all rise out of their beds, the long night shall fly away, and the day of eternity shall never end. Seeing these things must be, what manner of persons ought we to be, in all good conversation?

72

As the brands of a fire, if once severed, will of themselves go out although you use no other means to extinguish them, so distance of place together with length of time (if there be no intercourse) will cool the affections of intimate friends, though there should be no displeasance between them.

A good name is as a precious ointment, and it is a great favour to have a good
repute among good men; yet it is not that which commends us to God, for by
His balance we must be weighed, and by His judgment we must be tried, and as
He passes the sentence, so shall we stand.

74

Well doth the apostle call riches "deceitful" riches, and they may truly be
compared to deceitful friends who speak fair and promise much but perform
nothing, and so leave those in the lurch that most relied on them; so is it with the
wealth, honours, and pleasures of this world which miserably delude men and
make them put great confidence in them, but when death threatens and distress
lays hold upon them, they prove like the reeds of Egypt that pierce instead of
supporting, like empty wells in the time of drought that those that go to find
water in them return with their empty pitchers ashamed.

75

It is admirable to consider the power of faith, by which all things are (almost)
possible to be done; it can remove mountains (if need were); it hath stayed the
course of the sun, raised the dead, cast out devils, reversed the order of nature,
quenched the violence of the fire, made the water become firm footing for Peter
to walk on; nay, more than all these, it hath overcome the omnipotent Himself,
as when Moses intercedes for the people, God saith to him, "Let me alone, that I
may destroy them," as if Moses had been able by the hand of faith to hold the
everlasting arms of the mighty God of Jacob. Yea Jacob himself when he
wrestled with God face to face in Penuel, "Let me go," saith that Angel. "I will
not let thee go," replies Jacob, "till thou bless me." Faith is not only thus potent
but it is so necessary that without faith there is no salvation; therefore with all
our seekings and gettings, let us above all seek to obtain this pearl of price.

76

Some Christians do by their lusts and corruptions as the Israelites did by the
 Canaanites, not destroy them but put them under tribute, for that they could do
(as they thought) with less hazard and more profit; but what was the issue, they
became a snare unto them, pricks in their eyes and thorns in their sides, and at
last overcame them and kept them under slavery; so it is most certain that those
that are disobedient to the command of God and endeavour not to the utmost to
drive out all their accursed inmates but make a league with them, they shall at
last fall into perpetual bondage under them unless the great deliverer Christ Jesus
come to their rescue.

77

God hath by his providence so ordered that no one country hath all commodities
within itself, but what it wants another shall supply that so there may be a mutual
commerce through the world. As it is with countries so it is with men; there was
never yet any one man that had all excellences, let his parts natural and acquired,
spiritual and moral, be never so large, yet he stands in need of something which
another man hath (perhaps meaner than himself) which shows us perfection is
not below, as also that God will have us beholden one to another.

Bibliography
Anne Bradstreet

Primary Sources:

The Tenth Muse Lately Sprung up in America. Or Severall Poems, compiled with great Variety of Wit and Learning, full of delight. London: Stephen Bowtell, 1650.

Several Poems Compiled with great variety of Wit and Learning, Full of Delight. Boston: John Foster, 1678.

Several Poems Compiled with great variety of Wit and Learning, Full of Delight. Boston: [James and Ann Franklin?],1758.

The Works of Anne Bradstreet in Prose and Verse (Edited by John Harvard Ellis, Charleston: Cutter, 1867). Reprint. New York: Peter Smith, 1962 (The edition cited in this text).

The Poems of Mrs. Anne Bradstreet (1612 - 1672). Together with Her Prose Remains. Introduction by Charles Eliot Norton. New York: Duedecimos, 1897.

The Complete Works of Anne Bradstreet. Edited by Joseph R. McElrath, Jr. and Allan P. Robb. Boston: Twayne, 1981.

Secondary Sources:

Bacon, Francis. **The Complete Essays of ...** New York: Washington Square Press, 1963.

Dolle, Raymond F. **Anne Bradstreet, A Reference Guide**. Boston: G. K. Hall, 1990.

Galinsky, Hans. "Anne Bradstreet, DuBartas und Shakespeare im Zusammenhang Kolonialer Verpflanzung und Umfromung europaischer Literatur: Ein Forschungsbericht und enie Hypothese." In **Festshift fur Walter Fischer**. Heidelberg: Carl Winter, 1959.

Gilbert Sandra M. and Susan Guber. **The Norton Anthology of Literature by Women**. New York: Norton, 1985.

Gilligan, Carol. **In a Different Voice: Psychological Theory and Women's Development**. Cambridge: Harvard, 1982.

Hutchinson, Robert. "Introduction." 1 - 35, in his **Poems of Anne Bradstreet**. New York: Dover, 1969.

Koehler, Lyle. **A Search for Power: The "Weaker Sex" in Seventeenth-Century New England**. Urbana: U of Illinois, 1980.

Martin, Wendy. "Part One: Anne Bradstreet," in **An American Triptych: Anne Bradstreet, Emily Dickenson, Adrienne Rich**. Chapel Hill: University of North Carolina Press, 1984.

Nietzsche, Friedrich **Daybreak**. New York: Cambridge U P, 1982.

_____ **Human All Too Human**. New York: Cambridge U P, 1986.

Rosenmeier, Rosamond. **Anne Bradstreet Revisited**. Boston: Twayne, 1991.

Sargent, Ritamarie. "Poetry and the Puritan Faith: The Elegies of Anne Bradstreet and Edward Taylor." in **A Salzburg Miscellany: English and America Studies, 1964-1984**. Vol. 1, 149-160. Salzburg: Universitat Salzburg, 1984

Schweitzer, Ivy. "Anne Bradstreet Wrestles with the Reaissance," **Early American Literature**, 23(1988), no. 3, 291-312.

Spinoza, Benedict de. **The Chief Works of ...** Vol II, New York: Dover Publications, 1951.

Sweet, Timothy. "Gender, Genre, and Subjectivity in Anne Bradstreet's Early Elegies." **Early American Literature**, 23(1988), no. 2, 152-174.

Walker, Cheryl. "Anne Bradstreet: A Woman Poet." In **Critical Essays on Anne Bradstreet**. 254-261. Eds. Pattie Cowell and Ann Stanford. Boston: G.K. Hall, 1983.

Westbrook, Perry D. "Anne Bradstreet." In **A Literary History of New England**. Bethlehem: Leigh University, 1988.

Wharton, Donald P. "Anne Bradstreet and the **Arbella**." In **Critical Essays on Anne Bradstreet**. 262-269. Eds. Pattie Cowell and Ann Stanford. Boston: G.K. Hall, 1983.

White, Elizabeth Wade. **Anne Bradstreet, "The Tenth Muse."** New York: Oxford, 1931.

Wittgenstein, Ludwig. **Tractataus logico-philosophicus**. Trans. D. F. Pears & B.F. McGuinness. London: Rutledge & Kegan Paul, 1961.

Mercy Otis Warren
Bequest of Winslow Warren
Courtesy, Museum of Fine Arts, Boston

Chronology

Mercy Otis Warren 1728 - 1814

1728 September 25, born in Barnstable, Cape Cod, Mass. First daughter and third child in a family of 13 children.

1735 Joined her brother James in his candidate studies for Harvard with tutor Rev. Jonathan Russell.

1743 Attended Harvard Commencement and met James Warren. Continued studies with her brother James as he prepared at home for M.A. degree.

1754 November married James Warren, went to live in the Warren family estate at Eel River, Plymouth, Mass.

1757 Moved to Winslow house, Plymouth Mass. October 18, son James born.

1759 March 24, son Winslow born; died 1791.

1762 April 14, son Charles born; died 1785.

1761 February 24, James Otis's famous civil rights speech: "taxation without representation is tyranny."

1764 March 21, son Henry born.

1765 James Warren elected to Massachusetts House of Representatives

1766 September 20, son George born; died 1800.

1772 March 26 and April 23 selections from **The Adulateur** appear in **Massachusetts Spy**. October meeting in the Winslow house at which the idea for the committees of correspondence originated.

1773 **The Adulateur** appears as a political pamphlet. May 24 and July 19, selections from "The Defeat" appear in **Boston Gazette**.

1775 January 23 and 26, selections from **The Group** appear in the **Boston Gazette** and the **Massachusetts Spy**. Later in the year **The Group** published as pamphlet in Boston, New York and Philadelphia.

1776   **The Blockheads** published in Boston.

1779   **The Motley Assembly** published in Boston.

1787   James Warren again elected to the Massachusetts House of
        Representatives. Became the Speaker of the House.

1788   **Observations on the New Constitution** published in Boston and New
        York.

1790   **Poems: Dramatic and Miscellaneous** published in Boston.

1805   **History of...the American Revolution** published in Boston.

1807   July through August, ten letters from John Adams and six letters from
        Mercy concerning her treatment of him in the **History**. Later published as
        Correspondence ... relating to her History... in Boston in 1876.

1814   October 19, died in Winslow house, Plymouth, Massachusetts.

3

Mercy Otis Warren

1728-1814

The following words are not the words of one of our founding fathers, but rather those of one of our founding mothers.

> If peace and unanimity are cherished, and the equalization of liberty, and the equity and energy of law, maintained by harmony and justice, the present representative government may stand for ages a luminous monument of republican wisdom, virtue and integrity. The principles of the revolution ought ever to be the pole-star of the statesmen, respected by the rising generation; and the advantages bestowed by Providence should never be lost, by negligence, indiscretion, or guilt. The people may again be reminded that the elective franchise is in their own hands; that it ought not to be abused either for personal gratifications, or the indulgence of partisan acrimony. This advantage should be improved, not only for the benefit of existing society, but with an eye to that fidelity which is due posterity. **History** 696. [1]

This quotation taken from **HISTORY OF THE RISE, PROGRESS AND TERMINATION OF THE AMERICAN REVOLUTION Interspersed with Biographical, Political and Moral Observations**, published in 1805, typifies the thinking of its author, Mercy Otis Warren.

Mercy Otis Warren, playwright, poet, historian and one of the greatest enlightenment thinkers in America, is barely known in American history. Nevertheless, throughout that same history she has been cited often for the greatness of her mind by those who have read her--from her contemporaries to ours.

In 1776 John Adams wrote of her "of all the Genius's which have yet arisen in America, there has been none superior."[2]   In 1801, Thomas Jefferson commented "I have long possessed evidence of her high station in the ranks of genius."   In 1848, Elizabeth Ellet considered Mercy Otis Warren "the most remarkable woman who lived in the days of the American Revolution... Seldom has one woman, in any age, acquired such ascendancy over the strongest by the mere force of a powerful intellect."   In 1881, Ednah Dow Cheney called Mercy Otis Warren the "most gifted" of American women. In 1896, in the first book-length study of Mercy Otis Warren, Alice Brown concludes "You begin by admiring her intellectual gifts and her force of character; finally it is her gentleness by which you are chiefly impressed."   Anne R. Marble, in 1901, proclaimed "Mistress Mercy Warren" the "real daughter of the American Revolution," telling how Mercy Otis Warren wrote speeches for some of the members of the Massachusetts Assembly until one member, having stumbled so often over her vocabulary and her classical allusions, confessed to the congress the source of his wisdom and eloquence. In 1902, John Fiske saw her as "one of the brightest and most highly cultivated in her time."[3]   By the 1950's scholars were characterizing Mercy Otis Warren's writings "as the best expression of this doctrine (anti-federalism)," and maintaining that her "fame rests more upon her powerful intellect and political influence than on (her) other talents and virtues." [4]

Not until the 1980's did such judgments finally begin to bring about the reappearance of some of her work. First, a facsimile edition of her plays and poetry were introduced with the citation of Mercy Otis Warren as "one of the most significant American women of her time (**Poems** vii)." Then in 1981 her "private poems" were published in **The New England Quarterly** with the observation that these personal poems "give us an insight into her innermost feelings about life, family, her epoch and her God ("Private Poems" 201)." Then, in 1988, her **History of the Rise, Progress and Termination of the American Revolution, Interspersed with Biographical, Political and Moral Observations** was edited for the first time and republished with the claim that

Mercy Otis Warren "was the most formidable female intellectual in 18th century America" (**History** xvi).[5]

Although those who have come to know her work, testify to the greatness of her intellect; still, no one has suggested that this woman thinker might also be a great political philosopher. Notwithstanding, her contemporaries, v.g. John Adams and Thomas Jefferson, through their non-philosophic writings, even sometimes in virtue of their letters to her, are denominated political philosophers. This anthology will show through both her life and her work that Mercy Otis Warren is an American political philosopher.

Mercy Otis was born on a large farm in Barnstable, Massachusetts on September 24, 1728. She was the first daughter and third child in a family of thirteen children. The Otises were a well established Massachusetts family. John Otis I had emigrated to Bear Cove in the Massachusetts Bay Colony in 1630, the same year the poet and moral philosopher, Anne Bradstreet, arrived in Salem. By the generation of John Otis III, Mercy's father, the family had acquired both wealth and position. John Otis III had tripled his father's assets, become the judge of the Probate Court, was captain of the local militia, and Barnstable's representative to the Massachusetts General Assembly. Mercy's older brother James Otis was prepared for Harvard College by the Reverend Jonathan Russell, his uncle. Like Anne Bradstreet, Mercy thereby had the advantage of sharing a brother's tutor who seems to have just as enthusiastically entered into her intellectual training as he did her brother's. Again like Anne, Mercy read as widely as possible developing a special regard for Sir Walter Raleigh's **History of the World**. Jonathan Russell loaned her his copy of this book "and encouraged her in the study of history in general, for which she had a passion. (Brown 23)" Elizabeth Wade White, in describing the effect of this book on Anne Bradstreet characterizes it as:

> That majestic philosophical study of the ancient kingdoms of men that was written while Sir Walter was a prisoner in the Tower of London, and published in 1614. The somber magnificence of style, the vast narratives of dynastic triumph and decay, and most of all the ever-present recognition of God's will and authority in the cycles of history, made this monumental work, which was generally admired of particular interest and importance to the Puritan. (61-62.)

As the **Iliad** and the **Odyssey** were to the educated of fifth century Athens, this was many young American's encyclopedic book.

Her brother James went to Harvard College in 1739, where he was a fellow student of James Warren. The Warrens were also a very prominent New England family. Richard Warren had arrived on the Mayflower and was a prosperous pilgrim. By the third generation of Americans, James's father conducted a very successful coastal and overseas trade business. Like Mercy's father, he exercised civic responsibilities: High Sheriff of Plymouth County, Captain in the local militia, and Plymouth's representative to the Massachusetts General Assembly.

After completing his baccalaureate at Harvard, James Otis returned to Barnstable where he began his studies for the M.A. degree. Mercy worked with him, probably doing her first reading of John Locke and David Hume at this time. James finished his Harvard M.A. degree in 1754 and after his sister's marriage, moved to Boston.

Mercy Otis married James Warren in November 1754 when she was 26 years old. They settled on the Warren family estate at Eel River and shortly, upon the prosperous development of James's commercial enterprises, bought a place of their own, the Windsor Mansion in Plymouth. Within a few years James had become the Sheriff of Plymouth county, a justice of peace, and a leading officer in the militia. Their lives, like the lives of their parents, brothers, sisters, and their friends, the John Adamses, the John Winthrops and others, began as provincial citizens of the Massachusetts's colony--conventional, responsible, and well to do. Positions of governmental, economic and social consequence followed Mercy and James Warren. But the special talent of Mercy and the special circumstances of the Revolution made a conventional life preposterous.

Hosting meetings of American patriots in her home, sharing enthusiasm for liberty and eventually independence, the sister of James Otis who had famously proclaimed "taxation without representation is tyranny," the spouse of a leading, if reluctant military and political leader, and herself the originator of the idea of Committees of Correspondence among the thirteen colonies, [6] Mercy Otis Warren became a more and more important voice on the behalf of America. In a culture where there were no women publicly involved in the formation of the new politics, many men who were, grew in their knowledge and respect for the thought of Mercy Otis Warren. Her correspondence with Abigail Adams is an example of how she raised the consciousness of women's issues with her friends and how she attempted to influence the institutions of a newly forming republic.

All Mercy Otis Warren's pre-1790 work appeared anonymously. On March 26, 1772 in Isaiah Thomas' **Massachusetts Spy** there appeared a synopsis and speeches from a play set in Upper Servia (Boston), mocking the conflict between a repressive government, lead by British appointed Massachusetts governor, Rapatio (Thomas Hutchinson), against a group of patriots under Brutus (James Otis). In the April 23, 1772 issue more of the same play was presented. In 1773 these satirical excerpts were published as an anonymously written political drama in the pamphlet **The Adulateur**. On May 24 and July 19, 1773 excerpts from a second Warren play appeared in the **Boston Gazette**. In this play, entitled "The Defeat," the action continues. The evil Tory governor is still controlling Upper Servia, and still the people are subject to "That Bane of Freedom, and the Badge of Slavery, / That Nurse of Vice, of Rapine and Distress,/ A Standing Army/" (Act III, Sc. 2); but by the end of the play the governor, "his abettors and creatures are totally defeated" (May 24, **Boston Gazette**.). Again the patriots are virtuous and good, the British and the colonial government are farcically dishonest and evil. The patriots win against the Tories, but do not gain their real goal: independence for America.

John Adams thought this work so effective that he wrote to James Warren, that he hoped the Boston Tea Party would be "celebrated by a certain poetical pen which has no equal I know of in this country." The Boston Tea Party was so celebrated, but anonymously in a poem in a newspaper, not in the form of drama as political encouragement. Eventually "The Squabble of the Sea Nymphs" became Mercy Otis Warren's most famous poem, when it was published as her work in 1790. In introducing the poem, Mercy makes it clear that "the author's own opinion of the equity or policy is not to be measured in this political sally that was written at the request of a friend" (**Poems** 202).

Mercy continued the political war of words by satirizing the councilors appointed by the British parliament after the removal of Governor Hutchinson. This time she presented not the contrast of the worthy patriots against the

69

government and the Tories, but merely an expose of the ridiculous fashion of the discontent among the Tories and the British troops leading to their colossal ineffectiveness in Boston. Scenes from this play first appeared in the **Boston Gazette** on January 23, 1775 and in the **Massachusetts Spy** on January 26, 1775. Unlike "The Defeat" of which no part was ever published and no manuscript yet found, this play, **The Group**, was published that same year in Boston, in Philadelphia, and in New York as a part of the new political pamphleteering in America. There begins with **The Group** a series of women characters who are outspoken, some of whom are trapped by abusive husbands, and some who even begin to recognize their oppression. At the end of this play a Tory women makes a final speech that leaves "Freedom" weeping on the stage (Act IV, sc. 3).

Late in 1775 General John Burgoyne of the British Forces wrote the play "The Blockade of Boston," satirizing the patriots of America for the entertainment of his officers and the loyalists living in Boston. This play has been lost, but Mercy Otis Warren's response is not. **The Blockheads or the Affrightened Officers** published in 1776 humorously portrays the British problems in Boston to be socially and politically unresolvable. Again the role of the women in the play magnifies the futility of seeking wealth, power and position by siding with the British. The drama itself ends with a monologue by a woman who has retreated with her family to Halifax, Nova Scotia, under the command of the British General William Howe. This woman typifies Tory values; she has sought through British allegiance to raise herself and her daughter socially and economically, but now she is living in a barn in the brutal wilderness of Canada, eating bait fish and weeping over her betrayal of New England. Her message concludes: "one tear my injur'd country weep for me, /And for that tear, may you ever be free (Epilogue)."

The last wartime Boston play written and published by Mercy Otis Warren was **The Motley Assembly**. It appeared as a pamphlet in 1779, treating the problems of a Boston freed from British domination but peopled with those who still held allegiance to Troy values, who are hoping for the defeat of the American states and the return of a social elite with British sensitivities. Once again women incriminate themselves against a ruder American democratic society, desiring a return to a society envisioned as cultured, mannered and elegant but satirized as a phony and plutocratic way of life. Two veterans of the American Revolution end the play prophesying a society that will bring an expiration and thorough reformation of Tory values. Even though this pamphlet is published with four references to its author as a man--friends, colleagues and many of the political leaders of America were aware of who this political and social pundit was.

These early dramas are all unfinished. It is most probable that Warren merely sketched out the plots, wrote scenes to meet the exigencies of rapidly developing political circumstances, and then set them before the public in periodicals and pamphlets. Rapid political and military changes in the independence movement necessitated new messages in new dramas with never the time nor the necessity to return to the completion of the original efforts.

General James Warren had been the paymaster general and a chief commissary officer for the supply and logistical support of the Revolutionary Army in Massachusetts. He and his wife, Mercy Otis Warren, saw some of their fellow citizens use wartime positions to increase personal fortunes. As post revolutionary society emerged, the new fame often brought with it the power to effect commercial rewards, which in turn brought greater desire for political control.

> In the Warren letters from the 1770's James's even more than Mercy's, one finds a note of exasperation, of impatience with those people who were not pulling their weight, who hoped to profit in honor, position, or wealth from the wartime exigencies (Weales 889).

These conclusions brought the Warrens's an increased sensitivity to the possibility of the corruption of national government offices for the purpose of increasing personal fame and wealth. On the other hand so many farmers were ever more suffering a decline in their standard of living. The desperate acts of the indebted farmers, most of whom suffered because they were veterans of the Revolutionary war, came to fruition as Shays rebellion. This armed insurrection moved against the courts which were sentencing debtors to prison. General Warren sympathized with their plight and was even suspected by some of complicity with the uprising.

Once again James and Mercy Otis Warren, now in their sixties, came back to the active political life. General Warren was elected to the Legislature on a post Shays wave of radicalism. He became Speaker of the Massachusetts House for the next two years, the period corresponding with the ratification of the Constitution. Mercy became the chief correspondent and theorist behind her husband, behind

Elbridge Gerry, the only Massachusetts delegate to refuse to sign the Constitution as it came out of the convention, and the leader behind the rest of that small number of Massachusetts anti-federalist republicans. This time both husband and wife went to press, he as "Helvidius Priscus" in a series of newspaper articles, she as the anonymous pamphleteer, "a Columbian Patriot." This time her work was not contemporarily known as hers even by their friends and past political allies. The first edition of her **Observations On The New Constitution** was distributed by Elbridge Gerry and, in spite of a number of denials, accredited to him. There were only a few copies published in Boston in 1788, but, later in 1788, Greenleaf printed 1,630 copies for the Federal Committee of New York to distribute to their local county committees in preparation for the New York debate on the adoption of the constitution.

Through her and her husband's criticism of growing public corruption, of a constitution that they, at that time, thought would lend itself to oligarchy, and through a widening knowledge of this criticism following from the voluminous correspondence of Mercy, the Warrens placed themselves outside the emerging federalist consensus. Even John Adams, who had been a long time friend, found their views increasingly repugnant. Their constant dread about the demise of republican principles after the revolutionary war, their fear of the "federal city," caused them to appear politically untrustworthy and even led General James Warren, in 1790, when he had been elected lieutenant governor of Massachusetts in the Hancock administration, to decline the post. From this point on the Warrens sank deeper and deeper into obscurity. More and more the politically active shunned or even impugned the reservations of the Warrens.

Mercy Otis Warren had concluded her **Observations** in 1788 by entreating that if America did accept this dangerous federalization, then the active political types should "strive to support the peace and the unanimity of his country though every other blessing should expire;" and that "the sublimer characters, the philosophic lovers of freedom who have wept over her exit, (should) retire to the calm shades of contemplation (19)." This, in a large way, is what **Poems: Dramatic and Miscellaneous** is; her retirement from the active political life and the beginning of her contribution through calm contemplation and indirect influence on the life of this republican democracy. The book, published in 1790, is the first published work bearing her name. It contained eighteen miscellaneous poems and two plays. Most of the poems had appeared anonymously in newspapers during the 70's and the 80's, and nine have political content. The dramas, **The Sack of Rome** and **The Ladies of Castile**, appeared for their first and only publication to this day. They, unlike the five wartime plays, are completed and polished works set outside her contemporary country. Each speaks directly to the problem of liberty and especially to the social and moral values that a new republic must protect if it is to survive. These themes dominate all Mercy Otis Warren's post revolutionary writings.

Mercy Otis Warren's prodigious correspondence continued, and with these last two plays, the poems, and the coming three volume history of the American Revolution, she retired into an even more indirect "behind the scenes" influence on public opinion and the formation of public policy. However, even after the Warrens' isolation by John Adams and the Federalist party, Mercy worked on Adams' behalf guiding her fellow anti-federalist Elbridge Gerry in avoiding a war with France in 1797. Jefferson took her public silence during the Adams administration as "a proof that she did not go with the current (Anthony 203)." In fact, she, her husband and her sons suffered great disfavor among their Massachusetts fellow citizens because of their dedication to the republicanism of Jefferson.

In 1805, her three volume **History of the Rise Progress and Termination of the American Revolution interspersed with Biographical, Political and Moral Observations** was published.

> [It] was the culmination of her literary career. Through it she satisfied a powerful urge to fuse her personal and public convictions. It served as a means to unite her ethical, political and philosophical concerns; it joined her personal religiosity with her ideological commitments; and it provided a vehicle for a female intellectual to be useful in a republican culture. **(History**, xvi).

In 1807, when John Adams read Mercy Otis Warren's analysis of his character in her **History**; he was hurt and angry. From July to August, there were ten letters from Adams and six replies from Mercy, all bitter. Not until November, 1811, through the good work of Elbridge Gerry, was the correspondence between these two old friends begun again on a friendly basis. Adams was 76 and she was 83. Once again they joined influences among their Massachusetts constituencies in support of the extremely unpopular War of 1812.

On the last day of her life, October 19, 1814, Plymouth was a War of 1812 garrison town, and she wrote "we are hourly expecting the depredation of the British," still alert to that sense of vigilance on the behalf of freedom that rose from her energy and **amor patriae**.

Introduction to
Observations on the New Constitution

When the Warrens studied the newly proposed federal constitution in 1788 they saw no relief for those who had indebted themselves as a result of this war and too many opportunities for the developing oligarchy in America. If governmental institutions were created that could control commerce in accordance with what those institutions themselves took to be the needs of the federal system--those who created and controlled such institutions would be making all others potential economic slaves to such a "federal city."[7] It was not that the convention was conspiratorial, but that "power without limitation or amenability may endanger the brightest virtue." Therefore, any articles of union must assure the people, and their separate states, of a frequent and constant return to their constituency, an assured rotation of the officers of a federal government, severe limits on the powers of any continental bureaucracy, a particular bill of rights and protection against "the insolence of any petty revenue officer to enter our houses, search, insult and seize at pleasure." The natural propensity of any "overbearing insolence of office" had to be checked in the constitution lest they replace the monarchical tyranny of a foreign ruler with an "aristocratic tyranny: of our own making."

For this reason Mercy Otis Warren, again in anonymity, argues that Massachusetts should have rejected the then proposed federal constitution. Instead, the people should ask that another constitution be written, one that provides rectificatory justice in the form of an equitable allowance, first, for all those who have incurred personal debt and loss on behalf of direct support of the War for Independence, and secondly, for the several states which publicly incurred war debt. This along with the inclusion of a bill of rights would create an instrument, an attitude and a motive for the freed people of the Confederated States to bind themselves "by the most indissoluble union, but without renouncing their separate sovereignties and independence and becoming tributaries to a consolidated fabric of aristocratic tyranny."

According to Mercy Otis Warren the simple principles from which the social, political and moral community arise are powerfully evident in the history of the world and in our personal experience. The character of humanity is

75

distinguished by the natural principles of self-defense and the love of distinction. When institutions, family, church, and government support, inculcate, and channel distinction toward equality and benevolence then a society flourishes. When institutions are regulated by the one or the few, rather than equally by all the citizens, human nature is such that the distinction, the power and the wealth accrue to the one and the few. Freedom is the instrument of society that allows each citizen the responsibility to gain sufficient wealth and to exert a shared power in the political community. When this fails to happen, as history so abundantly shows "from the days of Nimrod to Caesar, and from Caesar to an arbitrary prince of the house of Brunswick" (**History** 3) in 18th century Britain, the arbitrary use of distinction, power and wealth ultimately leads to democratic revolution. However, history also shows that oftentimes the patriots of the new freedom become caught up in "an alteration of manners, the blending of characters and new trains of ideas" which in turn create "the rage of accumulation and the taste for expensive pleasures ... Thus the hurry of spirits, that ever attends the eager pursuit of fortune and a passion for splendid enjoyments leads to the forgetfulness" of the very virtues that gain and maintain freedom (**History** 4). Then, once again there grows up the horrible accretion of personal power, distinction and the oppression of the many who provide the fodder for such accumulation.

To prevent this from happening to the new union of American states, Mercy argues for a constitution that requires safeguards against the use of the federal system for commercial advantage. Many of her criticisms were answered by the Bill of Rights, by subsequent amendments, and by the spirit and traditions formed through the beginnings of U.S. history. However, a number of her odious projections still plague us: the accumulation of wealth through long service in the Congress, a federal court system with practically dictatorial jurisdiction over the states, a tax revenue bureaucracy with powers that preceed judicial review, a "federal city" governed by an aristocratic officialdom not directly subject to its citizens.

Governmental institutions can guide, protect and preserve the individuals of a country in the formation of attitudes, manners, ethical principles and even the character of the arts and sciences developed in such a culture. The springs of action and the strength of social ties, however, ultimately depend upon the

76

"feelings of the heart" (**History** 4) and when we search our hearts carefully, in the light of Mercy Otis Warren's analysis, we can see the constitution as originally proposed and its convention as "betray[ing] the rights of the people, under the specious and popular pretence of **justice, consolidation** and **dignity**." For freedom is established and maintained on the underlying realization of benevolent character, allowed and encouraged through social institutions, the family, the church and the government, as the means and the way to restrain the personal desire for wealth and power and to encourage equal access to power and wealth in a republic of "rational liberty" (**History** 43).

This is not the understanding of freedom of John Adams, who held that the principle of freedom is the silence of law, and that that principle depends upon a civil constitution which will regulate the natural inequalities of men in such a fashion as to preserve the rights of all, by creating a republican government of the best and the wisest (Adams, VI,65). Nor is it the conception of freedom of Thomas Jefferson, who maintains that freedom of thought and speech is the primary guarantee of all the other liberties in a democratic republic; that with it and through it, the government will adapt itself to new and different situations, or be overturned (Jefferson 530).

This constitution was adopted. Mercy Otis Warren lost her plea for longer deliberations and for a better instrument to preserve the original virtues and spirit of the American Revolution. In the **Observations**, as was noted above, she agreed to a complete acceptance of the judgment of the people of the "confederated states." She did accept this judgment and went on to see the development of this constitution and its government as a protector of her concept of freedom, truly based on the principles she had elaborated:

> Perfection in government is not to be expected from so imperfect a creature as man; experience has taught, that he falls...Perhaps genius has never devised a system more congenial to their wishes, or better adapted to the conditions of man, than the American constitution. At the same time it is left open to amendments whenever its imperfections are discovered by the wisdom of future generations, or when contingencies may arise either here or abroad, to make alterations necessary. On the principles of republicanism was this constitution founded; and on this it must stand (**History** 692).

Freedom for Mercy Otis Warren is a fundamental principle of republicanism. The civil constitution, however, is not its only agency. The family, the church and the culture, as well as the government, must assure each member of the right and the opportunity to gain sufficient wealth and distinction and, thus, to share in the fullness of this country.

The difference in Mercy Otis Warren's formulation of the concept of freedom is only one example of her unique understanding of political concepts which follows from a fully developed political philosophy. John Adams once said of his differences with Thomas Jefferson in political philosophy "Whether you or I are right, posterity must judge." Hopefully, someday the study of the political philosophy of Mercy Otis Warren will be a part of our understanding of the history and the foundation of the United States of America. And hopefully, it will become, equally with Adams' and Jefferson's philosophy, subject to the judgment of posterity.

Mercy Otis Warren believed in the elemental reality of two human passions: survival and distinction. Reason and religion must find institutional ways to regulate and guide these passions if the social fabric is to be preserved and promoted. These two original forces animated all of her work, from the earliest satirical political drama, through her voluminous correspondence to her final monumental history of the War of Independence. The nature of humanity is such that unchecked desire leads to despotic rule. Republics throughout history have self-destructed because of the growth of personal avarice and political ambition.

> Public opinion, when grounded on false principles, and dictated by the breath of ambitious individuals, sometimes creates a tyranny, felt by the minority more severely, than that usually inflicted by the hand of the sceptred monarch (**History**, 695).

An understanding of these fundamental principles of all human action energize all the enthusiasms and all the fears that drive Mercy Otis Warren's political philosophy.

> The study of human character opens at once a beautiful and a deformed picture of the soul. We find a noble principle implanted in the nature of man, that pants for distinction. This principle

78

operates in every bosom and when kept under control of reason and the influence of humanity, it produces the most benevolent effects, but when the checks of conscience are thrown aside, or the moral sense weakened by the sudden acquisition of wealth or power, humanity is obscured, and if favorable coincidence of circumstances permits profligacy, tyranny, and the wanton exercise of arbitrary sway (**History**, 3).

This original spring of goodness must be guided by a system of government that furthers human benevolence. If the social, moral and political circumstances are roughly equal, then a democratic institution can keep open the avenues of freedom and opportunity for all. On the other hand if the rich and the poor, the politically powerful and a large weakened populace grow, with them will grow the arbitrary use of power. Eventually such a concentration of power will destroy a republic and lead to absolute tyranny and moral anarchy.

In 1888, **Observations** was reprinted still being attributed to Elbridge Gerry by Paul Leicester Ford in his centennial celebration, the **Pamphlets on the Constitution of the United States**. By the 1950's research into the life and the letters of Mercy Otis Warren, specifically a letter to Catherine Macauley in England, established Mercy's authorship of the pamphlet. It's republication has remained rare. One is in the 1962 Quadrangle Books edition of Richard Henry Lee's **Letters from a Federal Farmer to the Republican**. **Observations** is there only as an additional example of the anti-federalist argument. The last and most careful publication is in Herbert J. Storing, ed., **The Complete Anti-Federalist**, 7 volumes, Chicago, 1981. **Observations** is in Volume 4, pages 270-287.

The political doctrine set forth by Mercy Otis Warren in these **Observations** is singular. Here is a distinct and distinguishing political philosophy. The concept of freedom, the institutions that support it, and their particular ways of doing so are uniquely and insightfully drawn in the terms of human achievement throughout the history of revolutions. It is a politically dangerous time when the citizens of a new republic create the instruments whereby their new freedom will be maintained. Mercy Otis Warren knows of the failures of the past --in her two completed and formal dramas **The Sack of Rome** and **The Ladies of Castile** she presented examples of those failures--here she refers to such failures as "the most mortifying instances of human weakness." Throughout her objections to various "ambiguities of expression" that fill this constitution, she appeals to arguments of the founders of the philosophy of English law, to Matthew Hale, and to William Blackstone, but always adding new distinctions and understandings to concepts of trial by jury, taxation rights, legislative limitation, the parameters of political office, etc. Mercy Otis Warren is one of the first philosophers to use the late 18th century term "responsibility." [8] She uses it twice in the **Observations**, once arguing that politically "annual election is the basis of responsibility," and secondly arguing that a Senate chosen for six years sets up a legislature "beyond all responsibility." Thus, use of one of the newest concepts in political philosophy is again a mark of the depth and the originality of Mercy Otis Warren's philosophy.

As you read and study this work, you will be in contact with a specification of political philosophy that Mercy Otis Warren wrote in a passion and under an assurance that its author would always remain anonymous. Hopefully that passion and the protection of that assumed anonymity will bring to you new insights into the practice of what political freedom should mean in a republic.

Endnotes

[1] All citations to works of Mercy Otis Warren will be by page number to: Lester Cohen's edition of **History of the Rise, Progress and Termination of the American Revolution**, cited **History**; Benjamin Franklin V's edition **The Plays and Poems of Mercy Otis Warren**, cited **Poems**. [See #7 below.]

[2] John Adams was denounced as "a better orator than critic" by a nineteenth century author who reprinted a few passages from Warren's "The Sack of Rome" while claiming that they "have little dramatic or poetic merit"(22). With his premise that "the qualities of genius" in women are merely "the similtude of that which in men is the characteristic...of the highest grade of mental inspiration"(7), the author finds her ideas of political partisanship to be "even in a woman...delightful"(23). (Rufus Wilmot Griswold. **The Female Poets of America**. Philadelphia: Cary and Hart, 1849,)

[3] In the same year, a librarian at Providence, Rhode Island, writes that Mercy Otis Warren's history is "of interest only to the special student, as one of the earliest connected narratives of the struggle" (William Eaton Foster, "Mercy Otis Warren," 148 in J.N. Larned. **The Literature of American History: A Bibliographical Guide.** Boston: Houghton, Mifflin, 1902).

[4] Sources for quoted citations in the order of their appearances: Adams: Alice Brown p. 163; Jefferson: Katharine Anthony, p.198; Elizabeth Ellet, p.46 ; Ednah Dow Cheney, p.71; Alice Brown, p.26; Anne Marble, p.163 & 175; John Fiske, p.68. Maud Macdonald Hutchenson, p.401; Katharine Anthony, p.15.

[5] In 1991 optimistic attention to Mercy Otis Warren's work even to her furniture continues:

Fran Mascolo in "Floor Bid Takes Chair for $130 Grand," **Boston Sunday Herald** (31 March 1991:56) explains that a table sold for a particularly high price because it was once owned by Mercy Otis Warren, and that a letter and autograph of hers sold for $1,000 over its estimated $200 value.

Susan Chira in "The New Heroes of American History," **International Herald Tribune** (11 July 1991:18) comments on how Sacramento, California's school children are learning that Mercy Otis Warren wrote political pamphlets during the American Revolution and the positive effect such knowledge is having.

Ellen K. Coughlin in **The Chronicle of Higher Education** (4 September 1991:A9) reviews Nina Baym's article on Warren in the summer issue of **The South Atlantic Quarterly** which suggests that Warren seeks to "enlarge the traditional understanding of women's `separate sphere.'"

[6] Contemporary scholarship credits the origination of the committees of correspondence usually to Samuel Adams or to Thomas Jefferson, but rarely to Mercy Otis Warren who proposed the idea in her own home in 1772. See, for example, Adrienne Koch, p. 6.

[7] All uncited quotations in this Introduction are taken from the **Observations** as it appears in this anthology.

8   The term responsibility first appears in Jeremy Bentham's **The Principles of Moral Legislation**, 1780, and then, in America in James Madison's **Notes on the Constitutional Convention**, 1787. Cf. Richard McKeon, **Freedom and History and Other Essays**, xxix.

OBSERVATIONS
ON THE NEW CONSTITUTION,
AND ON THE FEDERAL AND STATE CONVENTIONS.
By a Columbian Patriot.
[Boston, 1788.}

Mankind may amuse themselves with theoretic systems of liberty, and trace its social and moral effects on sciences, virtue, industry and every improvement of which the human mind is capable; but we can only discern its true value by the practical and wretched effects of slavery; and thus dreadfully will they be realized, when the inhabitants of the Eastern States are dragging out a miserable existence, *only* on the gleanings of their fields; and the Southern, blessed with a softer and more fertile climate, are languishing in hopeless poverty; and when asked, what is become of the flower of their crop, and the rich produce of their farms—they may answer in the hapless stile of the Man of La Mancha, -- "The steward of my Lord has seized and sent it to Madrid." -- Or, in the more literal language of truth, The *exigencies of* government require that the collectors of the revenue should transmit it to the *Federal City.*

Animated with the firmest zeal for the interest of this country, the peace and union of the American States, and the freedom and happiness of a people who have made the most costly sacrifices in the cause of liberty, -- who have braved the power of Britain, weathered the convulsions of war, and waded thro' the blood of friends and foes to establish their independence and to support the freedom of the human mind; I cannot silently witness this degradation without calling on them, before they are compelled to blush at their own servitude, and to turn back their languid eyes on their lost liberties -- to consider, that the character of nations generally changes at the moment of revolution. -- And when patriotism is discountenanced and public virtue becomes the ridicule of the sycophant -- when

83

every man of liberality, firmness and penetration who cannot lick the hand
stretched out to oppress, is deemed an enemy to the State --then is the gulph of
despotism set open, and the grades to slavery, though rapid, are scarce perceptible
-- then genius drags heavily its iron chain -- science is neglected, and real merit
flies to the shades for security from reproach -- the mind becomes enervated, and
the national character sinks to a kind of apathy with only energy sufficient to
curse the breast that gave it milk, and as an elegant writer observes, "To bewail
every new birth as an increase of misery, under a government where the mind is
necessarily debased, and talents are seduced to become the panegyrists of
usurpation and tyranny." He adds, "that even sedition is not the most indubitable
enemy to the public welfare; but that its most dreadful foe is despotism which
always changes the character of nations for the worse, and is productive of nothing
but vice, that the tyrant no longer excites to the pursuits of glory or virtue; it is not
talents, it is baseness and servility that he cherishes, and the weight of arbitrary
power destroys the spring of emulation." [1] If such is the influence of government
on the character and manners, and undoubtedly the observation is just, must we
not subscribe to the opinion of the celebrated *Abbe Mable?* "That there are
disagreeable seasons in the unhappy situation of human affairs, when policy
requires both the intention and the power of doing mischief to he punished; and
when the senate proscribed the memory of *Caesar* they ought to have put *Anthony*
to death, and extinguished the hopes of Octavius." Self defence is a primary law of
nature, which no subsequent law of society can abolish; this primeval principle, the
immediate gift of the Creator, obliges every one to remonstrate against the strides
of ambition, and a wanton lust of domination, and to resist the first approaches of
tyranny, which at this day threaten to sweep away the rights for which the brave
sons of America have fought with an heroism scarcely paralleled even in ancient
republics. It may be repeated, they have purchased it with their blood, and have
gloried in their independence with a dignity of spirit, which has made them the
admiration of philosophy, the pride of America, and the wonder of Europe. It has
been observed, with great propriety, that " the virtues and vices of a people when
a revolution happens in their government, are the measure of the liberty or slavery

---

[1]Helvitius

they ought to expect -- An heroic love for the public good, a profound reverence for the laws, a contempt of riches, and a noble haughtiness of soul, are the only foundations of a free government."[2] Do not their dignified principles still exist among us? Or are they extinguished in the breasts of Americans, whose fields have been so recently crimsoned to repel the potent arm of a foreign Monarch, who had planted his engines of slavery in every city, with design to erase the vestiges of freedom in this his last asylum. It is yet to be hoped, for the honor of human nature, that no combinations either foreign or domestic have thus darkened this Western hemisphere.—On these shores freedom has planted her standard, dipped in the purple tide that flowed from the veins of her martyred heroes; and here every uncorrupted American yet hopes to see it supported by the vigor, the justice, the wisdom and unanimity of the people, in spite of the deep-laid plots, the secret intrigues, or the bold effrontery of those interested and avaricious adventurers for place, who intoxicated with the ideas of distinction and preferment have prostrated every worthy principle beneath the shrine of ambition. Yet these are the men who tell us republicanism is dwindled into theory—that we are incapable of enjoying our liberties --and that we must have a master. -- Let us retrospect the days of our adversity, and recollect who were then our friends; do we find them among the sticklers for aristocratic authority? No, they were generally the same men who now wish to save us from the distractions of anarchy on the one hand, and the jaws of tyranny on the other; where then were the class who now come forth importunately urging that our political salvation depends on the adoption of a system at which freedom spurns? — Were not some of them hidden in the corners of obscurity, and others wrapping themselves in the bosom of our enemies for safety? Some of them were in the arms of infancy; and others speculating for fortune, by sporting with public money; while a few, a very few of them were magnanimously defending their country, and raising a character, which I pray heaven may never be sullied by aiding measures derogatory to their former exertions. But the revolutions in principle which time produces among mankind, frequently exhibits the most mortifying instances of human weakness; and this alone can account for the extraordinary appearance of a few names, once

---

[2]Abbe Mable

distinguished in the honourable walks of patriotism, but now found in the list of the Massachusetts assent to the ratification of a Constitution, which, by the undefined meaning of some parts, and the ambiguities of expression in others, is dangerously adapted to the purposes of an immediate *aristocratic tyranny,* that from the difficulty, if not impracticability of its operation, must soon terminate in the most *uncontrolled despotism.*

All writers on government agree, and the feelings of the human mind witness the truth of these political axioms, that man is born free and possessed of certain unalienable rights— that government is instituted for the protection, safety and happiness of the people, and not for the profit, honor, or private interest of any man, family, or class of men -- That the origin of all power is in the people, and that they have an incontestible right to check the creatures of their own creation, vested with certain powers to guard the life, liberty and property of the community: And if certain selected bodies of men, deputed on these principles, determine contrary to the wishes and expectations of their constituents, the people have an undoubted right to reject their decisions, to call for a revision of their conduct, to depute others in their room, or if they think proper, to demand further time for deliberation on matters of the greatest moment: it therefore is an unwarrantable stretch of authority or influence, if any methods are taken to preclude this peaceful and reasonable mode of enquiry and decision. And it is with inexpressible anxiety, that many of the best friends of the Union of the States -- to the peaceable and equal participation of the rights of nature, and to the glory and dignity of this country, behold the insidious arts, and the strenuous efforts of the partisans of arbitrary power, by their vague definitions of the best established truths, endeavoring to envelope the mind in darkness the concomitant of slavery, and to lock the strong chains of domestic despotism on a country, which by the most glorious and successful struggles is but newly emancipated from the specter of foreign dominion. -- But there are certain seasons in the course of human affairs, when Genius, Virtue, and Patriotism, seems to nod over the vices of the times, and perhaps never more remarkably, than at the present period; or we should not see such a passive disposition prevail in some, who we must candidly suppose, have liberal and enlarged sentiments; while a supple multitude are paying a blind and idolatrous homage to the opinions of those who by the most precipitate steps are treading down their dear bought privileges; and who are endeavoring by all the arts of insinuation, and influence, to betray the people of the United States, into an acceptance of a most complicated system of government; marked on the one side with the *dark, secret* and *profound intrigues,* of the statesman, long practiced in the purlieus of despotism; and on the other, with the ideal projects of young *ambition,* with its wings just expanded to soar to a summit, which imagination has painted in such gaudy colors as to intoxicate the *inexperienced votary,* and to send *him* rambling from State to State, to collect materials to construct the ladder of preferment.

But as a variety of objections to the *heterogeneous phantom,* have been repeatedly laid before the public, by men of the best abilities and intentions; I will not expatiate long on a Republican *form* of government, founded on the principles of monarchy -- a democratic branch with the features of aristocracy -- and the extravagance of nobility pervading the minds of many of the candidates for office, with the poverty of peasantry hanging heavily on them, and insurmountable, from their taste for expense, unless a general provision should be made in the arrangement of the civil list, which may enable them with the champions of their cause to " *sail down the new pactolean channel.*" Some gentlemen, with labored zeal, have spent much time in urging the necessity of government, from the embarrassments of trade -- the want of respectability abroad and confidence of the public engagements at home. -- These are obvious truths which no one denies; and there are few who do not unite in the general wish for the restoration of public faith, the revival of commerce, arts, agriculture, and industry, under a lenient, peaceable and energetic government: But the most sagacious advocates for the party have not by fair discussion, and rational argumentation, evinced the necessity of adopting this many headed monster; of such motley mixture, that its enemies cannot trace a feature of Democratic or Republican extract; nor have its friends the courage to denominate a Monarchy, an Aristocracy, or an Oligarchy, and the favored bantling must have passed through the short period of its existence without a name, had not Mr. *Wilson,* in the fertility of his genius, suggested the happy epithet of a *Federal Republic.* -- But I leave the field of general censure on

87

the secrecy of its birth, the rapidity of its growth, and the fatal consequences of suffering it to live to the age of maturity, and will particularize some of the most weighty objections to its passing through this continent in a gigantic size. -- It will be allowed by every one that the fundamental principle of a free government is the equal representation of a free people. -- And I will first observe with a justly celebrated writer, "That the principal aim of society is to protect individuals in the absolute rights which were vested in them by the immediate laws of nature, but which could not be preserved in peace, without the mutual intercourse which is gained by the institution of friendly and social communities." And when society has thus deputed a certain number of their equals to take care of their personal rights, and the interest of the whole community, it must be considered that responsibility is the great security of integrity and honor; and that annual election is the basis of responsibility, -- Man is not immediately corrupted, but power without limitation, or amenability, may endanger the brightest virtue -- whereas a frequent return to the bar of their Constituents is the strongest check against the corruptions to which men are liable, either from the intrigues of others of more subtle genius, or the propensities of their own hearts, -- and the gentlemen who have so warmly advocated in the late Convention of the Massachusetts, the change from annual to biennial elections; may have been in the same predicament, and perhaps with the same views that Mr. *Hutchinson* once acknowledged himself, when in a letter to *Lord Hillsborough*, he observed, "that the grand difficulty of making a change in government against the general bent of the people had caused him to turn his thoughts to a variety of plans, in order to find one that might be executed in spite of opposition," and the first he proposed was that, "instead of annual, the elections should be only once in three years:" but the Minister had not the hardiness to attempt such an innovation, even in the revision of colonial charters: nor has any one ever defended Biennial, Triennial or Septennial Elections, either in the British House of Commons, or in the debates of Provincial assemblies, on general and free principles: but it is unnecessary to dwell long on this article, as the best political writers have supported the principles of annual elections with a precision, that cannot be confuted, though they may be darkened, by the sophistical arguments that have been thrown out with design, to undermine all the barriers of freedom.

2. There is no security in the proffered system, either for the rights of conscience or the liberty of the Press: Despotism usually while it is gaining ground, will suffer men to think, say, or write what they please; but when once established, if it is thought necessary to subserve the purposes, of arbitrary power, the most unjust restrictions may take place in the first instance, and an *imprimatur* on the Press in the next, may silence the complaints, and forbid the most decent remonstrances of an injured and oppressed people.

3. There are no well defined limits of the Judiciary Powers, they seem to be left as a boundless ocean, that has broken over the chart of the Supreme Lawgiver, " *thus far shalt thou go and no further,* " and as they cannot be comprehended by the clearest capacity, or the most sagacious mind, it would be an Herculean labor to attempt to describe the dangers with which they are replete.

4. The Executive and the Legislative are so dangerously blended as to give just cause of alarm, and everything relative thereto, is couched in such ambiguous terms -- in such vague and indefinite expression, as is a sufficient ground without any objection, for the reprobation of a system, that the authors dare not hazard to a clear investigation.

5. The abolition of trial by jury in civil causes. -- This mode of trial the learned Judge Blackstone observes, "has been coeval with the first rudiments of civil government, that property, liberty and life, depend on maintaining in its legal force the constitutional trial by jury." He bids his readers pause, and with Sir Matthew Hale observes, how admirably this mode is adapted to the investigation of truth beyond any other the world can produce. Even the party who have been disposed to swallow, without examination, the proposals of the *secret conclave,* have started on a discovery that this essential right was curtailed; and shall a privilege, the origin of which may be traced to our Saxon ancestors—that has been a part of the law of nations, even in the feudatory systems of France, Germany and Italy—and from the earliest records has been held so sacred, both in ancient and modern Britain, that it could never be shaken by the introduction of Norman customs, or any other conquests or change of government shall this inestimable

privilege be relinquished in America -- either thro' the fear of inquisition for unaccounted thousands of public monies in the hands of some who have been officious in the fabrication of the *consolidated system,* or from the apprehension that some future delinquent possessed of more power than integrity, may be called to a trial by his peers in the hour of investigation.

6. Though it has been said by Mr. *Wilson* and many others, that a Standing-Army is necessary for the dignity and safety of America, yet freedom revolts at the idea, when the Divan, or the Despot, may draw out his dragoons to suppress the murmurs of a few, who may yet cherish those sublime principles which call forth the exertions, and lead to the best improvements of the human mind. It is hoped this country may yet be governed by milder methods than are usually displayed beneath the bannerets of military law. -- Standing armies have been the nursery of vice and the bane of liberty from the Roman legions to the establishment of the artful Ximenes, and from the ruin of the Cortes of Spain, to the planting of the British cohorts in the capitals of America: -- By the edicts of an authority vested in the sovereign power by the proposed constitution, the militia of the country, the bulwark of defence and the security of national liberty if no longer under he control of civil authority; but at the rescript of the Monarch, or the aristocracy, they may either be employed to extort the enormous sums that will be necessary to support the civil list -- to maintain the regalia of power -- and the splendor of the most useless part of the community, or they may be sent into foreign countries for the fulfillment of treaties, stipulated by the President and two-thirds of the Senate.

7. Notwithstanding the delusory promise to guarantee a Republican form of government to every State in the Union -- If the most discerning eye could discover any meaning at all in the engagement, there are no resources left for the support of internal government, or the liquidation of the debts of the State. Every source of revenue is in the monopoly of Congress, and if the several legislatures in their enfeebled state, should against their own feelings be necessitated to attempt a dry tax for the payment of their debts, and the support of internal police, even this may be required for the purposes of the general government.

8. As the new Congress are empowered to determine their own salaries, the requisitions for this purpose may not be very moderate, and the drain for public moneys will probably rise past all calculation: and it is to be feared when America has consolidated its despotism, the world will witness the truth of the assertion -- "that the pomp of an Eastern monarch may impose on the vulgar who may estimate the force of a nation by the magnificence of its palaces; but the wise man judges differently, it is by that very magnificence he estimates its weakness. He sees nothing more in the midst of this imposing pomp, where the tyrant sets enthroned, than a sumptuous and mournful decoration of the dead; the apparatus of a fastuous funeral, in the center of which is a cold and lifeless lump of unanimated earth, a phantom of power ready to disappear before the enemy, by whom it is despised ! "

9. There is no provision for a rotation, nor anything to prevent the perpetuity of office in the same hands for life; which by a little well timed bribery, will probably be done, to the exclusion of men of the best abilities from their share in   the offices of government.-- By this neglect we lose the advantages of that check to the overbearing insolence of office, which by rendering him ineligible at certain periods, keeps the mind of man in equilibrio, and teaches him the feelings of the governed, and better qualifies him to govern in his turn.

10. The inhabitants of the United States, are liable to be dragged from the vicinity of their own country, or state, to answer the litigious or unjust suit of an adversary, on the most distant borders of the Continent: in short the appellate jurisdiction of the Supreme Federal Court, includes an unwarrantable stretch of power over the liberty, life, and property of the subject, through the wide Continent of America.

11. One Representative to thirty thousand inhabitants is a very inadequate representation; and every man who is not lost to all sense of freedom to his country, must reprobate the idea of Congress altering by law, or on any pretence whatever, interfering with any regulations for time, places, and manner of choosing our own Representatives.

12. If the sovereignty of America is designed to be elective, the circumscribing the votes to only ten electors in this State, and the same proportion in all the

others, is nearly tantamount to the exclusion of the voice of the people in the choice of their first magistrate. It is vesting the choice solely in an aristocratic junto, who may easily combine in each State to place at the head of the Union the most convenient instrument for despotic sway.

13. A Senate chosen for six years will, in most instances, be an appointment for life, as the influence of such a body over the minds of the people will be coequal to the extensive powers with which they are vested, and they will not only forget, but be forgotten by their constituents -- a branch of the Supreme Legislature thus set beyond all responsibility is totally repugnant to every principle of a free government.

14. There is no provision by a bill of rights to guard against the dangerous encroachments of power in too many instances to be named: but I cannot pass over in silence the insecurity in which we are left with regard to warrants unsupported by evidence -- the daring experiment of granting writs of assistance in a former arbitrary administration is not yet forgotten in the Massachusetts; nor can we be so ungrateful to the memory of the patriots who counteracted their operation, as so soon after their manly exertions to save us from such a detestable instrument of arbitrary power, to subject ourselves to the insolence of any petty revenue officer to enter our houses, search, insult, and seize at pleasure. We are told by a gentleman of too much virtue and real probity to suspect he has a design to deceive -- "that the whole constitution is a declaration of rights," -- but mankind must think for themselves, and to many very judicious and discerning characters, the whole constitution with very few exceptions appears a perversion of the rights of particular states, and of private citizens.-- But the gentleman goes on to tell us, "that the primary object is the general government, and that the rights of individuals are only incidentally mentioned, and that there was a clear impropriety in "being very particular about them." But, asking pardon for dissenting from such respectable authority, who has been led into several mistakes, more from his predilection in favor of certain modes of government, than from a want of understanding or veracity. The rights of individuals ought to be the primary object of all government, and cannot be too securely guarded by the most explicit declarations in their favor. This has been the opinion of the Hampdens, the

Pyms, and many other illustrious names, that have stood forth in defence of English liberties; and even the Italian master in politicks, the subtle and renowned Machiavel acknowledges, that no republic ever yet stood on a stable foundation without satisfying the common people.

15. The difficulty, if not impracticability, of exercising the equal and equitable powers of government by a single legislature over an extent of territory that reaches from the Mississippi to the Western lakes, and from them to the Atlantic Ocean, is an insuperable objection to the adoption of the new system. -- Mr. *Hutchinson*, the great champion for arbitrary power, in the multitude of his machinations to subvert the liberties in this country, was obliged to acknowledge in one of his letters, that, "from the extent of country from north to south, the scheme of one government was impracticable." But if the authors of the present visionary project, can by the arts of deception, precipitation and address, obtain a majority of suffrages in the conventions of the states to try the hazardous experiment, they may then make the same inglorious boast with this insidious politician, who may perhaps be their model, that "the union of the colonies was pretty well broken, and that he hoped to never see it renewed."

16. It is an undisputed fact that not one legislature in the United States had the most distant idea when they first appointed members for a convention, entirely commercial, or when they afterwards authorized them to consider on some amendments of the Federal union, that they would without any warrant from their constituents, presume on so bold and daring a stride, as ultimately to destroy the state governments, and offer a *consolidated system,* irreversible but on conditions that the smallest degree of penetration must discover to be impracticable.

17. The first appearance of the article which declares the ratification of nine states sufficient for the establishment of the new system, wears the face of dissension, is a subversion of the union of Confederated States, and tends to the introduction of anarchy and civil convulsions, and may be a means of involving the whole country in blood.

18. The mode in which this constitution is recommended to the people to judge without either the advice of Congress, or the legislatures of the several states is very reprehensible -- it is an attempt to force it upon them before it could be

thoroughly understood, and may leave us in that situation, that in the first moments of slavery in the minds of the people agitated by the remembrance of their lost liberties, will be like the sea in a tempest, that sweeps down every mound of security.

But it is needless to enumerate other instances, in which the proposed constitution appears contradictory to the first principles which ought to govern mankind; and it is equally so to enquire into the motives that induced to so bold a step as the annihilation of the independence and sovereignty of thirteen distinct states. -- They are but too obvious through the whole progress of the business, from the first shutting up the doors of the federal convention and resolving that no member should correspond with gentlemen in the different states on the subject under discussion; till the trivial proposition of *recommending* a few amendments was artfully ushered into the convention of the Massachusetts. The questions that were then before that honorable assembly were profound and important, they were of such magnitude and extent, that the consequences may run parallel with the existence of the country; and to see them waved and hastily terminated by a measure too absurd to require a serious refutation, raises the honest indignation of every true lover of his country. Nor are they less grieved that the ill policy and arbitrary disposition of some of the sons of America has thus precipitated to the contemplation and discussion of questions that no one could rationally suppose would have been agitated among us, till time had blotted out the principle on which the late revolution was grounded; or till the last traits of the many political tracts, which defended the separation from Britain, and the rights of men were consigned to everlasting oblivion. After the severe conflicts this country has suffered, it is presumed that they are disposed to make every reasonable sacrifice before the altar of peace. -- But when we contemplate the nature of men and consider them originally on an equal footing, subject to the same feelings, stimulated by the same passions, and recollecting the struggles they have recently made, for the security of their civil rights; it cannot be expected that the inhabitants of the Massachusetts, can be easily lulled into a fatal security, by the declamatory effusions of gentlemen, who, contrary to the experience of all ages would persuade them there is no danger to be apprehended, from vesting

94

discretionary powers in the hands of man, which he may, or may not abuse. The very suggestion, that we ought to trust to the precarious hope of amendments and redress, after we have voluntarily fixed the shackles on our own necks should have awakened to a double degree of caution. -- This people have not forgotten the artful insinuations of a former Governor, when pleading the unlimited authority of parliament before the legislature of the Massachusetts; nor that his arguments were very similar to some lately urged by gentlemen who boast of opposing his measures, "*with halters about their necks.*"

We were then told by him, in all the soft language of insinuation, that no form of government, of human construction can be perfect -- that we had nothing to fear -- that we had no reason to complain -- that we had only to acquiesce in their illegal claims, and to submit to the requisition of parliament, and doubtless the lenient hand of government would redress all grievances, and remove the oppressions of the people: -- Yet we soon saw armies of mercenaries encamped on our plains -- our commerce ruined -- our harbors blockaded -- and our cities burnt. It may be replied that this was in consequence of an obstinate defence of our privileges; this may be true; and when the *"ultima ratio"* is called to aid, the weakest must fall. But let the best informed historian produce an instance when bodies of men were entrusted with power, and the proper checks relinquished, if they were ever found destitute of ingenuity sufficient to furnish pretenses to abuse it. And the people at large are already sensible, that the liberties which America has claimed, which reason has justified, and which have been so gloriously defended by the swords of the brave, are not about to fall before the tyranny of foreign conquest: it is native usurpation that is shaking the foundations of peace and spreading the sable curtain of despotism over the United States. The banners of freedom were erected in the wilds of America by our ancestors, while the wolf prowled for his prey on the one hand, and more savage man on the other; they have been since rescued from the invading hand of foreign power, by the valor and blood of their posterity; and there was reason to hope they would continue for ages to illumine a quarter of the globe, by nature kindly separated from the proud monarchies of Europe, and the infernal darkness of Asiatic slavery. -- And it is to be feared we shall soon see this country rushing into the extremes of confusion and violence, in consequence of the proceeding of a set of gentlemen who disregarding the purposes of their appointment, have assumed powers unauthorized by any commission, have unnecessarily rejected the confederation of the United States, and annihilated the sovereignty and independence of the individual governments. — The causes which have inspired a few men to assemble for very different purposes with such a degree of temerity us to break with a single stroke the union of America, and disseminate the seeds of discord through the land may be easily investigated, when we survey the partisans of monarchy in the state conventions, urging the adoption of a mode of government that militates with the former professions and exertions of this country, and with all ideas of republicanism, and the equal rights of men.

Passion, prejudice, and error, are characteristics of human nature; and as it cannot be accounted for on any principles of philosophy, religion, or good policy; to these shades in the human character must be attributed the mad zeal of some, to precipitate to a blind adoption of the measures of the late federal convention, without giving opportunity for better information to those who are misled by influence or ignorance into erroneous opinions. — Literary talents may be prostituted, and the powers of genius debased to subserve the purposes of ambition or avarice; but the feelings of the heart will dictate the language of truth, and the simplicity of her accents will proclaim the infamy of those, who betray the rights of the people, under the specious, and popular pretence of *justice, consolidation,* and *dignity.*

It is presumed the great body of the people unite in sentiment with the writer of these observations, who most devoutly prays that public credit may rear her declining head, and remunerative justice pervade the land; nor is there a doubt if a free government is continued, that time and industry will enable both the public and private debtor to liquidate their arrearages in the most equitable manner. They wish to see the Confederated States bound together by the most indissoluble union, but without renouncing their separate sovereignties and independence, and becoming tributaries to a consolidated fabric of aristocratic tyranny. -- They wish to see government established, and peaceably holding the reins with honor, energy, and dignity; but they wish for no *federal city* whose *"cloud cap't towers"* may screen the state culprit from the hand of justice; while its exclusive jurisdiction may protect the riot of armies encamped within its limits. -- They deprecate discord and civil convulsions, but they are not yet generally prepared with the ungrateful Israelites to ask a king, nor are their spirits sufficiently broken to yield the best of their olive grounds to his servants, and to see their sons appointed to run before his chariots. -- It has been observed by a zealous advocate for the new system, that most governments are the result of fraud or violence, and this with design to recommend its acceptance --but has not almost every step towards its fabrication been fraudulent in the extreme? Did not the prohibition strictly enjoined by the general Convention, that no member should make any communication to his Constituents, or to gentlemen of consideration and abilities in the other States, bear evident marks of fraudulent designs? -- This circumstance is regretted in strong terms by Mr. Martin, a member from Maryland, who acknowledges "He had no idea that all the wisdom, integrity, and virtue of the States was contained in that Convention, and that he wished to have corresponded with gentlemen of eminent political characters abroad, and to give their sentiments due weight"— he adds, "so extremely solicitous were they, that their proceedings should not transpire, that the members were prohibited from taking copies of their resolutions, or extracts from the Journals, without express permission, by vote." - And the hurry with which it has been urged to the acceptance of the people, without giving time, by adjournments, for better information, and more unanimity has a deceptive appearance; and if finally driven to resistance, as the only alternative between that and servitude, till in the confusion of discord, the reins should be seized by the violence of some enterprising genius, that may sweep down the last barrier of liberty, it must be added to the score of criminality with which the fraudulent usurpation at Philadelphia, may be chargeable. -- Heaven avert such a tremendous scene and let us still hope a more happy termination of the present ferment: -- may the people be calm and wait a legal redress; may the mad transport of some of our infatuated capitals subside; and every influential character through the States, make the most prudent exertions for a new general Convention, who may vest adequate powers in Congress, for all national purposes, without annihilating the individual governments, and drawing blood from every pore by taxes, impositions and illegal restrictions. -- This step might again re-establish the Union, restore tranquility to the ruffled mind of the inhabitants, and save America from the distresses, dreadful even in contemplation. -- "The great art of governing is to lay aside all prejudices and attachments to particular opinions, classes or individual characters to consult the spirit of the people; to give way to it; and in so doing, to give it a turn capable of inspiring those sentiments, which may induce them to relish a change, which an alteration of circumstances may hereafter make necessary." -- The education of the advocates for monarchy should have taught them, and their memory should have suggested that "monarchy is a species of government fit only for a people too much corrupted by luxury, avarice, and a passion for pleasure, to have any love for their country, and whose vices the fear of punishment alone is able to restrain; but by no means calculated for a nation that is poor, and at the same time tenacious of their liberty -- animated with a disgust to tyranny -- and inspired with the generous feeling of patriotism and liberty, and at the same time, like the ancient Spartans have been hardened by temperance and manly exertions, and equally despising the fatigues of the field, and the fear of enemies," --and while they change their ground they should recollect, that Aristocracy is a still more formidable foe to public virtue, and the prosperity of a nation -- that under such a government her patriots become mercenaries -- her soldiers cowards, and the people slaves. -- Though several Sate Conventions have assented to, and ratified, yet the voice of the people appears at present strong against the adoption of the Constitution. -- By the chicanery, intrigue, and false coloring of those who plume themselves, more on their education and abilities, than their political, patriotic, or private virtues -- by the imbecility of some, and the duplicity of others, a majority of the Convention of Massachusetts have been flattered with the ideas of amendments, when it will be too late to complain. -- While several very worthy characters, too timid for their situation, magnified the hopeless alternative, between the dissolution of the bands of all government, and receiving the proffered system in *toto*, after long endeavoring to reconcile it to their consciences, swallowed the indigestible panacea, and in a kind of sudden desperation lent their signature to the dereliction of the honorable station they held in the Union, and have broken over the solemn compact, by which they were bound to support their own excellent constitution till the period of revision. Yet Virginia, equally large and respectable, and who have done honor to themselves, by their vigorous exertions from the first dawn of independence, have not yet acted upon the question; they have wisely taken time to consider before they introduce innovations of a most dangerous nature: -- her inhabitants are brave, her burgesses are free, and they have a Governor who dares to think for himself, and to speak his opinion (without first pouring libations on the altar of popularity) though it should militate with some of the most accomplished and illustrious characters.

Maryland, who has no local interest to lead her to adopt, will doubtless reject the system -- I hope the same characters still live, and that the same spirit which dictated to them a wise and cautious care, against sudden revolutions in government, and made them the last State that acceded to the independence of America, will lead them to support what they so deliberately claimed. -- Georgia apprehensive of a war with the Savages, has acceded in order to insure protection. -- Pennsylvania has struggled through much in the same manner, as the Massachusetts, against the manly feelings, and the masterly reasonings of a very respectable part of the Convention: They have adopted the system, and seen some of its' authors burnt in effigy -- their towns thrown into riot and confusion, and the minds of the people agitated by apprehension and discord.

New Jersey and Delaware have united in the measure, from the locality of their situation, and the selfish motives which too generally govern mankind; the Federal City, and the seat of government, will naturally attract the intercourse of strangers -- the youth of enterprize, and the wealth of the nation to the central States.

Connecticut has pushed it through with the precipitation of her neighbor, with few dissentient voices; -- but more from irritation and resentment to a sister State, perhaps partiality to herself in her commercial regulations, than from a comprehensive view of the system, as a regard to the welfare of all. -- But New York has motives, that will undoubtedly lead her to rejection, without being afraid to appeal to the understanding of mankind, to justify the grounds of their refusal to adopt a Constitution, that even the framers dare not to risque to the hazard of revision, amendment, or reconsideration, least the whole superstructure should be demolished by more skilful and discreet architects. I know not what part the

Carolinas will take; but I hope their determinations will comport with the dignity and freedom of this country -- their decisions will have great weight in the scale. But equally important are the small States of New Hampshire and Rhode Island: -- New York, the Carolinas, Virginia, Maryland, and these two lesser States may yet support the liberties of the Continent; if they refuse a ratification, or postpone their proceedings till the spirits of the community have time to cool, there is little doubt but the wise measure of another federal convention will be adopted, when the members would have the advantage of viewing, at large, through the medium of truth, the objections that have been made from various quarters; such a measure might be attended with the most salutary effects, and prevent the dread consequences of civil feuds. -- But even if some of those large states should hastily accede, yet we have frequently seen in the story of revolution, relief spring from a quarter least expected.

Though the virtues of a Cato could not save Rome, nor the abilities of a Padilla defend the citizens of Castile from falling under the yoke of Charles; yet a *Tell* once suddenly rose from a little obscure city, and boldly rescued the liberties of his country. -- Every age has its Bruti and its Decci, as well as its Ccesars and Sejani: -- The happiness of mankind depends much on the modes of government, and the virtues of the governors; and America may yet produce characters who have genius and capacity sufficient to form the manners and correct the morals of the people, and virtue enough to lead their country to freedom. Since their dismemberment from the British empire, America has, in many instances, resembled the conduct of a restless, vigorous, luxurious youth, prematurely emancipated from the authority of a parent, but without the experience necessary to direct him to act with dignity or discretion. Thus we have seen her break the shackles of foreign dominion, and all the blessings of peace restored on the most honorable terms: She acquired the liberty of framing her own laws, choosing her own magistrates, and adopting manners and modes of government the most favorable to the freedom and happiness of society. But how little have we availed ourselves of these superior advantages: The glorious fabric of liberty successfully reared with so much labor and assiduity totters to the foundation, and may be blown away as the bubble of fancy by the rude breath of military combinations, and politicians of yesterday.

It is true this country lately armed in opposition to regal despotism -- impoverished by the expenses of a long war, and unable immediately to fulfil their public or private engagements that appeared in some instances, with a boldness of spirit that seemed to set at defiance all authority, government, or order, on the one hand; while on the other, there has been, not only a secret wish, but an open avowal of the necessity of drawing the reins of government much too taught, not only for a republicanism, but for a wise and limited monarchy. -- But the character of this people is not averse to a degree of subordination, the truth of this appears from the easy restoration of tranquility, after a dangerous insurrection in one of the states; this also evinces a little necessity of a complete revolution of government throughout the union. But it is a republican principle that the majority should rule; and if a spirit of moderation should be cultivated on both sides, till the voice of the people at large could be fairly heard it should be held sacred. -- And if, on such a scrutiny, the proposed constitution should appear repugnant to their character and wishes; if they, in the language of a late elegant pen, should acknowledge that "no confusion in my mind, is more terrible to them than the stern disciplined regularity and vaunted police of arbitrary governments, where every heart is depraved by fear, where mankind dare not assume their natural characters, where the free spirit must crouch to the slave in office, where genius must repress her effusions, or like the Egyptian worshippers, offer them in sacrifice to the calves in power, and where the human mind, always in shackles, shrinks from every generous effort." Who would then have the effrontery to say, it ought not to be thrown out with indignation, however some respectable names have appeared to support it. -- But if after all, on a dispassionate and fair discussion, the people generally give their voices for a voluntary dereliction of their privileges, let every individual who chooses the active scenes of life strive to support the peace and unanimity of his country, though every other blessing may expire -- And while the statesman is plodding for power, and the courtier practicing the arts of dissimulation without check - while the rapacious are growing rich by oppression, and fortune throwing her gifts into the lap of fools, let the sublimer characters, the philosophic lovers of freedom who have wept over her exit, retire to the calm shades of contemplation, there they may look down with pity on the inconsistency of human nature, the revolutions of states, the rise of kingdoms, and the fall of empires.

Bibliography
Mercy Otis Warren

Primary sources:

The Adulateur, a Tragedy. Boston: Edes and Gill, 1773.

"The Defeat," in the **Boston Gazette**, May 24, 1773 and July 19, 1773.

The Group, a Farce. Boston: Edes and Gill, 1776.

The Blockheads: or The Affrightened Officers, a Farce. Boston: Edes and Gill, 1776.

The Motley Assembly, a Farce. Boston: Nathaniel Coverly, 1779.

Observations on the New Constitution, and on the Federal and State Conventions. By a Columbian Patriot. Boston, 1788.

Poems, Dramatic and Miscellaneous. Boston: T. Thomas and E.T. Andrews, 1790.

History of the Rise, Progress and Termination of the American Revolution, interspersed with Biographical and Moral Observations. 3 vols. Boston: Ebenezer Larkin, 1805.

Correspondence between John Adams and Mercy Warren relating to her History of the American Revolution. Fifth series, vol 4. Boston: Massachusetts Historical Society Collections, 1878.

Warren Family Letters and Papers, 1763-1814. Pilgrim Museum, Plymouth, Massachusetts.

Mercy Warren Papers, Massachusetts Historical Society, Boston.

The Plays and Poems of Mercy Otis Warren. Introduction Benjamin Franklin V, Delmar, New York: Scholars Facsimiles, 1980.

History of the Rise, Progress and Termination of the American Revolution, interspersed with Biographical, Political and Moral Observations. Ed. Lester H. Cohen, 2 vols. Indianapolis: Liberty Classics, 1988.

"The Private Poems of Mercy Otis Warren." **The New England Quarterly**, 54 (June 1981) 199-224.

Secondary Sources:

Adams, John. **The Works of John Adams**, Edited C. F. Adams. Boston: Charles Little and James Brown, 1851.

Anthony, Katharine. **First Lady of the Revolution**. New York: Doubleday, 1958.

Brown, Alice. **Mercy Warren**. New York: Scribners, 1896.

Cheney, Ednah Dow. "Women of Boston," in **The Memorial History of Boston**. ed. Justin Winsor. Vol IV, Boston: Osgood & Co. 1881.

Ellet, Elizabeth F. **The Women of the American Revolution**. 3 vols. New York: Baker and Scribners, 1850.

Fiske, John. **Essays Historical and Literary**. New York: Macmillan, 1902.

Griswold, Rufus Wilmot. **The Female Poets of America**. Philadelphia:Carey and Hart, 1849.

Hutchenson, Maud Macdonald. "Mercy Otis Warren 1728-1814," **The William and Mary Quarterly** 10 (July 1953) 378-402.

Jefferson, Thomas. **The Complete Jefferson**. Ed. S.K. Padover. New York: Duell, Sloan, & Pearce, 1943.

Koch, Adrienne **Adams and Jefferson: "Posterity must Judge."** Chicago: Rand McNally, 1963.

Marble, Anne Russell. "Mistress Mercy Warren: Real Daughter of the American Revolution," **The New England Magazine** (April 1903), 28-99.

McKeon, Richard P. **Freedom and History and Other Essays**. Chicago: University of Chicago Press, 1990.

Weales, Gerald. "The Quality of Mercy, or Mrs Warren's Profession," **The Georgia Review** (Winter, 1979) 881-294.

White, Elizabeth Wade. **Anne Bradstreet "The Tenth Muse."** New York: Oxford, 1971.

Judith Sargent Murray
Courtesy of the Frick Art Reference Library

Chronology

Judith Sargent Murray 1751-1820

1751   Born 1 May to Judith and Winthrop Sargent.

1769   Marries John Stevens.

1770   Portrait painted by John Singleton Copley.

1778   As professed Universalist is barred from First Church.

1779   Writes essay "Equality of the Sexes."

1782   Publishes catechism **Some Deductions...**

1784   Publishes essay: "Desultory Thought Upon the Utility of Encouraging a
       Degree of Complacency in the Female Bosoms" in **Gentleman's and
       Lady's Town and Country Magazine**, Boston.

1785   Husband John Stevens flees to St. Eustatius.

1786   John Stevens dies.

1788   Marries Rev.John Murray Oct. 6 in Salem, Christmas
       re-ordained in Gloucester where they live.

1789   Son George born, dies a few days later.
       (Publishes in **Massachusetts Magazine** 1789-94 under
       pseudonym Constantia.)

1790   Publishes "Apostrophe to the Shade..." July in **Universal Asylum and
       Columbian Magazine**; publishes 6 poems:
       "Lines,...death of an Infant" January.
       "Verses, wrote at a Period...with Uncertainty" February.
       "Lines to Philenia" April.
       "On Equality of the Sexes" March, April.
       "On the Domestic Education of Children" May.
       "Prologue to `Variety'" June.
       Travels to Philadelphia and New York:
       Attends Universalist convention-writes letters to parents.

Visits President George and Martha Washington, John and Abigail Adams, Ben Franklin and Dr. Benjamin Rush.

1791   Daughter Julia Maria born August. 22.
Publishes poetry and prose:
"Prologue to the West Indian" March.
"Valedictory Epilogue" April.
"Apology for an Epilogue" May.
Prose-Description of Bethlehem, June.
Description of Gray's Gardens, July.

1792   Publishes essays:
Gleaner Essays #'s 1-31 February 92-August 94.
Repository Essays #'s 1-27 September 92- July 94.

1793   Moves to Boston, 5 Franklin Place.

1794   Publishes 3 poems:
"Occasional Epilogue to `The Contrast'" March,
"Solution to the Rebus in the February Magazine" March.
"Reflections in the manner of Hervey..."June.

1795   Play "The Medium" produced at Federal Street Theater.

1796   Play "The Traveller Returned" produced.

1798   Publishes **The Gleaner** in 3 vols.

1802   (Publishes in **Boston Weekly Magazine** 1802-05), under pseudonym Honora-Martesia)
Publishes in **Hymns and Odes** ode/hymn for George Washington
Publishes 3 poems: "On Rocking Cradle" October.
"Birth Day Invitation." November. "Lines" December.

1803   Publishes 4 poems:
"Death of Salt" January. "Expiring Amity" February.
"On Blending..." and "An Hypothesis" March.

1805   Publishes "Ode to Time" under pseudonym Honora.

1809   John Murray has paralyzing stroke.

1812 - 1813   Edits John Murray's 3 vols. **Letters & Sketches of Sermons**.

1812   Julia Maria marries Adam Louis Bingamon from Mississippi upon
completion of his studies at Harvard.

1813   Julia in Boston, grand-daughter Charlotte born.

1815   John Murray dies.

1816   Finishes last fourth of Rev.J. Murray's autobiography
(ten editions, 1816-1891).

1820   July 6 Judith at 69 years old dies at Natches, Mississippi on plantation
"Fatherland", is buried Bingamon Cemetery, leaves in will $200 to needy
widows of Gloucester.
Charlotte dies Natchez the following year.

4

Judith Sargent Murray

1751-1820

As the frigates and schooners noisily loaded and unloaded in the Gloucester harbor in the 1760's, a young girl and her brother quietly studied Latin and Greek; she with a vehement thirst for knowledge; he with college in mind. She married; he entered Harvard. This disparity in opportunity was keenly perceived by the young woman. In a letter to her brother she laments that her parents followed custom regarding her education:

> It was the mode to confine the female intellect within the narrowest bounds, and by consequence, I was robbed of the aid of education-- I shall feel the effects of this irrational deprivation, as long as I shall continue an inhabitant of this world.(Mississippi Archives Paper on the Collection (Z/1827.00):1)

Before the close of the Revolutionary War that began on the heels of her brother's graduation, Judith Sargent began writing. The climate that Mercy Otis Warren, twenty-three years her senior, helped bring about, enabled the younger Judith to articulate her ideas of radical new freedoms for eighteenth century women.

Judith's essays on political philosophy have been singled out.[1] Principally a writer of essays, she also wrote poetry, drama, and a catechism. In addition, she edited two volumes of sermons by her second husband, Rev. John Murray, the Father of the Universalist Church in America, and consequent to his death, completed his autobiography. Except for the writing she did on her husband's behalf, most of her work forwarded feminist philosophy. Like Mary Astell, a century before her in England, Judith wrote and published full essays on women and education. Mary Astell, having been named the "first systematic feminist in England"(Hill 52); Judith Sargent Murray may yet be called the "first systematic feminist in America" or "Mother of American Feminism".[2]

Inspired with hope, Judith Sargent envisioned for the generation of women coming after her an encouraging future: "I expect to see our young women forming a new era in female history" (**Gleaner**, LXXXVIII,189), the "new era" for women meaning better education, more opportunities for independence, and participation in national concerns.   Hope increased when Judith learned of women's many past accomplishments and heard that her contemporary in Germany, Dorothy Schlözer, had received a Ph.D., a first for a woman at Göttingen University.   But in face of this optimistic portend, she is spared the pessimistic reality that it will be another hundred years before Gottingen University grants such a degree to another woman, and that Harvard will not grant a degree to a woman for nearly two-hundred years.   She is also spared the most distressing knowledge, that her own work would be practically forgotten for nearly two centuries.

The "feminist revolution" of the late twentieth century is acknowledging Judith Sargent Murray.   Her essays articulating her philosophy of feminism, "On the Equality of the Sexes," written in 1779 and published in 1790, and "Desultory Thoughts Upon the Utility of Encouraging Self-Complacency in the Female Bosom" published in 1784, were the earliest feminist writings published in English speaking America, preceding Mary Wollstonecraft's **Vindication of the Rights of Women**, printed in England in 1792. **Vindication** is generally given credit for being the earliest important feminist document on the improvement of women's educational and political status.   Murray's feminist philosophy profoundly affected her life, her publications, her correspondence, and her posterity.

Born on Cape Ann in Gloucester, Massachusetts, Judith Sargent was named for her distinguished mother, Judith Sanders and her grandmother Judith Robinson (Sargent, Emma 50-1).[3]   Judith Sargent was "early noted for quickness of perception, love of study and ease in acquiring knowledge"(Eddy **U in Gl** 195); for this reason and because she was born into a wealthy family, Judith was as well educated as any woman of her time.   Like Anne Bradstreet and Mercy Otis

112

Warren, Judith was allowed to study with her brother. She and Winthrop, two years younger, were tutored by Rev. John Rogers, a Harvard graduate. It is evident that Judith continued independent study, for her works demonstrate a wide acquaintance with philosophers from Socrates and Plutarch to Descartes and Rousseau, and with subjects from rhetoric and philosophy to history and poetry.[4] Judith became a member of one scholarly circle, Joseph Dennie's of Boston. In contrast, her brother Winthrop, belonged to the Society of the Cincinnati, the American Academy of Arts and Sciences, the American Philosophical Society and the Massachusetts Historical Society.[5]

In 1769, at eighteen Judith married twenty-eight year old John Stevens. Stevens commissioned the building of the large, elegant house which still stands overlooking the Gloucester seaport (Sargent, Emma 50). The Stevens lived there for seventeen years, and though they were childless, they helped raise several parentless nieces and nephews. During these years Judith published anonymously a catechism for parents' use with their children and later an essay on young women's self-esteem in the **Gentleman's and Lady's Town and Country Magazine**. Although Stevens' family was wealthy, owning land and three schooners, after the war John Stevens found himself in debt and his holdings at auction, whereupon he fled to the West Indies, dying there a year later on St. Eustatius in 1786.

Two years later in December 1788 in Salem, Judith married her second husband, the Universalist preacher Rev. John Murray. A widower from England and Ireland, Rev. Murray had come to this country in 1770; then, by request of Winthrop Sargent in 1774, had come to Gloucester where he lived with the Stevens as a boarder. Rellyian Universalism was already known and admired by the Sargents when Murray first came to preach in Gloucester, albeit such choice of a liberal religion was unusual for people of the Sargent's class (Carpenter 50). Rev. Murray not only promoted religious liberalism, but contributed substantially to religious freedom by effecting a tax change that liberated all denominations from having to support First Church (52).[6]

The Murray's had two children when Judith was nearly forty and John was nearly fifty--the first, a son George, born in 1789, died shortly after birth, the second, a daughter Julia Maria, was born in 1791.[7] In the year between the births of their children, 1790, the Murrays organized a Universalist convention in Philadelphia where Judith met Benjamin Franklin and Benjamin Rush, two men who had been influential in establishing the Young Ladies Academy of Philadelphia in 1787, an academy based on proposals of John Locke. After the meeting, Judith's praise of Dr. Rush was published in an article in a London magazine. The convention at an end, the Murrays spent time with George and Martha Washington in New York, attended sessions of Congress, and met with John and Abigail Adams. Judith's observations on the meetings in New York are vividly described in letters to her parents and preserved in part in the **Universalist Quarterly**. Thomas Jefferson who rarely attended church, came to hear Rev. John Murray preach. Although a popular preacher, John Murray committed little to paper, depending heavily upon Judith's writing. Both for her interest in Universalism and for her writing about its American founder, Judith is mentioned in articles and books on the history of Universalism in America.

Being married to John Murray put Judith in the adverse position of being socially persecuted for religious views; nevertheless, John Murray's enthusiasm was a help to her. It was after their marriage that Judith began publishing in the **Massachusetts Magazine**, "the most successful of the eighteenth century magazines in New England" (Pendleton 41). John Murray encouraged her to publish **The Gleaner**; his argument was that she would need the money which it would make from subscriptions once he was gone (Eddy **U in Gl** 190). **The Gleaner** obtained 729 subscribers from a rather large geographical area. A second edition to be printed in England failed because the person in charge died (Eddy **Univ in Am** 188-9). John believed Judith's "literary gifts were for the time distinguished," (Demarest 8) and he "took pride in her gifts" (407).

In her first publication, a catechism appearing in 1782, Judith Sargent Murray demonstrates her inventiveness when she allows the child rather than authority to ask the questions. Despite the fact that the catechism has yet to be included in bibliographies of her work, it is in the preface of this catechism that Murray begins her feminist revolution. Having written her first treatise on feminism, "On the Equality of the Sexes," in 1779, she did not publish it until 1790, which was after both the catechism and her next essay in a 1784 edition of **Gentleman's and Lady's Town and Country Magazine** were published. The

Massachusetts Magazine published Judith Murray's poems under the name Constantia from 1789-94 and from 1792-94 her essays, "gleanings from the pen of Mr. Virgilius," her repository essays, letters under a variety of pseudonyms, and her epilogues and prologues to popular dramas. After the Murrays moved from Gloucester to metropolitan Boston in 1793, Judith submitted dramatic productions to the public. Her comedies "The Medium" and "The Traveller Returned" were produced anonymously on the Boston Federal Theater stage in the years 1795 and 1796, with runs from one to three days. Controversies ensued in the papers concerning their authorship and their quality.[8] Judith Murray declined to publish in the **Massachusetts Magazine** after 1794, probably to avoid making an issue of the religious proselytizing charges against her. Once **The Gleaner** was published in three volumes in 1798, Judith Murray continued to publish poems from 1802-05 in the **Boston Weekly Magazine** under the names "Honora-Martesia" and "Honora." During her husband's six years of paralyzing illness, until his death in 1815, she edited his sermons (1812) and wrote the last four chapters of his autobiography (1816), all the while providing him with daily care.

In addition to writing for publication, Judith Sargent Murray continually wrote letters. Many of the contemporaries she corresponded with used pennames, sometimes more than one. Abigail Adams used "Portia" and Mercy Otis Warren "Marcia" and indeed, the newspaper critic of her plays, Robert Treat Paine, used "Menander" as a pseudonym. Murray won the right to use the pseudonym "Constantia" when another writer began to use the same name. This "Constantia" consequently changed her name to "Constantia-Philenia" and then to "Philenia."[9] Among other correspondents were Martha Washington and possibly Hannah Adams, the religious historian, who wrote to request John Murray for his definition of the Universalist religion that it might be included in her dictionary of religions.

Judith Sargent Murray began the first deliberate, "networking" by citing contemporary women writers by actual name or pseudonym in her essays.[10] Ever attempting to persuade the public of the need to recognize not only women writers but American writers, Murray is well aware that but few American women writers have been recognized in their homeland. She was encouraged by the international recognition achieved by such English women writers as Mary Wollstonecraft and the playwright Elizabeth Simpson Inchbald, whose comedies appeared on the Boston stage the same years as did her own. Although Judith Sargent Murray challenged the thinking of her day, and "celebrated the `excellency of our sex'"(Woloch 82), it is poignant to note that her most important essay, "On the Equality of the Sexes," was not reprinted until nearly the 1970's, and even then, short as it is, only in part (Kraditor 30, Rossi 18).

In 1820 Judith Murray at sixty-nine years of age having moved from New England to Natchez, Mississippi died in June on her daughter Julia Maria Murray Bingamon's plantation, "Fatherland." She was followed in death by her granddaughter Charlotte in 1821; the same year that her grandson Adam was born. Julia died the next year, 1822, to be buried alongside her mother. The infant Adam grew up to marry Ellen Livingston of New York; their daughter Julia Maria Bingamon with her early death in 1865 brought an end to Judith Sargent Murray's direct descendants.

After her death, Judith Sargent Murray's unpublished work and most of her letters, stored at an antebellum estate in Mississippi, were reported destroyed by mildew. However, some of that work, twenty copy books of letters, four volumes of poetry and a volume of essays was discovered only recently in 1986, and it has not yet been transcribed from her handwriting.[11] When these works are available for study, the full substance of her philosophy will become known.

Murray was the first American to have a play performed on a Boston stage (Seilhamer 248, Field 118); her essays were possibly the first to be published separately in a book in this country; the thread of a story around the adopted Margaretta throughout many of her **Gleaner** essays presents an early form of the novel (Field 53). Aware of ill treatment of Afro-Americans, she attempted to ameliorate situations in her own community by word and deed;[12] her feminist philosophy anticipated Mary Wollstonecraft and Margaret Fuller; her feminist theology, though unique, was not noted for nearly two hundred years (Kraditor 30, Rossi 17). With her insistent mentioning of women scholars of her day, Murray began to make the history she claimed women would form and to set in evidence the tradition that we are here attempting to further demonstrate, a philosophical tradition that has yet to be proved. "Pioneer" though she was for her early accomplishments, Judith Sargent Murray's work remains in obscurity (Field 53).

For all her effort expended in articulating ideas, seeing them published, and doing so without overstepping the boundaries of propriety, it was said of her work, that it was "as well forgotten as remembered"(Sargent 53). Judith Sargent Murray was not acknowledged even by feminists in the nineteenth century; Mary Wollstonecraft not Murray is listed among early feminists by such enthusiasts as Susan B. Anthony. Ednah Dow Cheney, in her history of women in Boston, refers to Murray only as poet and playwright. Introduced to the twentieth century by Vena Bernadette Field in 1930 and Chester A. Jorgensen in 1940, Murray is considered to have been a "very minor" writer of little significance (Field 53). In the late twentieth century the sociologists Aileen Kraditor and Alice Rossi introduced a small portion of Murray's hitherto unpublished work and more recently the historians Linda Kerber and Mary Beth Norton have begun to promote her as a leading figure. However, she is omitted as a philosopher in such valuable works as Mary Ellen Waithe's **A History of Women Philosophers.**

From comments made about her by those who knew her then or knew her later through her works, Judith Sargent Stevens Murray appears to have been gracious, a person desirous of influencing her world without offending it and hopeful of achieving some morsel of literary immortality. A young girl listening to Judith read her "sublime poetry," concluded that "Nature has formed her of its finest material and to compleat her has given her a soul superior to any I have met with (Sargent,Emma 51)". A cousin referred to her as "a most kind, affectionate excellent lady" (53). Benjamin Rush and John Adams praised her. Rev. Richard Eddy quotes remembrances of her "having uncommon beauty of person, and a superior mind"(**U in Gl** 189),of having "remarkable personal beauty, gifted with wonderful conversational powers"(**UQ** 211) and of being a "commanding person, of very strong determination and nerve, but always discriminating, intelligent, and polite"(212). Another biographer infers that she possessed "a strong affectional magnetism, as well as...masculine energy and intellect"(Demarest 8). To these epitaphs one twentieth century scholar believes her to have been "a dynamic force in whatever arena she entered"(Ferguson 2); another has written a fitting summary: "Judith Murray's mind was as catholic and resilient as her heart was exquisite and tender"(Jorgenson 73). Wordless, the Copley portrait, the famous eighteenth century canvas, depicting Judith Sargent Stevens at eighteen with vigilant yet calm

117

presence, reminds us of who she was and what she wanted for us. The true power of her ideas and depth of her mind have yet to be discovered and made available as a legacy to American philosophers, men and women.[13] This is but a beginning.

Endnotes

1   Chester Jorgenson in his 1940 "Gleanings from Judith Sargent Murray" **American Literature** (March 1940) considers her most important contribution to be her political theory.

2   An American who wrote feminist poems and essays before Judith Sargent Murray, Sor Juana Ines de la Cruz, a Mexican nun of the seventeenth century has recently been referred to as "first American feminist" by Dorothy Shones (Merrim, Stephanie. **Feminist Perspectives on Sor Juana Ines de la Cruz**, Detroit: Wayne State UP, 1991):11) This title "first" is fitting for Sor Juana, while the title "mother" is fitting for Murray.

3   Judith Sargent's great-great grandfather Andrew Robinson (b. 1679), grandson of John Robinson, pastor of the Pilgrims, constructed the first "schooner" which he named from the Icelandic word for skipping stones (Sargent 48). Her father and grandfather both named Winthrop were descendants of William Sargent who arrived in this country in 1678. Her father, a ship owner and merchant was a political leader and one of the ratifiers of the Federal Constitution. A member of First Church, he became a Universalist despite adverse affects of bigotry on "mind and fortune"(50). The eldest of eight children of whom four survived, Judith with her two brothers Winthrop and Fitz-William achieved notable success. Winthrop, who received an A.M. degree from Harvard in 1771, after a trip to Europe in 1775 became aide-de-camp to Major General Robert House in Washington's army, and was later appointed first governor of the Mississippi Territory. His grandson Fitz-William, a noted surgeon, was father to the painter John Singer Sargent. Winthrop built a home called "Gloster Place" in Natchez, Mississippi near Judith's daughter. He died there in January 1820, six month's before Judith. Judith's other brother, also named Fitz-William became a wealthy merchant whose business took him to China, Russia, and India where he founded the India Company (Field 16).

    Judith was cousin to the artist Henry Sargent and great-grand aunt to the artist John Singer Sargent.

4   "Though the study of English literature and the belles lettres did not then form a part of college preparation..." both Winthrop and his sister Judith developed a fondness for poetry (Field 16).

5   Although no American women belonged to these organizations at the time, the Russian Dashkova, "Catherine the Little," who in 1783 was head of both the academy of science and the academy of art in Russia, was elected the first woman member of the Philosophy Society of Philadelphia (Alic 179) and, in fact, was invited by Benjamin Franklin to visit Philadelphia (Mamonova 16).

6   Universalism was an optimistic religion which believed in universal salvation. Though not widely accepted, it claimed a long chronology: tenth century philosopher John Scotus Erigena and the seventeenth century mystic Jane Lead came to its defense (Eddy **U in A**,I,7-11). In 1863 it made history by ordaining Olympia Brown, the first woman to receive ordination in a graduation. In 1961 the Universalist Church merged with the Unitarian.

7   An account of Judith Sargent Murray's extremely difficult birthing can be found in a letter by John Murray which is at present on view at her home in Gloucester.

[8] As late as 1968, corrections were still being made concerning the authorship of "The Medium" by "a Citizen of the United States." Marius B. Peladeau's article claiming Royall Tyler to be the author, is refuted by G. Thomas Tanselle who points out in the **NEQ** that Arthur Hobson Quinn in 1923 had disproved that claim. Murray was "most laudatory" in her praise of Tyler and wrote an epilogue to one of his dramas, but she wrote her own dramas as well.

[9] Sarah Wentworth Morton or possibly Susannah Rowson was the poet (Philenia) with whom Judith Murray had an exchange in the **Massachusetts Magazine** over the use of Murray's pen-name "Constantia." According to one source, Morton, having acquired the name long after Judith Murray had used it, conceded from then on to use "Constantia-Philenia" and finally "Philenia." Apparently, Murray held no rancor as she mentions "Philenia" proudly in her Gleaner essay, but in a letter to Joseph Dennie, Morton mentions the occasion with umbrage (Pendleton 75).

[10] Mary Astell, from whom Judith Sargent Murray might have inherited the feminist baton, urged women to support one another. Astell herself had many women friends; for example, she wrote an introduction to a book by one of her friends, Lady Mary Wortely Montague.

[11] Rev. Gordon D. Gibson discovered the papers believed to have been lost since 1881 (Richard Eddy's article in the **Universalist Quarterly** reported the loss from evidence of Murray's niece, Mrs. Worcester) in a library at an antebellum mansion in Natchez, Mississippi. The papers were then donated to the Mississippi Department of Archives and History, and ultimately microfilmed for use at several libraries. Unfortunately, Murray wrote commending the volumes to "posterity" that she had burned all correspondence prior to 1774. These contained the history of her "juvenile life."

[12] In a letter to her brother Winthrop in May, 1785 Judith Sargent Stevens writes about her attempt to find work on a "fishing vessel" for the Afro-American servant Winthrop had left behind in Gloucester. To her dismay she finds it impossible because "a single objection was in their opinion sufficient--He was a <u>Negro</u>". It is possible that she wrote a play called <u>The African,</u> but it has not been recovered.

[13] The new found letters spanning nearly a fifty year period, once they become published, will provide us with a portrait of Judith Sargent Murray in her own words. To illustrate:
    In a letter dated November 27,1807 to her sister she writes that her ill husband "helpless as an infant" has caused her mind to be "shaken as by a mighty tempest" and contemplates her own mortality--"when I am ready to sink beneath the garden of existence." Still, she looks forward to the joy of approaching Christmas "which taught our senses to anticipate".
    In other letters dated January 1810 she speaks of her worries over expenses of hiring nurses and the necessity of purchasing more candles during her husband's long illness, and tells of such pleasures as learning to add figures "scientifically" from young William Fitz William Sargent, a student at Harvard.
    In other letters Judith Sargent Murray contrasts her views with Mary Wollstonecraft's, describes the British fleet in Gloucester's harbor, responds to Jedidiah Morse with a theological argument on behalf of her husband.

Introduction to the Selections

"On the Equality of the Sexes" and "Female Abilities" presented here establish clearly, that before the word existed, Judith Sargent Murray, did in fact, write "feminist" philosophy.[1] "Feminist," the word which names the concern for women expressed by theorists like Murray, according to the OED was not actually coined until 1894, a hundred years after Murray's first works were published. Earlier American women had voiced feminist ideas--Anne Bradstreet maintained a firm feminist outlook in her poetry and aphoristic ethics; Mercy Otis Warren raised and articulated feminist issues in plays and private letters; and, Abigail Adams often gave and quoted feminist arguments in her correspondence. However, it was Murray who not only articulated feminist concerns but developed a feminist philosophy. Nominating her "philosopher" would not have been possible in her own time; presention of her as "philosopher" today is not yet generally accepted.[2]

To discover Murray's feminist perspective is not difficult; however, to discover her systematic feminist philosophy one must resort to examining a number of her works not immediately identifiable as pertinent, sort out the subject matter, method and principle of her philosophy from this variety of sources, and detect the consistency of thought abiding in her rhetoric of expression.

Judging from the scant notice of her these two hundred years, it is difficult to believe that Judith Sargent Murray actually probed profoundly the vital feminist questions of her day as when she asked:

> Is it reasonable that an intelligent being be allowed no other ideas,
> than those which are suggested by the mechanism of a pudding,
> or the sewing of the seams of a garment? (**E of S** 134).

But, traced through a variety of genres and literary conventions of the time, Murray's philosophy does becomes clear. Through disparate modes of presentation--a poem, an essay and a fictitious letter regarding that essay--one discovers a consistent philosophy. To reveal her philosophy in a manner inoffensive to her public, Murray relied on such rhetorical devices as irony, humor, and various personae. At times she included contradictory visions of popular concepts of women in the same way that propaganda is used by intellectuals in repressive societies. The subtlety of the underlying consistency has belied those who read her as contradicting herself, hence the reason for addressing the difficulties in discovering Murray's feminist philosophy not only through various works but through her use of rhetoric as well.

Murray's situation was unusual: "Many Americans of the eighteenth century could read but not write, paper and ink were costly, quill pens time consuming (DePau 98). Few women could even sign their names. Still, with all her advantages of pen and ink, Murray felt the repression.[3] Murray articulates the rhetorical line she must walk through metaphor in the preface of her first published work, **Some Deductions...as Assistant to the Christian Parent**. The metaphorical line, the constraint of psychological space in which eighteenth century women were confined becomes a continuing theme:

> When a Female steps without the Line in which custom hath
> circumscribed her, she naturally becomes an Object of
> Speculation:...I shall be accused of Arrogance, Heresy,
> Licentiousness...(**Some Deductions** iii)

To write is to step out of bounds for a woman.[4] To write something with authority is censurable. These consequences occur not for reasons but from "custom." "The Door of science barred to us, the Path of Truth ...the Page of Revelation, lies open before us:(iii)" Custom denying us truth through science, we women, nevertheless, are allowed to find truth in Scripture, examples there provide proof.

Murray repeats the image of a confining space in her essays: "On the Equality of the Sexes" she notes "in the contracted circle I have moved;" she observes in "Some Desultory Thoughts Upon the Utility of Encouraging a Degree of Self-Complacency, Especially in Female Bosoms" that women's progress has been "consigned" to "narrow bounds;" and in **The Gleaner** she again writes that women are "circumscribed in their education within very narrow limits." Ever aware of the "circle" of limitations surrounding her, Judith Sargent Murray attempts to reason the circle away and then to step outside it, always motioning her sex to follow. Between the dichotomy of being either silent or strident, she finds a prudent method in a polished style that shelters her ideas in conventions.

Appropriateness of time, perhaps, was also a consideration. She refrains from publishing for six years the essay "On the Equality of the Sexes," which was written four years before the catechism. Writing under the pseudonyms-Constantia, Honora-Martesia, and Honora, or under no name at all, e.g. when her plays were produced, or under various fictitious names as authors of letters--also granted her more leeway and more freedom of expression.

In the final essay of her three volume compilation, **The Gleaner**, Murray reveals why she took on a masculine disguise as its author, the gleaner, "Mr. Virgilius." Still, she does not go so far as to reveal her name:

> Observing, in a variety of instances, the indifference, not to say contempt, with which female productions are regarded, and seeking to arrest attention, at least for a time, I was thus furnished with a very powerful motive for an assumption, which I flattered myself would prove favorable to my aspiring wishes. Another strong inducement to the assumption and continuance of my disguise was the opportunity it afforded me of making myself mistress of the unbiased sentiments of my associates...further reason for concealment; I was ambitious of being considered independent as a writer;(313)

To demonstrate her precarious situation, Murray quotes Rousseau, who claimed that behind every woman writer there was sure to be a man guiding the pen, and she quotes another who claimed that should a woman dare to consult a man, he would pass for the "original inventor"(315). Hence, Murray's feminist philosophy is set forth with rhetorical and timely prudence.

That Murray's feminist philosophy was inter-related with her political philosophy, suggests to some that her greatest importance is not as a defender of women's rights so much as an interpreter of the American federal union: "her mind ...[is] best revealed in her concept of liberty..." (Jorgenson 76). Friend of the Warrens and the Adams, daughter of a politically active father, wife of an army chaplain, and admirer of George Washington, Murray was intensely interested in the new political climate--such was the fire that kindled her notions of feminine freedom. Murray develops a rationalist /federalist philosophy that differs from anti-federalist Mercy Otis Warren.[5]

Linda Kerber and Jane DeHart-Mathews consider Murray a political theorist because her "essays provide the most fully developed articulation of the idea that political independence should be the catalyst for female autonomy"(84). True as these conclusions are, underlying her political theory is the fact that the subject of all her philosophy, is the institution, be that institution national, political, academic, religious, civic or domestic, public or private. For this reason, historians, educators, sociologists and literary critics observe her as one of their own. It is the same subject matter that informs her metaphysics, epistemology, and ethics. We exist as individuals animated by God; we learn as individuals, as parents, as citizens; we act as individuals, couples, citizens etc. Reality is in the institutional experience--the problems she sees in the issues of institutions concern women; the correction of the problems concern women.

Judith Sargent Murray begins an inquiry by looking to first principles, i.e. metaphysical foundations. For it is only with knowledge of these principles, that she can move on to practical application. Murray initiates the articulation of her philosophical principles in the preface of her catechism:

> Whatsoever is essential to the ethereal Spark, which animates these transient tenements, will exist when the Distinctions of Male and Female, shall be forever absorbt. (iii)

The spirit which animates the body of both male and female is sexless.[6] How spirit is related to matter follows upon contemplation of immortality in "Spirit Independent of Matter" (**GL**, II,LXII) and in her poem "On Blending Spirit with Matter" in which she deduces that the spirit cannot be superior to its material home-"As is the House, so is the Master too." Yet the spirit must be present, or we would never be able to overcome the "comfortless" plan of our impending death, nor become strengthened and meet with truth; thus the spirit's presence must be an inspired one, one that allows for a kind of transcendence of reason. Reason is the "harbinger" of truth in her playful poem "An Hypothesis;" truth is brought forward through the "mental mine of reflection." Through nightly visits to Absolute Truth, the soul replenishes the "mine." Hence Murray's metaphysics establishes that the mind is inspirated by an immortal independence that energizes reason. The following works illustrate how through reason, transcendence is achieved.

124

"On the Equality of the Sexes"

Before Murray addresses epistemological and ethical problems in "On the Equality of the Sexes," she once again enunciates first principles. In the poetical introduction Murray recalls the "spirit mingling with the clod" as "unfettered, to no sex confin'd." Here two problems emerge: one involving the spirit, the other the "clod" or "house." First, it can be inferred that if the spirit is asexual, the intellectual powers of the sexes, being of the spirit, must also be asexual and therefore equal; it is the spirit the "inborn powers of the soul" (Gl,LXII,270).[7]

The second problem, the material of the "clod" or mind, is addressed in the prologue to the essay . Murray hypothesizes that nature would not be "partial in her distributions" to men and women. In the essay proper, it becomes clear to Murray that women are not lower intellectually than men, but that the "lordly" sex still consigns women to being "imbeciles" and then disallows them the power to improve. So, to prove that the intellectual powers of the mind are equal, Murray examines empirically the four categories of intellectual power: imagination, memory, reason, and judgment from the standpoint of "reason, nature and experience."

Once this inquiry is complete, Murray examines two related ethical issues; the first, preparation for afterlife. Murray takes up this argument in "Letters of Mary Vigililius to Margaret": "The mind is only in its dawn of being;--but for the valuable acquirements which it attains while here, are not upon its emancipation, lost; for otherwise--they are rather introductory to that career, which is to be continued and perfected in future worlds"(**GL**,XLIV,106). Thus women's souls as well as men's, need preparation for their future existence of divine contemplation.

The other ethical issue, moral superiority, is taken up at the close of the essay. Murray cites with evidence from Scripture that despite their claims, men are not morally superior. In her catechism, Murray had given the following answer to a question about Adam and Eve: "The Woman, we are informed, was first in the Offense"(10). The prevalent idea that "first" meant "worst" she takes to task in what Alice Rossi calls the "earliest example of this argument"(17). In an addendum in the form of a letter to "On Equality..." Murray argues that while Eve sinned believing she was gaining wisdom, Adam was not so deceived and thus sinned with full realization that it was a sin.

Murray concludes that there are no pink souls and blue souls "our souls are by nature equal to yours; the same breath of God animates, enlivens, and invigorates"(134). She points out that arguments from the analogy of physical strength to intellectual strength are not philosophically sound and are thus irrelevant. What is at issue is that neither the spirit that unites with the body in the mind nor the body is intellectually or morally superior in the male sex.

Having addressed the ethical issues, Murray lastly takes up issues of economics. She argues that economics of equality follows from the principle of equality, so that if men protect women, women take care of men's domestic needs--neatness, food, peaceful family relationships. It is an even trade. And again, there could be a gain on the distaff side, domestic duties being what they are leave more time for study than do the "employments of the other sex"(224). Murray also focuses on economics in her 1795 drama, "Virtue Triumphant," when her heroine Eliza refuses to marry until her "social and financial position are established" (Quinn 126).[8]

It is on metaphysical and epistemological principles that Murray adds an historical foundation and upon these builds her theories of education, psychology and feminist philosophy. With reflection and system, Murray deduces that according to nature, mental powers are equal. Why is it important to know this? For Murray it is the ethical well-being of women themselves, for their families and for their country as well as for the spiritual, psychological and educational disposition needed for a positive sense of identity, for the sake of all learning including the manual trades, and in preparation for eternity, for all this a firm philosophical foundation is necessary.[9]

Between "On the Equality of the Sexes" and its sequel "Observations on Female Abilities" published nearly ten years later, Murray wrote two essays on the psychological requirements for learning. The first addressed the needs of young women in learning "everything mental within their grasp," and the second addressed the needs of young children: how a thirst for ethical living should be fostered, and how a healthy system of discipline should be established. In her essay "On the "Equality of the Sexes" Murray referred to how women both thought and felt. She extended her interest to the psychological result of the deprivation of education and the psychological preparation needed for its gain. These two essays prepare for the subsequent "Female Abilities" essays.

First:

"Desultory Thoughts Upon the Utility of Encouraging a Degree of Self-Complacency in Female Bosoms"

The purpose of the essay "Desultory Thoughts...," published in the **Gentleman's and Lady's Magazine** in 1784, was to articulate what should be the "groundwork" of education, "to teach young minds to aspire," so that with application and intense study external grace and mental accomplishments could be acquired, i.e. "everything in the compass of mortality"(251). What is needed is positive re-enforcement. The phrase most repeated is "to reverence yourself," by which words Murray means respect your "intellectual existence." To do that a girl must be addressed as a rational being and from her beginning be "habituated to reflect"(252). Praised by her family and having learned to estimate her true value, she will neither have a low estimation of herself nor be prey to flatterers but will instead be able to meet life protected. Thus she will not "throw herself away upon the first" who professes love, and thereby suffer not only unhappiness but possibly material want as well (253).

Socrates' "know thyself" becomes transformed by Murray to "reverence thyself" to which she adds the practical hypothesis, that not only will a woman be better armed in the world with self-knowledge and self-esteem, but that she will also be better able to fend off needless material deprivation. The historian Linda Kerber considered this essay a "prescient argument." Its aim, to encourage women to "reverence" themselves, however, is still an issue today. Ironically, Mary Astell had proposed the beginnings of these same ideas in the seventeenth century.[10]

Second:

"On the Domestic Education of Children"

Published in **Massachusetts Magazine** in 1790, "On the Domestic Education of Children" again lays groundwork, i.e. the psychological preparation, but now addressing the pre-school situation. She asks, "do blows ever produce a salutary effect upon a gentle or generous disposition?" and follows with "...what

127

shall we substitute instead of those violent and coercive measures?"(272). She answers through the example of Martesia, an exemplary mother. Martesia makes a point of being even tempered around her children. Her "irregular passion" is kept away from their observation. "Tenderly concerned" and deeply interested in their happiness, she impresses them, however, with an idea of her "superior abilities." This idea insures that her "authority will be readily acknowledged, and her decisions will obtain the requisite weight"(276).

Always reasonable, Martesia also gives examples of being humane and benevolent. To create "finer feelings of the soul" she recites stories to promote "interest of virtue" and "to excite commiseration." Thus, children learn from habit to become generous. But if a child's misdemeanor should be discovered, consequences are dealt according to its seriousness: a trivial fault remains a secret between the child and the mother; a great offense is proclaimed throughout the house; a greater offense results in banishment from notice by the entire household, but when the child is penitent, the crime is cancelled. The hypothesis is that when "the boys" depart for school (girls, of course, remain at home) the psychological preparation, mental and moral, begun at home will continue at school (276).

In the eighteenth century, "use the rod or spoil the child" and the idea of schools existing only for boys were the realities. Here Murray addresses the pre-school preparation for learning and living for both sexes. Keep in mind that Murray had explained in the previous essay that girls should have an education which omitted nothing, which of course, they could not obtain as well at home with their mothers as at Harvard.[11]

Speaking further in the essay "Sentiments on Education" in **The Gleaner**, Murray remarks that "few parents are endowed by nature, or qualified by improvement." Having seen the results of bad parenting, she concludes that it might be better if youths were placed "under the tutelage of the State" (GL,XXXV,5-6). (This idea, for different reasons, will be restated by such women as Frances Wright in the nineteenth century and Charlotte Perkins Gilman and Voltairine De Cleyre in the early twentieth.)

In summary, these essays prove that it is not just the Enlightenment's reason, that Murray's philosophy regards, but the development of the whole person, the person as child in the home, child at school, child becoming adult. An Enlightenment feminist, Murray wants balance, "spirit blending with matter."[12]

THE GLEANER: "Observations on Female Abilities"

When Judith Sargent Murray compiled in 1798 a number of her writings into three volumes entitled **The Gleaner**, she left out "On the Equality of the Sexes," and included instead a four chapter addition, entitled "Female Abilities" explaining that she did not think the "subject exhausted." Perhaps, relinquishing the deductive approach in the earlier essay in order "to prove, by examples, that the minds of women are naturally as susceptible of every imporvement, as those of men" (Gl.III,197), she believed this new appeal would be more persuasive to a wider audience. Note that she not only accepts the vision of Wollstonecraft as to the numbers of women to be educated and to the breadth of their education but wants to extend it: "improving on the opinions of a Wollstonecraft, we are ready to contend for the quantity, as well as the quality, of mind." Her rhetorical sensibilities further inspire her to write these chapters in the form of an oration and as a case in law.

Presented in what might be termed a "little lawsuit," this series of essays prefigures Margaret Fuller's "great lawsuit." Murray's suit argues that history and current cases give evidence that women's achievements prove equal to those of men. Fuller's suit contends that conditions exist which could now offer women fuller achievement than men have yet attained.

First, Murray begins the oration with the classical "exordium" in which she congratulates her countrywomen, lauds the opening of academies and articulates the future as she sees it. Next she presents the brief, the argument and a summary of what will be covered (narratio and expositio). In the second chapter she explains why this method is most suitable, and then explains that the "court, is...convened; the jury are empaneled, and we proceed to the examination of the witnesses"(198). She continues the chapter by outlining ten areas of proof and proceeds with the first four. These four pertaining to interior strength are the virtues of endurance, resourcefulness, heroism and bravery--which women in fact have demonstrated.[13] The third chapter concerns the six remaining virtues, those pertaining to relationships, to country and government, that prove women have been patriotic, influential, energetic and eloquent, faithful, strong, and capable of literary achievements. Lists of women who have exhibited these virtues in their accomplishments prove women's capability to perform equally with men. Examples range from ancient Greece to seventeenth century Europe. Chapter four continues by detailing women who have succeeded in the present eighteenth century. Thus, to further her first deductive essay, Murray now presents inductive evidence of the equality of the sexes:

> Our evidences tend to prove them alike capable of enduring hardships; equally ingenious and fruitful in resources; their fortitude and heroism cannot be surpassed; they are equally brave; they are as patriotic, as influential and as eloquent; as faithful and as persevering in their attachments; as capable of supporting with honor the toils of government, and equally susceptible of every literary acquirement(Gl.III,198).

But is it only equality of the sexes that Murray is arguing? No, now she is proving further that women have the civic virtues "capable of supporting...the toils of government" i.e., capable of being citizens in the full sense of the word. Why the formal oration and court case? This rhetorical constraint allowed Murray to argue the audacious conclusion without ever overstepping the bounds of propriety. As a matter of fact, her ideas were so foreign, that it would take the new nation from 1798 to 1920 to fully appropriate her suggestion by enfranchising women.

In the guise of a letter to the Gleaner by "Martha Studious" at the end of the same third volume in which these chapters occur, Murray adds names of two more women, Margaret of Valdemer, a fourteenth century widow who discharged admirably the duties of governing and Dorothy Schlözer, a mineralogist who became the first woman in Germany to receive a Ph.D. in Göttingen (1787). [14]

Conclusion

In summary, Judith Sargent Murray begins her philosophical investigations on feminism with a metaphysical inquiry into the nature of spirit, mind and matter. The inquiry leads her to conclude that although we all alike share divine spirit, that spirit is limited, not by sex, but by our materiality. That materiality is limited by the "order of nature"(GL,LXXXIX,196), not by sex. Reflective powers allow a fuller participation in the spirit. These powers divided into imagination, reason, judgment and memory are proved, according to both reason and historical illustration, to be shared by both men and women according to individual natural talents and efforts. These powers need the institution of education for effective exercise in both this world, at home and in government, and the next. Hence, this inquiry concludes that women should be as well educated as men.

The subject matter of Murray's feminist philosophy is institutions: the institutions of family and school in early life, later the institutions of the single life, the married life which may include parenting, and the civic life. Her method of inquiry into these institutions is to look at the problems and discover their resolution. Her principle is reflexive: the discovering of a problem and the correcting of that problem. Her assumption is that institutions arise to resolve problems and that problems can be solved through reasoning.

Aware of the power of rhetoric, Murray was also aware of the power of linguistics. Speaking of a Massachusetts independent scholar in the field of agriculture, Murray refers to her as "husbandwoman" rather than "husbandman" (GL,XCL,221). This person is one who "realizes all that independence which is proper to humanity" (222)--a goal which she hopes will make the term "helpless widow" as non existent as "helpless widower"(219). In a 1794 article in **Massachusetts Magazine** Murray also took to task the demeaning phrase "female curiosity" claiming that "curiosity" which "predominates in a superior degree in the female bosom...[and as] the origin of every mental acquisition [should therefore] cease to be considered a term of reproach" (Norton 239).

Murray's "new era in female history" did brighten in the next century, but now at the close of the twentieth century we see that future as still moving toward Murray's goal of women's full development and participation in domestic and civic institutions:

> "The lustre of those minds,(is) still enveloped in a veil of mortality," but "...the curtain will be thrown back, and posterity will contemplate, with admiration, their manifold perfections" (III,217), and "that half of the human species which hath hitherto been involved in the night of darkness," will be advancing with alacrity "toward the irradiating sun of science" (Norton 295).

131

In her eighteenth century style, Murray's redefinition of women and her redefinition of women's place appear at once dated and contemporary. Constraint is her theme and virtue; her words are both radical and moderate. Pious, she was yet worldly; an idealist, also practical. With humor and good sense, she both philosophizes and exhorts. By presenting here two of her essays on feminist philosophy, the intention is to let her be heard and thus to merit the "crown of applause" she so wanted herself and others to hear and to have (E of S 134).

Endnotes

1 Murray mentions these three women in "Observations on Female Abilities." It has been said that nearly a hundred years before Murray, feminism "arose from Marie de Gournay's brain in full armor" (201).

2 Some have said that "the United States did not produce its own philosopher of feminism until the publication of Margaret Fuller's **Woman in the Nineteenth Century** in 1845" (Sinclair 51).

3 Murray's situation was unusual: "Many Americans of the eighteenth century could read but not write, paper and ink were costly, quill pens time consuming (98 DePau). Few women could even sign their names. "After the war, as before, English Common law remained in effect. Lawyers, moreover, continued to rely on Sir William Blackstone's **Commentaries**. These 1765 **Commentaries on the Laws of England**, assert that the "'very being or legal existence of a woman is suspended during the marriage'"(Woloch 78). American eighteenth-century lawyers and their successors relied on this code. It would not be changed until such nineteenth century agitators beginning with Frances Wright sought its demise. Old English Common Law had held that husband and wife were one, and the husband was the one. With all her advantages, Judith Sargent Murray felt this repression.

4 Lack of space is a frequent, feminine theme. Mercy Otis Warren, Murray's contemporary also used this image of confined space for women. In her poem "To a Patriotic Gentleman Who Presented a Small Book of Bark Requesting a poem Might be written Therein" Warren writes "...I quit the pen, and keep within the bounds,/The narrow bounds prescrib'd to female life, the gentle mistress; and the prudent wife." from **Miscellaneous Poems**.

Before either of these eighteenth century women used that image of space, the seventeenth century Dutch scholar, Anna Maria Van Schurman wrote of women "The higher minds among us may not be cramped within such narrow confines; nor should the peak of soaring intelligence be crushed down against nature" (Birch, 76-77) and Mary Astell urges women to "dare to break the enchanted Circle that custom has plac'd us in" (Hill 141).

Shortly after Murray, the American Eliza Southgate, echoed Murray's phrases with "stepping beyond the limits" (Cott 105).

Julia Ward Howe in 1874 laments that girls have "only so much room allowed them as may not cramp the full sweep of the other sex" (28). Space for women continues to be a feminist theme--from the novelist Virginia Woolf's plea for a room of one's own, to the philosopher Julia Kristeva's "signifying space" in her essay "Women's Time." Kristeva's essay relates space to the "very notion of identity...challenged" in our "new theoretical and scientific space" (Keohane 51-2). The philosophers of language too, are asking how are women to step out of the "web" of masculine speech, using an image very much like that of Murray's "circle." Andrea Nye tells us, "One cannot simply step painlessly outside the web of one's" patriarchical world (232).

5 Murray's defined Federalism as a

> "superstructure" in which "each individual receives from the common fund and where every member contributes his quota, for the benefit of the whole" (**GL**,XXVI,253)

and as the way to a "peaceful" government that involves also her concept of liberty as "system" "regulations" "laws" and "subordination" as opposed to "licentiousness," a "heaven descended goddess, rational and refined," liberty's "movements are authorized by reason; knowledge is her

harbinger; wisdom administereth unto her; and all her interpositions are mildly beneficient..."(**GL**,XXVI,260);
as well as that of justice

> "Justice is enthroned far above all law" rather than blind, Murray personifies her as "the goddess of fire" with "a subtle essence, which should penetrate through, and pervade the inmost recesses of the soul; by every insignia of light I would surround and designate her while among the ornaments which composed her crest, a broad and never closing eye"...Justice should feel, hear and see, but truth alone should be the pole star" (**GL**, XXIII,219-20).

Murray teasingly suggests in the guise of Modestus Mildmay that an article be added to the Constitution providing for a sinecure "providing for the establishment of <u>real genius</u>, whether it be found in the male or female world" (**GL**,V,52).

6 Londa Schiebinger points out in **The Mind Has No Sex**? that Francois Poullain de la Barre, a Cartesian, claimed in 1673 that based on new scientific evidence in anatomy, the mind had no sex, "L'esprit n'a point de sexe"(1). Marie de Gournay (207) and Sor Juana Ines de la Cruz (366) also make that statement, and Judith Drake argues in her 1696 **An Essay in Defense of the Female Sex** that unlike men's bodies which were made for action, women's bodies were made for thought. Although, the idea of minds having no sex was used in 1884 to support women's admission to the Academie Francaise, William Whellell in 1834 had declared that "there is sex in minds." "Before and since Poullain's time, the question of sex in the mind has been the topic of intense political debate--a debate whose history has, until recently, been neglected"(273).

7 This philosophical argument continues, for example Hilda Hein's recent essay concludes:"While spirituality may be characterized by intelligence, it is not reducible to it....neither men nor women have a monopoly on spirituality...." (Gould 139-40).

8 Although Eliza is found to have station and wealth via a "deus ex machina," she has proved herself equal to Charles in worth; now, with economic equality, she becomes independent and thus marriageable. With no other means besides marriage and/or private contract available to women by which to gain financial independence, this resolution was timely.

Though the rich varieties of characterizations entertain, Murray "fashioned her plays to fit her theory of drama as a means of moral instruction" (Ferguson 89). For Murray the theater was "a very powerful engine in forming the opinion and manners of a people" (**GL**,XCVI,262) on the equality of women, patriotism, propriety, religion, class distinction, and in face of anti-theater sentiment, on the value of theater itself (Ferguson 262). Murray valued the fact that "Socrates, Cicero and even Cato, have mingled with the audience of a theater" (**GL**,XXIV,228). Murray's first play was performed early in 1795, the ban on theaters in Boston during the Revolutionary War having been lifted in 1793. To her second play at its third performance Murray added this apology:

> Who would not tolerate a female pen?
> Women, perhaps, were born a match for men:
> But natal rights by education crampt,
> The sex's inequality is stampt...(20)

9 Why now? The Revolution, with its rhetoric of liberty and equality created a different climate; how different it would come to be, no one knew. In the human rights issues raised, women discerned questions that needed serious debate. Not yet citizens, were women educable to participate more fully in the political realm? Indeed, were they as "human" as men? The church and state now separate, who would provide the moral leadership; indeed, were women innately as good as men? Although economic upheavals in the war were often shouldered by women, were women capable of handling their economic affairs?

Perhaps opportunities were at hand: "As Murray argued, the Republic had defined an ideal filled with political implications for woman: she was to be clearheaded and in control of her own emotions so that she could in turn control her husband and her children and thereby guarantee the virtuous behavior on which the security of the Republic depended" (Kerber 230). In fact, the historian Mary Beth Norton believes this "Gloucester woman" wanted to "accomplish a break with the past," but in order to do so she had to establish a foundation for the future (252).

10 A further irony is that it was a decade after this forward -looking essay was published that the American Philosophical Society awarded a prize for an essay on education with the backward view that considered the male child only (Kerber 210).

11 Current discussion by Judith Hughes notes Locke's ideas about the rationality of children (Griffiths 79-85); Murray is more definite than Locke about children's rationality. Although her theory of education is divulged through various kinds of writing, it is philosophically consistent. She is amenable, as Jean Nostrand Dorgan notes, to her contemporary, Wollstonecraft, in claiming, for example, that education is based on experience and individualized instruction, and to twentieth century philosopher John Dewey in arguing the importance of curiosity (185, 80).

12 Christine Pierce's essay "Postmodernism and other Skepticisms" in **Feminist Ethics** edited by Claudia Card makes the case that feminism is not necessarily postmodern, but rather a "a balance" recognizing with skepticism white masculine Enlightenment rationalism while maintaining a pluralistic understanding of its strengths.

13 In arguing that women have been courageous, a virtue Aristotle claimed to be male, Murray praises woman warriors, but then later appears to contradict herself when she claims that "we are not desirous to array the sex in martial habiliments; we do not wish to enlist our women as soldiers...we only contend for the capability ..."(217). Murray was probably aware of such women in the Revolutionary War as Deborah Samson, Mary Ludwig Hays (Molly Pitcher) or Margaret Corbin. Although Mary and Margaret entered the war at the side of their husbands, Deborah of Plymouth, was a common soldier for three years; twice wounded, she fought under the name of Private Robert Shirtliffe and was eventually awarded a pension. In any event, Murray rhetorically makes the point that women can and have been soldiers, but leaves the full discussion open.

14 At the time **The Gleaner** was published, Schlözer, born in 1770, had not as yet been honored by the Academy of Science in Paris. Murray's dates are not completely accurate, the year of Schlözer's graduation being listed as 1790 rather than 1787.

On the Equality of the Sexes

To the Editors of the Massachusetts Magazine,
Gentlemen, The following essay is yielded to the patronage of candor.--If it has been anticipated, the testimony of many respectable persons, who saw it in manuscript as early as the year 1779, can obviate the imputation of plagiarism.

On the Equality of the Sexes

That minds are not alike, full well I know,
This truth each day's experience will show;
To heights surprising some great spirits soar,
With inborn strength mysterious depths explore;
Their eager gaze surveys the path of light,
Confest it stood to Newton's piercing sight.

Deep science, like a bashful maid retires,
And but the ardent breast her worth inspires;
By perseverance the coy fair is won.
And genius, led by study, wears the crown.

But some there are who wish not to improve,
Who never can the path of knowledge love,
Whose souls almost with the dull body one,
With anxious care each mental pleasure shun;
Weak is the level'd, enervated mind,
And but while here to vegetate design'd.
The torpid spirit mingling with its clod,
Can scarcely boast its origin from God;
Stupidly dull--they move progressing on--
They eat, and drink, and all their work is done.
While others, emulous of sweet applause,

On the Equality of the Sexes

Industrious seek for each event a cause,
Tracing the hidden springs whence knowledge flows,
Which nature all in beauteous order shows.
         Yet cannot I their sentiments imbibe,
Who this distinction to the sex ascribe,
As if a woman's form must needs enroll,
A weak, a servile, an inferior soul;
And that the guise of man must still proclaim,
Greatness of mind, and him, to be the same:
Yet as the hours revolve fair proofs arise,
Which the bright wreath of growing fame supplies;
And in past times some men have sunk so low,
That female records nothing less can show.
But imbecility is still confin'd,
And by the lordly sex to us consign'd;
They rob us of the power t'improve,
And then declare we only trifles love;
Yet haste the era, when the world shall know,
That such distinctions only dwell below;
The soul unfetter'd, to no sex confin'd,
Was for the abodes of cloudless day design'd.
         Mean time we emulate their manly fires,
Though erudition all their thoughts inspires,
Yet nature with equality imparts,
And noble passions, swell e'en female hearts.

ON THE EQUALITY OF THE SEXES

   Is it upon mature consideration we adopt the idea, that nature is thus
partial in her distributions? Is it indeed a fact, that she hath yielded to one half of

the human species so unquestionable a mental superiority? I know that to both sexes elevated understandings, and the reverse, are common. But suffer me to ask, in what the minds of females are so notoriously deficient, or unequal. May the intellectual powers be ranged under these four heads--imagination, reason, memory, and judgment.

The province of imagination hath long since been surrendered up to us, and we have been crowned undoubted sovereigns of the regions of fancy. Invention is perhaps the most arduous effort of the mind; this branch of imagination hath been particularly ceded to us, and we have been time out of mind invested with that creative faculty. Observe the variety of fashions (here I bar the contemptuous smile) which distinguish and adorn the female world; how continually they are changing, insomuch that they almost render the wise man's assertion problematical, and we are ready to say, there is something new under the sun. Now what a playfulness, what an exuberance of fancy, what a strength of inventive imagination, doth this continual variation discover? Again, it hath been observed, that if the turpitude of the conduct of our sex, hath been ever so enormous, so extremely ready are we, that the very first thought presents with an apology, so plausible, as to produce our actions even in an amiable light.

Another instance of our creative powers, is our talent for slander; how ingenious are we at inventive scandal? what a formidable story can we in a moment fabricate merely from the force of a prolific imagination? how many reputations, in the fertile brain of a female, have been utterly despoiled? how industrious are we at improving a hint? suspicion how easily do we convert into conviction, and conviction, embellished by the power of eloquence, stalks abroad to the surprise and confusion of unsuspecting innocence. Perhaps it will be asked if I furnish these facts as instances of excellency in our sex. Certainly not; but as proofs of a creative faculty, of a lively imagination. Assuredly great activity of mind is thereby discovered, and was this activity properly directed, what beneficial effects would follow. Is the needle and kitchen sufficient to employ the operations of a soul thus organized? I should conceive not. Nay, it is a truth that those very departments leave the intelligent principle vacant, and at liberty for speculation.

On the Equality of the Sexes

Are we deficient in reason? we can only reason from what we know, and if an opportunity of acquiring knowledge hath been denied us, the inferiority of our sex cannot fairly be deduced from thence.

Memory, I believe, will be allowed us in common, since every one's experience must testify, that a loquacious old woman is as frequently met with, as a communicative old man; their subjects are alike drawn from the fund of other times, and the transactions of their youth, or of maturer life, entertain, or perhaps fatigue you, in the evening of their lives.

"But our judgment is not so strong--we do not distinguish so well." --Yet it may be questioned, from what doth this superiority, in this determining faculty of the soul, proceed. May we not trace its source in the difference of education, and continued advantages? Will it be said that the judgment of a male of two years old, is more sage than that of a female of the same age? I believe the reverse is generally observed to be true.

But from that period what partiality! how is the one exalted, and the other depressed, by the contrary modes of education which are adopted! the one is taught to aspire, and the other is early confined and limited. As their years increase, the sister must be wholly domesticated, while the brother is led by the hand through all the flowery paths of science. Grant that their minds are by nature equal, yet who shall wonder at the apparent superiority, if indeed custom becomes second nature; nay if it taketh the place of nature, and that it doth the experience of each day will evince. At length arrived at womanhood, the uncultivated fair one feels a void, which the employments allotted her are by no means capable of filling. What can she do? to books she may not apply; or if she doth, to those of the novel kind, lest she merit the appellation of a learned lady; and what ideas have been affixed to this term, the observation of many can testify. Fashion, scandal, and sometimes what is still more reprehensible, are then called in to her relief; and who can say to what lengths the liberties she takes may proceed. Meantime, she herself is most unhappy; she feels the want of a cultivated mind. Is she single, she in vain seeks to fill up time from sexual employments or amusements. Is she united to a person whose soul nature made equal to her own, education hath set him so far above her, that in those entertainments which are productive of such rational

139

felicity, she is not qualified to accompany him. She experiences a mortifying consciousness of inferiority, which embitters every enjoyment. Doth the person to whom her adverse fate hath consigned her, possess a mind incapable of improvement, she is equally wretched, in being so closely connected with an individual whom she cannot but despise. Now, was she permitted the same instructors as her brother (with an eye however to their particular departments) for the employment of a rational mind an ample field would be opened. In astronomy she might catch a glimpse of the immensity of the Deity, and thence she would form amazing conceptions of the august and supreme Intelligence. In geography she would admire Jehovah in the midst of his benevolence; thus adapting this globe to the various wants and amusements of its inhabitants. In natural philosophy she would adore the infinite majesty of heaven, clothed in condescension; and as she traversed the reptile world, she would hail the goodness of a creating God. A mind, thus filled, would have little room for the trifles with which our sex are, with too much justice, accused of amusing themselves and they would thus be rendered fit companions for those, who should one day wear them as their crown. Fashions, in their variety, would then give place to conjectures, which might perhaps conduce to the improvement of the literary world; and there would be no leisure for slander or detraction. Reputation would not then be blasted, but serious speculations would occupy the lively imaginations of the sex. Unnecessary visits would be precluded, and that custom would only be indulged by way of relaxation, or to answer the demands of consanguinity and friendship. Females would become discreet, their judgments would be invigorated, and their partners for life being circumspectly chosen, an unhappy Hymen would then be as rare, as is now the reverse.

  Will it be urged that those acquirements would supercede our domestick duties. I answer that every requisite in female economy is easily attained; and, with truth I can add, that when once attained, they require no further mental attention. Nay, while we are pursuing the needle, or the superintendency of the family, I repeat, that our minds are at full liberty for reflection; that imagination may exert itself in full vigor; and that if a just foundation is early laid, our ideas will then be worthy of rational beings. If we were industrious we might easily find time to arrange them upon paper, or should avocations press too hard for such an indulgence, the hours allotted for conversation would at least become more refined and rational. Should it still be vociferated, "Your domestic employments are sufficient" --I would calmly ask, is it reasonable, that a candidate for immortality, for the joys of heaven, an intelligent being, who is to spend an eternity in contemplating the works of Deity, should at present be so degraded, as to be allowed no other ideas, than those which are suggested by the mechanism of a pudding, or the sewing the seams of a garment? Pity that all such censurers of female improvement do not go one step further, and deny their future existence; to be consistent they surely ought.

Yes, ye lordly, ye haughty sex, our souls are by nature equal to yours; the same breath of God animates, enlivens, and invigorates us; and that we are not fallen lower than yourselves, let those witness who have greatly towered above the various discouragements by which they have been so heavily oppressed; and though I am unacquainted with the list of celebrated characters on either side, yet from the observations I have made in the contracted circle in which I have moved, I dare confidently believe, that from the commencement of time to the present day, there hath been as many females, as males, who by the mere force of natural powers, have merited the crown of applause; who, thus unassisted, have seized the wreath of fame.

I know there are those who assert, that as the animal powers of the one sex are superior, of course their mental faculties also must be stronger; thus attributing strength of mind to the transient organization of this earth born tenement. But if this reasoning is just, man must be content to yield the palm to many of the brute creation, since by not a few of his brethren of the field, he is far surpassed in bodily strength. Moreover, was this argument admitted, it would prove too much, for ocular demonstration evinceth, that there are many robust masculine ladies, and effeminate gentlemen. Yet I fancy that Mr. Pope, though clogged with an enervated body, and distinguished by a diminutive stature, could nevertheless lay claim to greatness of soul; and perhaps there are many other instances which might be adduced to combat so unphilosophical an opinion. Do we not often see, that when the clay built tabernacle is well nigh dissolved, when it is just ready to mingle

141

with the parent soil, the immortal inhabitant aspires to, and even attaineth heights the most sublime, and which were before wholly unexplored. Besides, were we to grant that animal strength proved any thing, taking into consideration the accustomed impartiality of nature, we should be induced to imagine, that she had invested the female mind with superior strength as an equivalent for the bodily powers of man. But waiving this however palpable advantage, for equality only, we wish to contend.

I am aware that there are many passages in the sacred oracles which seem to give the advantage to the other sex; but I consider all these as wholly metaphorical. Thus David was a man after God's own heart, yet see him enervated by his licentious passions! Behold him following Uriah to death, and show me wherein could consist the immaculate Being's complacency. Listen to the curses which Job bestoweth upon the day of his nativity, and tell me where is his perfection, where his patience--literally it existed not. David and Job were types of him who was to come; and the superiority of man, as exhibited in scripture, being also emblematical, all arguments deduced from thence, of course fall to the ground.

The exquisite delicacy of the female mind proclaimeth the exactness of its texture, while its nice sense of honor announceth its innate, its native grandeur. And indeed, in one respect, the preeminence seems to be tacitly allowed us, for after an education which limits and confines, and employments and recreations which naturally tend to enervate the body, and debilitate the mind; after we have from early youth been adorned with ribbons, and other gewgaws, dressed out like the ancient victims previous to a sacrifice, being taught by the care of our parents in collecting the most showy materials that the ornamenting our exterior ought to be the principal object of our attention; after, I say, fifteen years thus spent, we are introduced into the world, amid the united adulation of every beholder.

Praise is sweet to the soul; we are immediately intoxicated by large draughts of flattery, which being plentifully administered, is to the pride of our hearts the most acceptable incense. It is expected that with the other sex we should commence immediate war, and that we should triumph over the machinations of the most artful. We must be constantly on our guard; prudence and discretion must be our characteristics; and we must rise superior to, and obtain a complete victory over those who have been long adding to the native strength of their minds, by an unremitted study of men and books, and who have, moreover, conceived from the loose characters which they have seen portrayed in the extensive variety of their reading, a most contemptible opinion of the sex. Thus unequal, we are notwithstanding forced to the combat, and the infamy which is consequent upon the smallest deviation in our conduct, proclaims the high idea which we formed of our native strength; and thus, indirectly at least, is the preference acknowledged to be our due.

And if we are allowed an equality of acquirements, let serious studies equally employ our minds, and we will bid our souls arise to equal strength. We will meet upon even ground, the despot man; we will rush with alacrity to the combat, and, crowned by success, we shall then answer the exalted expectations which are formed. Though sensibility, soft compassion, and gentle commiseration, are inmates in the female bosom, yet against every deep laid art, altogether fearless of the event, we will set them in array; for assuredly the wreath of victory will encircle the spotless brow. If we meet an equal, a sensible friend, we will reward him with the hand of amity, and through life we will be assiduous to promote his happiness; but from every deep laid scheme for our rule, retiring into ourselves, amid the flowery paths of science, we will indulge in all the refined and sentimental pleasures of contemplation.

And should it still be urged, that the studies thus insisted upon would interfere with our more peculiar department, I must further reply, that early hours, and close application, will do wonders; and to her who is from the first dawn of reason taught to fill up time rationally, both the requisites will be easy. I grant that niggard fortune is too generally unfriendly to the mind, and that much of that valuable treasure, time, is necessarily expended upon the wants of the body; but it should be remembered, that in embarrassed circumstances our companions have as little leisure for literary improvement, as is afforded to us; for most certainly their provident care is at least as requisite as our exertions. Nay, we have even more leisure for sedentary pleasures, as our avocations are more retired, much less laborious, and, as hath been observed, by no means require that avidity of attention which is proper to the employments of the other sex. In high life, or, in other words, where the parties are in possession of affluence, the objection respecting time is wholly obviated, and of course falls to the ground; and it may also be repeated, that many of those hours which are at present swallowed up in fashion and scandal, might be redeemed, were we habituated to useful reflections.

But in one respect, O ye arbiters of our fate! we confess that the superiority is indubitably yours; you are by nature formed for our protectors; we pretend not to vie with you in bodily strength; upon this point we will never contend for victory. Shield us then, we beseech you, from external evils, and in return we will transact your domestic affairs. Yes, your, for are you not equally interested in those matters with ourselves? Is not the elegancy of neatness as agreeable to your sight as to ours; is not the well favored viand equally delightful to your taste; and doth not your sense of hearing suffer as much, from the discordant sounds prevalent in an ill regulated family, produced by the voices of children and many et ceteras?

Constantia.

By the way of supplement to the forgoing pages, I subjoin the following extract from a letter wrote to a friend in the December of 1780.

And now assist me, O thou genius of my sex, while I undertake the arduous task of endeavoring to combat that vulgar, that almost universal error, which hath, it seems enlisted even Mr. P---under its banners. The superiority of your sex hath, I grant, been time out of mind esteemed a truth incontrovertible; in consequence of which persuasion, every plan of education hath been calculated to establish this favorite tenet. Not long since, weak and presuming as I was, I amused myself with selecting some arguments from nature, reason, and experience, against this so generally received idea. I confess that to sacred testimonies I had not recourse. I held them to be merely metaphorical, and thus regarding them, I could not persuade myself that there was any propriety in bringing them to decide in this **very important debate.** However, as you sir, confine yourself entirely to the sacred oracles, I mean to bend the whole of my artillery against those supposed proofs, which you have from thence provided, and from which you have formed an entrenchment apparently so invulnerable.

And first, to begin with our great progenitors; but here, suffer me to promise, that it is for mental strength I mean to contend, for with respect to animal powers, I yield them undisputed to that sex, which enjoys them in common with the lion, the tiger, and many other beasts of prey; therefore your observations respecting the rib, under the arm, at a distance from the head, etc. etc. in no sort militate against my view.

Well, but the woman was first in the transgression. Strange how blind self love renders you men; were you not wholly absorbed in a partial admiration of your own abilities, you would long since have acknowledged the force of what I am now going to urge. It is true some ignoramuses have, absurdly enough informed us, that the beauteous fair of paradise, was seduced from her obedience, by a malignant demon, in the guise of a baleful serpent; but we, who are better informed, know that the fallen spirit presented himself to her view, a shining angel still; for thus, saith the critics in the Hebrew tongue, ought the word to be rendered. Let us examine her motive--Hark! the seraph declares that she shall attain a perfection of knowledge; for is there aught which is not comprehended under one or other of the terms good and evil.

It doth not appear that she was governed by any one sensual appetite; but merely by a desire of adorning her mind; a laudable ambition fired her soul, and a thirst for knowledge impelled the predilection so fatal in this consequences. Adam could not plead the same deception; assuredly he was not deceived; nor ought we to admire his superior strength, or wonder at his sagacity, when we so often confess that example is much more influential than precept. His gentle partner stood before him, a melancholy instance of the direful effects of disobedience; he saw her not possessed of what wisdom which she had fondly hoped to obtain, but he beheld the once blooming female, disrobed of that innocence, which had heretofore rendered her so lovely. To him then deception became impossible, as he had proof positive of the fallacy of the argument, which the deceiver had suggested. What then could be his inducement to burst the barriers, and to fly directly in the face of that command, which immediately from the mouth of Deity he had received, since, I say, he could not plead the fascinating stimulus, the accumulation of knowledge, as indisputable conviction was so visibly portrayed before him.

What mighty cause impelled him to sacrifice myriads of beings yet unborn, and by one impious act, which he saw would be productive of such fatal effect, entail undistinguished ruin upon a race of beings, which he was yet to produce. Blush, ye vaunters of fortitude; ye boasters of resolution; ye haughty lords of creation; blush when ye remember, that he was influenced by no other motive than a bare pusillanimous attachment to a woman! by sentiments so exquisitely soft, that all his sons have, from that period, when they have designed to degrade them, described as highly feminine. Thus it should see, that all the arts of the grand deceiver (since means adequate to the purpose are, I conceive, invariably pursued) were requisite to mislead our general mother, while the father of mankind forfeited his own, and relinquished the happiness of posterity, merely in compliance with the blandishments of a female.

The subsequent subjection the apostle Paul explains as a figure after enlarging upon the subject, he adds, "This is a great mystery; but speak concerning Christ and the church." Now we know with what consummate wisdom the unerring father of eternity hath formed his plans; all the types which he has displayed, he has permitted materially to fail, in the very virtue for which they were famed. The reason for this is obvious, we might otherwise mistake his economy, and render that honor to the creature, which is due only to the creator. I know that Adam was a figure of him who was to come. The grace contained in this figure, is the reason of my rejoicing, and while I am very far from prostrating before the shadow, I yield you--fully in all things the pre eminence to the second federal head. Confiding faith is pre-figured by Abraham, yet he exhibits a contrast to affiance, when he says of his fair companion, she is my sister. Gentleness was the characteristic of Moses, yet he hesitated not to reply to Jehovah himself, with unsaintlike tongue he murmured at the waters of strife, and with rash hands he breaks the tables, which were inscribed by the finger of divinity. David, dignified with the title of the man after God's own heart, and yet how stained was his life. Solomon was celebrated for wisdom, but folly is wrote in legible characters upon his almost every action. Lastly, let us turn our eyes to man in the aggregate. He is manifested as the figure of strength, but that we may not regard him as anything more than a figure, his soul is formed in no sort superior, but every way equal to the mind of her, when in the emblem of weakness, and whom he calls the gentle companion of his better days.

OBSERVATIONS ON FEMALE ABILITIES

The Gleaner, Vol. III, Essay LXXXVIII: 188-196.

> Amid the blaze of this auspicious day,
> When science points the broad refulgent way,
> Her iron scepter prejudice resigns,
> And sov'reign reason all resplendent shines.

The reader is requested to consider the four succeeding numbers as supplementary to an essay which made its appearance, some years since, in a periodical publication of a miscellaneous nature. The particular paper to which I advert, was entitled, **The Equality of the Sexes**; and, however well I may think of that composition, as I do not conceive that the subject is exhausted, I have thought proper, treading in the same path, to set about collecting a few hints which may serve as additional, illustrative, or ornamental.

And, first, by way of exordium, I take leave to congratulate my fair country-women, on the happy revolution which the few past years has made in their favor; that in those infant republics, where, within my remembrance, the use of the needle was the principal attainment which was thought necessary for a woman, the lovely proficient is now permitted to appropriate a moiety of her time to studies of a more elevated and elevating nature. Female academies are every where establishing, and right pleasant is the appellation to my ear.

Yes, in this younger world, "the Rights of Women" begin to be understood; we seem, at length, determined to do justice to The Sex; and, improving on the opinions of a Wollstonecraft, we are ready to contend for the quantity, as well as quality of mind. The younger part of the female world have now an inestimable prize put into their hands; and it depends, on the rising generation to refute a sentiment, which still retaining its advocates, grounds its arguments on the incompatibility of the present enlarged plan of female education, with those necessary occupations, that must ever be considered as proper to the department and comprised in the duties of a judiciously instructed and elegant woman; and, if our daughters will combine their efforts, converts to the new regulations will every day multiply among us. To argue against facts, is indeed contending with both

148

wind and tide; and, borne down by accumulating examples, conviction of the utility of the present plans will pervade the public mind, and not a dissenting voice will be heard.

I may be accused of enthusiasm; but such is my confidence in the sex, that I expect to see our young women forming a new era in female history. They will oppose themselves to every trivial and unworthy monopolizer of time; and it will be apparent, that the adorning their persons is not with them a primary object. They will know how to appreciate personal advantages; and, considering them as bestowed by Nature, or Nature's God, they will hold them in due estimation: Yet, conscious that they confer no intrinsic excellence on the temporary possessor, their admeasurement of real virtue will be entirely divested of all those prepossessing ideas, which originate in a beautiful exterior. The noble expansion conferred by a liberal education will teach them humility; for it will give them a glance of those vast tracts of knowledge which they can never explore, until they are accommodated with far other powers than those at present assigned them; and they will contemplate their removal to a higher order of beings, as a desirable event.

Mild benignity, with all the modest virtues, and every sexual grace--these they will carefully cultivate; for they will have learned, that in no character they can so effectually charm, as in that in which nature designed them the pre-eminence. They will accustom themselves to reflection; they will investigate accurately, and reason will point their conclusions: Yet they will not be assuming; the characteristic trait will still remain; and retiring sweetness will insure them that consideration and respect, which they do not presume to demand. Thinking justly will not only enlarge their minds, and refine their ideas; but it will correct their dispositions, humanize their feelings, and present them the friends of their species. The beauteous bosom will no more become a lurking-place for invidious and rancorous passions; but the mild temperature of the soul will be evinced by the benign and equal tenor of their lives. Their manners will be unembarrassed; and, studious to shun even the semblance of pedantry, they will be careful to give to their most systematic arguments and deductions, and unaffected and natural appearance. They will rather question than assert; and they will make their

149

communications on a supposition, that the point in discussion has rather escaped the memory of those with whom they converse, than that it was never imprinted there.

It is true, that every faculty of their minds will be occasionally engrossed by the most momentous concerns; but as often as necessity or propriety shall render it incumbent on them, they will cheerfully accommodate themselves to the more humble duties which their situation imposes. When their sphere of action is enlarged, when they become wives and mothers, they will fill with honor the parts allotted them. Acquainted, theoretically, with the nature of their species, and experimentally with themselves, they will not expect to meet, in wedlock, with those faultless beings, who so frequently issue, armed at all points, from the teeming brain of the novelist. They will learn properly to estimate; they will look, with pity's softest eye, on the natural frailties of those whom they elect partners for life; and they will regard their virtues with that sweet complacency, which is ever an attendant on a predilection founded on love, and happily combining esteem. As mothers, they will assume with alacrity their arduous employment, and they will cheerfully bend to its various departments. They will be primarily solicitous to fulfil, in every instance, whatever can justly be denominated duty; and those intervals, which have heretofore been devoted to frivolity, will be appropriated to pursuits, calculated to inform, enlarge, and sublime the soul--to contemplations, which will ameliorate the heart, unfold and illumine the understanding, and gradually render the human being an eligible candidate for the society of angels.

Such, I predict will be the daughters of Columbia; and my gladdened spirit rejoices in the prospect. A sensible and informed woman--companionable and serious--possessing also a facility of temper, and united to a congenial mind--blest with competency--and rearing to maturity a promising family of children--Surely, the wide glove cannot produce a scene more truly interesting. See! the virtues are embodied--the domestic duties appear in their place, and they are all fulfilled--morality is systematized by religion, and sublimed by devotion--every movement is the offspring of elegance, and their manners have received the highest polish. A reciprocation of good offices, and a mutual desire to please, uniformly distinguishes the individuals of this enchanting society--their conversation, refined and elevated, partakes the fire of genius, while it is pointed by information; and they are ambitious of selecting subjects, which, by throwing around humanity, in its connection, additional luster, may implant a new motive for gratitude, and teach them to anticipate the rich fruition of that immortality which they boast. Such is the family of reason--of reason, cultivated and adorned by literature.

The idea of the incapability of women, is, we conceive, in this enlightened age, totally inadmissible; and we have concluded, that establishing the expediency of admitting them to share the blessings of equality, will remove every obstacle to their advancement. In proportion the nations have progressed in the arts of civilization, the value of the sex hath been understood, their rank in the scale of being ascertained, and their consequence in society acknowledged. But if prejudice still fortifies itself in the bosom of any; if it yet enlifteth its votaries against the said despot and its followers, we produce, instead of arguments, a number of well attested facts, which the student of female annals hath carefully compiled.

Women, circumscribed in their education within very narrow limits, and constantly depressed by their occupations, have, nevertheless, tinged the cheek of manhood with a guilty suffusion, for a pusillanimous capitulation with the enemies of their country. Quitting the loom and the distaff, they have beheld, with indignation, their husbands and their sons flee in battle: With clasped hands, and determined resolution, they have placed themselves in their paths, obstructing their passage, and insisting, with heroic firmness, on their immediate return to death or conquest! They have anxiously examined the dead bodies of their slaughtered sons; and if the fatal wounds were received in front, thus evincing that they have bravely faced the foe, the fond recollection of their valor has become a source of consolation, and they have sung a requiem to their sorrows! Women, in the heat of action, have mounted the rampart with undaunted courage, arrested the progress of the foe, and bravely rescued their besieged dwellings! They have successfully opposed themselves to tyranny and the galling yoke of oppression! Assembling in crowds, they have armed themselves for the combat--they have mingled amid the battling ranks--they have fought heroically--and their will-timed and well-concerted measures have emancipated their country! They have hazarded

151

the stroke of death in its most frightful form; and they have submitted to bonds and imprisonment, for the redemption of their captive husbands!

The character of the Spartan women is marked with uncommon firmness. At the shrine of patriotism they immolated nature. Undaunted bravery and unimpeached honor, was, in their estimation, far beyond affection. The name of Citizen possessed, for them greater charms than that of Mother; and so highly did they prize the warrior's meed, that they are said to have shed tears of joy over the bleeding bodies of their wounded sons!

When Europe and Asia were infested by armed multitudes, who, emigrating for purposes of devastation and settlement, perpetrated the most ferocious acts, among all those various tribes of unprincipled invaders, no discriminating line seems to have marked the sexes; wives submitted to similar hardships with their husbands; equally they braved the impending danger; and their efforts and their sufferings were the same. Nor can their habits of endurance and patient fortitude admit a rational doubt.

The women of Hungary have rendered themselves astonishingly conspicuous in their wars against the Ottoman Empire--But proofs abound; and numerous actions might be produced to evince, that courage is by no means exclusively a masculine virtue. Women have frequently displayed an intrepidity, not to be surpassed by men--neither is their bravery the impulse of the moment. They not only, when trained by education and inured by subsequent habit, rise superior to the fears of death; but, with unimpassioned and sedate composure, they can endure life--they can struggle with the fatigues and inconveniences--they can fulfil the duties, and they can support the irremediable calamities of war. They have achieved the most surprising adventures; indulgences have been extended to them on the well-fought field; and they have expired with the weapons of death in their hands! Actuated by devotional zeal, and stimulated by the sublime expectation of an opening heaven, and a glorious immortality, they have rushed into the flames, have ascended the scaffold, have suffered the dismemberment of their bodies, have submitted to the tortures of dislocation, and to the most excruciating racks, in defense of truth! nor hath the voice of murmuring or complaint escaped their lips!

Abilities

Women have publicly harangued on religion--they have presented themselves as disputants--they have boldly supported their tenets--they have been raised to the chair of philosophy, and of law--they have written fluently in Greek, and have read with great facility the Hebrew language. Youth and beauty, adorned with every feminine grace, and possessing eminently the powers of rhetoric, have pathetically conjured the mitred fathers and the Christian monarchs to arm themselves for the utter extirpation of the enemies of their holy religion.

In the days of knight-errantry, females, elevated by the importance with which they were invested, discriminated unerringly between the virtues and the vices, studiously cultivating the one, and endeavoring to exterminate the other; and their attainments equalled the heroism of their admirers; their bosoms glowed with sentiments as sublime as those they originated; generosity marked their elections; the impassioned feelings, the burst of tenderness, were invariably blended with honor; and every expression, every movement, was descriptive of the general enthusiasm. Pride, heroism, extravagant attachments; these were common to both sexes. Great enterprises, bold adventures, incredible bravery--in everything the women partook the color of the times; and their taste and their judgment were exactly conformed. Thus the sexes are congenial; they are copyists of each other; and their opinions and their habits are elevated or degraded, animated or depressed, by precisely the same circumstances.

The Northern nations have generally been in the habit of venerating the female sex. Constantly employed in bending the bow, in exploring the haunts of those animals, who were the victims of their pleasures and their passions, or of urging against their species the missive shafts of death, they nevertheless banished their ferocity, and assumed the mildest manners, when associating with their mothers, their sisters, their mistresses, or their wives. In their ample forests, their athletic frames and sinewy arms were nerved for battle, while the smiles of some lovely woman were the meed of valor; and the hero who aspired to the approbation of the beautiful arbitress of his fate, authorized his wishes, and established his pretensions, by eminent virtue, and a long series of unbroken attentions.

153

Abilities

A persuasion, that the common Father of the universe manifests himself more readily to females than to males, has, at one period or another, obtained, more or less, in every division of the globe. The Germans, the Britons, and the Scandinavians--from these the supposition received an easy credence. The Grecian women delivered oracles--the Romans venerated the Sibyls--among the people of God, the Jewish women prophesied--the predictions of the Egyptian matron were much respected--and we are assured, that the most barbarous nations referred to their females, whatever they fancied beyond the reach of human efforts: And hence we find women in possession of the mysteries of religion, the arcana of physic, and the ceremonies of incantation. Writers assert, that several nations have ascribed to women the gift of prescience, conceiving that they possessed qualities approximating to divinity; and the serious German embosomed in his native woods, renders a kind of devotional reverence to the female sex.

Such is the character of those periods, when women were invested with undue elevation; and the reverse present the sex in a state of humiliation, altogether as unwarrantable. The females among the savages of our country, are represented as submitting to the most melancholy and distressing oppression; slaves to the ferocious passions and irregular appetites of those tyrannical usurpers, who brutally and cruelly outrage their feelings. They encounter for their support, incredible hardships and toils, insomuch that, weary of their own wretched existence, the women on the banks of the Oronoko, urged by compassion, not infrequently smother the female infant in the hour of its birth; and she who hath attained sufficient fortitude to perform this maternal act, esteems herself entitled to additional respect. Commodore Byron, in his account of the inhabitants of South America, informs us, that the men exercise a most despotic authority over their wives, whom they consider in the same view they do any other part of their property, and dispose of them accordingly: Even their common treatment of them is cruel; for, although the toil and hazard of procuring food lies entirely on the women, yet they are not suffered to touch any part of it, till their imperious masters are satisfied, and then he assigns them their portion, which is generally very scanty, and such as he has not an appetite for, himself.

Abilities

Thus have the sex continued the sport of contingencies; unnaturally subjected to extremes; alternately in the mount of exaltation, and in the valley of unmerited degradation. Is it wonderful, then that they evince so little stability of character? Rather, is it not astonishing, that their attainments are so numerous, and so considerable? Turning over the annals of different ages, we have selected a number of names which we purpose, in our next essay, to cite, as vouchers of the sex's merit; nor can we doubt, that their united suffrages will, on a candid investigation, effectually establish the female right to that quality with their brethren, which, it is conceived, is assigned them in the Order of Nature.

The Gleaner, Vol. III, Essay LXXXIX: 196-205.

> The historic page with many a proof abounds,
> And fame's loud trump the sex's worth resounds;
> The patriot's zeal, the laurel'd warrior's claim,
> The scepter'd virtues, wisdom's sacred name,
> Creative poesy, the ethic page,
> Design'd to form and meliorate the age,
> With heroism, with perseverance fraught,
> By honor, truth, and constancy enwrought,
> And those blest deeds which elevate the mind,
> With female genius these are all combin'd:
> Recording story hands their virtues down,
> And mellowing time awards their fair renown.

Plutarch, in one of his invaluable compositions, speaking of men and women, thus expresses himself--"The talents and the virtues are modified by the circumstances and the persons, but the foundation is the same." This celebrated and truly respectable biographer has yielded every thing that we wish; and the testimony of so nice a distinguisher must be considered as a very powerful auxiliary.

Abilities

It is not our purpose to analyze the properties of mind; we are inclined to think, that accurately to discriminate, or draw the intellectual line, is beyond the power of the best informed metaphysician within the purviews of humanity. Besides, as we write for the many, and as it is notorious that a number of well attested facts have abundantly more weight with the multitude, than the finest spun systems which ever issued from the archives of theory, we shall proceed to summon our witnesses, arranging their testimonies with as much order, as the cursory turning over a number of volumes to which a deficiency in memory necessitates us to apply, will permit; and here, (lest the patience of our readers should reallocate at the idea of the motley circle, to which they may apprehend they are to be introduced) we take leave to inform them, that we shall be careful to abridge, as much as possible, the copious depositions which may present.

Many centuries have revolved, since the era, when writers of eminence, giving a catalogue of celebrated women, have had the number to amount to eight hundred and forty-five: From these, and succeeding attestors, we shall select a few, not perhaps the most striking, but such as occur the most readily. Our object is to prove, by examples, that the minds of women are naturally as susceptible of every improvement, as those of men. In the course of our examination, an obvious conclusion will, we conceive, force itself on every attentive and ingenuous reader. If the triumphs and attainments of the sex, under the various oppressions with which they have struggled, have been thus splendid, how would they have been augmented, had not ignorant or interested men, after clipping their wings, contrived to erect around them almost insurmountable barriers. Descartes expatiated on the philosophical abilities of the sex; and, if their supporting themselves with astonishing equanimity under the complicated oppressions to which they are not infrequently subjected, may be called the practice of any branch of philosophy, the experience of every tyrant will evince their proficiency therein. But the highly respectable and truly honorable court, is, we presume convened; the jury are empaneled, and we proceed to the examination of the witnesses, leaving the pleadings to those silent suggestions and inferences, which, we are assured, will voluntarily enlist themselves as advocates in every ingenuous bosom. The pending cause, as we have before observed, involves the establishment of the female intellect, or the maintaining the justice and propriety of considering women, as far as relates to their understanding, in every respect, equal to men. Our evidences tend to prove them--

First, alike capable of enduring hardships.

Secondly, equally ingenious, and fruitful in resources.

Thirdly, their fortitude and heroism cannot be surpassed.

Fourthly, they are equally brave.

Fifthly, they are patriotic.

Sixthly, as influential.

Seventhly, as energetic, and as eloquent.

Eighthly, as faithful, and as persevering in their attachments.

Ninthly, as capable of supporting, with honor, the toils of government. And

Tenthly, and lastly, they are equally susceptible of every literary acquirement.

And **first**, they are alike capable of enduring hardships. A proposition so self-evident, supercedes the necessity of either arguments or witnesses. On the women of Brittany, and the females among the savages of our own country, fatigues almost incredible are imposed. Imbecility seems to have changed sexes; and it is in these instances, masculine weakness and feminine vigor. The sex, enervated and sinking amid the luxuries and indulgences of an Asiatic climate, are elsewhere hardly and courageous, and fully adequate to all those exertions requisite to the support of themselves and their supine oppressors; and these well authenticated facts, are I conceive, alone sufficient to prove the powerful and transforming effects of education, and subsequent habits. But we need not take a voyage to Brittany, nor penetrate the haunts of savages, to prove that some are capable of suffering. They are the enduring sex; and, by the irreversible constitution of nature, they are subjected to agonies unknown to manhood; while I do not recollect that they are exempted from any of the calamities incident to humanity.

Secondly, they are equally ingenious, and fruitful in resources. Female ingenuity will not, we apprehend, be controverted; every day furnishes fresh proof of their invention, and their resources are a consequence. We select, however, a corroborating instance, which, from its salutary effect, seems to claim a preference. .

A certain sovereign, of avaricious memory, was so fond of amassing treasure, that he arbitrarily compelled a very large proportion of his subjects to labor in the mines; but while his majesty's ingots were rapidly augmenting, the grounds remained uncultivated; famine advanced with hasty strides; and the dreary prospect every moment gathered darkness. No one possessed sufficient intrepidity to remonstrate--the despot's lot was fate--from his decrees there was no appeal-- and the love of life, although its eligibles may be in a great measure diminished, is generally a paramount passion. In this emergency, the ingenuity of the queen suggested a resource that snatched the nation from the horrors of that dearth which had seemed so inevitable. She secretly employed an artist to produce an exact imitation of those luxuries, in which the king most delighted, a variety of fish and fowl--bread and fruits of the most delicious kind, made of pure gold, were expeditiously completed, and displayed in order on the costly board--the table was highly decorated--and when everything was complete, the king, (after having been purposely diverted from taking his customary refreshment) was ushered into the banqueting room. His Majesty took a seat--for a moment, astonishment suspended even the clamors of hunger, and his mind was occupied by admiration of the imagination of the queen, and the deceptive abilities of the artist. The event was proportioned to the most sanguine expectations of the lady. The mines were suddenly dispeopled, and the earth again produced the necessary support.

Thirdly, their fortitude and heroism cannot be surpassed. Listen to a woman of Sparta, reduced by melancholy casualties to a state of servitude--she was captured, and afterwards sold as a slave. The question was put by him on whom her very existence seemed to depend--"What knowest thou?" "To be free," was her characteristic reply: But the unfeeling despot, uninfluenced by indubitable indications of a noble mind, proceeded to impose his ignominious commands; to which she dispassionately returned, "you are unworthy of me;" and instantly resigned herself to death. Fortitude and heroism was a conspicuous trait in, and

158

gave uncommon dignity to, the character of the Roman ladies. Arria, the wife of Paetus, a Roman of consular dignity, is an illustrious instance of that transcendent elevation, of which the female mind is susceptible. With persevering firmness, and a tenderness not to be exceeded, she continued unwearied in her endeavors to procure the life of her husband--long she cherished hope; but, when the pleasing vision fled, and the portending storm was bursting over their heads: In that tremendous moment, while the disappointed man, trembling on the verge of dissolution, had not the courage to point the deadly--with that exquisite delicacy, true fortitude, and faithfulness of affection, which is so highly sexual, she first imprinted on her own bosom the characters of death; and, animated by that sublime, consciousness becoming a being more than half celestial, she then presented him the pointed dagger, with this consolatory assurance--"Paetus, this gives me no pain."

But fortitude and heroism are not confined to the Greek and Roman ladies; we have pledged ourselves not to multiply examples unnecessarily, otherwise a crown of witnesses presenting, we could with difficulty suppress their testimony. Yet we find it impossible so speedily to close this part of our examination; and from the multitude of examples in the Island of Great Britain, we produce the Lady Jane Gray, who seemed an exemplification of every virtue and every grace which has been attributed to the male or female character. The excellent understanding she received from nature was opened and improved by uniform application. At sixteen, her judgment had attained a high degree of maturity. She was at that age an adept both in the Greek and Latin languages; and she was able to declare that her Greek Plato was a more pleasing entertainment to her than all those enchanting pleasures usually so captivating to the unexperienced mind. Nurtured in the bosom of parental affection, and of tender friendship--happy in the distinguishing regards of her sovereign, and permitted the sublime enjoyment of intellectual pursuits, she had no ambition for the pageantry of royalty, and her advancement to the throne was an era, over which she dropped the melancholy tear. We are sensible that in adverting to these traits in a character, affectingly interesting, we do in fact anticipate other divisions of our subject; but, contemplating a mind thus richly furnished, it is difficult to consider separately, endowments so nicely blended, and reflecting on each other such unusual luster.

The passage of the Lady Jane, from the throne to the scaffold, was very short--her imposed queenship continued only ten days; yet she seemed displeased at their duration, and she received, with heroic fortitude, the message of death. The lover and the husband, whose vows she had recently accepted, was also under sentence of death; and, on the morning assigned for their martyrdom, he solicited for a parting interview; with solemn firmness she refused his request--yet her resolution originated not in a deficiency of tenderness; but it was nerved by an apprehension that her sensibilities, thus stimulated, might surmount her fortitude. With modest resignation she pursued her way to the place of execution--the officers of death, bearing the body of her husband, while the headless trunk yet streamed with blood, met her on her passage--neither of them had completed their seventeenth year--she looked--she sighed--and then, reassuming her composed sedateness, desired her conductors to proceed--she mounted the scaffold with an accelerated step--she addressed the surrounding spectators--she committed the care of her person to her woman; and, with a countenance descriptive of serene dignity, bowed her head to the executioner. Thus perished a spotless victim of despotism and of bigotry in the bloom of youth and beauty, rich in innocence, and adorned with every literary accomplishment and sexual grace. Latest posterity will lament her fate, and many hearts will join to execrate the sanguinary measures which procured it. Under this head we produce but one more testimony.

Miss Anna Askew, a young lady of great merit, and possessed also of a beautiful exterior, lived during the tyranny of Henry VIII of England; a despot, who seemed to conceive the female world created on purpose to administer to his pleasures, or to become the victims of his cruelty and implacability. Miss Askew was arraigned as a transgressor; her crime was a denial of the real presence in the eucharist; and for this atrocious offense, she was rigorously imprisoned and subjected to a series of barbarities that would have disgraced even savage inhumanity. Yet, in a situation which involved trials, that in a succeeding reign proved too mighty for the resolution even of the virtuous Cranmer, her heroism and fortitude continued unshaken. With unyielding firmness she vindicated the truth of her opinion, and her hourly orisons were offered up to her Father God. The chancellor, a bigoted Catholic, sternly questioned her relative to her abettors; but she nobly disdained to present an accusation, the consequences of which she so rigorously experienced: Her unbending integrity furnished the pretence, and she was, without further delay, put to the torture; but still her fortitude receded not; and her heroic silence evinced her abundantly superior of their unmanly cruelties. The enraged chancellor, in whose presence she suffered, transported with diabolic zeal, grasping with his own hands the cords, violently stretched the rack, and almost tore her body asunder; while yet unappalled, her fortitude forsook her not, and her triumph over her barbarous tormentors was complete.

Her death-warrant was next made out, and she received the sentence which condemned her to the flames, as an emancipation from every evil. All her joints dislocated by the rack, she was borne to the place of execution; and there, after being bound to the stake, was offered her life on condition of retracting her supposed error; but she consistently rejected an existence to be purchased only by the forfeiture of that consciousness of rectitude, which the virtuous so well know how to prize; and as the flames that were her passport to regions of blessedness, enkindled around her, a song of thanksgiving was on her lips, and her exultation evidently augmented.

Fourthly, they are equally brave. Bravery is not a quality which figures gracefully in the list of female virtues, nor are we anxious it should take rank in the catalogue--far from it; we should rather lament to see it become a characteristic trait. We would have women support themselves with consistent firmness under the various exigencies of life, but we would not arm them with the weapons of death: Yet, when contending for equality of [soul], it may be necessary to prove the capability of the female mind, to rear to perfection whatever seeds may be adventitiously implanted therein. We therefore proceed to produce a witness or two on this part of the question; and, consulting our records, we assign the precedence, all circumstances considered, to a young woman of Lemnos, an island in the Archipelago.

This magnanimous female beheld the streaming wounds of her expiring father, in the fatal moment in which he was slaughtered on the field of battle; and, instead of yielding to those tender sensibilities originating in nature, and generally associated with valor--instead of lamenting his fate by sighs and tears, or the wordy exclamations of clamorous sorrow, she undauntedly seized that sword and shield now rendered useless to the venerable warrior, and, arming herself therewith, reanimated the dispirited soldiers, led them once more to the charge; bravely opposed the Turks, who, having forced a gate, were rapidly advancing; and gloriously avenged the death of her father, by driving them back to the shore, and compelling them to take refute in their vessels.

Jane of Flanders next presents: This lady, during the imprisonment of her husband, nobly supported the declining honors of her house: With her infant son in her arms, she met the assembling citizens, and pathetically deploring her misfortunes, she secured their exertions in her favor. She sustained with unyielding firmness the attacks of a vigilant and active foe. In the frequent sallies made by the garrison, she herself led on her warriors. At the head of three hundred horses, with her own hand she set fire to the tents and baggage of the besiegers, thus necessitating them to desist from the general assault which they were in the moment of commencing; and, although intercepted in her return to the citadel, she nevertheless fought her way through one quarter of the French camp, and rejoined her faithful friends in triumph!

Margaret of Anjou is a decisive proof that courage is not exclusively the property of man--Brave, indefatigable and persevering--fruitful in resources--supporting by her genius and her exertions a pusillanimous husband--repeatedly emancipating him from prison, and replacing him on a throne which he had lost by imbecility, and which he was unable to retain--and equal to every thing which depended on undaunted courage, she headed her armies in person; directed their arrangements; and proceeded from rank to rank, animating them to her undaunted intrepidity and judicious conduct; and, when borne down by misfortunes, and apparently destitute of every resource, suddenly she emerged, and, followed by numerous armies, again appeared in the field; nor did she submit to fate, until she had fought, as a general and a soldier, twelve decisive battles!!!

The French women--Charlotte Corde---But our depositions unexpectedly multiplying, a recollection of our engagement can alone suppress their evidence.

The Gleaner, Essay XC:205-217.

> This joy to tread the splendid paths of fame,
> Where countless myriads mental homage claim;
> Time honor'd annals careful to explore,
> And mark the heights which intellect can soar.

Fifthly, they are equally patriotic. We have, in some measure, forestalled this article. The Grecian women have produced their testimonies, and that preference which they demonstrably manifested to the character Citizen; estimating it beyond the endearing appellations, wife and mother, incontrovertibly establishes their sex's capability of experiencing with an ardor not to be exceeded, the patriotic glow; and yet it is true, that sexual occupations frequently humiliating, and generally far removed from whatever has a tendency to elevate the mind, may rationally be supposed to chill, in the female bosom, the fine fervors of the amor patriae.

Women are not usually exercised in those extensive contemplations which engage the legislator: They are not called on to arm in their country's cause; to appear in the well fought field, or to put their lives at hazard: But when they part with him in whom is centered their dearest hopes, who blends the character's lover, friend, husband and protector--when they resign to the hostile career the blooming youth whom from infancy they have watched with all a mother's tenderness, and whose rich maturity hath become the pride and consolation of their declining life-- in those moments of anguish, their heroism and their fortitude are indisputably evinced. Nor is the patriotism of the chief arrayed for the battle; nor his, who devotes himself with all a statesman's integrity to the public weal, condemned to an ordeal more severe.

The patriotism of the Roman ladies, procured a senatorial decree that funeral orations should be pronounced from the rostrum in their praise: Repeatedly they saved their country. And the patriotism of the mother and wife of Coriolanus, while it snatched Rome from impending ruin, devoted to inevitable destruction the husband and the son: Hence towered the temple consecrated to feminine honor; and it must be confessed they had purchased this distinction at a very high price. The venerable Senate, too, again interposed; public thanks were decreed; and men were ordered, on all occasions, to yield precedence to women.

Sixthly, they are as influential. The ascendency obtained by females, is so notorious, as to have become proverbial. Instances are multiplied, wherein women have bent to their purposes the strongest masculine understanding. Samson, the victim of female blandishments, is not a singular instance. The example edited under the last article, is in point. Coriolanus rejected with unbending severity supplicating friendship, garbed in senatorial robes; succeeding deputies plead in vain--The ministers of religion, clothed in sacerdotal habits, joined in solemn procession--they crowded around the warrior, commissioned to advocate a sinking people's cause; still, however, he continued obdurate, inflexibly firm and steady to his plans. But Veturia and Volumnia, his wife and mother, attended by the most illustrious of the Roman ladies, appear--they shed torrents of tears--they embrace his knees--the hero is disarmed--his heart is melted--his resentment and his resolutions vanish together--and Rome is saved.

Seventhly, they are as energetic, and as eloquent. Women always decree with fervor: Did it depend on them, their movements would be decisive. Their expressions are often as strongly marked, as they are vehement; and both their plans and the execution thereof, are endowed with all the vigor that existing regulations will permit. Their eloquence is indisputable. possessing a richness of fancy; their words are sufficiently copious; and education, when they are indulged with its aids, prescribes the proper rules. Aspasia, of Miletus, it is well known, taught the immortal Socrates rhetoric and politics. And, when Rome groaned under the enormous cruelties of her second Triumvirate, the three barbarians by whom she was enslaved, and who had armed themselves for the destruction of her citizens, as if desirous of spreading every possible calamity, seized not only the lives, but the treasures of the people, and equally greedy of gold as of blood, after exhausting every other mode of plunder, turned their rapacious views on those respectable matrons, who had hitherto been exempted from pecuniary exactions; an exorbitant tax was levied on every individual female, and the consternation occasioned by this unheard of assumption, was proportioned to the distress of which it was productive.

In this extraordinary emergency, the oppressed females earnestly solicited the aid of those advocates who were appointed to plead the cause of the injured and defenseless; but the orators, fearful of incurring the displeasure of those who had usurped the power of life and death, refused to interfere; and no means of redress appearing, submission to an imposition acknowledged grievous, seemed inevitable: It was, however, reserved to the talents and exertions of Hortensia to furnish the desired aid.

This lady inherited all the abilities of her father; and she presented herself a voluntary advocate for her sex. With modest intrepidity she opened, conducted, and closed the pleadings. Persuasion dwelt on her tongue: Her arguments resulting from rectitude, were pointed by reason: And it will be conceived that her rhetorical powers must have been of the first rate, when it is remembered that the countenances of the tyrants betrayed sudden and evident tokens of that remorse which was then first enkindled in their bosoms; the hue of guilt pervaded their cheeks and they hastily repealed the injurious decree. For the brow of Hortensia, fame prepared an immortal wreath: To the utmost gratitude of her contemporaries she was entitled: Her triumph was the triumph of virtue and of talents: She enkindled even in the callous breasts of assassins, the almost extinguished sparks of humanity; and she stands on the page of history, a pattern of dauntless courage, and an example of genuine eloquence.

Eighthly, they are as faithful and as persevering in their attachments. Here countless witnesses crowd on retention, and the greatest difficulty is in choosing judiciously. Repeatedly have I seen the faithfully attached female, firmly persevering in that affection which was first implanted in the soil of innocence, and fondly watching with tender anxiety every symptom of the diseased man: With patient assiduity she hath hung over the couch, and fought to mitigate the pangs of him, whose licentious conduct had brought ruin on herself and her unoffending children! Had circumstances been reversed, divorce would have succeeded--a hospital must have sheltered the helpless woman; and, had she received from the man she had injured any trivial attention, the unmerited gratuity would have resounded through the circle of their connections, been dwelt on with rapture, and echoed by every tongue. But when virtue is the basis; when acts of kindness cement the union, the sex in many instances have set no bound to that faithful attachment which their hearts have exultingly acknowledged. Filial duty--conjugal affection--persevering constancy--these receive in the female bosom the highest perfection of which they are, in the present state, susceptible.

The young Roman, supporting her imprisoned parent by the milk of her own chaste bosom, if unparalleled in history, would yet, in like situation, obtain many imitators; and the feelings of a daughter would prompt, for the relief of the authors of her being, the noblest exertions. The celebrated Mrs. Roper, eldest daughter of Sir Thomas Moore, continued his affectionate solace during his imprisonment: With heart-affecting anguish she rushed through the guards to catch, from the illustrious martyr, a last embrace. Bending under a weight of calamity, she obtained permission to pay him sepulchral honors; and, regardless of the tyrant's power, she purchased the venerable head of the meritorious sufferer: Yet, too noble to permit the consequences to fall upon another, with dauntless courage she became her own accuser; and, loaded with fetters for two crimes, "for having watched the head of her father as a relic, and for having preserved his books and writings," appeared with unconcern before her judges--justified herself with that eloquence which virtue bestows on injured merit--commanding admiration and respect--and spent the remainder of her life in solitude, in sorrow, and in study.

But women, unable to support existence, when deprived of those with whom they have exchanged the nuptial vow, have mounted the funeral pile, and hastened to rejoin their deceased partners in other worlds. Portia, the daughter of Cato Uticensis, and wife of Brutus, hearing of the death of her husband, disdained to live; and when debarred access to the usual weapons of destruction, made her exit by resolutely swallowing burning coals of fire! Julia, the wife of Pompey, expired upon seeing his robe stained with the blood which she imagined had issued from his veins. Molsa Tarquinia, rendered illustrious any genius and literature, of unblemished virtue, and possessing, also, a beautiful exterior, although one of the brightest ornaments of the Court of Ferrara, and receiving from the people of

Rome, that unprecedented honor, the freedom of their city, mourned, nevertheless, through a long life, until the hour of her dissolution, the husband of her youth, Artemisia, wife of Mausolus, rendered herself illustrious, and obtained immortality, by her devotion to the memory of her husband. The Mausoleum, which she reared in honor of him, was considered as one of the seven wonders of the world; and it gave name to all those succeeding monuments, which were distinguished by extraordinary marks of magnificence. Artemisia expired, the victim of inconsolable regret and tender sorrow , before the Mausoleum was completed. Victoria Colonna, Marchioness of Pescaira, ardently engaged in literary pursuits, which fame did ample justice to her productions; yet, separated by the stroke of death, in the morning of her days, from an illustrious and gallant husband, appropriated her remaining years to unceasing grief, lamenting, in her pathetic essays, the long-lost hero. The celebrated Mrs. Rowe, equally conspicuous for genius and virtue, continued faithful and persevering in her attachment to her deceased husband; nor could a length of years abate her regrets.

Ninethly, they are capable of supporting, with equal honor, the toils of government. Semiramis appears to have associated all the virtues and vices which have received the masculine stamp--she extended her empire from Ethiopia to India, and subdued many nations--her buildings and gardens were also magnificent--and she governed, in many respects, judiciously. Artemisia, queen of Caria, and daughter of Lygdamis, possessing, during the minority of her son, sovereign authority, distinguished herself, both by her counsels and her personal valor. Amalasuntha governed with the greatest justice, wisdom, and prudence. Julia Mammaea educated her son, Alexander Severus, implanting in his bosom the seeds of virtue, and adorning him with every princely accomplishment; He was worthy of the high rank to which he was raised, and disposed to become the father of his people: His mother presided in his councils; the era of their administration was tumultuous and hazardous, and disastrous termination is one of the events which the student of history will not fail to deplore.

Zenobia united genius and valor--she was dignified by the title of Augusta. After the demise of her husband, the supreme authority devolving upon her, she governed with rectitude, firmness, and intrepidity. She preserved the provinces in their allegiance, and added Egypt to her dominions. Moreover, when led into captivity, she knew how to bring into subjection, her feelings; she endured misfortune with the heroism of a noble spirit, and found a solace for the loss of royalty, and the pageantry of a throne, in those rational pursuits, which solitude and freedom from care uninterruptedly permit. Longinus was her preceptor and friend; and she was worthy of his tuition and preferable attachment. Elizabeth of England was endowed with energetic talents; her reign was glorious for the people over which she presided; she was undoubtedly a great politician, and governed with uniform vigor; she is characterized as possessing much penetration, and an understanding fruitful of resources; her sovereign negotiations were conducted with propriety and dignity; her mind was opened and polished by all the aids of an extensive education, and adversity was among her preceptors. Christina, queen of Sweden, governed her subjects twenty-one years with uniform wisdom and unimpeached prudence, when she magnanimously resigned her crown; thus giving a rare example of an elevation of intellect, which has not been surpassed.

Tenthly, and lastly, they are equally susceptible of every literary acquirement. Corinna, it is said, triumphed a fifth time over the immortal Pindar, who had publicly challenged her to contend with him in the poetical line. Sappho, the Lesbian poet, was admired by the ancients--she produced many poems, and was addressed as the tenth Muse. Sulpicia a Roman lady, who lived under the reign of Domitian, was called the Roman Sappho. Hypatia, beautiful, learned, and virtuous, the daughter of Theon, presided over the Platonic school at Alexandria, about the close of the fourth century; she was judged qualified to succeed her father in that distinguished and important office; her wisdom was held in universal esteem; and from her judgment no one thought proper to appeal:Persons clothed in public authority, even the first magistrates, deliberated with her on the most urgent and important emergencies; this unavoidably drew around her succeeding circles of men; yet she maintained her intercourse with characters of various descriptions, without the shadow of an impeachment of her reputation, until basely traduced, in a single instance, by bigoted and interested caluminators. Cassandra, a Venetian lady, attained an accurate skill in languages, and made great proficiency in the learning of her time; she composed with facility, both in numbers and in prose, in the language of Homer, Virgil, and Dante; she was a proficient in the philosophy of her own and preceding ages; she rendered theology harmonious; she supported theses with brilliancy; she lectured publicly at Padua; she blended the fine arts with her serious studies; and the mild complacency of her character: She received homage from sovereign pontiffs, and sovereign princes; and she continued an ornament of her sex, and of humanity, one hundred and two years.

The daughter of Sir Thomas Moore, Mrs. Roper, already cited under the eighth article, whose virtues were polished by literary attainments, corresponded in Latin with the celebrated Erasmus, and successfully appropriated many years of her life to study: Her daughter inherited her erudition, and her amiable qualifications. The Seymours, sisters, and nieces of a king, wrote elegantly in Latin.   Isabella of Rosera, in Spain, by her substantial arguments, natural deductions, and able rhetoric, greatly augmented the number of believing Jews; the great church of Barcelona was open for the exertion of her pulpitorial abilities; and she acquired much honor by her commentaries upon the learned Scotus.   France knew how to estimate the talents of the Duchess of Retz; she pursued her studies amid the seducing pleasures of a court; and, although young and beautiful, spoke the ancient languages with propriety and elegance.   Mary Stuart, queen of Scotland, possessing all the advantages of exterior, and every sexual grace, assiduously cultivated her mind: she could, we are informed, write and speak six languages; her numbers enchanted the Gallic ear; and, at an early age, she pronounced before the French Court a Latin oration, calculated to convince her hearers, that literary pursuits are proper to the female sex. Beauty could not plead in vain; the lovely speaker exemplified, in her own character and attainments, the truth, she inculcated; she was, herself, that happy combination, the practicability of which she labored to impress; and conviction undoubtedly irradiated the minds of her audience.

In the thirteenth century, a young lady of Bologna, pursuing, with avidity, the study of the Latin language, and the legislative institutions of her country, was able, at the age of twenty-three, to deliver, in the great church of Bologna, a Latin oration, in praise of a deceased person, eminent for virtue; nor was she indebted for the admiration she received, to the indulgence granted to her youth, or sex.   At the age of twenty-six, she took the degree of a Doctor of Laws, and commenced her career in this line, by public expositions of the doctrines of Justinian: At the age thirty, her extraordinary merit raised her to the chair, where she taught the law to an astonishing number of pupils, collected from various nations. She joined to her profound knowledge, sexual modesty, and every feminine accomplishment; yet her personal attractions were absorbed in the magnitude and splendor of her intellectual abilities; and the charms of her exterior only commanded attention, when she ceased to speak. The fourteenth century produced, in the same city, a like example; and the fifteenth continued, and acknowledged the pretensions of the sex, insomuch that a learned chair was appropriated to illustrious women.

Issotta Nogarolla was also an ornament of the fifteenth century; and Sarochisia of Naples was deemed worthy of a comparison with Tasso. Modesta Pozzo's defense of her Sex did her honor; she was herself, an example of excellence. Gabrielle, daughter of a king, found leisure to devote to her pen; and her literary pursuits contributed to her usefulness and her happiness. Mary de Gournay rendered herself famous by her learning. Guyon, by her writings and her sufferings, hath evinced the justice of her title to immortality. Anna Maria Schurman of Cologne, appears to have been mistress of all the useful and ornamental learning of the age which she adorned: She was born in 1607; her talents unfolded with extraordinary brilliancy: In the bud of her life, at the age of six years, she cut, with her scissors, the most striking resemblances of every figure which was presented to her view, and they were finished with astonishing neatness. At ten, she was but three hours in learning to embroider. She studied music, painting, sculpture and engraving, and made an admirable proficiency in all those arts. The Hebrew, Greek and Latin languages were familiar to her; and she made some progress in the oriental tongues. She perfectly understood French, English and Italian, and expressed herself eloquently in all those languages; and she appropriated a portion of her time, to the acquirement of an extensive acquaintance with geography, astronomy, philosophy, and other sciences: Yet she possessed so much feminine delicacy, and retiring modesty, that her talents and acquirements had been consigned to oblivion, if Vassius, and other amateurs of literature, had not ushered her, in opposition to her wishes, upon the theater of the

170

world: But when she was once know, persons of erudition, of every description, corresponded with her; and those in the most elevated stations, assiduously sought opportunities of seeing and conversing with her.

Mademoiselle Scudery, stimulated by necessity, rendered herself eminent by her writings. Anna de Parthenay possessed great virtues, great talents, and great learning; she read, with facility and pleasure, authors in the Greek and Latin languages; she was a rational theologician; she was a perfect mistress of music; and was as remarkable for her vocal powers, as for her execution on the various instruments which she attempted. Catherine de Parthenay, niece to Anna, married to Renatus de Rohan, signalized herself by her attention to the education of her children; and her maternal cares were crowned with abundant success: Her eldest son was the illustrious for her genius and piety, as for her birth. She was mistress of the Hebrew language; her numbers were beautifully elegant; and she supported, with heroic firmness, the calamities consequent upon the siege of Rochelle.

Mademoiselle le Fevre, celebrated in the literary world by the name of Madame Dacier, gave early testimonies of that fine genius which her father delighted to cultivate. Her edition of Callimachus was received with much applause. At the earnest request of the Duke de Montansier, she published an edition of Florus, for the use of the dauphin; she exchanged letters with Christina, Queen of Sweden; she devoted herself to the education of her son and daughter, whose progress were proportioned to the abilities of their interested preceptress: Greek and Latin were familiar to her; and she was often addressed in both those languages, by the literati of Europe. Her translation of the Iliad was much admired. She is said to have possessed great firmness, generosity, and equality of temper, and to have been remarkable for her piety. Maria de Sèvigne appropriated her hours to the instruction of her son and daughter; she has enriched the world with eight volumes of letters, which will be read with pleasure by every critic in the French language. The character of Mary II, Queen of England, and consort to William of Nassau, is transcendently amiable. She is delineated as a princess, endowed with uncommon powers of mind, and beauty of person. She was extensively acquainted with history, was attached to poetry, and possessed a good taste in compositions of this kind. She had a considerable knowledge in architecture and gardening; and her dignified condescension, and consistent piety, were truly admirable and praiseworthy--Every reader of history, and lover of virtue, will lament her early exit. The Countess of Pembroke translated from the French, a dramatic piece; she gave a metrical edition of the Book of Psalms, and supported an exalted character.

Anna Killigrew, and Anna Wharton, were eminent, both for poetry and painting; and their unblemished virtue, and exemplary piety, pointed and greatly enhanced the value of their other accomplishments. Catherine Phillips was, from early life, a lover of the Muses; she translated Corneille's Tragedy of Pompey into English; and in this, as well as the poems which she published, she was successful. Lady Burleigh, Lady Bacon, Lady Russell, and Mrs. Killigrew, daughters of Sir Anthony Cook, received from their father a masculine education; and their prodigious improvement was an ample compensation for his paternal indulgence: They were eminent for genius and virtue, and obtained an accurate knowledge of the Greek and Latin languages. The writings of the Duchess of Newcastle were voluminous; she is produced as the first English lady who attempted what has since been termed polite literature. Lady Halket was remarkable for her erudition; she was well skilled, both in physic and divinity. Lady Masham, and Mary Astell, reasoned accurately on the most abstract particulars in divinity, and in metaphysics. Lady Grace Gethin was happy in natural genius and a cultivated understanding; she was a woman of erudition; and we are informed that, at the age of twenty, "she treated of life and morals, with the discernment of Socrates, and the elegance of Xenophon" --Mr. Congreve has done justice to her merit. Chudleigh, Winchelsea, Monk, Bovey, Stella, Montague--these all possess their respective claims. Catherine Macauley wielded successfully the historic pen; nor were her exertions confined to this line--But we have already multiplied our witnesses far beyond our original design; and it is proper that we apologize to our readers, for a transgression of that brevity which we had authorized them to expect.

Abilities

The Gleaner, Essay XCI:217-224.

> Nor are the modern Fair a step behind,
> In the transcendent energies of mind:
> Their worth conspicuous swells the ample roll,
> While emulous they reach the splendid goal.

We take leave to repeat, that we are not desirous to array the sex in martial habiliments; we do not wish to enlist our women as soldiers; and we request it may be remembered, that we only contend for the capability of the female mind to become possessed of any attainment within the reach of masculine exertion. We have produced our witnesses; their depositions have been heard; the cause is before the public; we await their verdict; and, as we entertain all possible veneration for the respectable jury, we shall not dare to appeal from their decision.

But while we do homage to the women of other times, we feel happy that nature is no less bountiful to the females of the present day. We cannot, indeed, obtain a list of the names that have done honor to their sex, and to humanity, during the period now under observation: The luster of those minds, still enveloped in a veil of mortality, is necessarily muffled and obscure; but the curtain will be thrown back, and posterity will contemplate, with admiration, their manifold perfections. Yet, in many instances fame has already lifted her immortalizing trump. Madame de Genlis has added new effulgence to the literary annals of France. This lady unites, in an astonishing degree, both genius and application! May her indefatigable exertions be crowned with the success they so richly merit--May no illiberal prejudices obstruct the progress of her multiplied productions; but, borne along the stream of time, may they continue pleasurable vehicles of instruction, and confer on their ingenious author that celebrity to which she is indisputably entitled. France may also justly place among her list of illustrious personages, the luminous name of Roland. Madame Roland comprised, in her own energetic and capacious mind, all those appropriate virtues, which are characterized as masculine and feminine. She not only dignified the sex, but human nature in the aggregate; and her memory will be held in veneration,

173

wherever talents, literature, patriotism, and uniform heroism, are properly appreciated.

The British Isle is at this moment distinguished by a constellation of the first magnitude. Barbauld, Seward, Cowley, Inchbald, Burney, Smith, Radcliff, Moore, Williams, Wollstonecraft, etc. etc.--these ladies, celebrated for brilliancy of genius and literary attainments, have rendered yet more illustrious the English name.

Nor is America destitute of females, whose abilities and improvements give them an indisputable claim to immortality. It is a fact, established beyond all controversy, that we are indebted for the discovery of our country, to female enterprize, decision, and generosity. The great Columbus, after having in vain solicited the aid of Genoa, France, England, Portugal, and Spain--after having combated, for a period of eight years, with every objection that a want of knowledge could propose, found, at last, his only resource in the penetration and magnanimity of Isabella of Spain, who furnished the equipment, and raised the sums necessary to defray the expenses, on the sale of her own jewels; and while we conceive an action, so honorable to the sex, hath not been sufficiently applauded, we trust, that the equality of the female intellect to that of their brethren, who have so long usurped an unmanly and unfounded superiority, will never, in this younger world, be left without a witness. We cannot ascertain the number of ingenious women, who at present adorn our country. In the shade of solitude they perhaps cultivate their own minds, and superintend the education of their children. Our day, we know, is only dawning--But when we contemplate a Warren, a Philenia, an Antonia, a Euphelia, etc. etc. we gratefully acknowledge, that genius and application, even in the female line, already gild, with effulgent radiance, our blest Aurora.

But women are calculated to shine in other characters than those adverted to, in the preceding essays; and with proper attention to their education, and subsequent habits, they might easily attain that independence, for which a Wollstonecraft hath so energetically contended; the term, helpless widow, might be rendered as infrequent and inapplicable as that of helpless widower; and although we should undoubtedly continue to mourn the dissolution of wedded amity, yet we

174

should derive consolation from the knowledge, that the infant train had still a remaining prop, and that a mother could assist as well as weep over her offspring.

That women have a talent--a talent which, duly cultivated, would confer that independence, which is demonstrably of incalculable utility, every attentive observer will confess. The sex should be taught to depend on their own efforts, for the procurement of an establishment in life. The chance of a matrimonial coadjutor, is no more than a probable contingency; and if they were early accustomed to regard this uncertain event with suitable indifference, they would make elections with that deliberation, which would be calculated to give a more rational prospect of tranquility. All this we have repeatedly asserted, and all this we do invariably believe. To neglect polishing a gem or obstinately to refuse bringing into action a treasure in our possession, when we might thus accumulate a handsome interest, is surely egregiously absurd, and the height of folly. The united efforts of male and female might rescue many a family from destruction, which, notwithstanding the efforts of its individual head, is now involved in all the calamities attendant on a dissipated fortune and augmenting debts. It is not possible to educate children in a manner which will render them too beneficial to society; and the more we multiply aids to a family, the greater will be the security, that its individuals will not be thrown a burden on the public.

An instance of female capability, this moment occurs to memory. In the State of Massachusetts, in a small town, some miles from the metropolis, resides a woman, who hath made astonishing improvements in agriculture. Her mind, in the early part of her life, was but penuriously cultivated, and she grew up almost wholly uneducated: But being suffered, during her childhood, to rove at large among her native fields, her limbs expanded, and she acquired a height of stature above the common size; her mind also became invigorated; and her understanding snatched sufficient information, to produce a consciousness of the injury she sustained in the want of those aids, which should have been furnished in the beginning of her years. She however applied herself diligently to remedy the evil, and soon made great proficiency in writing, and in arithmetic. She read everything she could procure; but the impressions adventitiously made on her infant mind still obtained the ascendency. A few rough acres constituted her patrimonial inheritance; these she has brought into a state of high cultivation; their productions are every year both useful and ornamental; she is mistress of agricolation, and at once a botanist and a florist. The most approved authors in the English language, of these subjects, are in her hands, and she studies them with industry and success.

She has obtained such a considerable knowledge in the nature of soils, the precise manure which they require, and their particular adaption to the various fruits of the earth, that she is become the oracle of all the farmers in her vicinity; and when laying out, or appropriating their grounds, they uniformly submit them to her inspection. Her gardens are the resort of all strangers who happen to visit her village; and she is particularly remarkable for a growth of trees, from which, gentlemen, solicitous to enrich their fruit-gardens, or ornament their parterres, are in the habit of supplying themselves; and those trees are, to their ingenious cultivator, a considerable income. Carefully attentive to her nursery, she knows when to transplant, and when to prune; and she perfectly understands the various methods of inoculating and ingrafting. In short, she is a complete **husbandwoman**; and she has, besides, acquired a vast stock of general knowledge, while her judgment has attained such a degree of maturity, as to justify the confidence of the villagers, who are accustomed to consult her on every perplexing emergency.

In the constant use of exercise, she is not corpulent; and she is extremely active, and wonderfully athletic. Instances, almost incredible, are produced of her strength. Indeed, it is not surprising that she is the idol and standing theme of the village , since, with all her uncommon qualifications; she combines a tenderness of disposition not to be exceeded. Her extensive acquaintance with herbs, contributes to render her a skilful and truly valuable nurse; and the world never produced a more affectionate, attentive, or faithful woman: Yet, while she feelingly sympathizes with every invalid, she is not herself subject to imaginary complaints; nor does she easily yield to real illness. She has lately been indisposed--and a life so valuable, when endangered, embodied a host of fears for its safety: With difficulty she was persuaded to lie down upon her bed; and the young woman who attended her, and to whom she had-endeared herself by a thousand good offices, after softly closing the shutters and door of her apartment, privately summoned the aid of a physician; and when the medical gentleman made his appearance, she accompanied him to the apartment of her friend; but behold, the bird was flown! and when pursued, she was found at a distance from her habitation, directing some laborers, who were employed in her service, and who, she was fearful, were not sufficiently attentive to her previous instructions. The event proved she had acted judiciously; for, braced by the fresh air, her nerves new strung, assumed their usual tone, her sickness vanished, and her native vigour returned.

Although far advanced in years, without a matrimonial connection, yet, constantly engaged in useful and interesting pursuits, she manifests not that peevishness and discontent, so frequently attendant on old maids; she realizes all that independence which is proper to humanity; and she knows how to set a just value on the blessings she enjoys.

From my treasury of facts, I produce a second instance, equally in point. I have seen letters, written by a lady, an inhabitant of St. Sebastian, (a Spanish emporium) that breathed the true spirit of commerce, and evinced the writer to possess all the integrity, punctuality and dispatch, which are such capital requilities in the mercantile career. This lady is at the head of a firm, of which herself and daughters make up the individuals--Her name is Birmingham. She is, I imagine, well known to the commercial part of the United States. She was left a widow in the infancy of her children, who were numerous; and she immediately adopted the most vigorous measures for their emolument. Being a woman of magnanimous mind, she devoted her sons to the profession of arms; and they were expeditiously disposed of, in a way the best calculated to bring them acquainted with the art of war. Her daughters were educated for business; and, arriving at womanhood, they have long since established themselves into a capital trading-house, of which, as has been observed, their respectable mother is the head. She is, in the hours of business, invariably to be found in her counting-house; there she takes her morning repast; her daughters act as clerks, (and they are adept in their office) regularly preparing the papers and letters, which pass in order under her inspection. She signs herself, in all accounts and letters, Widow Birmingham; and this is the address by which she is designated. I have conversed with one of our captains, who has often negotiated with her the disposal of large and valuable cargoes. Her consignments, I am told, are to a great amount; and one of the principal merchants in the town of Boston asserts, that he receives from no house in Europe more satisfactory returns. Upright in their dealings, and unwearied in their application, these ladies possess a right to prosperity; and we trust that their circumstances are as easy, as their conduct is meritorious.

"Would you, good Mrs. Gleaner, station us in the counting-house?" No, my fair country-woman, except circumstances unavoidably pointed the way. Again I say, I do but hold up to your view, the capability of your sex; thus stimulating you to cultivate your talents, to endeavor to acquire general knowledge, and to aim at making yourselves so far acquainted with some particular branch of business, as that it may, if occasion requires, assist in establishing you above that kind of dependence, against which the freeborn mind so naturally revolts. Far be it from me, to wish to unsex you--I am desirous of preserving, by all means, those amiable traits that are considered as characteristic-- I reverence the modesty and gentleness of your dispositions--I would not annihilate a single virtue; but I would assiduously augment the faithfulness and affection of your bosoms. An elegant panegyrist of your sex, hath assigned you the superiority in the feelings of the heart; and I cannot more emphatically conclude my subject, than in his beautifully pathetic language: "The pleasures of women must arise from their virtues. It is by the cradle of their children, and in viewing the smiles of their daughters, or the sports of their sons, that mothers find their happiness. Where are the powerful emotions of nature? Where is the sentiment, at once sublime and pathetic, that carries every feeling to excess? Is it to be found in the frosty indifference, and the sour severity of some fathers? No--but in the warm and affectionate bosom of a mother. It is she, who, by an impulse as quick as involuntary, rushes into the flood to preserve a boy, whose imprudence had betrayed him into the waves--It is she, who, in the middle of a conflagration, throws herself across the flames to save a sleeping infant--It is she, who, with dishevelled locks, pale and distracted, embraces with transport, the body of a dead child, pressing its cold lips to hers, as if she would reanimate, by her tears and caresses, the insensible clay. These great expressions of nature--these heart-rending emotions, which fills us at once with wonders, compassion and terror, always have belonged, and always will belong to Women. They possess, in those moments, an inexpressible something, which carries them beyond themselves; and they seem to discover to us new souls, above the standard of humanity."

Bibliography
Judith Sargent Murray

Primary Sources:

Books and Manuscripts:

(One volume of essays, four volumes of poetry and twenty copy-books of letters, discovered in Mississippi in 1986 by Gordon D. Gibson and now residing in the Mississippi Department of Archives and History [Z/1827.00] as yet have not been published)

The Gleaner: A Miscellaneous Production in Three Volumes. Boston: I. Thomas and E.T. Andrews, 1798.

Some Deductions from the System Promulgated in the Page of Divine Revelation: Ranged in the Order and Form of a Catechism: Intended as Assistant to Christian Parent, MDCCLXXXII (40 pp.) Norwich, Connecticut: Printed by John Trumbull, 1782.

---- Portsmouth, New Hampshire, 1782. (32 pp.)

Life of John Murray, By Himself. With Continuations by Judith Sargent Murray. Boston, 1816.

Letters and Sketches of Sermons. 3.vols.John Murray (edited by Judith Sargent Murray) Boston:Joshua Belcher, 1812-13.

Prose Publications:

"Desultory Thoughts Upon the Utility of Encouraging a Degree of Self-Complacency, Especially in Female Bosoms," **Gentleman's and Lady's Town and Country Magazine**   (October 1784):251-53.

"On the Equality of the Sexes," (Constantia) **Massachusetts Magazine** (April, March 1790):132-35, 223-24. (Letter subjoined 224-26).

"On the Domestic Education of Children," **Massachusetts Magazine** (May 1790):275-77.

"Description of Bethlehem," **Massachusetts Magazine** (June 1791): 365-70.

Abilities

"Description of Gray's Gardens, in Pennsylvania," **Massachusetts Magazine** (July 1791):413-16.

"The Gleaner," **Massachusetts Magazine** (February 1792-August 1794).

"The Repository," **Massachusetts Magazine** (September 1792-July 1794).

"Reflections in the manner of Hervey--occasioned by the death of an Infant Sister," **Massachusetts Magazine** (June 1794).

Poetry:

Massachusetts Magazine:

"Lines, Occasioned by the Death of an Infant," (January 1790):57.

"Verses, wrote at a Period of American contest, replete with Uncertainty," (February 1790) 120.

"New Epilogue to The Recruiting Officer," (March 1790) 194.

"Lines to Philenia, by Constantia," (April 1790) 248-49.

"Prologue to Variety" 2 (June 1790) 371.

"Apology for an Epilogue," 3 (April 1791) 266.

"Valedictory Epilogue," 3 (April 1791) 266.

"Occasional Epilogue to The Contrast," 4 (March 1794) 179-80.

"Solution to the Rebus in the February Magazine" (March 1794) 182-3.

Boston Weekly Magazine:

"On Rocking a Cradle," 1 (30 October 1802)

"Birth Day Invitation" 1 (20 November 1802) 52.

"Lines Occasioned by the Departure of a Friend," 1 (4 December   1802) 24.

"Death of Saltonstall." 1 (15 January 1803) 52.

"Expiring Amity," 1 (26 February 1803) 24.
    America, Vol. 1, 1891.

"On Blending Spirit with Matter" 1(5 March 1803) 80.

"An Hypothesis," 1 (19 March 1803) 88.

"Ode to Time," 14 (December 1805).

Universal Asylum and Columbian Magazine:
"Apostrophe to the Shade of the justly celebrated founder of Pennsylvania,"(19
    July 1790)

"Ode." **Hymns and Odes**: Composed on the Death of George Washington.
    Portsmouth, N. H.:   Charles H. Pierce, 1802. 4 pp.

Plays: published in Volume III of **The Gleaner**

The Medium; or Virtue Triumphant. Boston, Federal Street Theater 2 March 1795.
The Traveller Returned, Boston, Federal Street Theater, 9 March 1796.

Letters:

Copy-books of letters, the Mississippi Department of Archives and History
    (Z/1827.00).
"Letter written to parents from Philadelphia, June 19, 1790 in **Universalism in**
"Two letters from Philadelphia," in the **Massachusetts Magazine**, Junr, 1791.
"Letter to Joseph Dennie" 9 April 1797 2 pp. Houghton-Harvard Library MS bms
    am 715 114
"Letters to Mercy Warren" **Warren-Adams Letters,** Vol. II, 4 March 1796, 328-
    29, 1 June   1805, 346. Mass. Hist. Soc.:Boston,1925.
"Extracts from letters" **Universalist Quarterly,** vols. 18,19 1881,1882.

Secondary Sources:

Alic, Margaret. **Hypatia's Heritage.** Boston: Beacon, 1986.

Berkin, Carol Ruth and Mary Beth Norton, **Women of America: A History**,
    Boston: Houghton   Mifflin, Co., 1979.

Ferguson, Ann L. The Plays of Judith Sargent Murray MA Thesis Indiania University 1982. 98 pp.

Field, Vena Bernadette, "Constantia: A Study of the Life and Works," **The Maine Bulletin**, 1931.

Gitlin-Emmer, Susan. **Roots of Our Strength: A Heritage of Unitarian and Universalist Women.** Boston:Univarian Universalist Women's Federation, 1980.

Bingham, Caleb. **The American Preceptor**. Boston: Manning and Loring, 1806.

Birch, Una. **Anna Van Schurman:Artist, Scholar, Saint**. New York: Longmans Green,1909.

Bosha, Francis J. "Judith Sargent Murray,"228-9. **A Dictionary of British and American Writers 1660-1800**. ed. Janet Todd. Totowa, New Jersey:Rowman and Allenhead, 1984.

Card, Claudia, ed. **Feminist Ethics**. Lawrence: University of Kansas, 1991.

Carpenter, Elton. "John Murray and the Rise of a Liberal Religion." MA Thesis Columbia 1937.

Cheney, Ednah Dow, "Women of Boston," in **The Memorial History of Boston** ed. Justin Winsor, vol. iv, Boston" James R. Osgood & Co., 1881, 331-56.

Cott, Nancy ed. **The Bonds of Womanhood:`Woman's Sphere' in New England, 1780-1835.** New Haven: Yale U P, 1977.

Demarest, Rev. G.L.ed. **The Life of Rev. John Murray, With a Contribution by Judith   Sargent Murray**, Boston: Universalist Publishing House, 1870.

DePau, Linda Grant and Conover Hunt, **"Remember the Ladies":Women in America 1750-1815**.

Dorgan, Jean Nostrand. "Eighteenth Century Voices of Educational Change: Mary Wollstonecraft and Judith Sargent Murray" Ed.D.Diss. Rutgers 1976.

Eddy, Rev. Richard "Mrs. Judith Murray," **Universalist Quarterly**, v.18 (April 1881) 194-213 and v.19 (April 1882) 140-150.

---------Universalism in America. Boston: Universalist Publishing House, 1891.
   vol. I 1636-1800 vol.2 1801-1886.

----------Universalism in Gloucester, Massachusetts, Gloucester, Mass.:Proctor
   Brothers, 1892.

Ellis, Harold Milton. "Joseph Dennie and His Circle," Bulletin of the University
   of Texas (July 15, 1915).

-----. "Judith Sargent Stevens Murray." 364-5. Dictionary of American
   Biography, XIII. New   York: Charles Scribner's,1934.

"Family History: John Murray." The Dolphin Vol.1, No.2 Dec.1978.

Gibson, Rev. Gordon D. "The Rediscovery of Judith Sargent Murray," lecture,
   Universalist Conference, Chicago, 1991.

Gould, Carol G.ed. Beyond Domination. Totowa, New Jersey: Rowman and
   Allanheld, 1984.

Griffiths, Morwenna, and Margaret Whitford. Editors. Feminist Perspectives in
   Philosophy.   Bloomington: Indiana University, 1988.

Hersey, Laura. "By Their Works"Biographical Sketches of Universalist
   Women. Boston: Assoc.of Universalist Women, 1954.

Hill, Bridget. The First English Feminist: Reflections Upon Marriage and
   Other Writings by Mary Astell. Gower: Maurice Temple Smith, 1986.

Hoffman, Ronald and Peter J. Albert Editors. Women in the Age of the
   American Revolution. Charlottsville:University Press of Virginia, 1989.

Hornblow, Arthur. A History of the Theater in America. Phila:J.J. Lippincott,
   1919.

Howe, Julia Ward,ed. Sex and Education (1874). New York: Arno,1972.

Humm, Maggie. Feminist Criticism: Women as Contemporary Critics. New
   York: St. Martins, 1986.

James, Janet Wilson. "Judith Murray." **Notable American Women.** Cambridge, Mass.:Belknap, 1971, 603-605.

Jorgenson, Chester, E. "Gleanings from Judith Sargent Murray," **American Literature** (March 1940): 3-79.

Keohane, Nannerl O., Michelle Z. Rosaldo, and Barbara C. Gelpi, Editors. **Feminist Theory: A Critique of Ideology.** Sussex, England: Harvester, 1982.

Kerber, Linda. "The Republican Mother: Women and the Enlightenment--An American Perspective." **American Quarterly** (Summer 1976):187-205.

----- **Women of the Republic:Intellect and Ideology in Revolutionary America.** Chapel Hill: No. Carolina, 1980.

------ and Jane De Hart-Mathews. **Women's America: Refocusing the Past.** New York:Oxford University Press, 1987.

Kraditor, Aileen, ed. **Up From the Pedestal: Selected Writings in the History of American Feminism.** Chicago:Quadrangle, 1968.

Lawton, James, "Judith Sargent Murray," **Dictionary of Literary Biography,** 240-242.

Mahowald, Mary B. "A Majority Perspective: Feminine and Feminist Elements in American Philosophy," **Cross Currents** 36:410-17.

Mamonova, Tatyana. **Russian Women's Studies.** New York: Pergamon Press, 1889.

Martin, Wendy. "Women and the American Revolution." **Early American Literature** Winter 1976/77):322-35.

McAlexander, Patricia Jewell. "The Creation of the American Eve: The Eighteenth-Century America." **Early American Literature** (Winter 1975):252-66.

McDowell, Tremaine. "Sensibility in the Eighteenth-Century American Novel." **Studies in Philology** (July 1927):231-40.

Mississippi State Gazette. Natchez, July 8, 1820.

Norton, Mary Beth. **Liberty's Daughters:The Revolutionary Experience of American Women, 1750-1800**, Boston: Little Brown, 1980.

Nye, Andrea. **Feminist Writers of the Seventeenth Century**. London: Croom Helm, 1988.

Pendleton, Emily and Milton Ellis. **Philenia: Life and Works of Sarah Wentworth Morton 1759-1846**. Orono, Maine: University Press, 1931.

Phillips. W. "John Murray Life of Himself" **North American Review.** 5(May 1817):55-63.

Quinn, A., **A History of the American Drama,** New York: Harper & Bros., 1923.

Robinson, Alice Jean McDonnell. "The Developing Ideas of Individual Freedom and the National Unity as Reflected in American Plays and the Theatre 1772-1819." Diss. Stanford 1965.

Rossi, Alice S. **The Feminist Papers: From Adams to de Beauvoir**.New York and London: Columbia University Press, 1973.

Sargent, Emma arr. **Eppes Sargent of Gloucester And His Descendants.** Boston: Houghton-Mifflin Co., 1923.

Sargent Murray Gilman Hough House Association. Gloucester, Mass.: Cape Ann Ticket and Label Company, 1941.

Schiebinger, Londa. **"The Mind Has No Sex?"**. Cambridge, Mass.: Harvard UP, 1989.

Seilhamer, George O. **History of the American Theater**. Phila: Globe, 1891.

Sinclair, Andrew, **The Emancipation of American Women,** New York: Harper & Row, 1965.

Skemp, Shelia L. "The Judith Sargent Murray Papers," **The Journal of Mississippi History.** (August 1991):241-50.

Skinner, Clarence R. and Alfred S. Cole. **Hell's Ramparts Fell: The Life of John Murray.** Boston: Universalist Publishing House, 1941.(article "Letters of John Murray" 240 pp.)

Spencer, Anna Garlin, **Women's Share in Social Culture.** New York: Arno, 1972.

Tanselle, G. Thomas. "Royall Tyler, Judith Sargent Murray and <u>The Medium</u>." **New England Quarterly** (March 1968):115-17.

Warren, Mercy Otis. **Plays and Poems of Mercy Otis Warren**: Facsimile Reproductions Compiled and with an Introduction by Benjamin Franklin V. Delmar, N.Y.: 1980.

Webb, Alison. **Theresa of Avila and the Rhetoric of Femininity**. Princeton, N.J.: Princeton UP, 1990.

Frances Wright
Engraving by J.C. Buttre
Dictionary of American Portraits, 1967

Chronology

Frances Wright 1795-1852

1795   Born 6 September Dundee, Scotland to James and Camilla Campbell Wright.

1798   Parents die. She is separated from her sister and brother.

1807   Reunited with younger sister Camilla.

1809   Reunited with brother Richard shortly before he is killed enroute to India. Grandfather, General Campbell, dies.

1813   Writes **A Few Days in Athens** and "Altorf."

1816   Travels from London to live with Prof. James Mylne, Glasgow.

1818   Sails from Liverpool to New York in August with sister.

1819   "Altorf" produced on February 19 at Park St.Theater.

1820   "Altorf" performed in Philadelphia, meets Pres. James Monroe May 10, sails from New York to Liverpool.

1821   Publishes **Views of Society and Manners in America** by an English woman.

1822   Meets Jeremy Bentham.

1823   Publishes **A Few Days in Athens**. Goes to Paris, meets and works with Lafayette.

1824   Returns to United States with Lafayette, meets Robert Owen and James and Dolly Madison in Washington, visits Jefferson at Monticello. Views Bunker Hill Monument with Lafayette.

1825   Becomes first woman to publicly oppose slavery. Purchases 320 acres in Tennessee from Andrew Jackson's friends 30 mi. NE of Memphis, the beginning of Nashoba. March, first slaves arrive.

1826　At Nashoba portrait of Fanny with Turkish pants costume.
　　　December deeds Nashoba (1,860 acres) to 10 persons.
　　　Visits New Harmony until June.
　　　In July Adams and Jefferson die.

1827　May, Robert Dale Owen to Nashoba, accompanies very ill Fanny to France.
　　　July, introduces him to Gen. Lafayette.
　　　In England attempts to recruit Mary Wollstonecraft Shelley.
　　　James Richardson's journal "Nashoba Book" is published in Lundy's
　　　Genius of Universal Emancipation.
　　　Sails from Europe November 4, arrives Nashoba December.
　　　Frances Trollope, recruited for Nashoba, stays 10 days.
　　　Camilla has married Richeson Whitby December 15.

1828　May, Camilla, Richeson, Owen leave Nashoba.
　　　June, Fanny leaves 30 slaves at Nashoba with caretaker.
　　　At New Harmony edits with Robert Dale Owen-**New Harmony Gazette**.
　　　July, gives public Fourth of July Address.
　　　Publishes "Institution of Nashoba" written on board American ship
　　　Edward bound for New Orleans Dec.1827, **Gleaner**(49-70).
　　　October leaves Nashoba, Camilla pregnant.
　　　. November, lectures Philadelphia and New York.

1829　January 21, the first signed editorial of **The FreeEnquirer**.
　　　First woman to edit newspaper since colonial days.
　　　February 21, hears Camilla had son in January.
　　　April 26 opening address; April 28 dedicates New York Hall of Science on
　　　Broome St.
　　　Publishes **Opening Address**.
　　　Publishes **Course of Popular Lectures**
　　　Lectures from Boston to New Orleans.
　　　Workingman's Party nicknamed "Frances Wright's Party."
　　　July 4, Fanny gives address in Philadelphia.
　　　August, lecture "The State of the Public Mind and the Measures which it
　　　calls for." Camilla's baby dies.
　　　September,lectures in Providence, R.I., Delaware against Wm.L. Garrison.
　　　October 17, leaves New York to lecture along Hudson.

1830　January, accompanied by Dr. William Phiquepal D'Arusmont, takes 30
　　　Nashobans to Haiti aboard ship **John Quincy Adams;**

March 25, returns; June, departs for Europe.
Publishes **Fables, An Address to the Industrious Classes, Address to the Conductors of New York**.
Sells **Sentinel** and **Advocate**,loses half of $6000 investment.

1831 February sister Camilla dies in France. ·
      Marries D'Arusmont.
      July daughter Sylva born.

1832 April 14 second daughter born.
      August, Robert Dale Owens visits in Paris.

1833 June lectures in England, D'Arusmont comes for her.

1834 Lectures in England.

1835 Returns to the United States, forbidden to speak in Philadelphia.
      Settles in Cincinnati.
      Publishes **Supplement to A Course of Lectures**.

1836 Becomes associate editor of **Boston Investigator**.
      May 15 lectures Cincinnati on "Chartered Monopolies."

1837 Publishes **Manual of American Principles**.

1838 Publishes **What is the Matter**. New York series of 5 lectures.

1839 June 16, sails with Sylva to Paris.

1840-52 crosses ocean seven times

1843 Publishes **Tracts on Republican Government and National Education**.

1844 Receives inheritance.

1845 In Paris finds her papers burned.

1848 Publishes **England the Civilizer**: Her History Developed in its Principles, by a woman.

1849 Publishes **Biography, Notes, and Political Letters of Frances Wright** (enlarged ed. 1972). Visits Nashoba.

1850   Files for divorce.

1852   Dies in Cincinnati 13 December at 57 years old. Buried Spring Grove
        Cemetery (D'Arusmont dies March 22, 1855 Paris)

5

Frances Wright

1795-1852

That Frances Wright should become "straw-woman" to her own arguments was, perhaps, unavoidable. Her life story as it was reported superimposed itself over what she had to say and what she did. Although it is not my intention to allow her life once again to overshadow her philosophy, an introduction to her life is necessary. One reason, is that her life exemplified a selfless commitment to her philosophical principle, the improvement of the human race; and the second, inspite of the calumny against her, her philosophical and historical contributions, and the compellingness of her story, she remains relatively unknown. As both a person and a philosopher of ethics, epistemology, politics and economics, Frances Wright was remarkable.

Born in eighteenth century Scotland, Frances Wright became nineteenth century America's adopted daughter. Orphaned at two and a half, Frances was raised in England. At eighteen, venting anger upon her Aunt Campbell who had fostered her, Frances, or Fanny as she was called, left London and Dawlish, England to live at Professor James Mylne's home in Scotland. Her older brother Richard, a young military officer, had been killed enroute to India. In 1818 Frances and her younger sister Camilla, now both of age traveled to the United States, which for the most part they made their lifetime home. In a poignant letter to Wollstonecraft's daughter, Mary Shelley, Frances commiserates with their shared "sad history" of "blighted affection," never having known their mothers.[1] Later, she would make sure in her writings on educational theories, that "orphans"

195

would "find here an open asylum" (Tract 2). Her public life was accompanied by this private "heart solitude of orphanship" (Life,9).[2]

At once independent and dependent, Wright searched for "parents" she had never known. When a grown woman, she wanted Lafayette to adopt both her and her sister. Upon finding her father's diary, Wright was elated to discover "the singular coincidence between father and daughter" espousing similar shared liberal views though "removed from all acquaintance with her Scotch relatives!"(Perkins 364).[3] Although Wright adopted this country, this country did not actually adopt her, partly because her extraordinary ideas were untimely. Rooted in the empiricism of the eighteenth century, her ideas carried beyond the nineteenth and perhaps the twentieth century. When she died in Cincinnati, Ohio in 1852, she had lived a life, according to the philosopher John Stuart Mill, as one of the most important women of her day (Eckhardt 1). Her tomb lists her works and reads:

> "I have wedded the cause of human improvement, staked on it my fortune, my reputation, and my life."

Nearly six feet tall, slender and graceful, with "steely" blue eyes and "conspicuous" bearing, she had commanding presence (Heineman 6). She wore her curly, red-brown hair short about her "classic head" (Lee 523). At nearly fifty she was still considered handsome, her walk "erect" and her brow "broad and magnificent" (Life 45). A "cultivated Englishwoman" she "was thoroughly versed in the literature of the day...and spoke French and Italian fluently" (Owen 296). Her personal attractiveness was matched by a gift of eloquence, but most impressive was her intellect. Her "strong, logical mind" (297) revealed extraordinary learning that was provided by "rare and extensive" libraries available to her early in life. As a young woman, during her three years in Scotland, she spent her winters in study, often making use of the library at the University of Glasgow (Life 49).

Before coming to this country in 1818, Frances Wright had written **A Few Days in Athens**, the play **Altorf**, and at least six other plays. Once here she lectured, wrote travel books and essays, edited newspapers, journeyed widely, met heads of state, presidents and prominent leaders, founded an experimental community and experienced its demise--all before she married and had children.

Her marriage to William Phiquepal D'Arusmont, which ended in divorce, produced two daughters, one, Sylva, survived infancy.[4]

Soon after arriving in the United States, Frances Wright began her unorthodox career. During their stay, she and Camilla traveled from Niagara Falls to Washington, D.C. where they met President James Monroe and observed slavery for the first time. In 1819, Frances's play "Altorf" was performed on the New York stage. For propriety's sake she declined to admit to its authorship, even as the audience applauded and shouted, "author, author!" But when in 1820 it was performed in Philadelphia, she opted to forego propriety and admit authorship. Unfortunately, for succumbing to public authorship and for deciding not to remove from the dialogue the words "burning kisses," she was repudiated.

That same year before returning to England, she also had a poem published on the front page of the Washington **National Intelligencer**. The following year 1821 her book **Views of Society and Manners in America,** signed vaguely "by an Englishwoman," was signed "par Miss Wright" in the French publication in 1822. In this book she happily concludes that American women were "assuming their place as thinking beings," a <u>view</u> that changes (422).

Her **Views** brought her attention and popularity in the United States and abroad.[5] Jeremy Bentham, the utilitarian, invited her to his Hermitage in England. Later, on business for Bentham in Paris, Wright met Lafayette, for whom she became a courier and with whom she attended sessions of the Chamber of Deputies. Soon employed by Lafayette to write his biography, she was acknowledged by many "grey-headed politicians and philosophers" as brilliant (Eckhardt 64). But after three years in Paris, she came to be disillusioned with the loss of liberalism in France. In 1824, in the company of Lafayette, Frances and Camilla returned to New York.

More mature and experienced, Wright witnessed the nation differently this second time. On her way to Monticello, where Lafayette would introduce Wright to ex-President Jefferson, she witnessed chained slaves being shipped off to slave markets; Frances was at once taken up with the inhumanity of slavery. In Washington, D.C. she observed the government first hand: attended many House debates, beheld John Quincy Adams winning the Presidency over Jackson, and met with Monroe and James and Dolly Madison.[6] These new travels and experiences led Frances Wright into ventures no contemporary woman dared: she established a Utopian community, become the first woman to edit a newspaper since Colonial days, the first woman to lecture publicly, the first woman to publicly denounce slavery, the first woman to call for public education for all children, and the only woman to have a political party, the "Fanny Wright Party," named after her.

The intellectual liberalism of Frances Wright's father--a graduate of Trinity College in Dublin, a correspondent of Adam Smith's and a disseminator of Thomas Paine's works--was evident early in Frances, for even as a child she abhorred the disparity between rich and poor. It was during this time in Washington, that she heard Robert Owen lecture on experimental communities. Robert Owen was the liberal manufacturer and first "city planner" of the model town of New Lanark in Scotland in 1800. Wright was inspired. Before Owen purchased the eleven year old German town of Harmonie (20,000 acres) on the Wabash River in Ohio, and renamed it "New Harmony" to establish with the aid of William Maclure their New Moral World and Community of Equality for whites (1825), Wright initiated her own community of Nashoba in Tennesee.

It was Owen's son Robert Dale, with whom Wright, six years his senior, had a long friendship. Together they wrote a number of pamphlets.[7] In 1826 Wright visited New Harmony, and in the spring of 1827 when "New Harmony had ceased to be a community" (Frances 449) Robert Dale accompanied Wright to Tennessee to visit the community she had founded, Nashoba. He then accompanied Wright to Europe in July to find support for the Nashoba project. In 1828 Wright began editing the **New Harmony Gazette** with Robert Dale. The next year, Robert Dale followed her to New York to edit **The Free Enquirer**, a weekly newspaper. Robert Dale Owen, who wrote an early book on birth control (1831) and generally encouraged her feminist ideas, stopped short of advocating enfranchisement (Oliver 61). Owen last saw Wright in Passey, France in 1832, when Owen and his new wife visited her. A politician as well as a writer and reformer, Owen became a member of the House of Representatives and the Minister to Naples. In 1836 their friendship ended.[8]

It was not political sociology but ethics that led Wright to develop a plan to assuage the damage of slavery. In 1824, Wright's plan to found an experimental commune was underway. The result, Nashoba, according to the Deed of Trust,

was "founded on the principle of community of property and labor," a concept of work-study for the re-education and gradual emancipation of slaves.[9] Begun in the autumn of 1824 (Institution 49) Nashoba was situated on the Wolf River near Memphis, Tennessee, in what came to be 320 acres, later enlarged to about 2,000 acres, of malaria infested swamp bordering Indian territory and inhabited by bears and wolves. Having bought a number of slaves, this eloquent Scotswoman attempted to persuade them to accept a new lifestyle. Her five-year-plan for Nashoba, published in September 1825 in the journal **Genius of Universal Emancipation** inaugurated her on a career as spokesperson and activist against the institution of slavery (Woloch 152).

After a trip to New Harmony in 1826, Wright revised these plans in "Explanatory Notes." The Nashoba plan, now allowed inter-racial marriage, and, to gain individual rights and independence for women, allowed marriage free from religious law.[10] Too radical for public digestion, her ideals were labeled "free love," and she was soundly denounced. An article written on December 4, 1827 aboard a ship bound for New Orleans and published in **The Gleaner** in 1828, clarified the philosophy of Nashoba and listed its ten regulations. Physically ill, Wright had left Nashoba in an attempt to gain European intellectual support for the Nashoban experiment. As the community log book recordings reveal, Wright unfortunately left Nashoba in what turned out to be, incompetent hands. By 1828 Nashoba was in financial chaos and by 1829 the community had disintegrated morally and physically.

It was in these years that Wright began to lecture from Boston to New Orleans, dazzling her audiences with her breadth of knowledge and shocking ideas--emancipation for women and slaves, education for women as well as men, free public education, and halls of science to replace the churches which she believed used religion to keep women uneducated and subservient.[11] To lecture, Wright changed her unique attire of the Turkish pants she wore for travel and work at Nashoba, for a toga-- "Her tall majestic figure...the plain white muslin which hung about her in folds that recalled the drapery of a Grecian statue..." (Perkins 214). Lillian O'Connor considers her lecture of July 4, 1828 at New Harmony Hall to be the beginning of a time when women addressed their ideas publicly; the next woman (Maria Stewart, an Afro-American Bostonian), would not lecture publicly until 1832. In 1829 Wright purchased a church in New York which she converted to the New York Hall of Science.[12] Here with Owen and others she set up a book store, a dispensary for medical information, provided a place for physical exercise and set up a lecture series. In addition, she published a weekly newspaper, **The Free Enquirer**; one of her followers edited the **Workingman's Advocate**. "Fanny Wright's vivid sense of impending revolution infected much of the Workingman's movement" (Schlesinger 184). Though the Workingman Party, also called "Fanny Wright's Party," collapsed in 1830, it succeeded in electing one of its people to the legislature in Albany.

In 1830, Nashoba in shambles, Wright was forced to leave New York at the height of political activity. But before she travelled south to move her former slaves to Haiti, she lectured up and down the Hudson. Accompanying her on the difficult trip to and from Haiti was Phiquepal D'Arusmont, a French physician and education reformer whom she had met at New Harmony. Later, to follow up on these former Nashobans' well being, Wright travelled to Haiti several times. Nashoba had been a radical attempt to solve a radical situation, which, had it worked, might have prevented the Civil War--an even more radical, but more familiar and acceptable solution. Nashoba, probably hopeless from the beginning, was, in the simple fact of its existence, a monument to Wright's foresight, idealism, courage and heart.

Always at her sister's side, Camilla endured seasickness from transatlantic travel and boils on her back caused from corsetry worn on the long horseback trips to and from Nashoba. From this physical abuse she recuperated in various countries and in cities from Boston, where she and her sister had attended the celebration of the Bunker Hill Monument with Lafayette, to Memphis. The Nashoba experiment at an end, Camilla, unhappily married and pregnant, abandoned her husband. The young son she delivered, much to both sisters' sorrow, lived less than a year. In 1831, the year following her son's death, alone in France, Camilla also died.

When Frances Wright found herself pregnant, she perceived a collision of her ideals and reality; her ideas about marriage and her experience of being an orphaned child, clashed. In July 1831, Wright returned to Paris via England and married D'Arusmont, the baby's father. Domestic life proved difficult for her, and she became plagued by recurring nervous complaints. In 1833 lecturing in London, she discovered the fame she once had was gone. Returning, then, to the United States in 1835, she resumed lecturing and became associate editor of the **Boston Investigator**. From 1836-7 Wright edited a monthly paper in Philadelphia, **Manual of American Principles**, hoping that its success would result in the establishment of a Popular Hall in Philadelphia, a forum for improving the human mind and voicing opinions, i.e. for "humankind herself"(7). It is in this paper that she focused on economic issues. Fearful that the United States is bankrupt, she warned that he "who holds the purse holds the power"(17).[13]

When Wright traveled and lectured, she often lived apart from her husband, a person with whom she was ill-suited. Perhaps because of this separation, her daughter Sylva, came to reject both her mother and her mother's ideas. Although saddened by this outcome, Wright was able to be very generous in her bequest to her daughter. Wright received a substantial inheritance in 1844, but because of the laws of the time, in order to gain her own inheritance, she was compelled to divorce D'Arusmont. To Sylva she also willed all her unpublished papers and letters. However, in 1845 upon learning that many of these letters accidentally burned, Wright had a temporary physical/mental breakdown. Even so, much of the work and letters which survived will also disappear when Sylva in turn passes them on to her children (Eckhardt 283). In 1848 Wright added to her fortune by publishing **England the Civilizer**, a philosophical assessment of England's history, and in 1849 her **Life, Letters and Lectures**. Living in Cincinnati in 1852, this activist leader, writer and political philosopher, having fallen on the ice and broken a hip, lingered in emotional and physical pain for nearly a year before she died (probably of colon cancer). Once a public figure, she was now at her death, obscure and virtually unacknowledged.

Bentham had said "if there are no heretics, it is only because there are no thinkers"(Bentham 15). In the introduction to her second course of lectures Wright addresses the persecution that all thinkers who have "raised their voice in favor of more equal distributions of knowledge and liberty" have received. Frances Wright had withstood caricaturists depicting her as a goose in a dress and epithets denouncing her as brazen, a female monster, a red harlot, "fallen and degraded fair one" (Lerner 95) and the "Priestess of Beelzebub." Emma Willard pronounced her ideas "ravings" (O'Connor 48) and Lyman Beecher railed against her. Despite the ad hominem invectives, only once did Wright direct her words against a particular person (Perkins 265).

Wright's work was read by Elizabeth Cady Stanton and Matilda J.Gage, and Wright was included in the Honor Roll of Susan B. Anthony (Eckhardt 283). In 1848 Antoinette Brown Blackwell, discussing the possibility of studying for the ministry in a letter to her friend Lucy Stone, ironically said, "Sometimes they warn me not to be a Fanny Wright man" (Lasser 35). But Wright was also referred to as a "pioneer Utopian" and one among "few of wider vision," (Coleman 52) one with "clairvoyance on many issues" (Eckhardt 283). There were other accolades as well. Her interviewer at the **Northern Star** in Dundee, Scotland in 1844 thought her to be "unquestionably the most intellectual female defender of liberty in the present age" (Lives 46). On the centenary of her birth, one writer judged her influence in "destroying intolerance and slavery" to have been "very great" (Holland 4624).

A criticism made time and again of Wright, that she lacked prudence and that her zeal outmatched her practical knowledge, is unfair. To have travelled, lectured, founded newspapers and written books demanded great practical wisdom. To have acted at all on her ideas is to her credit. That some of her ideas demanded a century-worth of effort to be appreciated is not to her discredit. Timidity of thought does not belong to a philosopher; timidity of action oftentimes does. Courage was Wright's great asset in both thinking and action.

Fanny Wright made profound personal sacrifices so that all citizens, women and Afro-Americans in particular, be freer, better educated, and in better economic straits. And although often a flamboyant public figure, she was cultured, well mannered and a well spoken person. One of "such great reserve" that a "most careful study of her writings yields little about herself" (Lee 527).[14]

Like her mother's great aunt, the intellectual Elizabeth Montague, Frances had a wide circle of friends.[15] Mrs. Craig Millar, her closest friend in Scotland, worried about "Fanny ...afloat on a full if dangerous sea, with streamers flying and sails set" (Perkins 19). Lafayette fondly called her the "tender child of my choice," Sismondi, the Swiss economist "a new St. Theresa," Dewitt Clinton "the most superior female of his acquaintance" (Eck. 103). Though often called "beloved

Fanny" by her friends, Wright's intensity, abruptness and arrogance at times turned many away. Still, like the Epicureans she admired, Wright attempted to cultivate a garden of sacred friendship.

Sisterhood for her meant "bonding together for mutual action" (Heineman 178). She was leader of a circle which included Julia Garnett, who moved to Berlin when she married; Harriet Garnett who moved to Paris, Julia Smith whose niece was Florence Nightingale; Helen Martineau, Harriet's sister-in-law, Mary Clarke; Mrs. Jameson and the prolific novelist, Frances Milton Trollope. This is the same Trollope, mother of seven children, who at age fifty-three followed Wright to Nashoba in 1827 with three of her children, but after ten miserable days in a roofless cabin, took leave. On the way up river she left one of her sons to be educated in New Harmony. Nearly bankrupt, Trollope arrived at Cincinnati for a prolonged stay and participated in designing and building a cultural shopping mall. Trollope's account of a Wright lecture in Cincinnati, praises Wright's "extraordinary gift of eloquence, her almost unequalled command of words, and the power of her rich and thrilling voice..."(Perkins 213). Given Trollope's most unpleasant experience as a result of Fanny Wright's recruitment and their opposing ideas on the value of American democracy, this is high praise.

Frances Wright's legacy is more than eloquence and activity on behalf of the betterment of humankind. As a contributor to her adopted country, she gave her country's citizens a philosophy to treasure and courageous living to emulate. Once her philosophy is studied within the context of the history of the discipline, she is destined for new appreciation.

Endnotes

---

[1] The letter from Frances to Mary Shelley (Paris 1827) continues, expressing the pain of loss--
"We must have buried and mourned and felt the chill of disappointment and sighed over the
moral blank of a heathen's world--...I have greatly suffered and widely observed." Although
Mary Shelley shared little of Frances's more radical positions, she was her true friend and felt a
shared compassion with her.

[2] Wright's plan for an egalitarian boarding school is echoed with humor in Charlotte Perkins
Gilman's utopian **Herland** which argued that the child "educated for citizenship" should be
raised in boarding school rather than "isolated" in the nuclear home (108, xxiii).

[3] A dispute among certain twentieth century authors disparage Wright in their interpretations of
the facts. One claims Her "mental baggage" did come from her father (Holbrook 171); another
that no connection existed between the liberal tendencies of father and daughter (Riegel 11).

[4] Sylva had two sons who, ironically, became ministers. One of Wright's grandson's, William
Norman Guthrie, became rector of St. Marks-in-the-Bowrie in New York City.

[5] The review of the "Views" in **The North American Review** issued in January 1822, begins
"This work has been so extensively read in America, that a review of it, at the present time, may
seem unnecessary" (15).

[6] An anecdote told to Frances Trollope about the Wrights' stay in Washington: "when the
Misses Wright were in Washington with Gen. Lafayette, they very frequently attended the
debates, and the most distinguished members were always crowding round them. For this
unwanted gallantry they apologized to their beautiful countrywomen by saying, that if they took
equal interest in the debates, the galleries would be always thronged by the members"(Domestic
Manners 175)

[7] In **Tracts**, which they both wrote, Wright articulates her "Plan of National Education" in
which she states: "The industrious classes have been called the bone and marrow of the nation;
but they are the nation itself." She wanted the "men of industry" to unite to establish schools in
the country where "no inequality may be allowed to enter," no children like the ones in New
England will be "worked to death," a "parent tax" will be distributed evenly, and property tax will
be distributed according to wealth. Wright's advocacy of State Guardianship was her solution to
the hunger and poverty she saw among children (Judith Sargent Murray's similar solution came
from witnessing poor parenting).

[8] Mary Shelley provides an insight into the friendship of Wright and Robert Dale Owen when
she wrote in a letter to Robert Dale, "Take care of our Fanny...she is neither so independent or so
fearless as you think;" shortly after this, in a letter to Mary Shelley, Wright remarks:"Dale
arrived, his sweet kind heart all unthawed, and truly when he left us for Harmony I think the very
last thin flake of Scotch ice had melted from him." (Leopold 52) What began the rift in their
friendship was an $11,000 debt that William McClure and Robert Dale owed to Frances, and
what clinched the rift was an exchange of words handled poorly on both sides.

9 Elizabeth Lee makes the point that "Miss Wright was not altogether without sympathy for the (slave) masters. She wrote: 'In facing the subject of slavery, it is necessary to bear in mind the position of the master as well as that of the slave, bred in the prejudice of colour, untaught to labour, and viewing it as a degradation. We must come to the slave-holder, therefore, not in anger, but in kindness; and when we ask him to change his whole order of life, we must show him the means by which he must do so, without complete compromise of his ease and his interests'"(521).

In the Delaware (a slave and Quaker state) lecture of 1829, Wright denounces the abolitionists for their stance of hatred for the slave-holder (Perkins 329).

Frances wrote to Mary Shelly from Paris in 1827 concerning her Nashoba experiment that "Many, of course, think me mad, and if to be mad means to be one of the minority, I am so, and very mad indeed, for our minority is small"(Lee 525).

10 The law at the time based on English Common Law still considered married women to be chattel. Frances Wright had arraigned this law in 1828 in both the **Free Enquirer** and the **New Harmony Gazette**, but married women's legal rights reform was not given a boost until Margaret Fuller's essay in July of 1843, and the National Women's Rights Convention of October of 1850 (Pancoast 56-7).

11 Wright lectured in many United States cities--Baltimore, Boston, Cincinnati, New York, Philadelphia and abroad as well; however, lost lectures and discrepancies in dates and places in various biographies make a clear chronology difficult, as yet, to completely ascertain. Celia Eckhardt, Helen Heineman, and Margaret Lane have increased the accuracy in their significant contributions.

12 This was the year that the first national correspondent, the self supporting journalist and author, Anne Newport Royall turned 60 years old. She had been at her trade since 1824 when she first came to Washington D.C.

13 Noah Webster noted that "Fanny Wright" and Jefferson held similar opinions regarding the transmission of debt to posterity, and that the democratic republicans of New York who praised Jefferson and rejected Wright on that issue were inconsistent.
(**Connecticut Herald**, New Haven 16 January 1838:3).

14 One study of her life suggests that perhaps even that biography was not from her own interview: the "miniature biography...published in her lifetime (1844), professedly from notes of her conversation taken by the editor of a Dundee newspaper...presents...unequivocal internal evidence of being written in English by a Frenchman, or translated from the French; ...it may be suspected that M. Darusmont had a hand in it" (Garnett 522).

15 Elizabeth Montague, admired by Samuel Johnson and others in her popular salon, upon the death of her husband became a farmer (Hill, 35). Perhaps it was from this ancestral heritage that Wright was willing to attempt Nashoba.

An Introduction to **"The Nature of Knowledge"**

Frances Wright, lectured with a scholar's knowledge of the philosophical traditions of Epicureanism, Empiricism and Utilitarianism. Her learned presentations were also dramatic. While addressing audiences composed of the advantaged and the disadvantaged from Boston to Chickasaw Bluffs in Tennessee, Wright often held high a copy of the Declaration of Independence of Independence as she argued that the "religious" words "created equal" meant what they said. They meant education for all--male and female, black and white, rich and poor. They meant a life without poverty, that is, equal opportunity for the "pursuit of happiness" for all who live under the Constitution. Her thrilling perception of these liberties awoke a nation, and they sustained her own spirit amidst a reception of mockery in her new country.[1]

Wright's political and ethical philosophy is founded upon the first principles she establishes in the initial lecture in her series of seven lectures on the theory of knowledge. With motivation from the Constitution, Wright formulated her philosophy founded upon Epicurus's matter of pleasure/pain, her own observations testing this underlying reality, and her own original approach to the principle of improvement, inchoate in her early publications. Unlike many of the women we are beginning to call "philosopher," Frances Wright called herself "philosopher." Like Leontium in her Epicurean, **A Few Days in Athens**, Frances Wright had "the noble majesty of mind, that asked respect and promised delight and instruction. Her features were not of Venus, but Minerva"(A Few Days 39). Mary Shelley's son is reported to have said of Wright, that "she was like Minerva"(Lee 523). But, believing her mental abilities overstated and her ideas too revolutionary, some critics thought calling her "philosopher" as unnerving to Minerva as Wright was to them. William C. Bryant dubbed her "The New Aspasia" as a joke. However, philosophers who knew her, Jeremy Bentham in England and Orestes Brown in America, were impressed with her powers of thought. Her influence on John Stuart Mill was significant.[2]

Today Frances Wright remains another woman philosopher whose works have not yet been given the judicious examination needed either for proper assessment or for establishment in the philosophical tradition. Yet, as thinker Wright was much more precise and consistent than some of her biographers suggest, and as writer and lecturer, she was a careful rhetorician. Joel Brown, her biographer and the articulate builder of her house, said in admiration, "Her language was as smooth as oil and as entertaining as it was smooth. Every word left the tongue finished..." He recalled seeing her memorizing speeches, whispering to herself as she walked three miles to see friends (Perkins). In her "Address to the Young Mechanics" in 1830, Wright lectured on the importance of eloquence and in her discussion of the bar, pulpit and senate, borrows from the rhetorics of Blair and Whately (O'Connor 163). For the first woman to lecture publicly, the sense of rhetoric was personally important, a subject worthy of a lecture for the good of the public at large--ironic because as subject matter, rhetoric was generally deemed not fit for women, its public use forbidden them.[3]

Milieu of Philosophical Tradition

When Wright was living at the home of James Mylne, Professor of Moral Philosophy in Scotland, she had opportunities to encounter the ideas of the 18th century Scottish rhetoricans and to read and listen to philosophy. She became acquainted with Reid's common-sense, Adam Smith's economics, and the political justice of Godwin (husband of Mary Wollstonecraft). Her ideas on education were influenced by the empiricist view of Locke. It was later in France that she encountered the contemporary socialism of Saint-Simon for whom marriage offered strict equality, and the "positivist sensations" of Comte. What validated for Wright what she had written of Epicurus on Religion, was her discovering Holbach's "System of Nature," and finding it surprisingly similar to her own. (Life 6,Letter #1).

Having read with admiration Epicurus, who espoused the good as pleasure, that is, pleasure primarily of the mind, it was reasonable that Wright be attracted to Bentham's idea of the good as the greatest happiness for the greatest number, and then establish her own principle as that of the improvement of humanity (Life 6). In this tradition, Wright bridged the philosophical step from Bentham to John

Stuart Mill, especially when she demonstrated the non-utility of women's subordination, and the necessity for women's education as a pre-requisite for power to improve (Donovan 13).

In her philosophical milieu, Wright was "somewhat at odds with her principal mentors" (Palmer 97). Wright claimed that the principles at the base of the Nashoba experiment were Godwin's (Eck. 151) . But she had also taken "Jefferson's philosophical radicalism" and extended it (195). Although, she held much in common with Bentham, in thought, style and deed, she often differed from him. Both disliked Blackstone's Commentaries on English Common Law, he because they were an outgrowth of change rather than a fixed system, she because they dehumanized and enslaved women. Both were interested in model communities, he in his brother Sam's experiment on the Black Sea, she with her own in Tennessee. Both determining the necessity of people's right to determine their own life, they differed on the sense of the masses; he tolerated democracy while she celebrated it.

Bentham knew John Stuart Mill from the time he was two years old. When Bentham met Wright, she was in her twenties and Mill was in his teens debating against the anti-Owenites in London. Wright made the connection between principle and progress before Mill did. She had made liberty a requirement for truth, not for his rational and intuitive truth, but for her rational and empirical truth. If Mill "marked the birth of the `liberal intellectual,' Wright was certainly the midwife of such birth" (Letwin 8).

Milieu of Her Own Works

Wright's first philosophical work, written when she was eighteen, demonstrates "no mean classical learning" (Lee 519). It is an imaginary account of the Epicurean school, one of the earliest ancient schools to include women. Initially entitled "Epicurus," it was renamed **A Few Days in Athens** "to soften the alarm of its first London publisher"(Life 5,Letter #1). Concluding with-- "Let Epicurus be your guide. The source of every enjoyment is within yourselves"--it threatened such nineteenth century readers as Lydia Marie Child, who eventually responded with a novel, **Philothea** published in 1836. **A Few Days** had two editions in London, two in New York, one in Boston and one in France. Lest her influence become too great, Bostonians "circled (negative) tracts about her." Though it "delighted Walt Whitman," Child "feared that Frances Wright's fictionalized account of Epicurus...would lead many astray" (Camaron 2). Child's novel, influenced by neo-Platonism, Swedenborgianism and Transcendentalism, emphasized **virtue** rewarded.

Wright's first work presented and published in this country was **Altorf** (1819-20), a play "Full of effective rhetoric and stirring situations" (Garnett 521). Its main theme, liberty, permeates her philosophy. It was her ideas on liberty, partly formed in England and then subjected to the kiln of the United States, that influenced John Stuart Mill's **Essay on Liberty** (1859).

When her volume of lectures was published in 1829, Wright was thirty-four years old. In the preface, she considers her motives for publishing her work, beginning with a review of her acquaintanceship with this country. Having read at seventeen with passion a history of America by the Italian Bocca, **Istoria della Rivoluzione Americana**, she wanted to see America for herself. It was her visit to this country, whereupon she composed letters to her friend Mrs. Craig Millar and then published twenty-eight of them in her **Views of Society and Manners in America**. Her "view" is that America presents a new society and culture. But this perspective in reality was more ideal than real.

On her first visit, Wright "mistook for the energy of enlightened liberty what was, perhaps rather the restlessness of commercial enterprise." A second visit in the "sober light of truth" made clear that the country "enshrined all the liberties," but did so imperfectly; nevertheless, she became a resident and citizen. Then, after four years of observing the discrepancies between theory and practice, especially in regard to black slaves and that race in general, "the neglected state of the female mind, and that consequent dependence of the female condition," and "the inaptness and corruption of the public press," she was led to "challenge the attention of the American people." For only by the "spread and increase of knowledge," she reasoned, can "man" meliorate the human condition. This "man," however, must be a "woman," for only women can deliver the "unbought truth"(iii).

The particular episode which precipitated her indignation against religious fervor was a Calvinist camp revival on the Ohio river that she concluded made women victims to unreasonableness.[4] Consequently, Wright believed that a course of lectures and a periodical publication would counteract "the ravings of zeal without knowledge"(Life 6). Hence she gave lectures on three Sundays in Cincinnati at the courthouse and then again in the theater. In the published volume of lectures, she writes that therein "contains the first, or introductory course, closing at the seventh lecture; in which I have attempted to sketch an outline of the field of truth, and, at the same time, to expose such existing errors as must tend to blind the intellectual sight to its perception"(ix). Here she intends to "proceed step by step--to outline and consider the details--to substantiate first principles" because "a certain order and arrangement are indispensable" otherwise "the most simple appear confused, and truths the most evident, difficult or doubtful." As a lecturer, she aimed to apply "herself to truth, rather than to "expose what is false"(x).

In addition to her course of seven lectures, and her supplementary four lectures, Wright wrote a series of seven letters, published in the **Northern Star** as "Political Letters." These letters discuss how she arrives at the distinction between theology and religion, what that distinction means in terms of a political religion, how civilizations have arisen from "religions," and how the present evil is connected with them. Within the discussion she digresses on her discovery of an order of inquiry which must be followed "by all the pioneers of truth, until the higher summit of synthetical perception is attained" (Life 6). While the course of seven lectures develops an epistemology, this series of letters gives evidence.

Wright's concrete ideas on the acquisition of knowledge were much like those in practice in the educational system of the Owens' experimental community, New Harmony. Here pupils were required to learn as much as possible by direct examination --thinking for themselves to prevent acquiring only ready-made opinions. One present day resident of the town can recall experiencing remnants of that school's educational philosophy in his youth. His anecdote concerns a lesson in the earth's rotation taught to him and a few other young boys by a retired teacher. The teacher had the boys outline the shadow of a tree on her lawn with dry oatmeal; then, after lemonade on her porch, return to the lawn to discover that the shadow of the tree had moved, the outline of oatmeal--a testimony to where it had been-- now fully in the sun. From their "measuring," they now not only **believed** that the earth rotated but **knew** it.[5]

Wright's epistemology influenced the economic and political theory in her last lengthy work, **England the Civilizer**, written in 1848 nearly 20 years after these lectures. This work first researches the historical principles of civilization where it finds that what is now in error is the separation of the scientific method of analysis from synthesis, that man's goal is gold rather than truth, that separation of male love of self and female love of species if not synthesized, both individual and species will perish. Second, it proposes a new world order of economy that attends to the "public rather than the individual good" where America will "gift our globe with her flag of federation" (467):

> All wretched must be comforted, fed, clothed, lodged. Cities must be relieved of their multitudes. The breath of heaven, and the green fields, and the fresh earth restored to man, and, with these, wholesome exercise, and occupation, and recreation. Age and childhood must be seen to. The work of duty and of love must be first accomplished, if we would open in a right spirit a new era. Society has been so long driven by the selfish principle singly, that it may be hard for her to receive inspiration from the generous. By the new order of economy both will be drawn into co-operative action....Women must give the tone in this; and place herself everywhere on the side of humanity, union, order, right reason, and right feeling.(467)

Frances Wright determines that only with effective intellectual power and effective moral power by which "men and women--shall exert equal influences in a state of equal independence"(22), is a future for civilization possible.[6]

Thus it seems clear that this introductory lecture on the nature of knowledge is introductory to her thinking and foundations much later in her **England the Civilizer**. In this lecture Wright introduces with new intelligibility the influences of English Utilitarianism and empiricism with American political and feminist philosophy. The interaction extends the political "created equal" to include women, "pursuit of happiness" to mean improvement and the role of "knowledge" or "things known" to be essential to both sexes and reflexive of each. This lecture most of all introduces Frances Wright's foundation for human improvement.

Endnotes

1   The hostility to view women as philosophers continued beyond her life span by such influential writers as Thomas de Quincey who proclaimed that "no woman ever was or will be a...philosopher" and furthermore that the "peculiar province" of women does not extend to "learning, technically so called" (125).

Both Judith Sargent Murray who wrote "The Equality of the Sexes" (1790) long before Frances Wright gave her first lectures and some years after, Sarah Grimke whose "Letters on Equality" (1837) claimed that Scripture had been misinterpreted in regard to women. Unlike Murray, Grimke maintained that the notion of equality between the sexes comes from the Bible but she denounces "clerical control over women's lives and beliefs" (Bartlett 11).

2   Orestes Brown heard Fanny Wright lecture at Utica, New York in the fall of 1829. Captivated by her command of the language, he became editor of The Free Inquiry and a member of the Workingman's Party.

3   When Antoinette Brown Blackwell is admitted to Oberlin College, she is not allowed to study rhetoric, even though she is studying to be a minister. Some women students formed a class outside the college to learn and practice the art of public speaking (1847-50).

4   Nancy Cott claims that women's sphere in the early nineteenth century was defined not by feminist rationality but by the religion of the Second Great Awakening (202). An article appearing in the **Christian Examiner** in 1834 castigates Wright as an infidel:

"Such is the system of Miss Frances Wright...no two people could be more different than Miss Wright as she is understood and represented, and Miss Wright, as she really is"(Ellis 33); her "abstract principles really are" a "shallow compound of assumptions and influences which constitute the hideous spectre,'Modern Philosophy'"(34).

5   Professor Howard A. Wilson, having grown up in New Harmony and having heard about and witnessed the vestiges of that educational system, gave such accounts in a telephone conversation March 18, 1989.

6   Curiously, Wright's vision reminds one of Judith Sargent Murray's. Though very different temperamentally, acquainted with variant philosophical traditions and living in different cultural moments in time, Frances Wright and Judith Sargent Murray value reason and empirical evidence. For both Murray and Wright, mental accomplishment is vital; Murray for the purpose of engaging with truth for institutional correction in this world and fulfillment in the next, and Wright for discovering the truth and for improvement of the species.

Similarly to Murray, Wright concludes that, "The mind has no sex but what habit and education give it" (Woloch 153). Wright argues: not so that "truth has any sex,"(Life 15), it is **only** women, because of their lack of corrupting institutionalized education, who can advance truths not yet acknowledged. It is only free inquiry by both men and women that can loosen "mental bondage" (21).

INTRODUCTORY ADDRESS,

To the Second Course

(As delivered for the second time in New York)

The circumstances under which I now meet this assemblage of the people of New York are, I believe, unparalleled in the history of the world. All nations have had their revolutions--all cities, in the hitherto unfortunate annals of the human race, their disturbances, and their disturbers; but truly, the sight and the sound is alike novel, of privilege and pretension arraying all the forces of a **would-be** hierarchy and a **would-be** aristocracy, to assassinate the liberties of a free state in the person of a single individual, and to outrage public order and public decency, by ribald slanders and incendiary threats, against the reputation and person of a woman. Truly the signs are novel which mark this hour, and truly the place assigned to myself by the clamor and artifice of a body of men, trembling for privileges and profits, and eager to drown with noisy words that which they cannot confute by argument might cower the strength of one less confident in her cause or less ardent for its success. But, so surely as I know the strength of the ground which I have assumed, and the weakness of that which **they** have to defend, will I stand fast, and stand firm. And did I need, in this hour, ought beyond or without conviction of the destined triumph of the cause I serve, and in the pure decision of wiser and happier generations to come, who (be what it may, the momentary issue of this hour, and its momentary consequences, to me) shall write my name and preserve my memory among those of the champions of human liberty and heralds of human improvement.

I know of none, from the modest Socrates and gentle Jesus, down to the least or the greatest reformers of our own time, who have remembered the poor, the ignorant, or the oppressed, raised their voice in favor of more equal distributions of knowledge and liberty, or dared to investigate the causes of vice and wretchedness, with a view to their remedy; I know of none, I say, who have not been the mark of persecution, drank the poison of calumny, or borne the cross

213

of martyrdom. What better and wiser have endured, I shall not lack courage to meet. Having put my hand to the plough, I will not draw back, nor, having met the challenge so long cast at human nature and human reason, alike by privilege and superstition, will I refuse to meet all hazards in their cause.

I have already pledged myself to show evidence for all my opinions; I pledge myself farther, to **show all my opinions,** for, so truly as I have taken man for my study, and his happiness for my object, do I believe that all my opinions can bring facts to their support, and will, sooner or later, find an echo in every thinking mind and feeling heart.

It hath been asked again and again, amid all the confusion of reports and assertions, threats and declamations, conjured up to fright the timidity of woman, and alarm the protecting tenderness of man, why I do not reply to the slander of enemies, and supply arguments to friends?

If among the present assemblage there be any who have followed all or some of my previous discourses, I would put it to their memory and their reason, if I, on those occasions, presented arguments and evidence for the opinions advanced; and if any one of those arguments has been by a single individual impugned. And I will here call upon you to observe, that my opponents have had the command of the whole press and all the pulpits of this city. To what account have these been turned? To heap on my name and person, outrage and abuse. To libel my audience, intimidate women, attack the interests of men, invoke the interference of the magistracy of the city, and threaten the lessees of this house with "riot, fire, and bloodshed."

My friends, I appeal to your reason, if by resorting to such measures, my opponents have not substantiated their own weakness, and supplied an acknowledgment, that so far as I have spoken they cannot gainsay me?

And now, then, I will ask, and that rather for the sake of good order and common sense, than for any personal interest of mine, if on the topics I **have** spoken, I have neither outraged your reason nor your feelings and remain unanswered by my enemies--if it be not at the least probable that on the topics I have **not** spoken, I may be rational also. I have nothing in my head or my heart to hold back from such of my fellow creatures, as may desire to read either, with a view to the eliciting of truth. I have already sketched out to you the subject matter of many future investigations, embracing all our weightiest duties and responsibilities, as reasoning and sentient beings.

But, as I have opened our discussions in order, so **in order** must I pursue them, if pursued at all. We cannot speak to all things at once, nor demonstrate the last problem in Euclid, ere we have substantiated the first.

In compliance with the wishes of a mass of the citizens, as conveyed to me by individuals, and attested by my own observations of the many disappointed of entrance in our former places of meeting, I have consented to redeliver my elementary course on the nature of all knowledge, physical and moral.

Without a thorough understanding of the primary truths which it has been my attempt, in this elementary course, familiarly to elucidate, the public mind must be unfit for any discussion; therefore it is, that I commence with these primary truths; and therefore it is, that I shall decline the discussion of all other topics, until our first premises being laid, we are supplied with a standard by which to test all existing opinions and existing practice.

Whenever hereafter I may be called, in peace and with seriousness, to deliver my views on any subject of general interest to my fellow beings, I will meet their wishes. My opinions, whatever they may be, I am not accustomed to **defend**, but I will willingly **explain**; and explain with that simplicity, which befits inquiry after truth, and that tenderness to the feelings of others, which I think I am not apt to forget.

Before we open our discussions of the evening, I would suggest to the audience, the propriety of bearing in mind the circumstances under which we meet, the former futile attempts to disturb our meetings in the Masonic Hall, and the possible presence of some mistaken and misguided individuals, ready to excite false alarm, and to take advantage of any the least disturbance, with a view to the injury of the cause of human improvement, which we are met to promote, and to the injury of the lessees of the building which we now occupy.

In case of any attempt to disturb our meeting, by cries of alarm, I beg the audience to bear in mind, that the house is under vigilant and double police.

I shall now, then, present you with the opening discourse, formerly delivered in the Masonic Hall. And, as it will be in matter and words the same, you will judge of the accuracy of the reports presented in your daily papers.

Lecture I

ON THE NATURE OF KNOWLEDGE

Who among us, that hath cast even an occasional and slightly observant glance on the face of society, but must have remarked the differing opinions, which distract the human mind; the opposing creeds and systems, each asserting its claim to infallibility, and rallying around its standard pertinacious disciples, enthusiastic proselytes, ardent apologists, fiery combatings, obsequious worshippers, conscientious followers, and devoted martyrs? If we extend our observation over the surface of our globe, and consider its diversified population, however varied in hue and feature, we find it yet more varied in opinions, in one opinion only invariably agreed, viz. that of its infallibility. The worshipper of sculptured idols bows before the image of his hand, and shrinks with unfeigned terror, if a sacrilegious intruder profane the sanctuary of his superstition. The adorer of the bright luminary which marks our days and seasons, sees in the resplendent orb, not a link in the vast chain of material existence, but the source of all existence; and so from the most unpretending savage, to the most lettered nation of a lettered age, we find **all** shaping their superstitions, according to the measure of their ignorance or their knowledge, and each devoutly believing his faith and practice to be the true and the just. Or let us confine our observation within the limits of the country we inhabit--how varying the creeds arising out of one system of faith! How contradictory the assertions and expectations of sects, all equally positive, and equally, we may presume, conscientious! How conflicting the opinions and feelings of men upon all subjects, trivial or important! until we are tempted to exclaim, "Where, then, is right or wrong but in human imagination, and what is truth more than blind opinion?" Few of us prone to study or observation, yet educated after existing methods, but must have asked these questions, and halted for a reply.

Should the problem here started be, I say not impossible, but even difficult of solution, lamentable must be the human condition to the end of time! Had truth no test--no standard--no positive, no tangible existence, behold us, then, sold to error, and, while to error, to misery, through all the generations of our race! But, fortunately, the answer is simple; only too simple, it would appear, for mystery-loving, mystery-seeking man, to perceive and acknowledge.

Let not the present audience imagine, that I am about to add one more to the already uncountable, unnameable systems, which distract the understandings of men, or to draw yet new doctrines and precepts from the fertile alembic of the human brain. I request you to behold in me an inquirer, not a teacher; one who conceives of truth as a jewel to be found, not to be coined; a treasure to be discovered by observation, and accumulated by careful, persevering industry, not invented and manufactured by learned art or aspiring quackery, like the once fashionable elixir of immortality and philosopher's stone. My object will be simply to take with you a survey of the field of human inquiry; to ascertain its nature, its extent, its boundaries, its limits; to discover, in the first place, what there is for us to know; secondly, the means we possess for acquiring such knowledge as is of possible attainment, and, thirdly, having satisfied ourselves as to what can be known, and as to what we know, to seek in our knowledge the test of our opinions.

It must be admitted, that, as all our opinions must rest upon some evidence, real or imagined, so upon the truth or falsehood of the evidence admitted, must rest the truth or falsehood of the opinions based thereupon. It is evident, therefore, that before we can reflect, we must have something to reflect upon; before we can think accurately respecting any thing, we must know accurately all relating to it; and wheresoever our knowledge be complete, will our opinion be just.

Seeing, then, that just opinions are the result of just knowledge, and perceiving, as we must all perceive, how much confusion arises to society out of the conflicting opinions, which divide alike nations and families into sects and parties, it is equally our interest and our duty, to aim at the acquisition of just knowledge, with a view to the formation of just opinions. And, as we shall hereafter have occasion to observe, just practice being the result of past opinions, and human happiness being the certain result of just practice, it is equally our interest and our duty to aim at the formation of just opinions, with a view to the attainment of happiness.

We shall, therefore, open our investigations by an inquiry into the nature and object of just knowledge; and if we succeed in ascertaining these, we will farther examine the causes which at present impede our progress, and the means best calculated at once to remove such impediments, and to advance us in the course which it is our interest to pursue.

If we consider man in comparison with other animals, we find him distinguished by one principle. This principle, which is shared by no other existence within the range of our observation, gives him all his pre-eminence. It constitutes, indeed, all existence. By its neglect or cultivation he remains ignorant and degraded, or becomes intelligent and happy; and, as he owes to it all that has elevated him above the brute in past time or at present, so in it may he find rich hope and promise for the future.

Much does it behove us, then, earnestly to consider this distinguishing principle of our nature. Much does it behove us to understand the fullness of its importance and its power, and to know that, as without it we should be as the beasts of the field, so with it we may rise in the scale of being, until every vice which now degrades, every fear which unnerves, and every prejudice which enchains us, shall disappear beneath its influence.

I advert to the simple but all-important principle of improvement. Weak as we are, compared to the healthy strength we are conscious would be desirable; ignorant as we are, compared to the height, and breadth, and depth of knowledge which extends around us far as the universal range of matter itself; miserable as we are, compared to the happiness of which we feel ourselves capable, yet in this living principle we see nothing beyond or above us, nothing to which we or our descendants may not attain, of great, of beautiful, of excellent. But to **feel** the power of this mighty principle, to urge it forward in its course, and accelerate the change in our condition which it promises, we must awaken to its observation.

Are we yet awake to this? Do we know what we are, or have we ever asked ourselves what we might be? Are we even desirous of becoming wiser, and better, and happier? and, if desirous, are we earnestly applied to effect the change?

Knowledge

It is probable that some vague desire of advancing in knowledge pervades every bosom. We find every where some deference paid to the great principle of our nature in the growing demand for schools and colleges. We seem to have discovered that the faculties of man demand care for their development; and that, like the marble of the quarry, he must be shaped and polished ere he will present the line of beauty.

But, alas! here is the difficulty. If agreed that something must be done, we see but darkly what that something is. While eager to be doing, we are still in doubt both as to the end to be attained and the means to be employed. While anxious to learn, we are but too often ignorant of the very nature of knowledge. We are unacquainted with her haunts and her habitation, and seek her where she is not to be found. It may be useful, then, before we engage in the labyrinth of learning, that we examine carefully what knowledge is.

If we ask this in our schools, we shall be told, that knowledge is an acquaintance with the structure of our own language; a familiarity with foreign, especially with dead languages. We shall, moreover, hear of history, geography, astronomy, etc. Do we ask the same in our colleges, we shall hear further of law, medicine, surgery, theology, mathematics, chemistry, and philosophy, natural and mental: and we shall be farther told, that when a youth has mastered all these sounding names, and puzzled through all the learning, useful or useless, attached to them--he is well taught and thoroughly educated. It may be so. And yet may he be also very ignorant of what it most imports him to know. Nay, more! in despite of an intimate acquaintance with all the most esteemed branches of knowledge, he may be utterly unacquainted with the object and nature of knowledge itself. Let us, then, enquire again, **what knowledge is.**

It is not, in the first place, acquaintance with ourselves? and secondly, with all things to which we stand in relation?

How are we to obtain this acquaintance? By observation and patient inquiry.

What are the means we possess from this observation and inquiry? Our senses; and our faculties, as awakened and improved in and by the exercise of our senses.

Knowledge

Let us now examine what are the objects really submitted to the investigation of our senses. These may be all embraced under the generic term matter, implying the whole of existence within the range of our inspection.

Were we to proceed minutely in our analysis, we should observe that matter, as existing around us, appears under three forms, the gaseous, the liquid, and the solid; and that under one or other of these forms may be accurately classed all that is submitted to our observation--all, in short, that we can see, hear, feel, taste, or smell. But to enter at present into such details would be foreign to our purpose.

I shall, therefore, pass on to observe that the accurate and patient investigation of matter, in all its subdivisions, together with all its qualities and changes, constitutes a just education. And that in proportion as we ascertain, in the course of investigation, the real qualities and actual changes of matter, together with the judicious application of all things to the use of man, and influence of all occurrences on the happiness of man, so do we acquire knowledge. In other words, knowledge is an accumulation of facts, and signifies **things known.** In proportion, therefore, as the sphere of our observation is large, and our investigation of all within that sphere careful, in proportion is our knowledge.

The view of knowledge we have here taken is simple; and it may be observed, that not in this case only, but in all others, accuracy and simplicity go hand in hand. All truth is simple, for truth is only fact. The means of attaining truth are equally simple. We have but to seek and we shall find; to open our eyes and our ears; without prejudice to observe; without fear to listen, and dispassionately to examine, compare, and draw conclusions.

The field of knowledge is around, and about, and within us. Let us not be alarmed by sounding words, and let us not be **deceived** by them. Let us look to things. It is things which we have to consider. Words are, or, more correctly, should be, only the signs of things. I say they **should be;** for it is a most lamentable truth, that they are now very generally conceived to constitute the very substance of knowledge. Words, indeed, should seem at present contrived rather for the purpose of confusing our ideas, than administering to their distinctness and arrangement. Instead of viewing them as the shadows, we mistake them for the substance; and conceive that in proportion as we enlarge our vocabulary, we multiply our acquirements.

Vain, then, will be the attempt to increase our knowledge, until we understand where we are to look for it, and in what it consists. Here is the first stepping stone. Let our foot but firmly strike it, and our after progress is easy.

And in what lies the importance of this first step in human knowledge? In the accuracy which it brings to all our ideas. It places us at once on firm ground, introduces us into the field of real inquiry, and lays the reign of the imagination in the hand of the judgment. Difficult were it to exaggerate the importance of the step which involves such consequences. Until we bring accuracy to our thoughts, and, we may add, accuracy to the words employed for their expression--we can make no progress. We may wander, indeed, and most certainly shall wander, in various paths; but they will be paths of error. The straight broad road of improvement it will not be ours to tread, until we take heed unto our feet, and know always whither we are going.

Imagine--and how easy is it to imagine, when we have but to look around us or within ourselves--imagine the confusion of hopes, desires, ambitions, and expectations, with which the scholar enters, and but too often leaves the halls of science. On entering them, he conceives that some mysterious veil, like the screen of the holy of holies, is about to be withdrawn, and that he is to look at things far removed from real life, and raised far above the vulgar apprehension. On leaving them, he has his memory surcharged with a confusion of ideas, and a yet more confusion of words. He knows, perhaps, the properties of ciphers and of angels; the names and classification of birds, fishes, quadrupeds, insects, and minerals; the chemical affinities of bodies; can measure star from star; analyze invisible substances; detail in chronological order the rise and fall of nations, with their arts, sciences, and sects of philosophy. He can do all this, and more; and yet, perhaps, is there neither arrangement in his knowledge, distinctness in his ideas, nor accuracy in his language. And, while so many wordy pedants, and hair-brained or shallow disputants, are sent forth from the schools of all countries, while those who do honor to their species, by rendering service in their generation, are, most generally, what is called self-taught. And the reason of this is evident. Our existing modes of education, being equally false and deficient. and the instruction of our schools full of fallacies, theories, and hypotheses, the more regularly a youth is trained in fashionable learning, the more confused is usually his perception of things, and the more prostrated his reason by the dogmatism of teachers, the sophism of words, and the false principles engrafted by means of pretended science, ostentatiously inculcated or real science, erroneously imparted. While, on the other hand, a vigorous intellect, if stimulated by fortunate circumstances to inquiry, and left to accumulate information by the efforts of its own industry, though its early progress may be slow, and its aberrations numerous, yet in the free exercise of its powers, is more likely to collect accurate knowledge, than those who are methodically fed with learned error and learnedly disguised truth.

I shall have occasion, in a more advanced stage of our inquires, to examine minutely the errors in the existing mode of instruction, and which are of a nature to perplex the human mind from infancy to age, and to make even learning an additional stumbling-block in the way of knowledge. For the present, I would confine myself to the establishing the simple position, that **all real knowledge is derived from positive sensations.**

In proportion to the number of senses we bring to bear upon an object, is the degree of our acquaintance with that object. Whatever we see, and feel, and attentively examine with **all** our senses, we **know**; and respecting the things thus investigated, we can afterwards form a correct opinion. Wherever, respecting such things, our opinions are erroneous, it is where our investigation of them has been insufficient, or our recollection of them imperfect; and the only certain way of rectifying the error, is to refer again to the object itself.

Things which we have not ourselves examined, and occurrences which we have not ourselves witnessed, but which we receive on the attested sensations of others, we may **believe**, but we do not **know**. Now, as these two modes of intellectual assent are generally, if not universally confounded; and, as their accurate distinction is, in its consequences, of immense importance, I shall risk the straining of your attention for a few minutes, while I attempt its elucidation.

To select a familiar, and at the moment a pertinent example. The present audience **know** that an individual is now addressing them, because they see her person, and hear her voice. They may **believe** that some other speaker occupies the pulpit of a church in this town, if assured to that effect by a person of ordinary veracity; but, let the testimony of that person be as well substantiated in their opinion as possible, the fact received through his reported sensations, they would **believe**; the fact of my presence, admitted upon their own sensations, they will **know**.

My hearers will understand that my object in presenting these definitions, is not to draw a mere verbal distinction, but a distinction between different states of the human mind; the distinction in words only being important, in that it is necessary to a clear understanding of the mental phenomena it is desirable to illustrate.

Did the limits of our present discourse permit such a development, or did I not apprehend to weary the attention, it would not be difficult to draw the line between knowledge and belief, and again between the different grades of belief, through all the varieties of intellectual assent from the matter-of-fact certainty supplied by knowledge down t the lowest stage of probability, supplied by belief. But having suggested the distinction, I must leave you to draw it for yourselves; requesting you only to observe--that, as your own positive sensations can alone give you knowledge of a thing, so is your belief of any thing stronger, in proportion as you can more accurately establish, or approach nearer to, the sensations of those whose testimony you receive.

Thus: if a friend, or, more particularly, if several friends of tried veracity and approved judgment, relate to us a circumstance of which they declare themselves to have been attentive spectators--our belief is of the highest kind. If they relate a circumstance which they shall have received from another, or from other individuals, for whose veracity and judgment they also vouch, our belief, though in a measure accorded, is very considerably weakened; and so on, until, after a few more removes from the original sensations of the reported spectators, our belief is reduced to zero.

But farther, it is here of importance to observe that belief--that is, the belief of a well trained mind--can never be accorded to the attested sensations of others, should those attested sensations be contradicted by our own well established experience, or by the unvarying and agreeing experience of mankind. Thus: should one, or twenty, or a thousand individuals, swear to the fact of having seen a man, by effort of his unaided volition; raise himself through the air to the top of the steeple in this city, we should believe--what? Not the eccentric occurrence, however attested, but one of two very common occurrences--either that the individuals were seeking to impose upon us, or that their own ignorant credulity had been deceived by false appearances.

But now let us suppose a case, very likely to be presented in form of an objection, although in reality capable of furnishing a forcible elucidation of the simple truth we are now attempting to illustrate. Let us suppose that some of our organs should become diseased--those of sight, for instance; and that we should, in consequence, imagine the appearance of an object not perceptible to more healthy individuals. If the phantasy presented nothing uncommon in any of its parts, or inconsistent with the course of previous sensations, we should at first, undoubtedly, yield credence to our eyes; until, in consequence, perhaps, of some incongruity, we should be led to appeal to our other senses, when, if they did not concur with the testimony of our vision, we should distinguish the appearance, immediately, for the effect of disease, and apply ourselves, on the instant, to its investigation and remedy.

But again, let us suppose (a case by no means uncommon in the history of the human pathology) that two of our senses should be diseased--our sight and our hearing; and that we should in consequence see the spectral illusion of a human being; and, farther, imagine such illusion to discourse with us. Our belief would be now strongly accorded to this two-fold evidence; but we should still have a resource in our sense of touch. Should this last not confirm the evidence supplied by our vision and our hearing, we should suspect as in the former case, the health of our organs, and consult on the subject with an able physician.

But let us now suppose that **all** the organs of sense, in some individual, should become suddenly diseased, and sight, hearing, feeling, taste, and smell, should **combine** to cheat him into the belief of existences not perceptible to the more healthy sensations of his fellow creatures. I do not conceive that such an individual, however, naturally strong or highly cultivated his judgment, and even supposing his judgment to retain its activity in the midst of the general disorder, could for any length of time struggle with the delusion, but must gradually yield intellectual assent to his diseased sensations, however incongruous these might be, or however at variance with past experience. I conceive that an individual thus diseased in all his organs of sense, must rapidly lose all control over his reasoning faculties, and present, consequently,to his fellow creatures, the afflicting spectacle of one laboring under mental insanity.

If we look to the unfortunate maniac, or to the sufferer tossing in fever delirium, we shall perceive how implicit the credence given to his diseased sensations. The phantoms which he hears, and feels, and sees, are all realities to him, and, as realities, govern his thoughts and decide his actions. How, in such cases, does the enlightened physician proceed? He does not argue with the incongruous ideas of his patient; he examines his disordered frame, and as he can restore healthy action to all its body parts, so does he hope to restore healthy sensations to the body, and accurate ideas to the mind. Here, then, we see, in sickness as in health, our sensations supplying us with all intellectual food. In fever, they supply us with dreams; in health, if accurately studied, with knowledge.

The object of these observations is to show, that as we can only **know** a thing by its immediate contact with our senses, so is **all knowledge compounded of the accurately observed, accumulated, and agreeing sensations of mankind.**

The field of knowledge, then, we have observed to be the field of nature, or of material existence around and within us. The number of objects comprised within the circle of human observation, is so multiplied, and the properties or qualities of these objects so diversified, that with a view to convenient and suitable divisions in the great work of inspecting the whole, and also with a view to the applying more order and method in the arrangement of the facts collated in the wide field of nature, they have been classed under different heads, each of which we may call **a branch of knowledge**, or, more succinctly, **a science**.

Thus: do we consider the various living tribes which people the elements? We class our observations under the head of natural history. Do we direct our attention to the structure and mechanism of their bodies: We designate the results

225

of our inspection under the heads anatomy and physiology. Do we trace the order of occurrences and appearances in the wide field of nature? We note them under natural philosophy. Do we analyze substances and search our their simple elements? chemistry. Do we apply ourselves to the measurement of bodies, or calculate the heights and distances of objects? geometry. And so on, through all the range of human observation, extending from the relative position of the heavenly bodies, and accurate calculation of their courses, to the uses, habits, structure, and physiology of the delicate plant which carpets our earth.

Now, all the sciences, properly so called, being compounded of facts, ascertained or ascertainable by the sensations of each individual, so all that is not so ascertainable is not knowledge, only belief, and can never constitute for us matter-of-fact certainty, only greater or less probability. In elucidation, we might remark that the facts we glean, in the study of chemistry, supply us with knowledge; those received upon testimony, as in the study of history, supply us with probabilities, or with improbabilities, as it may be, and constitute belief.

Now, again--as our knowledge is supplied by our own individual sensations, and our belief by the attested sensations of others, it is possible, while pretending to communicate knowledge, only to communicate belief. This we know to be the system pursued in all our schools and colleges, where the truths of the most demonstrable sciences are presented under the disguise of oral or written lessons, instead of being exposed, in practical illustrations, to the eye, and the ear, and the touch, in the simple, incontrovertible fact. This method, while it tends to hide and perpetuate the errors of teachers, so does it also inculcate credulity and blind belief in the scholar, and finally establishes the conclusion in the mind, that knowledge is compounded of words, and signs, and intellectual abstractions, instead of facts and human sensations.

Greatly, very greatly to be desired, is a just mode of instruction. It would not only shorten the road of knowledge, it would carpet it with flowers. We should then tread it in childhood with smiles of cheerfulness; and, as we followed its pleasant course, horizon after horizon would open upon us, delighting and improving our minds and feelings, through life, unto our latest hour. But if it is of

226

the first importance to be launched aright in infancy, the moment we distinctly perceive what knowledge is, we may, at any age, start boldly for its attainment.

I have said, we may start **boldly**--ay! and there lies the surety of our success. If we bring not the good courage of minds covetous of truth, and truth only, prepared to hear all things, examine all things, and decide upon all things, according to evidence, we should do more wisely to sit down contented in ignorance, than to bestir ourselves only to reap disappointment. But let us once look around upon this fair material world, as upon the book which it behooves us to read; let us understand, that in this book there are no puzzling mysteries, but a simple train of occurrences, which it imports us to observe, with an endless variety of substances and existences, which it imports us to study--what is there, then, to frighten us? what is there not rather, to encourage our advance?

Yet how far are we from this simple perception of simple things! how far from that mental composure which can alone fit us for inquiry! How prone are we to come to the consideration of every question with heads and hearts preoccupied! how prone to shrink from any opinion, however reasonable, if it be opposed to any, however unreasonable, of our own! How disposed are we to judge, in anger, those who call upon us to think, and encourage us to inquire! To question our prejudices, seems nothing less than sacrilege; to break the chains of our ignorance nothing short of impiety!

Perhaps at this moment, she who speaks is outraging a prejudice--(shall I be forgiven the word?) Perhaps among those who hear me, there are who deem it both a presumption and an impropriety for a woman to reason with her fellow creatures.

Did I know of a surety, this prejudice to prevail among my hearers, I should, indeed, be disposed to reason with **them**. I should be tempted to ask, whether truth had any sex; and I should venture farther to ask, whether they count for nothing, for something or for every thing, the influence of women over the destinies of our race.

Shall I be forgiven for adverting, most unwillingly, to myself? Having assumed an unusual place, I feel, that to my audience some explanation is due.

Knowledge

Stimulated in my early youth, by I know not what of pitying sympathy with human suffering, and by I know not what persuasion, that our race was not of necessity born to ignorance, and its companion, vice, but that it possessed faculties and qualities which pointed to virtue and enjoyment; stimulated, at once, by this pity for the actual condition of man, and this hope of a possible melioration, I applied myself to the discovery of the causes of the one, and of the means for effecting the other.

I have as little the inclination to obtrude on you the process of investigation and course of observation I followed through the period of an eventful youth, as you would probably have to listen to them. Suffice it, that I have been led to consider the growth of knowledge, and the equal distribution of knowledge, as the best--may I say, the only means for reforming the condition of mankind. Shall I be accused of presumption for imagining that I could be instrumental in promoting this, as it appears to me, good work? Shall I appear additionally presumptuous for believing that my sex and my situation tend rather to qualify than to incapacitate me for the undertaking.

So long as the mental and moral instruction of man is left solely in the hands of hired servants of the public--let them be teachers of religion, professors of colleges, authors of books, or editors of journals or periodical publications, dependent upon their literary labors for their daily bread, so long shall we hear but half the truth; and well if we hear so much. Our teachers, political, scientific, moral, or religious; our writers, grave or gay, are **compelled** to administer to our prejudices, and to perpetuate our ignorance. They dare not speak that which, by endangering their popularity, would endanger their fortunes. They have to discover not what is true, but what is palatable: not what will search into the hearts and minds of their hearers, but what will open their purse strings. They have to weigh every sentiment before they hazard it, every word before they pronounce it, lest they wound some cherished vanity, or aim at some favorite vice. A familiar instance will bring this home to an American audience.

I have been led to inspect, far and wide, the extensive and beautiful section of this country which is afflicted with slavery. I have heard in the cities, villages, and forests of this afflicted region, religious shepherds of all persuasions haranguing their flocks, and I have never heard **one** bold enough to comment on the evil which saps the industry, vitiates the morals, and threatens the tranquility of the country. The reason of this forbearance is evident. The master of the slave is he who pays the preacher, and the preacher must not irritate his paymaster. I would not here be understood to express the opinion, that the preaching of religious teachers against slavery would be desirable. I am convinced of the contrary--convinced that it would be of direful mischief to both parties, the oppressor the oppressed. To judge from the tone but too generally employed by religious writers in the northern states, where (as denunciation against the vice of the south risks no patronage and wins cheap credit for humanity) negro philanthropy is not so scarce--to judge, I say, from the tone employed by northern religionists, when speaking of their southern neighbors, and their national crime and affliction, one must suppose them as little capable of counselling foreign as home offenders--as little capable of advising in wisdom as of judging in mercy, or speaking with gentleness. The harshest physician with which I am acquainted is the religious physician. Instead of soothing, he irritates; instead of convincing, he disgusts; instead of weighing circumstances, tracing causes, allowing for the bias of early example, the constraining force of implanted prejudice, the absence of every judicious stimulus, and the presence of every bad one; he arraigns, tries, convicts, condemns--himself accuser, jury, judge, and executioner; nobly immolating interests which are not his, generously commanding sacrifices which he has not to share, indignantly anathematizing crimes which he cannot commit, and virtuously kindling the fires of hell to consume sinners, to whose sins, as he is without temptation so **for** whose sins he is without sympathy. I would not be understood, therefore, as regretting in this matter the supineness of the southern clergy; I would only point it out to you, desirous that you should observe how well the tribe of Levi know when and where to smite, and when and where to spare.

And though I have quoted an instance more peculiarly familiar to Americans, every country teems with similar examples. The master vice, wherever or whatever it be, is never touched. In licentious aristocracies, or to look no farther than the towns and cities of these states, the rich and pampered few are ever spared, or so gently dealt with, as rather agreeably to tickle the ear, than to probe the conscience, while the crimes of the greatly-tempted, greatly-suffering poor, are visited with unrelenting vigor.

Is any discovery made in science, tending to open to us farther the book of knowledge, and to purge our minds of superstitious beliefs in occult causes and unsubstantiated creed--where has it ever found opposers--or, might we not say, persecutors? Even among our hired preachers and licensed teachers of old doctrines and old ways. Is any inquiry instituted into the truth of received opinions and the advantage of existing practice--who are the last to encourage it? nay, the foremost to cry out "heresy!" and stop the mouth of knowledge? Who but those who live by the ignorance of the age, and the intolerance of the hour? Is any improvement suggested in our social arrangements, calculated to equalize property, labor, instruction, and enjoyment; to destroy crime by removing provocation; vice, by removing ignorance; and to build up virtue in the human breast by exchanging the spirit of self abasement for that of self respect--who are the foremost to treat the suggestions as visionary, the reform as impossible? Even they who live by the fears and the vices of their fellow creatures; and who obtain their subsistence on earth by opening and shutting the door of heaven.

Nor, as we have seen, are our licensed and pensioned teachers the only individuals interested in disguising the truth. All who write for the public market, all who plead in our courts of law, all who harangue in our halls of legislature, all who are, or who aspire to be, popular servants or popular teachers of the people, all are **compelled** to the support of existing opinions, whether right or wrong--all, more or less, do, and more or less must, pander to the weaknesses, vices, and prejudices of the public, who pays them with money or applause.

I have said not only that they do, but that they **must**; and most assuredly they must conciliate the popular feeling, or forego the popular favor. Here is intended no satire upon any individuals, professions, nor employments. The object is merely to expose a fact, but a fact highly important to be known; that as to be popular, men must not speak truths, so, when we would hear truths, we must seek them from other mouths and other pens than those which are dependent upon popular patronage, or which we ambitions of popular admiration.

Knowledge

And here, then, is the cause why I have presumed to reason with my fellow creatures; why, in my earliest years, I devoted myself to the study of their condition, past and present; why I searched into their powers and their capabilities, examined their practice, and weighed their opinions; and why, when I found these both wanting, I volunteered to declare it. I believe that I see some truths important for my fellow beings to know; I feel that I have the courage and the independence to speak that which I believe; and where is the friend to his species that will not say, **"Happy, most happy shall it be for human kind, when all independent individuals, male or female, citizens or foreigners, shall feel the debt of kindness they owe to their fellow beings, and fearlessly step forth to reveal unbought truths and hazard unpopular opinions."**

Until this be done, and done ably, fearlessly, and frequently, the reign of human error must continue; and, with human error, human vice, and human suffering. The advocates of just knowledge must be armed with courage to dare all things, and to bear all things, for the truths they revere; and to seek, as they may only find, the reward of their exertions in the impression, great or little, slow or rapid, as it may be, which their exertions may produce on public opinion, and through the public opinion on the public practice.

We have now sufficiently considered, so far as I have found possible in a single discourse on so wide a topic, the main subject of our introductory inquiries: viz. the nature and object of just knowledge. We have examined, also, some of the errors vulgarly entertained on the subject, and many of the impediments which now obstruct our advances in the road of improvement. We have seen that just knowledge is easy of acquirement, but that few are interested in revealing its simple principles; while many are driven by circumstances to interpret or dissemble them. We have remarked that, to accelerate the progress of our race, two means present themselves; a just system of education, and a fearless spirit of inquiry; and that while the former would remove all difficulties from the path of future generations, the latter would place far in advance even the present. We have also observed on the advantage which would accrue to mankind, if all independent individuals would volunteer the task, for which appointed teachers and professional men are now but too frequently unfit, by devoting themselves to the

231

promulgation of truth, without regard to fashionable prejudice. I have been led, also, incidentally to advert to the influence exerted over the fortunes of our race by those who are too often overlooked in our social arrangements and in our civil rights--I allude to women.

Leaving to a future opportunity the more complete development of the important subject, we have this evening approached--the nature of all knowledge-- as well as the equally important subject of youthful education, I shall, at our next meeting, consider the other two enumerated means of improvement, viz. by free inquiry. And as this is for us of the present generation the **only** means, so shall I endeavor to show how much it is our interest, and how imperiously it is our duty to improve it to the uttermost.

It is with delight that I have distinguished, at each successive meeting, the increasing ranks of my own sex. Were the vital principle of human equality universally acknowledged, it would be to my fellow beings without regard to nation, class, sect, or sex, that I should delight to address myself. But until equality prevail in condition, opportunity, and instruction, it is every where to the least favored in these advantages, that I most especially and anxiously incline.

Nor is the ignorance of our sex a matter of surprise, when efforts, as violent as unrelaxed, are every where made for its continuance.

It is not as of yore. Eve puts not forth her hand to gather the fair fruit of knowledge. The wily serpent now hath better learned his lesson; and, to secure his reign in the garden, beguileth her **not** to eat. Promises, entreaties, threats, tales of wonder, and, alas! tales of horror, are all poured in her tender ears. Above, her agitated fancy hears the voice of a god in thunders; below, she sees the yawning pit; and, before, behind, around a thousand phantoms, conjured from the prolific brain of insatiate priestcraft, confound, alarm, and overwhelm her reason!

Oh! were that worst evil withdrawn which now weighs upon our race, how rapid were its progress in knowledge! Oh! were men--and, yet more, women, absolved from fear, how easily, and speedily, and gloriously would they hold on their course in improvement! The difficulty is not to convince, it is to **win attention**. Could truth only be heard, the conversion of the ignorant were easy. And well do the hired supporters of error understand this fact. Well do they **know**

232

that if the daughters of the present, and mothers of the future generation, were to drink of the living waters of knowledge, their reign would be ended--"their occupation gone." So well do they know it, that, far from obeying to the letter the command of their spiritual leader, "Be ye fishers of men," we find them every where **fishers of women**. Their own sex, old and young, they see with indifference swim by their nets; but closely and warily are their meshes laid, to entangle the female of every age.

Fathers and husbands! Do ye not also understand this fact? Do ye not see how, in the mental bondage of your wives and fair companions, ye yourselves are bound? Will ye fondly sport yourselves in your imagined liberty, and say, "it matters not if our women be mental slaves?" Will ye pleasure yourselves in the varied paths of knowledge and imagine that women, hoodwinked and unawakened, will make the better servants and the easier playthings? They are greatly in error who so strike the account; as many a bankrupt merchant and sinking mechanic not to say drowning capitalist, could bear witness. But setting aside dollars and cents, which men, in their present uncomfortable state of existence, are but too prone exclusively to regard, how many nobler interests of the mind and the heart cry "treason!" to this false calculation?

At our next meeting, we shall consider these interests, which will naturally present themselves during our investigations on the subject of free inquiry. In what just knowledge consists we have cursorily examined; to put ourselves in the way of attaining that knowledge, be our next object.

Introduction to Lecture II
"Of Free Inquiry,
Considered as a Means for Obtaining Just Knowledge"

Questions about the nature of truth early on in her studies brought Frances Wright to two conclusions: "Truth had still to be found" and "men were afraid of it" (Perkins 9). Wright's study of chemistry and physics influenced her curiosity about the nature and utility of truth, about the need for both sexes to be equally engaged in its pursuit, and about "truths" which are misknown. One of these mis-known "truths" concerns the relationship between theology and religion. The "truth" about religion reveals that this country's "religion" is this country's "love of liberty" because that is what binds this country together (Life 24, Letter#5). Inquiry into this truth becomes an ethical issue that demands both sexes be equally engaged in its pursuit.

Wright argues that liberty could not have been attained without knowledge; for liberty to be maintained, it must be by education. Born free and equal, we do not live so, even though political institutions claim to be established on the notion of equality and the Declaration of Independence sets forth the principle--"Equality is the soul of liberty" (25) with "the golden words":"`All men are born free and equal'"(27). The republic cannot be governed by a public voice if the public mind is unenlightened. Further, Wright claims that for women to engage in inquiry, they must engage as a body, and that unless there is co-operation by both sexes, rich and poor, inquiry will not be effective. This "joint enterprise of both women and men" is currently an ethical consideration of modern women philosophers (Almond 56).[1] Although Wright does not mention race as a part of the equation here, it was a part of her pre-Civil War philosophy in the Nashoba equation.

In her "Institution of Nashoba" Wright defines political liberty as "liberty of speech and of action, without incurring the violence of authority or the penalties of law," and moral liberty as "the free exercise of the liberty of speech and of action, without incurring the intolerance of popular prejudice and ignorant public opinion." Her experience with liberty in practice made clear that the distance between theory and practice is great (51). Among discrepancies Wright pointed out were the penalties to which married women were legally subjected. Nevertheless, more than a decade would elapse before action would begin to gain more equitable legal status for married women (Woloch 191).[2]

Wright repeats the argument that Judith Sargent Murray made, that the way to move forward in a republic is through education. She assumes Murray's thesis that the sexes are equal and concentrates on education, not only because equal education is reasonable, but primarily because it is ethical.[3] Without full participation in inquiry, equality and liberty for all is not possible. In a broader and deeper sense Wright comes back to her Epicurean classroom, where women's opinions on ethical issues are taken seriously, turning Spinoza's question, "Are women subject to ethics" upside down--unless men honor the ethics of women, they will remain in an unethical situation (Kristeva 52-3).

In questioning how we "justly" allow liberty to ourselves without doing injury to either ourselves or others, Wright again anticipates John Stuart Mill, especially in the case she presents of the relationship between parents and daughters (29-30). Here she counsels parents to allow their children to experience the consequences of their actions, doing no more than guiding the "free exercise" of their senses; the same "natural liberties" extended to daughters as well to sons.

Thus, in this lecture on free inquiry, Wright bases her philosophy on political ethics as she demonstrates the ethical necessity of inquiry for which liberty must be the religion, and equality and education must be synonymous. With vision beyond that of most philosophers of her time, she prepares us for the additional issue of race as she works out the issue of women on the ethical road to the collective "whole family" of humankind's improvement (37).

Endnotes

1 The current debate in philosophy by Alison Jagger, Sandra Harding and many others about the role of women philosophers and the nature of philosophy by women, carries Wright's concern for inclusiveness in epistemology and ethics into new inquiry.

2 Later, Sarah Grimke offered a critique of Blackstone in regard to couverture. In addition to the legal concern, she reiterates the social and moral concern of Judith Sargent Murray that so long as women are "dressed as dolls" for the purpose of catching a husband, they will never be able to raise themselves from a subordinate position.

3 Judith Sargent Murray, Priscilla Mason, Frances Wright and following her Maria Stewart continued the ongoing contention in this country begun abroad centuries earlier that the key to the improvement for gender and race was education.

Lecture II

OF FREE INQUIRY, CONSIDERED AS A MEANS FOR OBTAINING JUST KNOWLEDGE

The subject we have to examine this evening, is that of free inquiry, considered as a means for the attainment of just knowledge.

At our last meeting, we endeavored to investigate the nature and object of just knowledge, together with the means proper for its attainment. We discovered these means to be two: a judicious education, and a free spirit of inquiry.

From the first and best means, a judicious education, we of the present generation are unfortunately excluded. Wherever our lot may have been cast, or whatever may be our attainments, we must all be conscious that we are what we are in spite of many disadvantages; and that, however wise or good our vanity may pronounce us to be, we should have been much wiser, and, consequently, better and happier, had a judicious education more carefully developed our tender faculties, and brought order and accuracy to all our nascent ideas. But the forest is grown; and, straight or crooked, the trees have to stand pretty much as early circumstances have inclined them. Still, something may be done; nay! if we bring fearless and determined spirits to the work, **much** may be done--much for ourselves, and every thing for our descendants. It rests with us to command, for the rising generation, that education, whose want we, in our own case, deplore. It rests with us to open, with a golden key, the gates of just knowledge for our children; and to marshal them in the smooth, broad, pleasant paths, which we ourselves have never trod. Equally true it is, that we cannot for ourselves, command that first, best means for attaining the first, best good. Our opinions have, unfortunately, to be changed, not simply formed; our advance in knowledge must involve forgetting as well as acquiring. We have not, in our own minds, to till a virgin soil, but one surcharged with weeds, soil. We may set the edge of our ploughshares, apply them with a steady and nervous hand, and scatter the good seed in good time to reap a harvest.

237

Inquiry

The second means for the attainment of knowledge is ours, if we choose to exercise it; that is, if we feel the importance of the object, and have courage to employ the means. The importance of the object we **must** feel, if we feel at all for ourselves or for our race; if we are not wholly indifferent to the rank we hold in the scale of being: not wholly indifferent to our moral excellence, to our mental elevation; to our own utility; to the liberty and happiness of our species through all the ages of time to come. And, if such be the mighty consequences depending on the object, shall we lack the courage to employ the means? And what means? to open our eyes and our ears; to throw wide the gates of our understanding; to dare the exercise of our intellectual faculties, and to encourage in others, as in ourselves, a habit of accurate and dispassionate investigation.

We have seen, also, that it is not our own improvement merely that it must be advanced or impeded according to our courage or timidity, but that of future generations, whose destiny it is ours to influence. Strongly, then, are we pledged to lay aside indolence and fear; and to engage honestly in the task of weeding out our prejudices and establishing our opinions.

There is a common error that I feel myself called upon to notice; nor know I the country in which it is more prevalent than in this. Whatever indifference may generally prevail among men, still there are many eager for the acquisition of knowledge; willing to inquire, and anxious to base their opinions upon correct principles. In the curiosity which motives their exertions, however, the vital principle is but too often wanting. They come selfishly, and not generously, to the tree of knowledge. They eat, but care not to impart of the fruit to others. Nay, there are who, having leaped the briar fence of prejudice themselves, will heap new thorns in the way of those who would venture the same.

And have Americans yet to learn that the interests of all are compounded of the interests of each? and that he who, in pursuing his own advantage, immolates one interest of his fellow beings, fails in justice as a man, commits treason as a citizen? And oh! what interest so dear as that of mental improvement? Who is without that interest? or of whom is not that interest sacred? Man, woman, child--who has not a claim to the exercise of his reason? or what injustice may compare with that which says to one, "thought is good for thee," and to another "knowledge is to thee forbidden?"

But will this imputation startle my hearers? Will they say, America is the home of liberty, and Americans brethren in equality. It is so? and may we not ask here as elsewhere, how many are there, not anxious to monopolize, but to universalize knowledge? how many, that consider their own improvement in relation always with that of their fellow beings, and who feel the imparting of truth to be not a work of supererogation, but a duty; the withholding it, not a venial omission, but a treachery to the race. Which of us have not seen fathers of families pursuing investigations themselves, which they hide from their sons, and, more especially, from their wives and daughters? As if truth could be of less importance to the young than to the old; or as if the sex which in all ages has ruled the destinies of the world, could be less worth enlightening than that which only follows its lead!

The observation I have hazarded may require some explanation. Those who arrogate power usually think themselves superior **de facto** and **de jure**. Yet justly might it be made a question whether those who ostensibly govern are not always unconsciously led. Should we examine closely into the state of things, we might find that, in all countries, the governed decide the destinies of the governors, more than the governors those of the governed; even as the laboring classes influence more directly the fortunes of a nation than does the civil officer, the aspiring statesman, the rich capitalist or the speculative philosopher.

However novel it may appear, I shall venture the assertion, that, until women assume the place in society which good sense and good feeling alike assign to them, human improvement must advance but feebly. It is in vain that we would circumscribe the power of one half of our race, and that half by far the most important and influential. If they exert it not for good, they will for evil; if they advance not knowledge, they will perpetuate ignorance. Let women stand where they may in the scale of improvement, their position decides that of the race. Are they cultivated?--so is society polished and enlightened. Are they ignorant?--so is it gross and insipid. Are they wise?--so is the human condition prosperous. Are they foolish?--so is it unstable and unpromising. Are they free?--so is the human character elevated. Are they enslaved?--so is the whole race degraded. Oh! that we could learn the advantage of just practice and consistent principles! that we could understand, that every departure from principle, how speciously soever it may appear to administer to our selfish interests, invariably saps their very foundation! that we could learn that what is ruinous to some is injurious to all! and that whenever we establish our own pretensions upon the sacrificed rights of others, we do in fact impeach our own liberties, and lower ourselves in the scale of being!

But to return. It is my object to show, that before we can engage successfully in the work of inquiry, we must engage in a body; we must engage collectively; as human beings desirous of attaining the highest excellence of which our nature is capable; as children of one family, anxious to discover the true and useful, for the common advantage of all. It is my farther abject to show that no co-operation in this matter can be effective which does not embrace the two sexes on a footing of equality; and, again, that no co-operation in this matter can be effective which does not embrace human beings on a footing of equality. Is this a republic--a country whose affairs are governed by the public voice--while the public mind is unequally enlightened? Is this a republic, where the interest of the many keep in check those of the few--while the few hold possession of the courts of knowledge and the many stand as suitors at the door? Is this a republic, where the rights of all are equally respected, the interests of all equally secured, the ambitions of all equally regulated, the services of all equally rendered? Is this such a republic--while we see endowed colleges for the rich, and barely **common schools** for the poor; while but one drop of colored blood shall stamp a fellow creature for a slave, or, at the least, degrade him below sympathy; and while one half of the whole population is left in civil bondage, and, as it were sentenced to mental imbecility.

Let us pause to inquire if this be consistent with the being of a republic. Without knowledge, could your fathers have conquered liberty? and without knowledge, can you retain it? Equality! where is it, if not in education? Equal rights! they cannot exist without equality of instruction. "All men are born free and equal!" they are **born**, but do they so **live**? Are they educated as equals? and, if not, can the be equal? and, if not equal, can they be free? Do not the rich command instruction, and they who have instruction must they not possess the power? and when they have the power, will they not exert it in their own favor? I will ask more; I will ask if two professions do not now rule the land and its inhabitants? I will ask whether your legislatures are not governed by lawyers and your households by priests? And I will farther ask, whether the deficient instruction of the mass of your population does not give to lawyers their political ascendency; and whether the ignorance of women be not the cause that your domestic hearths are invaded by priests? Are not these matters of popular interest? matters for popular inquiry? We shall examine tomorrow whether you have not now in your hands all the means necessary for equalizing instruction, not merely among your children but yourselves; so far, at least, as to place your liberties beyond risk of attainder.

This examination will involve all your interests, national and social. Your political institutions have taken equality for their basis; your declaration of rights, upon which your institutions rest, sets forth this principle as vital and inviolate. Equality is the soul of liberty; there is, in fact, no liberty without it--none that cannot be overthrown by the violence of ignorant anarchy, or sapped by the subtlety of professional craft. That this is the case your reasons will admit; that this is the case your feelings **do** admit--even those which are the least amiable and the least praiseworthy. The jealousy betrayed by the uncultivated against those of more polished address and manners, has its source in the beneficial principle to which we advert, however, (in this, as in many other cases,) misconceived and perverted. Cultivation of mind will ever lighten the countenance and polish the exterior. This external superiority which is but a faint emanation of the superiority within, vulgar eyes can see and ignorant jealousy will resent. This, in a republic, leads to brutality; and, in aristocracies, where this jealousy is restrained by fear, to servility. Here it will lead the wagoner to dispute the road with a carriage; and, in Europe, will make the foot passenger doff his hat to the lordly equipage with spatters him with mud, while there he mutters curses only in his heart. The unreasoning observer, will refer the conduct of the first to the **republican institutions**--the reflecting observer, to the **anti-republican education**. The instruction befitting free men is that which gives the sun of knowledge to shine on all; and at once secures the liberties of each individual, and disposes each individual to make a proper use of them.

Equality, then we have shown to have its seat in the mind. A proper cultivation of the faculties would ensure a sufficiency of that equality for all the ends of republican government, and for all the modes of social enjoyment. The diversity in the natural powers of different minds, as decided by physical organization, would be then only a source of interest and agreeable variety. All would be capable of appreciating the peculiar powers of each; and each would perceive that his interests, well understood, were in unison with the interests of all. Let us now examine whether liberty, properly interpreted, does not involve, among your unalienable rights as citizens and human beings, the right of equal means of instruction.

Have ye given a pledge, sealed with the blood of your fathers, for equal rights of all human kind sheltered within your confines? What means the pledge? or what understand ye by human rights? But understand them as ye will, define them as you will, how are men to be secured in **any** rights without instruction; how to be secured in the **equal exercise** of those rights without **equality of instruction**? By instruction understand me to mean knowledge--**just knowledge**; not talent, not genius, not inventive mental powers. These will vary in every human being; but knowledge is the same for every mind, and every mind may and **ought to be** trained to receive it. If, then, ye have pledged, at each anniversary of your political independence, your lives, properties, and honor, to the securing your common liberties, ye have pledged your lives, properties, and honor, to the securing of your **common** instruction. Or will you secure the end without securing the means? ye shall do it, when ye reap the harvest without planting the seed.

Oh! were the principle of human liberty understood, how clear would be the principle of human conduct! It would light us unerringly to our duties as citizens. It would light us unerringly to our duties as men. It would lead us aright in every action of our lives; regulate justly every feeling and affection of our hearts, and be to us a rule more unerring than laws, more binding than oaths, more enforcing than penalties. Then would passion yield to reason, selfishness to justice, and equal rights of others supply the sole, but the sure, immutable limits of our own.

As we have somewhat swerved from our leading subject to consider the nature of equality, let us again pause to consider that of liberty. We have seen that they are twin sisters; and so were they viewed by the effulgent mind of Jefferson, when from his fearless pen dropped the golden words. "All men are born free and equal." Those words his fellow citizens and descendants will have interpreted, when they shall have shed on the minds of the rising generation, and as far as possible on their own, the equal effulgence of just knowledge; before which every error in opinion and every vice in practice will fly as the noxious dews of night before the sun.

Let us, then, pause to consider these immortal words, graven by an immortal pen on the gates of time, "All men are born free and equal."

All men are born free and equal! That is: **our moral feelings acknowledge it to be just and proper, that we respect those liberties in other, which we lay claim to for ourselves; and that we permit the free agency of every individual, to any extent which violates not the free agency of his fellow creatures.**

There is but one honest limit to the rights of a sentient being; it is where they touch the rights of another sentient being. Do we exert our own liberties without injury to others--we exert them justly; do we exert them at the expense of others--unjustly. And, in thus doing, we step from the sure platform of liberty upon the uncertain threshold of tyranny. Small is the step; to the unreflecting so imperceptibly small, that they take it every hour of their lives as thoughtlessly as they do it unfeelingly. Whenever we slight, in word or deed, the feelings of a fellow creature; whenever, in pursuit our own individual interests, we sacrifice the interest of others; whenever, through our vanity or our selfishness, we interpret our interests unfairly, sink the rights of others in our own, arrogate authority, presume upon advantages of wealth, strength, situation, talent, or instruction; whenever we indulge idle curiosity respecting the private affairs, opinions, and actions of our neighbors; whenever, in short, we forget what in justice is due to others, and, equally, what in justice is due to ourselves, we sin against liberty--we pass from the rank of freemen to that of tyrants or slaves. Easy it were to enumerate the many laws by which, as citizens, we violated our common liberties; the many regulations, habits, practices, and opinions, by which, as human beings, we violate the same. Easy it were? Alas! and say I so? when to enumerate all these our sins against liberty, would be well nigh to enumerate all that we do, and feel, and think, and say! But let us confine ourselves within a familiar though most important example.

Who among us but has had occasion to remark the ill-judged, however well-intentioned government of children by their teachers; and, yet more especially, by their parents? In what does this mismanagement originate? In a misconception of the relative position of the parent or guardian, and of the child: in a departure, by the parent, from the principle of liberty, in his assumption of rights destructive of those of the child; in his exercise of authority, as by right divine, over the judgment, actions, and person of the child; in his forgetfulness of the character of the child, as a human being, born "free and equal" among his compeers; that is, having equal claims to the exercise and development of all his senses, faculties, and powers, with those who brought him into existence, and with all sentient beings who tread the earth. Were a child thus viewed by his parent, we should not see him, by turns, made a plaything and a slave; we should not see him commanded to believe, but encouraged to reason; we should not see him trembling under the rod, nor shrinking from a frown, but reading the wishes of others in the eye, gathering knowledge wherever he threw his glance, rejoicing in the present hour, and treasuring up sources of enjoyment for future years. We should not see him doubting at each emergency how to act, shifting his course with the shifting wind, and, at last, making shipwreck of mind and body on the sunken rocks of hazard and dishonest speculation, nor on the foul quicksands of debasing licentiousness.

What, then, has the parent to do, if he would conscientiously discharge that most sacred of all duties, that, weightiest of all responsibilities, which ever did or ever will devolve on a human being? What is he to do, who, having brought a creature into existence, endowed with varied faculties, with tender susceptibilities, capable of untold wretchedness or equally of unconceived enjoyment; what is he to do, that he may secure the happiness of that creature, and make the life he has given blessing and blessed, instead of cursing and cursed? What is he to do?--he is to encourage in his child a spirit of inquiry and equally to encourage it in himself. He is never to advance an opinion without showing the facts upon which it is grounded; he is never to assert a fact, without proving it to be a fact. He is not to teach a code of morals any more than a creed of doctrines; but he is to direct his young charge to observe the consequences of actions on himself and on others; and to judge of the propriety of those actions by their ascertained consequences. He is not to command his feelings any more than his opinions or his actions; but he is to assist him in the analysis of his feelings, in the examination of their nature, their tendencies, their effects. Let him do this, and have no anxiety for the result. In the free exercise of his senses, in the fair development of his faculties, in a course of simple and unrestrained facts; he will seize upon virtue, for he will have distinguished beneficial from injurious actions; he will cultivate kind, generous, just, and honorable feelings, for he will have proved them to contribute to his own happiness and to shed happiness around him.

Who, then, shall say, inquiry is good for him and not good for his children? Who shall cast error from himself, and allow it to be grafted on the minds he has called into being? Who shall break the chains of his own ignorance, and fix them, through his descendants, on his race? But, there are some, who, as parents, make one step in duty, and halt at the second. We see men who will aid the instruction of their sons, and condemn only their daughters to ignorance. "Our sons," they say, "will have to exercise political rights, may aspire to public offices, may fill some learned profession, may struggle for wealth and acquire it. It is well that we give them a helping hand; that we assist them to such knowledge as is going, and make them as sharp witted as their neighbors. But for our daughters," they say--if indeed respecting them they say anything--"for our daughters, little trouble or expense is necessary. They can never **be any thing**; in fact, they **are nothing**. We had best give them up to their mothers, who may take them to Sunday's preaching; and with the aid of a little music, a little dancing, and a few fine gowns, and fit them our for the market of marriage."

Am I severe? It is not my intention. I know that I am honest, and I fear that I am correct. Should I offend, however, I may regret, I shall nor repent it; satisfied to incur displeasure, so that I render service.

But to such parents I would observe, that with regard to their sons, as to their daughters, they are about equally mistaken. If it be their duty, as we have seen, to respect in their children the same natural liberties which they cherish for themselves--if it be their duty to aid as guides, not to dictate as teachers--to lend assistance to the reason, not to command its prostration,--then have they nothing to do with the blanks or the prizes in store for them, in the wheel of worldly fortune. Let possibilities be what they may in favor of their sons, they have no calculations to make on them. It is not for them to ordain their sons magistrates nor statesmen; nor yet even lawyers, physicians, or merchants. They have only to improve the one character which they receive at the birth. They have only to consider them as **human beings**, and to ensure them the fair and thorough development of all the faculties, physical, mental, and moral, which distinguish their nature. In like manner, as respects their daughters, they have nothing to do with the injustice of laws, nor the absurdities of society. Their duty is plain, evident, decided. In a daughter they have in charge a human being; in a son, the same. Let them train up these **human beings**, under the expanded wings of liberty. Let them seek **for** them and **with** them, just knowledge; encouraging, from the cradle upwards, that useful curiosity which will lead them unbidden in the paths of free inquiry; and place them, safe and superior to the storms of life, in the security of well-regulated, self-possessed minds, well-grounded, well-reasoned, conscientious opinions, an self-approved, consistent practice.

I have as yet, in this important matter, addressed myself only to the reason and moral feelings of my audience; I could speak also to their interests. Easy were it to show, that in proportion as your children are enlightened, will they prove blessings to society and ornaments to their race. But if this be true of all, it is more especially true of the now more neglected half of the species. Were it only in our power to enlighten part of the rising generation, and should the interests of the whole decide our choice of the portion, it were the females, and not the males, we should select.

When, now a twelvemonth since, the friends of liberty and science pointed out to me in London, the walls of their rising university, I observed, with a smile, that they were beginning at the wrong end: "Raise such an edifice for your young women, and ye have enlightened the nation." It has already been observed, that women, where placed, however high or low in the scale of cultivation, hold the destinies of humankind. Men will ever rise or fall to the level of the other sex; and from some causes in their conformation, we find them, however armed with power or enlightened with knowledge, still held in leading strings even by the least cultivated female. Surely, then, if they knew their interests, they would desire the improvement of those who, if they do not advantage, will injure them; who, if they elevate not their minds and meliorate not their hearts, will debase the one and harden the other; and who, if they endear not existence, most assuredly will dash it with poison. How many, how omnipotent are the interests which engage men to break the mental chains of women! How many, how dear are the interests which engage them to exalt rather than lower their condition, to multiply their solid acquirements, to respect their liberties, to make them their equals, to wish them even their superiors! Let them inquire into these things. Let them examine the relation in which the two sexes stand, and ever must stand, to each other. Let them perceive, that, mutually dependent, they must ever be giving and receiving, or they must be losing:--receiving or losing in knowledge, in virtue, in enjoyment. Let them perceive how immense the loss, or how immense the gain. Let them not imagine that they know aught of the delights which intercourse with the other sex can give, until they have felt the sympathy of mind with mind, and heart with heart; until they bring into that intercourse every affection, every talent, every confidence, every refinement, every respect. Until power is annihilated on one side, fear and obedience on the other , and both restored to their birthright--equality. Let none think that affection can reign without it; or friendship, or esteem. Jealousies, envyings, suspicions, reserves, deceptions--these are the fruits of inequality. Go, then! and remove the evil first from the minds of women, then form their condition, and then from your laws. Think it no longer indifferent whether the mothers of the rising generation are wise or foolish. Think it not indifferent whether your own companions are ignorant or enlightened. Think it not indifferent whether those who are to form the opinions, sway the habits, decide the destinies, of the species--and that not through their children only, but through their lovers and husband--are enlightened friends of capricious mistresses, efficient coadjutors or careless servants, reasoning beings or blind followers of superstition.

There is a vulgar persuasion, that the ignorance of women, by favoring their subordination, ensures their utility. 'Tis the same argument employed by the ruling few against the subject many in aristocracies; by the rich against the poor in democracies; by the learned professions against the people in all countries. And let us observe, that if good in one case, if should be good in all; and that, unless you are prepared to admit that you are yourselves less industrious in proportion to your intelligence, you must abandon the position with respect to others. But, in fact, who is it among men that best struggle with difficulties?--the strong-minded or the weak? Who meet with serenity adverse fortune?--the wise or the foolish? Who accommodate themselves to irremediable circumstances? or, when remediable, who control and mould them at will?--the intelligent or the ignorant? Let your answer in your own case, be your answer in that of women.

If the important inquiry which engaged our attention last evening was satisfactorily answered, is there one who can doubt the beneficial effects of knowledge upon every mind, upon every heart? Surely it must have been a misconception of the nature of knowledge which could alone bring it into suspicion. What is the danger of truth? Where is the danger of fact? Error and ignorance, indeed, are full of danger. They fill our imagination with terrors. They place us at the mercy of every external circumstance. They incapacitate us for our duties as members of the human family, for happiness as sentient beings, for improvement as reasoning beings. Let us awake from this illusion. Let us understand what knowledge is. Let us clearly perceive that accurate knowledge regards all equally; that truth, or fact, is the same thing for all humankind; that there are not truths for the rich and truths for the poor, truths for men and truths for women; there are simply **truths**, that is, **facts**, which all who open their eyes, and their ears, and their understandings can perceive. There is no mystery in these facts. There is no witchcraft in knowledge. Science is not a trick; not a puzzle. The philosopher is not a conjuror. The observer of nature who envelopes his discoveries in mystery, either knows less than he pretends, or feels interested in

withholding his knowledge. The teacher whose lessons are difficult of comprehension, is either clumsy or he is dishonest.

We observed, at our last meeting, that is was the evident interest of our appointed teachers to disguise the truth. We discovered this to be a matter of necessity, arising out of their dependence upon the public favor. We may observe yet another cause, now operating far and wide--universally, omnipotently--a cause pervading the whole mass of society, and springing out of the existing motive principle of human action--competition. Let us examine, and we shall discover it to be the object of each individual to obscure the first elements of the knowledge he professes--be that knowledge mechanical and operative, or intellectual and passive. It is thus that we see the simple manufacture of a pair of shoes magnified into an art, demanding a seven years' apprenticeship, when all its intricacies might be mastered in as many months. It is thus that cutting out a coat after just proportions is made to involve more science, and to demand more study, than the anatomy of the body it is to cover. And it is thus, in like manner, that all the branches of knowledge, involved in what is called scholastic learning, are wrapped in the fogs of pompous pedantry; and that every truth, instead of being presented in naked innocence, is obscured under a weight of elaborate words, and lost and buried in a medley of irrelevant ideas, useless amplifications, and erroneous arguments. Would we unravel this confusion--would we distinguish the true from the false, the real from the unreal, the useful from the useless--would we break our mental leading strings--would we know the uses of all our faculties--would we be virtuous, happy, and intelligent beings--would we be useful in our generation-- would we possess our own minds in peace, be secure in our opinions, be just in our feelings, be consistent in our practice--would we command the respect of others, and--far better--would we secure our own--let us inquire.

Let us inquire! What mighty consequences, are involved in these little words! Whither have they not led? To what are they not yet destined to lead? Before them thrones have given way. Hierarchies have fallen, dungeons have disclosed their secrets. Iron bars, and iron laws, and more iron prejudices, have given way; the prison house of the mind hath burst its fetters; science disclosed her treasures; truth her moral beauties: and civil liberty, sheathing her conquering sword, hath prepared her to sit down in peace at the feet of knowledge.

Let us inquire! oh, words fraught with good to man and terror to his oppressors! Oh words bearing glad tidings to the many and alarm only to the few! The monarch hears them, and trembles on his throne! The priest hears them, and trembles in the sanctuary; the unjust judge--and trembles on the judgment seat. The nations pronounce them and arise in their strength. Let us inquire; and behold, ignorance becomes wise, vice forsakes its errors, wretchedness conceives of comfort, and despair is visited by hope. Let us inquire! --when all shall whisper these little words, and echo them in their hearts, truly the rough places shall be made smooth, and the crooked paths straight. Let us inquire; and behold, no evil but shall find its remedy, no error but shall be detected, and no truth but shall stand revealed! Let us inquire! These little words, which presume in nothing, but which promise all things, what ear shall they offend? what imagination shall they affright? Not yours, sons of America! Not yours. What hold ye of good or great? what boast ye of rights, of privileges, of liberty, beyond the rest of the nations, that by inquiry hath not been won, by inquiry improved and protected? Let us inquire, said your ancestors when kingly and priestly tyranny smote them on the banks of the Thames or the Seine. Let us inquire, said your fathers, when imperious princes and arrogant parliaments questioned their charters and trampled on their rights. Let us inquire, said Henry, said Jefferson, said Franklin, said the people and congress of '76. Let us inquire; and behold, the inquiry gained to them and their descendants a country--lost to kings and their empires a world!

And shall the sons fear to pronounce, in peace, under the shadow of the olive and the laurel planted by their fathers--shall they, I say, fear to pronounce those little words which, by their ancestors, were uttered under ban and forfeiture, outlawry, and excommunication, in prison, and under scaffolds, before the bayonets of tyranny and the threatening thunders of leagued armies?

Or, is the race of human improvement ended, and the work of reform completed? Have we attained all truth, rectified all error, so that, sitting down in wisdom and perfection, we may say, "our duty is achieved, or destiny fulfilled?" Alas for our nature, alas for our condition, alas for reason and common sense, if such should be the answer of our presumption, such the decision of our ignorance! Where is the mind so vast, the imagination so sublime, that hath conceived the farthest limits of human improvement, or the utmost height to which human virtue may attain? Or, say! where is the heart so insensible, the mind so debased, that, looking abroad on the face of society, as now disfigured with vice, rapine, and wretchedness, can seriously think and feel farther inquiry superfluous, father reformation impossible?

Did the knowledge of each individual embrace all the discoveries made by science, all the truths extracted by philosophy from the combined experience of ages, still would inquiry be in its infancy, improvement in its dawn. Perfection for man is in no time, in no place. The law of his being, like that of the earth he inhabits, is **to move always, to stop never**. From the earliest annals of tradition, his movement has been in advance. The tide of his progress hath had ebbs and flows, but hath left a thousand marks by which to note its silent but tremendous influx.

The first observations of Indian and Egyptian astronomers; the first application of man to civil industry; the first associations of tribes and nations, for the purpose of mutual protection; the invention of an alphabet, the use of each ornamental, and, far better, of each useful art,--stand as so many tide-marks in the flood of recorded time, until, applying a lever to his own genius, man invented the printing press, and opened a first highway to inquiry. From that hour, his progress has been accelerating and accelerated. His strides have been those of a giant, and are those of a giant growing in strength. Mighty was the step he made, when, in Germany, he impeached the infallibility of Rome; mightier yet when, in England, he attacked the supremacy of kings; mightier by far, when appealing to his own natural rights, he planted in this new world the more new standard of equal liberty; and mightier still shall be his impulse in the onward career of endless improvement, when, rightly reading and justly executing his own decree, he shall extend to every son and daughter within the confines of these free states, liberty's first and only security--virtue's surest and only guide--national, rational, and equal education.

Something towards this has been done, and in no division of this promising republic more than in New England and the commonwealth of New York. But, as it may hereafter by my attempt to show, in the efforts yet made and making, the masterspring hath not been touched, the republican principle hath not been hit, and, therefore, is the reform imperfect.

If this be so--and who that looks abroad shall gainsay the assertion?--if this be so--and who that looks to your jails, to your penitentiaries, to your houses of refuge, to your hospitals, to your asylums, to your hovels of wretchedness, to your haunts of intemperance, to your victims lost in vice and hardened in profligacy, to childhood without protection, to youth without guidance, to the widow without sustenance, to the female destitute and female outcast, sentenced to shame and sold to degradation--who that looks to these shall say, that inquiry hath not a world to explore, and improvement yet a world to reform!

Let us inquire. Who, then, shall challenge the words? They are challenged. And by whom? By those who call themselves the guardians of morality, and who **are** the constituted guardians of religion. Inquiry, it seems, suits not them. They have drawn the line, beyond which human reason shall not pass--above which human virtue shall not aspire! All that is without their faith, or above their rule, is immorality, is atheism, is--I know not what.

My friends, I will ask you, as I would ask them would they meet the question, what means we possess for settling the point now at issue between the servants of faith and the advocates of knowledge, but what are supplied by inquiry?

Are we miserable creatures, innately and of necessity; placed on this earth by a being who should have made us for misery here and damnation hereafter; or are we born ductile as the gold and speckless as the mirror, capable of all inflection and impression which wise or unwise instruction may impart, or to which good or evil circumstance may incline? Are we helpless sinners, with nought but the anchor of faith to lean upon? Or are we creatures of noblest energies and sublimest capabilities, fitted for every deed of excellence, feeling of charity, and mode of enjoyment? How shall we know who hath the right and who hath the wrong but by inquiry? Surely the matter is not small, nor the stake at issue trifling. Every interest dearest to the heart, every prospect most exhilarating to the mind, is involved in the question and trembles on the decision.

Inquiry

Oh! then, let us gird up our minds in courage, and compose them in peace. Let us cast aside fear and suspicion, suspend our jealousies and disputes, acknowledge the rights of others and assert our own. And oh! let us understand that the first and noblest of these rights is, the cultivation of our reason. We have seen what just knowledge is; we have ascertained its importance to our worldly prosperity, to our happiness, to our dignity. We have seen, that it regards us, not only individually, but relatively and collectively. We have seen that to obtain it, we have but to seek it, patiently and fearlessly, in the road of inquiry; and that to tread that road pleasantly, securely, profitably, we must throw it open to both sexes--to all ages--to the whole family of humankind.

It now remains for us to distinguish what are the most important subjects of human inquiry. The field of knowledge is wide and the term of our existence short. With many of us life is considerably spent and much charged with worldly and domestic occupation. Still have we leisure sufficient, if we be willing to employ it, for the acquisition of such truths as are most immediately associated with our interests and influential over our happiness.

At our next meeting we shall inquire what these truths of primary importance are, together with the means now in your hands for their general distribution and popular acquisition.

Bibliography

Frances Wright

Primary Sources:

Drama:

Altorf, A Tragedy Philadelphia: R. Carey & Sons, 1819.

Books, Pamphlets, Speeches:

A Few Days in Athens. London: Longman, Hurst, Rees, Orms and Brown, 1822. 166 pp.

Views of Society and Manners in America in a Series of Letters from that Country to a Friend in England During the Years 1818, 1819 and 1820. London: Longman, Hurst, Rees, Orme, and Brown, 1822. German editions 1822,1824.

"Institution of Nashoba." **The Gleaner.** July 1828 :49-70.

"Address delivered at New Harmony Hall on 4th of July, 1828" in **The Disseminator,** vol.1, p.214.

"Address to the People of Philadelphia, at the Walnut Street Theater, 1829." New York: G.H. Evans. pp.15.

Course of Popular Lectures. New York: Office of Free Enquirer. 1829.

Introductory Address. Delivered at opening of the Hall of Science, April 26, 1829. New York; George Evans, printer, 1829. 18 pp.

Address on the State of the Public Mind. New York: Office of the Free Enquirer, 1829.

A Lecture on Existing Evils and Their Remedy in Philadelphia, June 2, New York: G.H. Evans, 1829. 16 pp.

Address, Containing a Review of the Times, May 9. New York: Office of the Free Enquirer, 1830. pp.20.

An Address to the Industrious Classes. New York: Office of the Free Enquirer, 1830.

Fables. New York: Office of the Free Enquirer, 1830. 20 pp.

Fanny Wright Unmasked by her Own Pen. Printed for Purchasers. 1830 (about Nashoba) pp.16.

The New Book of Chronicles (as rendered from the original Hebrew, by a learned Rabbi) New York:Office of Free Enquirer, 1830.

Parting Address, June. New York: Office of the Free Enquirer, 1830. 22 pp.

Supplement: Course of Lectures. Containing the last four lectures delivered in the United States, 1835.

What is the Matter; A political Address as delivered in Masonic Hall, Oct. 28th, 1838. Published by the author. 21 pp.

Tracts on Republican Government and National Education, J. Watson, 1843.

England the Civilizer: Her History Developed in its Principles; with reference to the Civilizational History of Modern Europe. London: Simpkin, Marshall, 1848. 470 pp.

Biography, Notes, and Political Letters of Frances Wright D'Arusmont. Dundee, Scotland: J. Myles 1844, New York: J. Windt, 1844 in 2 vols., Boston: J.P.Mendun, 1848,1849.

Life, Letters and Lectures:1834-1844. New York: Arno Press ,1972.

New Harmony's Fourth of July Tradition: Speeches of Robert Owen, William Owen, Frances Wright, Raintree Books, 1976.

(Authorship Uncertain, sometimes attributed to Frances Wright **Xerxes the Great** in 5 Acts. Phila: G.Palmer, 1815).

Newspapers edited:

255

The New Harmony and Nashoba Gazette. 1828.

The Free Enquirer. 1828-32.

The Boston Investigator. 1836.

Manual of American Principles. vol.I,1-7. 1837.

Letter:
To Mary Wollstonecraft Shelley, Paris, July 15,1827.1
Houghton Archives, Harvard University

Secondary Sources:

Almond, Brenda. "Women's Right: Reflections on Ethics and Gender." **Feminist Perspectives in Philosophy.** Editors Morweena Griffiths and Margaret Whitford. Bloomington: Indiana U P, 1988.

Anthony, Katherine. "Frances Wright." **Dictionary of American Biography**. New York: Charles Smith, 1936:549-50.

-------."Frances Wright" 549-50. **Biography of Ancient and Modern Celebrated Free Thinkers**, 1958.

Bartlett, Elizabeth Ann ed. **Sarah Grimke:Letters on the Equality of the Sexes and Other Essays** 1838. New Haven: Yale UP, 1988.

Boyer, Paul S. "Frances Wright." **Notable American Women**. Editors Edward T.James et.al.Cambridge, Mass: Belknap, 1971:675-680.

Brown, Anna B.A. "Dream of Emancipation." **New England Magazine** vol.38 494-498.

Cameron, Kenneth Walter, **Philothea...by Lydia Maria Child**, Hartford: Transcendental Books, 1975.

Coleman, McAlister. **Pioneers of Freedom** (1929). New York: Liberty Press, 1968.

Cott, Nancy F. **The Bonds of Womanhood: "Woman's Sphere in New England, 1780-1835**. New Haven: Yale UP, 1977.

Donovan, Josephine. **Feminist Theory.** New York: Frederick Unger, 1985.

Earnest, Ernest. **The American Eve in Fact and Fiction 1775-1914.** Chicago: University of Illinois Press, 1974.

Eckhardt, Celia Morris. **Fanny Wright, Rebel in America.** London: Harvard U P, 1984.

Ellis, G.E. "Characteristics of Modern Fidelity"(Frances Wright Darusmont, her Character and Projects). **Christian Examiner.** 17(September 1834):23 & 33.

Emerson, O.B. "Frances Wright and Her Nashoba Experiment," **Tennessee Historical Quarterly** (1947):41-52.

Everett, E. "Mrs. Frances Wright: Society and Manners of America." **North American Review.** 9(January 1822):15-26.

Garnett, Richard. "Frances Darusmont": 521-22. **The Dictionary of National Biography.** vol.V. Editors Leslie Stephen & Sidney Lee. London: Oxford UP,1959-60.

Gilbert, Amos. **Memoir of Frances Wright.** Cincinnati: Longman,1855.

Gilman, Charlotte Perkins. **Herland** (1915). New York: Pantheon, 1979.

Hale, Sarah Josepha. "Frances Darusmont"342-43. **Women's Record.** New York: Harper and Bros., 1876.

Hammerton, Sir J.A. **Concise Universal Biography.** vol.3, London: Educational Book (1934-35) 1975.

Heineman, Helen. **Restless Angels: The Friendship of Six Victorian Women.** Athens, Ohio: Ohio U P, 1983.

------. **Frances Trollope.** Boston: Twayne, 1984.

Hill, Bridget. **Women, Work, and Sexual Politics in Eighteenth-Century England.** Oxford: Basil Blackwell, 1989.

Holbrook, Stewart H. **Dreamers of the American Dream**. Garden City, New York: Doubleday, 1957:169-175.

Holland, F.M. "Frances Wright." **The Open Court**. 9(5 September 1895):4623-34.

Kolmerton, Carol A. "Frances Wright." **American Women Writers.** Ed.Lina Mainero. New York: Frederick Unger,1979:548-60.

Kristeva, Julia. "Woman's Time." **Feminist Theory**. Editors Nannerl O. Keohane et.al, Sussex, England: Harvester Press, 1982.

Lane, Margaret. **Frances Wright and the `Great Experiment'**. Manchester, England: Manchester UP, 1972.

Lasser, Carol & Marlene Deahl Merrill. **Friends & Sisters: Letters.** Urbana: Univ. of Ill. Press, 1982.

Lee, Elizabeth. "Frances Wright, the First Woman Lecturer." **Gentleman's Magazine.** May 1894:518-28.

Leopold, Richard William. **Robert Dale Owen**. Cambridge: Harvard UP,1940.

Lerner, Gerda. **The Grimke Sisters from South Carolina**. New York: Schocken, 1971.

Letwin, Shirley Robin. **The Pursuit of Certainty**. England: Cambridge UP, 1965.

Maxwell, Alice S. **Virago! The Story of Anne Newport Royall** (1769-1854) London: McFarland, 1985.

Nye, Andrea. **Feminist Theory and the Philosophy of Man**. London: Croom Helm, 1988.

O'Connor, Lillian. **Pioneer Women Orators.** New York:Columbia U. P., 1954.

Oliver, Robert T. **Public Speaking in Re-Shaping of Great Britain.** Newark: University of Delaware, 1987.

Owen, Robert Dale. "Frances Wright, General Lafayette, and Mary Wollstonecraft Shelley: A Chapter of Autobiography" **Atlantic Monthly** 192 (October

1873) 448-59.

------. **Threading My Way**. 1874. New York: Augustus M. Kelley, 1967.

Palmer, Phyliss M. "Frances Wright" Thesis, University of Indiana, 1973.

Pancost, Elinor and Anne E. Lincoln. **The Incorrigible Idealist**. Bloomington: Principia, 1940.

Perkins, A.J.G. and Theresa Wolfson. **Frances Wright: Free Enquirer.** London: Harper & Harper, 1939.

Riegel, Robert E. **American Feminists** Lawrence: University of Kansas, 1963.

Riley, Woodbridge. **American Thought.** New York: Henry Holt, 1915.

Rossi, Alice S. **The Feminist Papers: Adams to de Beauvoir.** N.Y. & London: Columbia U. P., 1973.

Rutherford, V. "A Study of the Speaking Career of Frances Wright in America." Dissertation, Northwestern University, 1960.

Schlesinger, Arthur Jr. **The Age of Jackson.** Boston: Little, Brown, 1946.

Schneider, Herbert W. **A History of American Philosophy**. New York: Columbia UP, 1963.

Sinclair, Andrew. **The Emancipation of the American Women.** New York: Harper, 1965.

Stephen, Leslie. **The English Utilitarians.** 1900 New York: Peter Smith, 1950.

Trollope, Francis Milton. **Domestic Manners of the Americans.** 2 vols. London(1832). Barre, Mass.:Imprint Society, 1969.

Waterman, William Randall. **Frances Wright** Diss. New York: Columbia U.P.,1924. (in **Studies in History, Economics, and Public Law** Vol.CXV).

Webster, Noah (Dectector). **Connecticut Herald**. New Haven (16 January 1838):3.

Wilson, Howard A. "Growing Up With a Past." **Yale Review** (Summer 1977)
628-40.

Wolloch, Nancy. **Women and the American Experience**. New York: Alfred A.
Knopf, 1984.

Woodward, Helen Beal. **The Bold Women**. New York: Farrar, Straus and
Young, 1953:24-52.

Ednah Dow Cheney
Reminiscences, 1902

Chronology

Ednah Dow Cheney 1824-1904

1824 Born, June 27 third child of Ednah Dow and Sargent Littlehale.

1837 Corresponds with Caroline Wells Healy on feminist issues.

1840 Attends "Conversations" with Margaret Fuller.
Attends Bronson Alcott's "Conversations."

1844 Ends Fuller's "Conversations."

1845 Meets Julia Ward Howe at meeting with Theodore Parker.

1848 Attends Bronson Alcott's "Conversations" for a second time.

1850 Father dies.
Ednah contracts typhoid fever.
Reads Plato with Ariana Smith Walker [(Anna)Sanborn].

1851 Helps found School of Design.

1853 Marries Seth Cheney.

1854 Sails for Liverpool Aug.2 for European trip together.
Seth completes portrait of her.

1855 Daughter Margaret born September 8.

1856 Husband dies.
Writes "Lesties'Handbook of Art" for **The North American Review**
(July).

1859 Aids in establishing New England Hospital for Women and
Children and takes position on its board.
Writes "The Life and Poems of Michael Angelo" **The North American
Review** (July).

1860 Takes part in women's rights convention.

1861   Begins to take active part in ministering to Black
soldiers of Civil War at Readville.

1863   Becomes Secretary of Teachers Committee of Freedman's Aid
Society.

1865   Calls roll when soldiers returned from the war.
Attends Freedman's Society Convention in New York.

1867   Writes review of Dr. Anton Heinrich Springer's history, published in
German, for **The Christian Examiner** (Sept.).

1868   Assists in founding New England Women's Club.
Writes "Art and Religion" for **The Radical** (July).
Writes "Vittoria Colonna" for **The Christian Examiner** (Jan.).

1869   "The Hope of the South" (1869):24.
Aids in founding the Horticultural School for Women.
Visits Freedman's schools in the South.
Writes "Hope of the South" for **The Christian Examiner** (Nov.).

1870   Submits "Special Report of the Commissioners of Education" to House of
Representatives,January 19.
Reads essay"The Value of Individuality in the Church and
State" at the Radical Club in Boston, April.

1871   Writes **Faithful**, **Social Games**,
For **The Radical** writes:
       "Value of Individuality to Church and State" (Feb.).
       "The Next Step in Popular Education (Aug.).
Lectures on horticulture before Massachusetts State
Agricultural Society.

1872   Contributes articles to **The Index** (1872 to 1882).
Writes **Sally Williams**.
Joins American Association for the Advancement of Women.
Delivers course of lectures on English literature at
Institute of Technology.

1874   Writes **Child of our Time**.
Writes "Child, Relations to the Home" for **Unitarian Review** (June).

1875　Writes **Biography of Susan Dimmock**, surgeon; **Patience**
Visits with Maria Mitchell of Vassar.

1876　Mother dies.

1877-78 Tours Europe with daughter.

1879　Lectures on "Art" at Concord School of Philosophy "Art".
Vice-president of Mass. School Suffrage Association.

1880　Lectures on "Color" and "Early American Art" at Concord.

1881　**Gleanings** published, "Women of Boston" essay published.
Memoirs of Seth Cheney, Artist published.
Poem "Apple Blossoms" published in Free Religious Association
pamphlet.

1882　Travels to California, Montreal.
Concord School of Philosophy "Nature" lecture.
Daughter Margaret "Daisy" dies.

1884　"Emerson and Boston" lecture.

1885　**Selected Poems of Michael Angelo** published. Reviewed.

1886　"Das Ewig Weibliche," Goethe essay published in F.B.
Sanborn's **The Life and Genius of Goethe.**

1888　**Poems By David A. Wasson** and **Louisa M. Alcott, the
Children's Friend** published.

1887-1902 President of New England Women's Hospital.

1888　"Conversations of A. Bronson Alcott" **Open Court** August.

1889　**Memoirs of John Cheney** and **Memoir of Margaret S. Cheney**
published.
Edits with memoir **Poems of Harriet Winslow Sewall**.
Attends Lake Mohonk Negro Conference.

1890   **Stories of Olden Time** published.   "The Mohonk Conference and the
       Education of Negroes" **Open Court** July.
       "Dramatic Poem by Ibsen" **Open Court** October.

1891   "The Mayflower" **Open Court** March.
       "Religious Prospects of Italy" **Open Court** July.

1892   **Life of Christian Daniel Rauch** published.

1893   **Memoirs of Lucretia Crocker and Abbey May**.

1895   Writes "Association for Advancement of Woman" for **Open
       Court** January.

1899   **Louisa M. Alcott, Life and Letters** published.

1900   **The Story of the Alcotts** published.
       "Lucretia Mott" address before Free Religious Association, Boston.

1901   Has her letter read at commemoration of Margaret Fuller on Fire Island.

1902   **Reminiscences** published.
       "Sketch of Dr. Zakrzewska's Life" **Open Court** July.

1903   Speaks on psychology at revival of Concord School.

1904   Dies 18 November at eighty years old.

6

Ednah Dow Cheney

1824-1904

A renaissance woman in the nineteenth century, Ednah Dow Cheney is unknown to present scholars; she does not exist in the roll calls of any scholarly tradition. She is buried in forgotten journals, in unread books, and in the correspondence of many: the transcendentalists, the suffragists, the abolitionists, artists, poets, educators, the religious, and all sorts of humanitarians. A practical philosopher as well as a theoretical one, Cheney not only wrote and taught philosophy, she lived it and nurtured it in the world around her. As an activist she was a religious Frances Wright bringing quiet fulfillment to Judith Sargent Murray's hopes. As a thinker she was both Mercy Otis Warren and Margaret Fuller's descendent. Hence, her life, which spanned nearly the same years as Queen Victoria's, can be characterized as one of both contemplation and service.

Cheney first demonstrated her activist nature when in grammar school she petitioned "for the privilege of Christmas," which was not yet an established national holiday as a day of vacation from school. A different choice of grammar schools might have made Cheney "a better scholar, but...(she would) not have developed so well...independence of thought" (Reminiscences 21). Nevertheless, she attended the best schools in Boston, the Pembertons' school and the Mt. Vernon school of Joseph Hale Abbot. Cheney's formal schooling ended at fifteen, at which time she said "So much for school days; now for education" (21). And so with anticipation, Cheney went on to attend the Conversations of Margaret Fuller, where at sixteen she was the youngest member. Before beginning those sessions,

Cheney, then Ednah Dow Littlehale, traveled with her father Sargent Littlehale, her mother Ednah Dow and her older sister to visit the northeastern states, Montreal and Quebec, returning in time to join in the 1840 Bunker Hill Monument celebration. The Littlehales were a close, comfortable family. Cheney's father, a Gloucester Universalist, Cheney, herself, became a Unitarian particularly drawn to Theodore Parker, a Unitarian transendentalist.

In addition to attending Fuller's classes for three years, Ednah attended the Conversations of Bronson Alcott. Alcott, who lectured on Pythagoras, Plotinus and Plato, claimed Cheney to be his best pupil in the Plato class. It was between the years 1840 and 1850 that Cheney, though at first skeptical, embraced transcendentalism.

Among the subjects of Cheney's wide reading were Plutarch, Homer, Locke, Brown, Stewart, Reid, Sismondi, Machiavelli, Schiller, and the historians Gibbon, Bulwer and Michelet. She, herself, lectured on Michelangelo and Goethe as poets, the playwrights Ford and Massinger, and the subjects nature and transcendentalism. Early on she wrote critiques of Henry Norman Hudson's lectures on Shakespeare for the **Boston Transcript**. As an aged woman, Cheney became "enamored of mental philosophy" or psychology, and, lectured on the subject at the revival of the Concord School of Philosophy in 1903 (Memorial 10). Cheney's advice about what to study, when asked by a young girl, was to encourage her to "learn to record...the processes of reasoning" and to investigate five subject matters: natural science, history ("history is philosophy teaching by examples"), mental philosophy, language and mathematics (Memorial 8-10).

In her memoirs, Cheney makes the point, that having once mastered Lindley Murray's grammar, she was brought to the conclusion that analysis of language and practice in defining were of great importance to any scholarship, hers in particular. Fluent in several languages, she comments that in reading **Paul et Virginie** to her grandmother, she translated from the French as she read; with friends she read Dante and other works in Italian. For her work on Goethe and on Springer's history, she translated from German.

Having been subjected to a variety of methods of argument in the company of Fuller, Alcott, Emerson and Parker among others, and having acknowledged the benefits of each in particular, Cheney adopted a pluralistic philosophy and a liberal point of view. Yet for new students, she recommended the conservative benefits of reading Locke, which are: his clear and consistent reasoning, his dryness and hardness, and his search into the laws of thought. She sees him as a good foundation for studying both the idealist and the sensationalist philosophers.

Like other transcendentalists, Cheney evolved her own unique philosophical perspective, method and interests. As Margaret Fuller developed a particular interest in music and Emerson in the art of writing, Cheney focused on painting and sculpture. Art was a subject of Cheney's writing. She was a friend of American artists Washington Allston and his only student Sarah Freeman Clarke. As Ednah Dow Littlehale she married the celebrated engraver, Seth Cheney. Their trip to Europe subsequent to the marriage encompassed meeting artists and visiting art galleries.

The following year an only daughter, Margaret Swan, named after several ancestral Margarets, and perhaps, Margaret Fuller, was born. Before the infant Margaret was a year old, Seth died.[1] Margaret grew up to attend Massachusetts Institute of Technology, and was on her way to becoming an important scientist when she died at age twenty-six, a victim of cholera.[2] What is significant is that, with both an artist and a scientist in her life, Cheney became aware of the relationships between the two apparently disparate kinds of study.

Activist

The tragedies in Cheney's life seem to have inspired her to more rather than less work. She wrote about and worked for improvement in women's education. Through Dr. Maria Zakrzewska in 1859 Cheney developed an interest in women's medical education. She succeeded Lucy Goddard as president of the New England Hospital for women and children in Boston. She helped found a school of design in 1851 which she hoped would allow women to become economically self-sufficient. She was a leader in founding a horticultural school for girls and the Girl's Latin School.

She also administered improvements in the education of Afro-Americans. She herself went to Readville, the encampment of the first Afro-American recruits for the Civil War, where she taught reading. She directed the Freedman Schools set up after the Civil War, making trips to the South to ensure their continuance.

She presented in-depth reports on education to the Massachusetts House of Representatives.

Cheney's educational projects were generally associated with the social and ethical issues of slavery and women's status. An intimate friend of Harriet Jacobs and Harriet Tubman as well as of Booker T. Washington, she often referred to the words of Frederick Douglass. It was Ednah Dow Cheney who stood beside Lt. Shaw's proud mother when the Black Regiment left for the Civil War, and it was she who called the diminished roll when the Black Regiment returned to Boston at the close of the war. Her pamphlets on suffrage were thought by some to be the most well written. In England she sat in the women's caged gallery at Parliament to listen to William Lloyd Garrison.

Cheney's interest in continuing education for adults led to her becoming a founding member of the New England Women's Club, where she was instrumental in instituting lecture series and a spirit of comradery, or what would now be called "networking."[3] As a member she often presented lectures; the list of both member and invited lecturers is a roster of the best minds in the New England area at the time (Sprague, see Index). She often wrote commentaries for **The Woman's Journal.**

An inspiration and friend to her contemporary women, Cheney wrote biographies that demonstrate the many women she felt deserved to be memorialized: Louisa May Alcott, author; Susan Dimmock, physician; Abby May, president of the Horticulture School for Women; Lucretia Mott, chairman of the mathematics department at Antioch College; Harriet Winslow Sewell, who had in turn collected the letters of Lydia Maria Child. Like Judith Sargent Murray, Cheney met the need women had to be acknowledged and also to be preserved for the legacy of all future women. Above all else, Cheney believed that the "emancipation of women has especially marked the nineteenth century. It is the most important and far reaching reform of the world"(168).

A woman of her age, Cheney was nevertheless an independent leader. Director in 1867 of the newly formed "Free Religious Association," she recruited speakers, and she herself occasionally preached at various churches at a time when few women held such privilege. She lectured on religion and individualism at the Radical Club in Boston, and published articles on ethics and other subjects related to religion. Her knowledge of various religions was broad, and her pluralistic views appear refreshingly modern. She wrote extensively for **The Index** (over 100 articles), **The Christian Examiner**, and other journals which supported a pluralistic approach to religion.

Scholar

Cheney at fifty was invited to be on the first faculty of the Concord School of Philosophy, its only woman. Although she continued to lecture for the school for nearly ten years, she was more than modest about it, "I had the painful feeling that I owed this invitation rather to the wish to do honor to women by giving them an equal position than to my own individual merits...it was my duty to appear as a representative woman and do the best I could." Over those years, she lectured with Alcott, Emerson, Elizabeth P. Peabody, William Torrey Harris and Julia Ward Howe among others. On her fiftieth birthday, when she was beginning her professorial career, Howe wrote a poem to Cheney with these apt lines:

Throned in philosophic ease,
Yet her heart its errand sees,
Near to human miseries.(235)

Cheney's lectures, beginning with a series on art and continuing on such topics as the relation of poetry to science, were often quoted and commented upon in the Boston papers. When nearly seventy-seven, she returned to lecture at a one day revival celebration of the school in 1903.

All through her life, Cheney authored books and articles. Her first book was a handbook for the Freedman's schools. She also wrote books of games for hospital patients, books for children, memoirs and biographies, poems, a sequel to Ibsen's **A Doll's House**, translations of Michelangelo's poetry, edited collections of David Atwood Wasson's and Harriet Winslow Sewell's poems, and authored books on art, most importantly the **Life of Christian Daniel Rauch**, a sculptor, and her own **Gleanings in the Field of Art**.[4] In addition to her articles in **The Woman's Journal** and other newspapers, Cheney wrote for the philosopher Paul Carus's **Open Court**.

Cheney's contributions to periodicals are philosophically consistent with her vision of the world and her method of exploring what she knew of it. "Clearness of

271

mind" is often attributed to her. Clearness is also attributable to her style, both in its artistic attention to concrete detail and in its systematic presentation of thought.

Assessment

Cheney's funeral service was referred to as being "more like a coronation than a funeral" by Alice Stone Blackwell in her obituary in **The Woman's Journal**. In that same paper Julia Ward Howe wrote that she was "a presence truly august and venerable."[5] In a memorial service for Cheney at the Women's Club of New England other accolades were given. For F.B. Sanborn she was a person of "philosophic character and culture" who "constantly looked at the problems of life in the genuine philosophic light" and who "put her theories of life in practice" (Memorial 6-11); for Eva Channing, Cheney was "herself so much greater than anything she wrote"(22).[6] A modern biographer saw her in the less flattering light as "social annotator and reformer" with a direct writing style that exhibited no "perceptual brilliance" (Kunitz 145). Alice Stone Blackwell related that her father Henry Blackwell fell in love with Cheney, never having met her, from reading her anti-slavery papers (Memorial 20). William Lloyd Garrison called Cheney "foremost among the leaders" (15). Harriet W. Sewall wrote a verse in Cheney's honor that praises the persuasiveness of her voice, her "candor, tolerance, freedom from pretenses" (Reminiscences 236). A present day scholar wrote of Cheney's life as being a "continuity between transcendentalism and good works" (Shakir 95). A recent assessment of Cheney's life:

> Ednah Dow Cheney has blessed the young with stories, and used
> her pen in the service of art and humanity, till one is at a loss
> whether to place her with reformers, artists, teachers, or literary
> women (Pearson 4).

People's words often illuminating their own character, Cheney's words are insightful. Contemplating in 1867 the history of her day Cheney wrote,

> With the dead weight of slavery lifted from our young energies,
> what giant strides may we not take in the march of humanity! Now
> we may turn, conscience free, to the great questions which the
> intellect presses upon us.... Universal suffrage, education for all, the
> right to existence guaranteed by the state, the harmony of capital

and labor, the advancement of science, the development of art,--all these grand problems may justly claim our attention; and we see that our era of revolutions still remains to be accomplished, not, we trust, by the sword, but by patient labor, and fidelity to truth (Springer's 175).

Thus, with a renaissance vitality did Ednah Dow Cheney write and work to confront these "grand problems" of her century and ours.

Endnotes

1 The marriage was a happy one; Seth was influenced by the example of his own father who unlike many nineteenth century men helped in every aspect with the children and who said: "God forbid that a woman should hold her peace because she is a woman. Methinks the apostle meant no such thing, but meant that they should let their light shine before men." (A C518-Seth's handwritten Memoirs-Schlesinger Library)

2 Had Margaret Swan Cheney lived, she would have been MIT's second woman receiving a degree. A room for women still exists at MIT in her name. Because women were not allowed to use the laboratories until 1876, much of women's lab work at that time had to be done in private.

3 In her widowhood "devoted not to weeds but to reform," she was present in 1868 at the house of Dr. Harriet Hunt when the New England Women's Club was instituted initiating the Women's Club Movement.(Pearson 3-4).

4 This 1890 publication, **Nora's Return** counters a sequel by Walter Besant in **Macmillan's Magazine.** Through chronological diary entries Nora and Helmar tell the story. Nora is accepted at nurse's training school, where she learns to speak and live the truth, and to make mistakes: "I am learning to know myself"(30). Meanwhile Helmar reads Plato for inspiration. In helping with the cholera epidemic, he succumbs to the disease. When Nora is nursing in a hospital, she finds her patient to be Helmar whom she brings back to health, but leaves before he finds out it was her. She is offered the position of superintendent of nurses, but rejects it when during her first visit to see children (New Year's Day), she finds in her room symbols for her . personhood: a bank book, keys, a watch, books and artworks.

5 Julia Ward Howe and Ednah Dow Cheney were best friends. They met in the study of Theodore Parker, attended Margaret Fuller's Conversations at Elizabeth Peabody's book shop and taught at Concord together. Howe comments on the beautiful Cheney silks and laces Cheney wore, even though dress meant little to her, and the long distant trips they took by train.
(Cheney delivered the eulogy at the memorial service for Elizabeth Peabody and wrote her tribute as well in **The Women's Journal** 20 January 1894).

6 Among others who commented at the memorial were Colonel Thomas W. Higginson, Caroline Severance, Lucia M. Peabody and among the epithets were "exemplar," "heirloom to children's children," "a link connecting us with that unfinished career of Margaret Fuller."

Introduction to "Art"

The first chapter of Ednah Dow Cheney's **Gleanings in the Fields of Art** is an essay on art. When Cheney developed her aesthetics, outlined mainly in this chapter, Boston was not a haven for artists, but it was beginning to acknowledge its own artists.[1] John Singleton Copley, John Singer Sargent, Gilbert Stuart, Thomas Sully, William Page, Richard Greenough, John and Seth Cheney, Washington Allston and Sarah Freeman Clarke were painters, sculptors and engravers who had made or were making their marks of achievement. Even with these superior talents, some Europeans found American artists to possess a "genius for mediocrity."[2] Boston's Quincy Market building (1832-) announced a classic revival in architecture, and New York City's St. Patrick's Cathedral (1853-88) evidenced a gothic revival. Still, nineteenth century progress in art was hindered by lack of instruction and interrupted by a Civil War. Nonetheless, America was in a dawn of interest in its own art and in its own artists by the late nineteenth century.[3]

Aesthetics, a discipline named by the German Alexander Gottlieb Baumgarten, nevertheless had a history prior to his eighteenth century. One preoccupation of aesthetical issues from the Pre-Socratics forward was the concept of beauty. For Democritus beauty was inspired by divine reason, and for Pythagoras beauty meant harmony. Aristotle, Plato, Plotinus and philosophers throughout history, have discussed the philosophy of art or aesthetics, and in doing so have examined such notions as imitation, nature and imagination. Other notions have entered the discussion as various subject matters, terms and methods evolved over the history of the philosophical discourse about art.

Ednah Dow Cheney was one of our most educated women in art in her time both in terms of study and experience. Familiar with the aesthetics of Michelangelo, Goethe and Hegel as well as with American transcendentalist perspective, Cheney also read and wrote on current philosophy of art education and art criticism. The subject of an engraving by her husband Seth, and of a line drawing by Allston, Cheney had closely observed the artist at work. Having journeyed to Europe on three occasions, she was acquainted with original works of art first hand at galleries and met with artists from France's Rosa Bonheur to

275

Scotland's David Scott. A student of both western and eastern philosophy and religion, and a student of both art and science, Cheney brought an eclectic approach to art theory.

Unlike other transcendentalists, in particular Emerson, Cheney developed her aesthetics specifically as an aesthetics of art, rather than of poetry or music.[4] The uniqueness of her aesthetics theory is determined in part by her analytical method and in part by her world view. Because Cheney's terminology is often similar to Emerson's, it would appear that her ideas would be similar as well, but they differ.

Emerson defined art broadly as "thought which...is good" (Nature 239) and beautiful; by good and beautiful he meant "alive, moving, reproductive" whether in "an oration, a statue, or a picture (248-49)".[5] When the essence of art is "thought," art is dependent upon the artist's power of insight into the object, a power which magnifies by detaching the "one" from the variety--its aim being to create a oneness, a whole again. Because art in this manner is always "flowing," being ever created from old into new into the old again, and one form and another into "oneness," it is ever in its "oneness" universal. Art, originating in the thought of nature, is nature's sequel, and in its creation as it becomes one, becomes one with nature. Thus art "flows" in a circular path, eventually coming full circle.[6]

Emerson was part of the milieu in which thinking about the fine arts in nineteenth century New England emerged. His intuitive method, however, was not shared by Cheney. Instead, Cheney dissects the layers of aesthetic issues, differentiating as she proceeds. Art is not thought in motion, or thought metamorphosed, but rather static phenomena which allows for exposition of its dichotomies: thought and non-thought, unity and difference, universal and individual. Because Cheney had shared in both the art world of her husband and in the scientific world of her daughter, it was possible for her to suit a "material" or scientific method to a "spiritual" subject matter. It was not the rivalry between the disciplines but rather their compatibility that Cheney witnessed and adopted.

Cheney had already at an early age sought to bring together disparate experiences. Hence, Cheney's aesthetic sense is consistent with her thinking about science and poetry, and about God and the universe. For Cheney, all is duality. Unlike Emerson, Cheney saw art not as one, but as two. The ultimate mystery of the one is not denied, but the reality of two is affirmed. God is "male and female," religion is "center and circumference" science is "observation and theory"; "poetry is thought and expression."[7]   There is science in poetry and poetry in science for both involve truth and fancy--"every great discovery has been anticipated by the imaginative mind before science was ready for it" (Scrapbook 1881). As poetry and science are dual in nature and dual parts of each other, art is not separate from nature but is nature and not-nature.

From the duality of God as divine woman and divine man comes all being, and all being is also dual.   Art represents, therefore, the eternal marriage: the masculine divinity, the feminine divinity, God-giving, God-receiving.   The one, the two, the resulting multiplicity, all must be recognized (Art and Religion 3).[8]   Thus art is both spirit and "subordinated" but "wholly recognized" matter, the one **and** the many, transcendent and non-transcendent.[9]

Hence, Cheney, a person of her time and place, is a transcendental aesthetician, but because of her unique method and emphasis, she might be called a renaissance-transcendentalist. Her emphasis on the province of art as being human means that the "spiritual truth" which co-exists in matter is not only thought but feeling.   That Cheney's "thought" includes "feeling" is perhaps indicative of her interest in "mental philosophy," nevertheless, it is not Benedetto Croce's "intense feeling"(Guide 25) but something different.[10]

Art as thought and feeling expresses the human soul and forms new spirit by awakening and expanding the soul through the imagination.   Thus art becomes us when we have in turn fitted our soul to receive it, and we become more fully human.   Rather than intuit, we prepare through the evolution and development of our human capabilities.   Eventually we become capable of discovering through analysis the relationships of the proportions, the "thought in a material form." Hence Cheney's philosophy submits the spiritual to the microscope of individuality as well as to the telescope of relationship.

Although art has an ethical nature, art is no more an ethics than it is a philosophy or a science.   In an essay on "Art and Religion," Cheney explains that it is the "corrective" nature of art to hold in balance the "two tendencies" of materiality and spirituality, as well as to prevent the possibility of "absorption in unity"(2).[11] As these tendencies must be checked in art, so too, the artist needs the "answering corrective of a free intellectual culture"(3).[12]

In the tradition of Michelangelo and Goethe, Cheney concedes the method of science in art in, for example, the materiality of color and anatomy;[13] in the tradition of Hegel, life itself is not art, the subject matter of art is "living thought," art being the most distinctly human discipline. Art is not, as it is for Emerson, a sequel to nature, but rather with humanity in its composite of nature and not-nature, art is consequent to human history and culture.

Art in Cheney's aesthetics is the "thought" in a material form, necessarily of and affected by a particular time and place. In Cheney's theory of aesthetics, art being a synthesis of opposites demands an analytical method to discover that dual nature. From the balance in its duality comes its ethical nature. Only through historical as well as natural realism is achievement of the highest "ideal" duality possible. This achieved "ideal" in art is capable of being appreciated insofar as the receiver is prepared to perceive it.

Cheney's aesthetics is important: it is the first aesthetics formulated by a woman in nineteenth century America; and it is the first aesthetics of our national character. Whether or not it has been considered as part of the canon, its unique transcendentalism enlarges the aesthetics of art tradition. That it was written at all, is our good fortune; that it become part of the canon of American aesthetics will be our gain.[14]

*Footnotes in following selection are added to the original work.

Endnotes

[1] Herbert Schneider claimed in his **History of American Philosophy** (New York: Columbia UP, 1963) "there is relatively little about American aesthetics...I have the impression, perhaps erroneous, that until the twentieth-century philosophies of the fine arts and natural sciences followed much the same lines as they did in Europe, and that therefore an American history would have little novelty or interest. This situation has certainly changed recently and future historians will have a longer and more complicated story to tell"xv.

[2] Mrs. Anna B. Jameson, a noted English critic of the nineteenth century met Washington Allston and other artists on a visit to the United States. She writes a chapter on Allston in her **Memoirs and Essays Illustrative of Art, Literature and Social Morals** in which this quote appears (New York: Wiley & Putnam, 1846).
      Cheney admits that "opportunities for the study of Art were very small" (Rem.184) and that "It was a dreary transitional time in Art" when American artists studied Italian or English schools of art, and "hardly recognized the new era in Art" coming through German schools and later the French (185) but she maintains that "we had a great living genius among us", Allston (184).

[3] Cheney lauds the opening of the Boston Art Museum on Sunday afternoons, free to the public (**The Index** Feb.1, 1877:55) In **The Woman's Journal** (19 May 1888):159 Cheney critiques an art exhibit by women looking upon it as "a forerunner of the success of American women in art."

[4] In Cheney's "Transcendentalism" she claims that "To Emerson, literature was the greatest of all the fine arts"(Rem.187) and to Fuller "`Music is the great art of the time'" (185) but that "It was impossible for any company to hold the Transcendental doctrines without greatly valuing Art, which always represents the Ideal"(183). "Transcendentalism is the philosophy of Ideal Art..."(185).

[5] Emerson's essay "Art" (Spencer Press 1936:239-50) and an address "The Method of Nature" delivered August 11, 1841 in Waterville College, Maine (**Nature, Addresses, and Lectures**. Boston:Houghton Mifflin, 1883:181-213) constitutes the essence of what he had to say on the subject. Generally, to discover Fuller's ideas on art, one must read comments within essays on a variety of subjects, but she clearly makes the above statements in the "text from Letter XI to the **Tribune**; in **At Home and Abroad** pp. 198-200, dated February 1847" (**Margaret Fuller: American Romantic** ed. Perry Miller. New York: Doubleday, 1963:265-68).
      Katherine Everett Gilbert explained Emerson's method as a sort of ladder approach to full circle, from the first rung one sees the apple, on the second Newton's globe, on the third Plato's universe, and on the fourth the transition of the apple's pervasiveness in the universe (**A History of Esthetics,** Bloomington: Indiana UP,1953:409-412).

[6] Fuller discerns the nature of art in general by bringing to bear, her own critical method. Rarely, however, does she clearly sort out the subject. Nevertheless, unlike Emerson, her method for understanding art enjoins one to stand close to rather than away from the object. One must look closely, drawing nearer and nearer to the soul "that causes and governs"(Fuller in Miller 267). A great work of art "demands a great thought, or a thought of beauty adequately expressed" (267). What one perceives from the close inspection becomes not the fact itself, but a symbol of the fact or thought such as art seeks to represent.(266). As symbol, art represents soul

in expression. Art becomes nature's metaphor-- the expression of the life or soul of the flower. As symbol or metaphor, most art imperfectly expresses the spirit and less fully represents it.

Cheney said of Fuller "Her method of thought was to seize the heart of the subject and develop from within" (Rem.209).

7   All of these dual distinctions are made in the lectures presented at the Concord School of Philosophy and kept in whole and in part in the Scrapbook with the exception of religion as "center-circumference." This distinction comes from her article "The Value of Individuality in the Church and State" read before the Radical Club in Boston in April, 1870 and published in **The Radical** in February 1871.

In letters written when she was thirteen, Cheney (Littlehale at the time) also reconciles fame with happiness, being a woman with enjoying "male" powers (Margaret McFadden, **Signs**, Summer 1990:832-47).

8   In her lead article "Art and Religion" in the July 1868 edition of **The Radical**:1-14, Cheney distinguishes between the fanaticism that results from the attempt of people to seek the one only at the expense of the plurality, "consciousness of the manifold"(1).

9   For comment on the transcendentalist notion that spirit is superior to form see (Urbanski 201)....

10   Benedetto Croce explains art as "vision or intuition"(8); it is "a yearning kept within the bounds of representation ...lyrical...or...the epic and drama of feeling"(25). Great works of art embody "a strong feeling, which has become the perfect representation throughout"(24). "Intense feeling" is what intuition expresses (25). **Guide to Aesthetics** [1913] New York: Bobbs Merrill, 1965).

11   The duality of art as spirit and matter and the relationship between art and religion is explained metaphorically.

"To theology may belong the pure white light of heaven, but art knows it only as it breaks into radiant color, or is tempered by shadow" (Art and Religion, 3).

12   Cheney makes note of the fact that women, for example the English artist Angelica Kaufman without "the bracing air of liberal thought, and free activity" was unable to reach her potential (Gleanings 313).

13   Cheney recognized that "The Transcendentalist group never entered fully into the great work of modern science"..."the methods of work were very different" yet the doctrines were in harmony (Rem. 189).

14   Not mentioned in Katherine Everett Gilbert's A History of Esthetics (Bloomington: Indiana UP, 1953) nor in any other history of aesthetics before or since, Ednah Dow Cheney has no prior documented part in either Western or American history of aesthetics.

"ART" from **Gleanings in the Field of Art**

Of the things of art are yet many things to be written, for I foresee that many excellent men will come after me who will all write well and better than I. I hold my art very little, for I know my faults--let every one try to better my work according to his power. Would God it were possible that I could now see the works and art of the great masters who are not yet born.

Albrecht Durer.[1]

The newly awakened interest in all art studies in America, during the last twenty years, and the broad, practical foundation of general instruction on which artistic education is placed, give a new promise for the future of art here, while at the same time the crudeness of thought upon the subject, the temptations to haste, superficiality, and show in execution, and to reliance upon fashion in the appreciation and enjoyment of artistic works, present very great dangers. Let no true lover of art feel that he cannot serve her, though he may lack the gift of creative genius. Perhaps nothing is more needed for art in our country than an educated and appreciative public, stimulating artists to efforts after true excellence. What do we mean by art? In its broadest sense, I should use this word for all that which seeks to express thought in a material form, without human activity which subordinates matter entirely to spirit, but which yet wholly recognizes the function of matter to express spirit, and by that expression to give to spiritual thought its vital force, and put it in human relation. Thus used, art may include all forms of life, since this object may be foremost in any action.

Human life itself is the greatest of all forms of art, unless we go still further and say, with Coleridge and Allston,[2] that creation is the art of God; since by it he

---

[1]   Albrecht Durer (1471-1528) was a German painter and engraver.
[2]   Samuel Taylor Coleridge (1772-1834) was an English poet and critic. Washington Allston (1779-1843) American painter, a romantic transcendentalist who painted Coleridge's portrait. He studied under Benjamin West in England and later practiced in Boston. He was a friend of Ednah Dow Cheney; she is said to be the model of an angel figure in his painting "Jacob's Ladder."

has uttered his thought and made matter the vehicle of expression. Art, religion, science, are all closely allied, and unite in their central thoughts, yet their manifestations are different. It is the object of science to observe facts, and so to arrange them as to develop their mutual relations and show the law which underlies them. She is bound only to examine carefully, to state clearly, and to reason logically. She is not bound to develop the spiritual meaning of these facts to make them useful in practical life, or to give them a binding force on the consciences of men, yet she works in harmony with art, furnishing to her both means of expression and a wider range of insight; so that, as Goethe says, "all that Science needs is needed for Art;" and with religion, by showing the universality of law, and revealing the infinite resources and immeasurable achievements of the Creative Power.[3] But religion has a higher function, not only to see the truth, not only to reveal the law, not only to enjoy the beauty in God's universe, but so to control the conscience and the will of intelligent beings as to bring the life of the individual into true relation with the universal, and bind men by duty as the universe is bound by law.

Art has a distinct province in human history, civilization, and life; and yet it stands in close relation with all other spiritual and material forces, and is never independent of them. It always recognizes both the spiritual and the material side of human nature, but varies in its manifestations from one extreme to the other. It differs from philosophy, natural science, or practical ethics. Philosophy investigates mental processes, and seeks to discover the laws which govern spiritual life. Natural science studies the phenomena of matter, and tries to establish relations between them from which laws may be deduced. Practical ethics regulate our action in life. Art simply seeks to express in outward form, what man can think and feel in his inmost soul. Art does not do this with a conscious effort to benefit man's material condition, or to improve his moral action; it does not enforce duty with authority, it only presents spiritual truths in such form as to appeal to the whole nature of man. Here is its great power. Its tendency is constantly to wholeness, to health,--since it appeals not to one faculty,

---

3   Johann Goethe (1749-1832) was a German poet and dramatist; Ednah Dow Cheney introduced his work to Emerson.

but to all; to the eye and the mind, the reason and the imagination, the heart and the passions.

And this, which gives it its power for good, makes also the danger of false art, since it finds us unarmed. He who appeals to our reason meets us with our defensive armor on; but he who appeals to the eye and the imagination takes us in our unguarded moments, and influences us before we are aware. So Plato well said, "Guard those who teach fables to the children." The licentious opera, the low-toned novel, will do far more harm than any direct immoral teaching.

It will be thought that I have omitted a great point in my definition of art, in not adding to the word **expression**, "beauty;" but I do not look upon beauty as the great direct object in art, any more than I look upon "happiness" as our "being's end and aim." However we define beauty, subjectively or objectively; in its derivation from certain ideas, or as affecting human beings; I cannot but see it as a result of harmony and proportion, truth and fitness, rather than as a separate object to be sought for by itself. So it is with happiness. It is a legitimate object, but not the first or leading object of life, and whenever it is made so, it defeats its own purpose, and happiness is lost in the very effort to gain it.

Perhaps there is not a better illustration of this truth as regards beauty than in the St. Catherine of the Sistine Madonna of Raphael,[4] of which Allston well says: "In this we see an evident rescript from the antique, with all the received lines of beauty, apparently faultless, yet without a single inflection which the mind can recognize as allied to our sympathies, and we turn from it coldly, as from the work of an artificer, not of an artist." As the happiest life will be that which has been devoted to the truest and most unselfish aims, with forgetfulness of self, so beauty will be the result of the truest art which has sought to express the noblest theme in the most fitting form.

A late critic says the object of art is to increase our happiness. I can as little accept this definition of art as of life, or of religion. Happiness may come in the process, and in the final result; but art as often will bring us a divine discontent, making us desire the impossible. It will make us alive and vital, so living that we

---

[4]   Raphael [Santi] (1483-1520), an Italian Renaissance painter, is famous for his Madonnas and his work for the Vatican.

ask not for happiness. Happiness, beauty, joy, and gladness will all flow in and mingle with its stream as with the current of our lives; but the Divine Ideal may be attained only at the cost of struggle, agony, and martyrdom.

Mr. Samuel Longfellow has written a very beautiful paper in which he has attempted to show that the law of use is the law of beauty, and he has given admirable illustration of his thought; for certainly as devotion to use eliminates more and more whatever is superfluous or contradictory from a tool or an instrument of any kind, it becomes more and more beautiful, and gratifies the taste as well as serves the convenience of man. [5] All the tools of agriculture, of navigation, of household use, are instances of this, and they all become attractive when used as symbols. Even the instrument of the most cruel punishment, stripped of all its accessories, and symbolical only of divine humanity triumphing over death, becomes the most beautiful of emblems.

The relation of art to use is natural, but not inevitable. An object may be thoroughly useful with no artistic expression; and yet artistic expression is not necessarily destroyed by use. The humblest craftsman may have ideas of love, of wisdom, of beauty, which he may put into his work without lessening its value for material ends; here the artist is added to the artisan. A square building well warmed and lighted would serve the purpose of use in accommodating the people who wished to hear preaching, better than a Gothic cathedral. But the cathedral itself is a work of art, built to express the religious aspirations of the age, and it speaks to the souls of the people though the preacher's voice is lost in it. It seems to have sported with the very laws of matter, and to have made solid stone spring upwards with the lightness of mist-wreaths of the morning. Railroad stations are not built primarily to express the grandeur of the great forces of civilization, but for the use of trains and passengers. Yet as more thought is put into their construction, and all that is cumbersome and inconvenient is got rid of, they will come, like the boat and the plough, to have a certain artistic expression and beauty of their own.

The simpler and nearer to nature daily life is, the easier it is for use to take on the conditions of beauty. The wigwam of the savage, the cottage of the

---

[5]   Samuel Longfellow (1819-1892) was a Unitarian clergyman and Harvard graduate.

peasant, are more often picturesque to the eye than the abode of the wealthy citizen. The bow and arrow of the Indian, the spear of the hunter, are far more picturesque than Colt's pistol or Sharp's rifle. Long ages have simplified it to this form of beauty. So we find a great charm in the common utensils of the older nations, especially of the Etruscans, whose very cooking-pans seem to be poetic. It is a very noble art which can unite the two functions of beauty and use. Art always works in limitations; and when the builder accepts the limitations of use, and yet makes them not hindrances, but stepping-stones, to the expression of thought, uniting in himself the artist and the artisan, marrying use and beauty, he is certainly performing a noble function. How much of this lies before us to be done! The Middle Ages, believing in heavenly aspirations, striving above all things to rise above the conditions of time and sense, gave us the Gothic architecture,--one of those organic creations of art, true to its time and place, which will never be surpassed in its way, and will never be repeated. All the imitations of our day are merely handsome buildings without originality or inspiration. It expressed the belief of that day; a belief which controlled men's thoughts and actions. We cherish the home to-day more than the church. Why should we not make that also a temple of art worthily expressing the love, truth, and earnest labor which are to consecrate it?

Here, too, the question of decorative art might come in. Is this a legitimate branch of art? It is certainly a worthy occupation to make life more comfortable, more cheerful, and more enjoyable, even if by only pleasing the eye or gratifying the ear; but decorations is not art unless it does more than this--unless it also speaks to the mind. Michel Angelo's prophets and sibyls do not cease to be the grandest art of the world because they decorate the ceiling of a chapel, but mere intricacies of carved lace-work do not become so because they are within the walls of a cathedral.[6] The exquisite tracery of the Alhambra has delighted the souls of poets for centuries, but it is not the careless play of frost work; it has a soul in it, and expresses in its delicate and seemingly wayward lines the same religious spirit as do the texts of the Koran interwoven in magic letters among its windings. A bit

---

[6]   Michelangelo (1475-1892), an Italian painter, sculptor, engineer and poet, often had his name Anglicized in 19th century.

of color stuck upon the wall because it is the fashion is not decorative art. A single flower so placed as to tell you its thought more clearly may become so. Still less can that be art which is meant to serve any purpose of display, or any gratification of the vanity of the possessor. Art is varied as life and nature are; the little chickweed is as good in its place as the apple tree with its glory of beauty in spring, and its wealth of use in autumn. So the true feeling for use and beauty may express itself humbly in the ordering of a household, or grandly in the building of a temple.

Another and even more important question is the relation of art to morals. We all feel that art is a valuable influence in the world, and have a sense of relation to goodness and morality connected with it, and yet we can easily point to periods in the history of nations when great excellence in art was found in connection with a most depraved moral condition. But we shall find that it is art surviving the influences which have already corrupted the state; and although the individual soul may always stand upright and assert its nobility, even in the basest times, as Jesus did in Jerusalem, Socrates at Athens, and Michel Angelo at Rome, yet the wave of corruption which carries the nation down carries art with it. But these instances show that no one need despair if his lot be cast in an unholy time; his own life may be kept true and pure, and he may speak his own faith in spite of it.

We ask from art a direct and immediate influence upon morals, but such is not her power. Art is no police officer to keep us in order; she does not enforce duty by law, or by reward and penalty; she teaches no code of morals. But as her power is to express that which is in the soul of humanity, so she impresses that same thought upon her receptive souls through the subtle power of imagination. It is not by direct didactic teaching, but by creating within us a sympathy with that which is high and noble, by calling out within us the same spirit, the same thought, which kindled the artist's soul, that we are helped by his work. He seldom succeeds when he has a direct, moral purpose in view, although I do not hold with some critics that such purpose is utterly fatal to art; but he fails because in his effort to point a special moral, he becomes narrow and partial, and loses that ideality, that relation to the Universal, which is the very life of art.

To the soul which is not fitted to receive it, art speaks a dead language; and the murderer will do his dreadful deed under the shadow of the Parthenon as under the light of the eternal stars. And as art can express the whole of humanity, so can it specially be used by those seductive passions which clothe corruption with beauty, and make the fiend appear like an angel of light. An artist once told me that he had never in any other form felt such expression of evil as came in strains of delicious music from the gardens of Paris. He fled from it as from the voice of the tempter. How, then, does art help to good morals, to good living? Must it be by direct lessons of the success attending the virtuous, and the misfortunes of the wicked, as Hogarth has painted it for us in the "Idle and the Industrious Prentice"?[7] These may have their influence, and in Hogarth's hands these lessons are powerful and artistic; but it is not by exhibiting the results, but the very essence of good and evil, that art affects us. We shudder away from Rembrandt's terrible picture of the Duke of Gueldres, though no human retribution has overtaken the impious son; we draw in love towards the holiness of St. Sebastian, though he is chained and tortured.[8]

Art has as true a relation to morals as education or religion has. The wise Catholic church has understood this, and has made use of the statue and the picture as well as the anthem and the chant, not so much to enforce a special dogma, though that purpose has not been wanting, as to influence the thoughts of her votaries by a subtle charm that brings them into such a frame of mind as she desires. For it is not by what it bids us to do that art influences us, but by what it makes us to be. It helps to form a new spirit within us, and out of that spirit are the issues of life. The pathetic picture of the poacher, it is said, led directly to the abolition of the Game Laws; but Ruskin looks at the "Beggar Boys" of Murillo, so lazily enjoying the sunshine and the melons of Seville, and asks, contemptuously, if they will lead to the founding of ragged schools?[9] Perhaps not directly, but they do give us a feeling of sympathy and brotherhood with the beggar boy--a sense of companionship, of gratitude that he is not an outcast from

[7]   William Hogarth (1697-1764) was an English painter and engraver.
[8]   Rembrant [Harmenszoon van Rijn] (1606-69) was a Dutch painter and etcher.
[9]   John Ruskin (1819-1900) the English writer and art critic is commenting on Bartolome Murillo (1618-1682), a Spanish painter.

the sweet influences of heaven, a loving and not contemptuous recognition; and would not those feelings lead us to relieve him when we saw him really in ignorance or misery? We especially need art to sweeten and round our benevolent desire to do good to our fellow-men, so that we shall consider them from their own standpoint, and do for them what they crave and need to have done to develop their own idea, not what we would like to have them do to carry out our pet schemes.

It is in this large way that art serves the cause of religion and of morals, by kindling the imagination, and taking us out of the petty round of self and narrow prejudices, --by putting that which is noble, pure, and high, before us in a form of beauty which wins our admiration and our life, and brings us for the time being into its own pure atmosphere. But it is only as we welcome this influence into our minds and hearts that it will do us good; it will not intrude itself upon us. Shelley said, "the true secret of morals is imagination."[10] It is the power of going out of ourselves, of imagining the life and needs of others, which enables us to love them and do rightly by them. Charles Reade expresses the same thought in his maxim, "Put yourself in his place: like Nature, the touch of art will make the whole world kin.[11]

The history of art follows the development of the history of the nation, --in religion, in morals, in high social ethics, in freedom, and the regard for the rights of all men. What is true of nations is true of every individual artist. Whatever else he paints, he cannot help painting himself. Selfish ends, a coarse, profligate life, may not prevent a man from drawing the form with exquisite skill, from blending colors in harmony, or moulding the marble to perfect symmetry, but it will make it impossible for him to infuse into his work that spirit of holiness and love which will give it an immortal worth. An artist may have sinned, and yet not have wholly debased his nature; and sometimes we may have the inspiration of his highest, and sometimes of his lowest thoughts, and so may find it hard to reconcile these differing expressions. One would hardly believe that the same soul gave us the highest type of the pure Saviour of humanity, and the mocking, seductive, half-

---

[10]   Percy Bysshe Shelley (1792-1822) was an English poet.
[11]   Charles Reade (1814-1884) was an English novelist.

devilish beauty of the Mona Lisa, but such contrasts were in the nature of Leonardo de Vinci himself.[12]   Art has indeed this lesson of liberality for us, teaching us how humanity touches the divine on one side, and the earthly on the other, and what noble possibilities may remain in men seemingly most degraded. Even such painters as Caravaggio and Spagnoletto, who seem in their coarsest works to have lost every vestige of refinement, will sometimes surprise us by a touch of beauty or tenderness.[13]   Goya's works generally seem only excellent scene-painting fit for the transient illusions of a theater, but in his picture of Saints Ruffina and Justina he has painted the life and inspiration of religious loyalty, which has worthily given it a place in the cathedral, although his models were of sinful women. And yet if you place his picture beside that of Murillo, whose whole nature is one of love and purity, you will at once feel the higher influence and truer art of his representation.[14]

The moral influence of art is so gentle that it is often only recognized when the whole soul is awakened to its needs. It is like the true specific, which is inert except to the patient to whose need it is exactly fitted; but who has not known the hour when some poem--how often the word of the Psalmist, or some picture, or a strain of music, never before heeded--has come to strengthen all the forces of good, or to calm the struggling passions? We seem to touch the whole of humanity through this medium, and to feel its whole power become ours. And here it is that the work of a true artist may not be lost, though he has not the genius or the skill to make his thought universally understood. If he does not speak to all, he may to one, and to that one with a power beyond that of all others. Variety is needful in art, and sometimes we shall find its divinity in the still small voice, when we could not in the thunder or the storm.

Therefore no art of the past is sufficient for us; every age, every generation has its peculiar thought and life, and must have its own fitting expression. So, too,

---

[12]   Leonardo de Vinci (1452-1519), an Italian artist and scientist, was an example of a Renaissance genius.
[13]   Michelangelo Caravaggio (1573-1610) was an Italian painter who introduced a new realism including the coarse with the religious. Spagnoletto (1592-1652), whose real name was Giuseppe Ribera was called "little Spaniard."
[14]   Francisco Goya (1746-1828), a Spanish painter and graphic artist often articulated through his art, social concerns.

the artist whom we condemn to mediocrity, if he has only spoken frankly and truly, may touch some heart, which the genius has failed to reach.

Art, too, offers us constant illustrations of religious and moral principles. I have called life the greatest of all arts, because it is the richest and grandest expression of spiritual thought and feeling in the most flexible and most expressive of all material forms. How truly art corresponds to life, may be seen by considering some of the established maxims of art, and seeing how truly they represent great spiritual and moral truths.

The first grand principle of art is, that it must be two-fold, representing both the spiritual and the material. It may be destroyed by the undue preponderance of either. "He that careth not for the things of his household is worse than the infidel," says the most spiritual of books. "Man shall not live by bread alone," says the same volume. This blending of the two elements is what makes human life so pre-eminently beautiful, and so vastly superior in degree, if not wholly different in kind, from that of any other race. The representation of spiritual thought by material manifestation is not arbitrary. The true artist does not make the fitting expression of his thought, he finds it. The universal creation is an artistic expression, and the intelligent creature re-discovers and re-presents it.

Michel Angelo, in his beautiful sonnet, speaks of chipping away the marble to find the image concealed there. But this correspondence must always be kept free and fluent. If it becomes fixed, as symbolism, as allegory, so that art cannot express the true thought which every soul of genius finds in nature, but must work according to tradition, art becomes cold and dead. Muller says: "This connection must absolutely be one imparted of necessity in the nature of man, not assumed from arbitrary regulation...Nature herself has established this sympathy of the mind with sensible forms, and on it all art depends."[15]

This correspondence must be ever fresh and original, or it loses its power as expression, and becomes traditional symbolism only;' and we must be content that it shall express itself in its won way, and not demand definiteness. We often hear it said, "I do not believe Shakespeare ever thought of the thousand meanings

---

[15]   Muller is probably Karl Otfried Muller (1797-1840), German archeologist and art historian.

which critics find in his works." That may be true, and therein is his fine ideality shown, that his words, always dramatic, and in keeping with the individual character and incident, are yet so central and universal in their relations as to suggest a thousand different thoughts to different minds; it is so with nature, which ever "wears the colors of the spirit." It is so with art, which suggests far more than it utters directly. It is even so with character and a lofty personality.

Again, the important thing in religion is the true relation of self to the universal, the subordination of the lower to the higher faculties, the relation of one to the All. This is also the very key-stone of true art, any impertinent self-assertion is fatal to it. The most beautiful detail is out of place if it hinders the harmony of the whole, and nothing however small, is unimportant if it helps the general effect. And yet there must be a clear organic unity to which all is related which gives a right to existence. William Page said once, "I had more trouble in painting out the foot of my Madonna, which everybody admired, than in anything else in the picture."[16]

So, too, every other artistic principle, even if a mere technical rule, we shall find to correspond with great truths in morals. "Never forget the straight line," Ingres would say to his pupils one morning.[17] Another time he would say, "There is no straight line in nature; everything curves, and that gives beauty." It is so in life; without the straight line of principle, of justice, of law, character is weak and unreliable; but it must also bend in mercy and charity, and perpetually remember its relation to others. "Look at the large lines, and large matter first," says the teacher of drawing. How many lives are wasted from not seeing this same principle in life when a petty object is allowed to keep us from great duties and noble joys.

The twofold character of art, which must express the spiritual, but always with the limitations of material form, makes its truths the truths of relation, and we can never have an absolute standard of art. It is what the young and uneducated, those sincerely desiring to follow the right, perpetually crave. As the child asks of every person in life or in fiction, "Papa! is he good?" --which question the

---

16   William Page (1811-1885) was an American artist and student of Morse.
17   Jean Auguste Ingres (1780-1885), a French painter, is greatly admired for his harmony of line.

experienced father finds it difficult to answer; so they say, "Give me a standard in art: tell me how I may know what is really good; what I ought to admire, and I will honestly try to do so." You ought **not** to admire the greatest thing in art until it seems admirable to you. There is no surer way of dulling your comprehension of it forever than by pretending raptures you do not feel. Many an observer who has written faithfully down in his note-book the bitter disappointment felt at seeing the celebrated statues or paintings, has been able afterwards to write against his words, as Mrs. Jameson did, "This was, indeed, ignorance!"[18] But the fashionable rhapsodist remain too often only that to the end. David Scott began by the severest criticism of Michel Angelo, and ended by being one of his greatest admirers, having written a profound analysis of his genius.[19]

It is quite unnecessary to be flippant in decrying that of which you are ignorant. You need not suppose that you can see at a glance what it took the artist years to produce; and you may modestly believe that what many generations have found good, speaks to other minds, although you do not understand it. The world is not anxiously awaiting your verdict, and you and it can both afford to wait for a fuller study and ripening of intelligence to appreciate any celebrated work. But far better is even the careless depreciation, than affected admiration. If you must speak, say at least only what you think and feel, and be quite willing to correct your judgment when you see reason to do so. The opinions of the most famous critics will soon show you how impossible it is to find any sure ground of authority. One will tell you that Michel Angelo was the corrupter in Italy. Another holds him so high that he can recognize no merit in his rivals.

Ruskin can see little merit in Claude, whom Allston is said to have called "the greatest of painters."[20]

In the battle about the Holbein Madonnas, eager critics have declared the picture, which has delighted Europe for three centuries, to be a miserable copy.[21]

---

18   Anna Brownell Jameson (1794-1860), an art critic, she was an English author born in Dublin.
19   David Scott (1806-1849), an historical painter in Scotland, painted Ralph Waldo Emerson's portrait.
20   Claude de Lorrain (1600-1682), was a French landscape painter whose real name was Gellee.
21   Hans Holbein both younger (1497-1543) and elder (1460-1524) were Dutch painters.

Still less is it necessary to take sides in all the controversies which have agitated the world of art, as all other worlds. Every human being has his idiosyncrasies, and what is full of interest to one, has little value for another. One is quite capable of enjoying the calm beauty of Poussin, but has no relish for the humor of Teniers or Hogarth.[22] One artist finds the designs of William Blake greater than those of Michel Angelo,[23] and another sees nothing but madness in his vagaries, but delights in the strong expression in Holbein's **Dance of Death.**

One thing may be good, and another very different from it not be bad. Perhaps the wisest of all rules for judging of works of art was that given to Allston by Coleridge: "Never judge a work of art by its defects." It may have a hundred faults, and yet have a value that outweighs them all; but until you can see the positive meaning in it you may pass it by. However peculiar your taste in art, you will find enough to gratify it, if you are simple and sincere in seeking it; and in studying what you really appreciate, your powers of comprehension and enjoyment will enlarge, until you will find the meaning and beauty of what was at first incomprehensible.

In a second-rate gallery in Europe, I one day busied myself with studying the works of the less famous painters. I tried to get into sympathy with their efforts, and to enter into their thoughts, and I found a rich satisfaction in detecting beauties I had passed by before, and a widening of my range of sympathies, which did not in the least prevent my feeling the transcendent superiority of the masterpieces of art.

Make any work of art which attracts you your own by loving, thorough study, and whatever critics may say of it, you will either exhaust that phase of expression and pass on to something higher, or finding in it what really speaks to you, you will be sure of what you have gained from it, and better fitted to appreciate everything.

As in the material world science finds a constant progress from unity to differentiation, so in tracing the history of art we shall find in its periods of activity-

---

22   Nicolas Poussin (1594-1665) French painter influenced Ingres. David Teniers (1610-90) was a Flemish painter.
23   William Blake (1757-1827) was an English poet and artist.

-its ascending nodes--a constant tendency to greater individual freedom: first to release from material fetters, and then from the bondage of tradition and its own past achievements. We shall see the former process most strikingly illustrated in Early Greek art, and the latter in the Renaissance in every country in Europe, all of which had felt the sway of Byzantine traditions and ecclesiastic rules; and all of which found new life in the study of Nature and the expression of human individuality.

But art must never forget the unity in the difference. Science may analyze and hold the part in the strongest light for the time, not stating its relation to the whole; but religion and art must always remember the whole. "The eye," says Goethe, "can never see a color without at the same time seeing the whole light with it." So it is in art. Whenever we find individual freedom carried so far as to obscure the relation of the universal, art ceases to be ideal, and becomes first prosaic and then meager and uninteresting. The greatest event in history is nothing, if the artist sees in it nothing but the action of the hour; the smallest incident is a grand subject if the whole of humanity is suggested by it.

This relation of the individual to the universal is the true source of the ideal. I never weary of Coleridge's definition, "The ideal is the true relation of the generic to the individual."

Perhaps no word has ever been more misused than this word Ideal. Sir Joshua Reynolds seems to use it to express a generalized form in which all individuality is lost.[24] Modern artists, especially modern amateurs, speak of a picture as idealized when it is made effeminate, and pretty, and all character is taken out of it. This is, of all work, the most unideal, since it has no idea in it; but only aims to please the fancy or delight the eye. But ideality raises the individual to its highest power by uniting it with the universal. Look at other idealizing forces: at Love, the greatest of all, that Supreme Artist, who can remake the world of nature and humanity for us. The mother idealizes her child, how? by confounding it indiscriminately with all other pretty children? No; but by finding in it the germ and promise of all humanity. There is no achievement too great for its future, nothing too perfect for it now; the whole universe is mirrored in her baby's

---

[24]   Sir Joshua Reynolds (1723-92) was an English painter.

eye; but at the same time the little bundle of flannel, which is a shapeless mass to the bachelor uncle, is wonderfully individual to her. She detects family traits and peculiarities in it, and is sure no baby was ever like it before. So it is with the lover, who sees all womanhood in his maiden, and yet knows the glance of her eye, the print of her foot, the tone of her voice from all others; and is angry that any one can mistake her for her twin sister.

It follows from the central idea of art that it always has two sides, one spiritual and one material, both essential to it, and either liable to be carried to such an extreme as to destroy its perfect balance and beauty.

It is customary to place the two words idealists and realists in opposition, and to class all schools or periods of arts, and all individual artists, according to these terms. But I think every true artist is and must be an idealist, and I should rather divide the two schools by the terms spiritualist and realist, which indicate the two poles of art, both legitimate, the one tending strongly to the universal-spiritual-immaterial side, the other to the particular human and material side. Realism does not acknowledge that it surrenders the ideal. Hazlitt says:

> The ideal is not the preference of that which exists **only** in the mind to that which exists in nature, but the preference of that which is fine in nature to that which is less so. But it is not that which is externally finer in nature, but it is the penetration into the finer meaning of nature that makes the idealist. He himself speaks of Wilson's genius, as it conveys not only the image but the feeling of nature; and of Poussin as able to give natural objects a sympathy with preternatural events, and to inform rocks, trees, and mountains with the presence of God.[25]

Hazlitt has been claimed as the leading critic of that school which makes direct imitation of nature the basis of all art. He says:

> The great works of art at present extant, as the Greek Statues, the pictures of the celebrated Italian masters, those of the Dutch and Flemish schools, to which we may add the comic productions of our own countryman, Hogarth, all stand unrivalled in the history of

---

[25]   William Hazlitt (1778-1830), an English writer and critic, is speaking of Richard Wilson (1714-82), English landscape artist who introduced classicism into art.

art, and they owe their pre-eminence and perfection to one and the same principle--the immediate imitation of nature.

When William Page, one of the most thoughtful of American artists, read this, he paused, and said: "I will agree henceforth to subscribe to every word that man has written." Yet Raphael gave a different version of his method when he said: "I make use of a certain idea in my own mind."

Both these tendencies in art are as essential as the two currents in a magnet, and yet it is very difficult to mark their boundaries or show their relation to true ideal art. Albert Durer, perhaps, expressed it as well as possible in saying "the artist must gather from nature into his mind, and out of nature produce his new creation;" or beginning from the other side, we may say, "that, having the thought in his mind, the artist must seek from nature the true means of representing it."

Here is the great mistake that imitation of nature is considered the end, not the means, of art. Goethe says: "Shall the artist only imitate nature? Why, the mirror can do that better than he;" and for us comes the photographic process, which is absolutely faithful to the material side, as far as form and shadow are concerned.

The spiritualist, like Blake, starts with a vision of his own soul, and gives to it as little outward semblance of nature as will make it recognized by another soul. But he does not give it that full and adequate expression which satisfies and delights those not already in possession of the thought, and so does not lead them into his meaning. He will always remain a seer rather than an artist, suggestive and interesting to the thinker, but not welcome to the popular heart.

The danger of the spiritualist is that he will be content to express his idea to his own satisfaction, and be angry that other men do not understand his language, because he scorns the very medium he is obliged to use. He gives up nature, which is the revelation of the universal, and confines himself to his own special inspiration; hence he becomes narrow, and vague, and usually repeats his one note again and again until he falls into sentimentality and mannerism. We rarely see either of those tendencies pure and unmixed, but we shall see this result of excessive tendency to the immaterial side abundantly illustrated in the history of

Christian art. Realism tends to run into the opposite extreme--to lay undue stress on the material form, to exaggerate the importance of accidental peculiarities, and to lose the idea in the expression. Instead of "study of nature," it adopts the phrase "imitation of nature," and finding it much more easy to imitate the surface than to catch the spirit, it remains content with that.

But the sincere realist who begins even with the imitation of details is often led into the true study and love of nature until he catches her secret; and so becomes an idealist. It is important to dwell a little on this subject because modern art has gone to great extremes, and its worst faults are due to a narrow understanding of that realism, which, nevertheless, has laid a foundation for some of its greatest merits.

The maxims of excessive realism attract us by their apparent regard for truth. Why should not every detail be given in art as well as in nature? When Jesus knelt in agony on the Mount of Olives, every twig on the trees, every leaf and leaflet, was as thoroughly carved out as in a botanical garden; why is it not so in Albert Durer's picture? But truth to fact is one thing; the truth of relation, the truth of expression, is another. You can read for yourself all the facts of that thrilling scene, but they may leave you unmoved; the artist gives you the life, the thought, the feeling, of the moment. Supposing him to have been really present, and to have told you of it, for the same purpose of rousing your deepest nature to sympathy and awe, would he have told you that the olive trees were of just such a height, that the branches followed each other in alternate order, that each leaf had a marked mid-rib, and their form was a narrow oval, and their edges smooth. He would never mention them unless to give you a sense of the solitude and stillness of nature so soon to be disturbed by the crime and passion of men.

So of the dress of the actors in a great scene; it must be so true to the actual that it will not impress you as false; but when Lear casts off his garments in the storm, do you care to know whether they are of serge or broadcloth? Nicety of detail is in place whenever it helps the expression--when it tells you anything you care to know in connection with the event or the feeling which the artist will portray. It is precisely by selecting for you the important and expressive features,

297

and throwing into the shade those of less value, that the artist helps you to see the scene with his finer imagination and deeper feeling.

Modern art has carried the tendency to realism to the most absurd extremes. Even in sculpture, which is expressly fitted for noble ideality, it has delighted in covering the human face with a veil in which every mesh was carefully made out; and in Berlin I saw a statue of the Fate spinning the thread of life in which an actual silk string was introduced. The texture of the cloth is made more prominent than the action of the wearer. In some of the Dusseldorf pictures I think an expert might almost say whether the button-holes were made by hand or by the machine. It seems difficult to disabuse people's minds of the idea that this is necessary for truth. Many things may be true, and yet are very impertinent. We do not care to see every process which has contributed to the result. Neither is it according to nature. We do not, and we cannot, see in nature every petty detail and the glorious whole at the same time.

"When the morning wind is blowing" in the tops of the oaks and pines, and the "green grass is bowing," we see all that belongs to the motion of the wind and the changes that it makes in the landscape,--we mark the light that touches the tops of the trees, the sharp outlines of the oak-leaves against the sky, and the cool shadows that rest below full of the silence and freshness of night; but we do not and cannot see every marking of the leaf, and every separate blade of grass. Put the tiniest grain, so conspicuous in the whole result, under the microscope, and a new world of beauty is revealed to you. This is nature's miracle, making every detail perfect, and yet losing them in the general effect. Art has not nature's means, and she must make up for the want of them, by throwing her emphasis upon that which is important to the purpose she has in view; and she makes this defect a new power by compelling our attention and securing our sympathy for the thought she has to express.

Almost from the very earliest dawn of human life we find in the scratches upon the rocks some trace of the natural desire to express ideas in visible form. It is the perpetual effort of the spiritual creative power in man to assert itself, and to supply the demands of a life which is not satisfied with a mere animal existence. Possibly it is evolved even from the consciousness of lower races, since we find the flowers are made beautiful to attract the insects, and we know how the lizard delights in the concord of sweet sounds, and the horse is excited by music. But without entering upon the disputed territory of science, history certainly does not deal with any people who have not shown, in some form, a striving after art. The South Sea Islander cover his own person with pictorial representations which have their meaning to him. The Aztec carved the images of his gods in stone. Where history is silent, the graven image, or the pictured wall, or the temple, or the ornamented tomb, have preserved for us the spirit and the character of the people. The researches of the last fifty years have brought to light treasures of ancient art which astound us, and which carry our minds back into the ages of which history reveals very little.

Egyptian art is a less remote means of illustration; and what life and power it has to this day! Even without the privilege of seeing its glorious works on her own soil, who can stand in the presence of her mighty monuments in the museums of Paris or London, Berlin or Florence, without feeling that the deep heart of humanity is speaking to you out of the ages so long gone by! With the details of their religious observance we care not to mingle; but from those grand, serene, peaceful deities comes a spirit of universal faith, and trust, and strength, which ministers to us as powerfully as the mountain and the sea.

Again, the Etruscans are almost unknown to us in history, which tells not wither they came, but only that they conquered by the stranger. Yet through their art they still live, and we may know of their religion, their society, and even of their daily household life, although their language is wholly lost to us. Their art was so strongly influenced by the Greek that it is difficult to separate it, yet there is an original character impressed upon it. The relation of the Divine to the Human seemed ever present in their religion, and one of their law-books taught the art of making human souls to gods. Yet their religious faith seems to have been narrowed by a perpetual reference to utility, seeking not to enter into the Divine Spirit, but to use it for the divination of human events. A rare humor is present in their work. The charming statue of **The Boy and Goose** is an instance of this. Their sculpture is extremely realistic, and one feels as if acquainted with the respectable citizens and fashionable ladies whose effigies were preserved in the tombs. Especially does the cheerfulness of the accompaniments of death strike us in comparison with the Christian symbolism, --it almost seems as if, in their constant communing with the spirit, they had come to that state which old Herbert ascribes to Adam, when

> He could to Heaven from Paradise go
> As from one room to another.[26]

In every period of art we find the same great principles exemplified. The art of the people represents its ethnological character, its social development, its political freedom, its material prosperity, but most of all the religious faith and the moral character of the people. Sometimes, indeed, the effect seems to come lingering after the cause, and we find the highest bloom of art when a nation has already begun to fall from its highest power, as we see both in Greek and Italian art; but it is only because individuals have preserved and represent that spirit which has ceased to control the nation.

And this is a lesson which I would wish to bring home to ourselves. What we do for art directly is valuable; but it is as nothing to what we do for her indirectly. If we become a base, sordid, unjust nation, caring only to heap up material wealth, it will be in vain to attempt any higher expression in art; if we forget the great principles of freedom and democracy, and seek to build up an aristocracy of wealth, or race, or inherited culture, our art will become narrow and traditional; if we care only for the intellect, and neglect love, and faith, and imagination, we may have a learned art; but we can only have an art that is truly original, noble, and beautiful, by cherishing and developing a national character of which it is the fitting expression.

---

26 George Herbert (1593-1633) was an English poet.

Introduction to **"The Reign of Womanhood"**

Why has Ednah Dow Cheney's feminist philosophy been neither a part of American feminism nor of American philosophy? Unfortunately, the foremost answer, if not only answer, lies in Cheney's obscurity. For the questions she addressed-- theological, philosophical and psychological--who is God, who are we, how are we to relate: we to God, and, male and female, to each other---are profound and relevant. So, now that Cheney's "The Reign of Womanhood" has been retrieved here, and once it is studied, perhaps it will be considered as a worthy contribution to the feminist philosophical tradition being made manifest.

Early on, the American feminist philosophical tradition was influenced from abroad. Anne Bradstreet celebrated Queen Elizabeth I in her seventeenth century poetry. Eighteenth century and early nineteenth century American women writers had no such woman leader in evidence and no fore-knowledge of Queen Victoria's coming. Coping with new concepts of freedom and their consequent meaning for women, they did have the work of Marie le Jars de Gournay, Anna van Schurman, Mary Astell and others to call upon. And with similar wisdom, Judith Sargent Murray, Frances Wright, and Maria Stewart likewise argued the necessity of making education women's highest priority.[1] Now, the nineteenth century fully on the way with an influential Queen on the throne in England once again, and more education for women already begun, participation of women in the political system became the new issue. The sea change of emphasis turned from education to suffrage and abolition of slavery. In Cheney's time Judith Sargent Murray's and Mercy Otis Warren's one hundred year old writings were near oblivion; Frances Wright's essays, generally considered too revolutionary, though they bridged the issues of education and abolition, were little valued. But Mary Wollstonecraft from England and Margaret Fuller from Boston, as much as the shadowy presence of Queen Victoria, were generally cherished.

It is curious, however, that when Ednah Dow Cheney writes her philosophy of women, she calls upon methods similar to those of Judith Sargent Murray. Like Murray she searches for metaphysical warrants and like Murray returns to Genesis in the Bible wherein a theory of human essence and Eve's essence in particular was germinated. As Murray's writings have demonstrated,

301

her metaphysical definition of human essence is trinitarian. The trinity of humanity - spirit, mind, and matter - made in God's image makes consequent that both male and female equally participate in God (spirit). Cheney's theory of God is also trinitarian, her trinity of God being -"spirit of life," male, and female. She reasons that if humanity is an image of God, then God must be equally male and female. Murray's narrative of Eve misunderstood as "tempter," contrasts with Cheney's historical exposition of Eve as "tempter and savior." Coming to a definition of divinity as "eternally womanly," Cheney redefines woman.[2]

Like Bradstreet and Murray, Cheney believes in establishing the tradition of accomplished women by citing them. In this address she looks to a range of indicators of women's progress. Although she lists but few representative women here, elsewhere she wrote biographies of women, some of whose lives would have been completely lost to posterity had she not written about them. In addition, as a part of a history of Boston, she catalogued the leading women in Boston's history and explained their roles, to include among them women of this text: Anne Bradstreet, Judith Sargent Murray, Mercy Otis Warren.[3]

Science becomes the milieu of Cheney's nineteenth century era as much as does religion. Insofar as science compounds the political issues and threatens the educational and social accomplishments of women, Cheney must take science into account. Some scientific theories confronting Cheney are those of Charles Darwin, who emphasizes the role of physical strength in evolution, and those of Dr. Edward H.Clarke, who claims that menstrual cycles debilitate serious academic work. Against Dr. Clarke's position, Julia Ward Howe compiled an anthology of inductive evidence.[4] In opposition to Darwin and his disciple Herbert Spencer, Antoinette Brown Blackwell wrote a philosophy of science. But in this address, Cheney does not argue about science's conclusions nor does she argue from science, she merely puts forth the scientific dialogue that relates to the issue at hand.

It is not to religion, politics or science, that Cheney looks for ultimate answers, but to metaphysics, albeit her thinking was influenced by the power evidenced in the reign of Queen Victoria, the progress of science and the hold of the Bible. But Cheney chooses for the underpinnings of her philosophy, the little known ancient traditions and contemporary doctrines which witness God as male

302

and female as her underpinnings. To build her own philosophical argument rooted in this tradition, Cheney chooses as her first materials the "new" words of Goethe, "the leading thinker and poet" of her time, "eternally womanly." In her argument, the human relationship of man to woman (the "man-ness" and "woman-ness" derived from God) becomes the ethical cornerstone, the foundation of which is the metaphysical truth of the duality of God.

Endnotes

1 The speeches of Maria W. Stewart, published under the title of **Productions of Maria W. Stewart**, were delivered in Boston in the early 1830's. Maria pleads "O woman, woman, would thou...store thy mind with useful knowledge..."31. Marilyn Richardson ed. **Maria W. Stewart, America's First Black Political Writer**. Bloomington: Indiana U P, 1987.

2 It is interesting to note that in Cheney's argument in this address, i.e. being a mother does not mean being a woman in the full sense, agrees with Mercy Otis Warren's Maria, heroine of her tragedy "The Ladies of Castile," who says "the wife--the mother--make me less than woman"(IV.v).

3 In "The Women of Boston." **The Memorial History of Boston: 1630-1880**. ed. Justin Winsor Vol.IV Boston: James R. Osgood, 1881, Ednah Dow Cheney lists and discusses chronologically many women leaders, scholars, writers, artists who have participated in Boston's history.

4 Dr. E.F. Clarke's **Sex in Education** is at issue here. As editor of **Sex and Education:A Reply to Dr. E.H. Clarke's "Sex in Education"** (Boston: Roberts Brothers, 1874) Julia Ward Howe gathers testimonies negating Clarke's conclusions in essays from eight men and women, and comments from representatives of Antioch,, Oberlin, and Vassar Colleges, and Michigan and Lombard Universities.

THE REIGN OF WOMANHOOD

Address by Mrs. Ednah D. Cheney in the Mechanics Institute, June 20, 1897, on the Occasion of the Unitarian Service in Commemoration of the Queen's Diamond Jubilee.

> So God created man in His own image, in the image of
> God created He him; male and female created He them.
> > --Genesis i.27.

This one verse contains a condensed statement of the great beginning of creation. First, God created man in His own image, and this is repeated, in the image of God created He him; then as dulaity begins to appear, male and female created He them, and the history of mankind in its struggle begins to be related.

The problem of our age is womanhood; and therefore on this day when we celebrate the longest, the most prosperous and peaceful reign which England has ever known, and under the beneficent guiding hand of a true woman, it is becoming for us to consider this great problem, not so much in its outward and practical form, which it will take our next century to work out, as in its inner meaning, and in reference to the eternal principles which alone will lead us to its final and triumphant solution.

For the true meaning of this primal question of sex does not consist alone of the outward form, which envelops the human spirit, but in its essential spirit. We are seeking to fathom the secret of life and to enter into the purposes of creation. We are trying, if not to comprehend, at least to apprehend the thought of God, when out of the peaceful unity of being He brought all this complex, warring, jarring life of creation, in which the two forces ever tending to reunion and mutual action are the necessary condition of all life. Sex as the most universal manifestation of the first step in creation is traceable throughout all life, and for perfect knowledge of it we must study it alike in the formation of the zoophyte as in the imagination of the angelic natures. Such cannot be the work of a brief hour. Only a sketch of the essential points can be given. This great mystery, how out of

305

the One comes first the two, and out of the twain again come the many, confronts us everywhere, in science, in life, in metaphysics, in religion.

We, as Unitarians, may rightfully give up the narrow form of a Trinity which saw the incarnation of God in one mystic Being alone, and not in all the wondrous world of life, but we cannot get away from the philosophic Trinity which recognizes the One, the All, the two through which unity acts, and the resulting third which is the Spirit of Life, making possible all this universe of infinite variety and yet underlying harmony.

You will find this Trinity, which has its representation in sex running through all the phenomena of life which we investigate by science. It is as true and as easily exemplified in the most practical mechanics, the most subtle chemistry, as in the sublimest astronomy.

"It is as high as heaven; it is deep as hell." No mythology can begin to read the riddle of the universe, but it has to meet the question of man and woman. Poetry is never weary of celebrating this relation, and finding every charm and glory of the universe but a symbol of its power and beauty. Law has a maxim that "everything has a woman in it." and until you get at the part she has played in the case you are groping in the dark. Goethe, who well knew the importance of this thought, has expressed his Trinity in the simplest form of the joy of family life.

After the birth of Euphorion, the mystical child of love, the chorus sing,

> Love in human wise to bless us,
> In a noble pair must be
> But divinely to possess us,
> It must form a perfect Three.

In the most ancient religions known to us the human mind has recognized that the duality which finds in life has its origin in the divine nature. Samuel Johnson says of the old Hindu writings that "they treat both sexes as equally necessary to the conception of Deity. Creation proceeds from the divine love or desire becoming twain, male and female."

Womanhood

The Hebrew saw the same truth expressed in the manifestation, "God created man in His own image; male and female created He them," and the latest scientist traces the whole evolution of this duality running through the mineral world, and becoming ever clearer through the whole range of vegetable and animal life, until it blooms out in the beauty of human love, and the whole earth in its springtide of beauty resounds with the divine epithalamium, the marriage song of insect and bird which call to each other from treetop to treetop, "God is love and we are His offspring."

The same thought runs through the Egyptian, Phoenician, Babylonian and other primitive religions. It becomes somewhat obscured in Christian theology, because of the tendency to dogma in the Christian church, but it has still always existed there in the essential thought of the Trinity, and in the very inadequate, though beautiful symbolism which accepted the Virgin Mary, the mother of Jesus, as the Divine Mother of mankind. And so necessary is this recognition to the human heart that the honor and love due to the primal Infinite God, or to His representative in humanity, the Divine Son, was almost obscured by the tenderer trust and affection given to the Queen of Heaven. In our own day this great thought has again found expression from the deep heart of Theodore Parker, whose reverent invocation to the Source of all good, as "our Father and Mother, too," will never be forgotten by those who were wont to hear it.

It is an interesting coincidence which shows how the highest things of heaven are mirrored in the humblest human life, that the poor widow whose welfare the great sculptor, Michael Angelo, made his care, addresses him in her letter of gratitude as "My father and my mother, too."

In his greatest poem, Faust, the German Goethe, the leading thinker and poet of our age, has given immortal expression to the thought of the divine womanhood, in the line which is spoken by the chorus Mysticus at the close of the man's life-long struggle, and which opens the way to his redemption:

"Das Ewig Weibliche zieht uns hinan."

(The Eternal Womanly leadeth us on.)

Womanhood

The word "eternal" makes the grand thought of this line. Woman is not an accident of creation, a necessity of earthly life, a second thought of God, who found man too lonely if left to himself, and who therefore made for him a pleasing toy to charm his leisure hours and soothe him when ill or weary. It is not woman as a minister to earthly pleasure that leadeth us on. It is the eternally womanly, as truly divine, as essential to the order of being as the manly, who is to lead the soul upward and onward, into that entire oneness with God which is redemption and Heaven. "What a promise of continual life and fresh creation is there in these words, what abounding love, what infinite hope." What leadeth us on? The attractive principle, the love which receives impulse and becomes creative. It is at once attraction which stimulates action and the centripetal power which holds action true to its center. While the degradation of womanhood is the most terrible evil of all time, our own fully included, while the actual manifestations of it, the fearful unspeakable, appalling sin, misery shame, the leprosy of soul and body resulting from it, fill us with a loathing, a horror, a despair of God and man, which almost turn the sun to blood and the dearest hopes of life to misery, there remains yet one Pole Star of Faith which shines through the gloomiest darkness and gives us hope that humanity can never wholly lose its way, but is bound to the eternal throne of God by the link that can never be wholly broken. The lowest, vilest man does not willingly lose his ideal of woman, does somehow cherish some feeling of motherhood, some belief in an unselfish love, some little gleam of romance in his heart, some sense that a woman's prayers are more powerful than his curses, some thought of the child that might have clung about his knees, some recognition that there is a power of love, an "eternally womanly" that may yet lead him upward and on to redeemed life out of the very jaws of death and hell. Hence, men judge actual women so severely as not answering to their ideal. You remember when the miners of California, living for months and years their wild, half-savage life, heard that an emigrant train was coming, bringing women in their company, they exclaimed: "Thank God, the women are coming to make us better." They knew not who they were; they might be the very refuse of the slums of the cities, driven out by dishonor and vice, but the men did not think of that; they recognized the "eternally womanly" and the first thought was the manly, noble one: "They have come to make us better." The natural religion of these rough men clung to their ideal and hoped thence their salvation. As Goethe said: "My idea of woman is not abstracted from the phenomena of actual life, but has been born within me. God knows how!"

Man's relation to woman is the great fact of his moral life. If he fails in it, no matter how the world may condone his fault, it saps the very strength of his manhood, and as Shakespeare so truly says, "Our pleasant vices are made the whips to scourge us." None but the poor victim can fully know how keen are the tortures, how bitter the humiliations that follow. But does man alone need to worship a lofty ideal born instead of the Spirit, but most blessed also when revealed in flesh and blood? Does not woman, too, need to feel the thrill of equal divinity in her partner and companion? When it is claimed that women should take their share of the active work and vital responsibility of the world's life we often hear men say, "Oh, we do not want woman brought down from her lofty pedestal; we want our ideal kept high and pure." Do you ever think that women, too, must have her ideal of man kept pure and holy? Can she touch pitch and not be defiled? Her ideal of man must match her own standard of spiritual purity and truth, or instead of leading him on she is dragged down to the dust with him. The whole meaning of sex is mutual relation and the one sex must be fit to mate the other. "All are needed by each one; nothing is fair or good alone." A man expressed to me the other day his hopelessness of the moral condition of his own sex, which he believed was sinking lower and lower in depravity. I could not, would not, despair with him, and I find my longing that a higher standard, a standard as high for them as for women, shall be held up before them, and that the women of actual life whom they meet day by day should demand of them the strictest fidelity to it.

If the human heart was not satisfied in its earliest efforts to draw near to the secrets of life without the recognition of the woman, the mother, in God, whence came then the debasing views of woman which have had such sway in the world and have produced such corruption and misery that we shrink from any effort to portray it? Even the morphism which, "making of God even such a one as themselves," has enlarged the selfish, narrow passions of humanity into universal proportions, until the great fact of evil and sin covered the whole existence of evil demanded a solution. Man must have been wholly divine, pure in his origin; what could have separated him from God? It must be a power almost equal to God that could thus strive against and often seemingly overcome him; and, as this power was subtle and wise after its kind, and knew that when the best is turned to evil it becomes the worst, so the evil power sought his instrument in woman, the embodiment of love, and she came to express in the popular theology, not the upward redeeming source of good, but the arch temptress to sin and evil. Thus woman in many mythologies is both the tempter and savior. She represents attractive love, and that love is capable of being the greatest incentive to good or the most fearful impulse to evil, as it is received and developed. So in Hebrew thought woman is the tempter; yet the pure mother bringing forth the son, that is,

> So God created man in His own image, in the image of
> God created He him; male and female created He them.
>
> --Genesis i.27.

This one verse contains a condensed statement of the great beginning of creation. First, God created man in His own image, and this is repeated, in the image of God created He him; then as duality begins to appear, male and female created He them, and the history of mankind in its struggle begins to be related.

The problem of our age is womanhood; and therefore on this day when we celebrate the longest, the most prosperous and peaceful reign which England has ever known, and under the beneficent guiding hand of a true woman, it is becoming for us to consider this great problem, not so much in its outward and practical form, which it will take our next century to work out, as in its inner meaning, and in reference to the eternal principles which alone will lead us to its final and triumphant solution.

For the true meaning of this primal question of sex does not consist alone of the outward form, which envelops the human spirit, but in its essential spirit. We are seeking to fathom the secret of life and to enter into the purposes of creation. We are trying, if not to comprehend, at least to apprehend the thought of God, when out of the peaceful restoring the whole, the harmony brings also salvation. So even the thought of fatherhood and motherhood became tainted with sin, and the monstrous doctrine, which lies like a heavy pall over the sweet region of theology, the doctrine of innate depravity and total alienation from God, being conceived and born in sin, has carried its message of doubt, despair, and hate into the fairest regions of life. Against it the doctrine of the divine motherhood is perpetually striving, and it is to the recognition of the holiness of the feminine principle that we must look for the regeneration of the world. Jesus set a little child in the midst of them and said, "Of such is the kingdom of heaven." Could He have been thinking of him as the offspring of the devil? In the Christian church the two opposite conceptions of woman have remained side by side struggling with each other; but where in the words of Jesus Himself, even when He speaks to one who calls herself a sinner, is there ever a want of recognition of the love to which all will be forgiven? There was a time when woman was the type of all evil, and when the deepest and holiest of human relations could not be consecrated within the walls of a church. It was a great step in the recognition of her nature when marriage was recognized as a sacrament, a symbol of that divine union which can alone promote harmony and life. Even now it is felt that the presence of woman desecrates many of the holy places of the church, and, while the Virgin is honored, and saints and martyrs are objects of prayer and devotion, the human, living mother is not received into the active service and honors of the church. Nor are our Protestant skirts free from the divine message if it come from the lips of a woman. Yet in all religions and all mythologies woman has had direct reception from divinity and become the inspired prophetess. There is one aspect of the religious veneration for woman which, while it has its deep meaning and beautiful expression, has yet worked great mischief because it is partial and not the whole truth. In the ancient religions we find that it is mainly as the human mother that woman is honored. As a wife she is loved indeed, but loved as a possession, and this love, so often selfish and exacting, allied so closely to selfish enjoyment and the lust of power, has thus become the greatest of dangers, the worst of foes to woman. It is only the mother who has always claimed a certain independent value and secured a measure of pure honor and respect, and even this feeling is vitiated by the selfish superstition that, as the father of sons whom she has brought to him the lasting glory of the man is secure. Thus even in the deepest corruption of womanhood something of purity and nobility and truth has lingered about the idea of motherhood, and its power to restore purity to the soul, and hope to the life, is acknowledged even in those whom the world counts as lost. The Koran says: "Woman is admitted to paradise only when she becomes a mother." If woman is not immortal by nature she is not worthy to become a mother. She cannot give immortal life to her son. Until it recognizes the true essential life of woman, Islam will always be a partial, not a universal religion. That this is the greatest distinctive function of earthly womanhood who will deny? But sin, falsehood, misery come in whenever we separate one function, however important, from the whole of life. Wholeness is holiness, and when we assume to cut off one part we destroy the harmony, we vitiate the purity of the whole. Fatherhood, too, is great and holy, so holy that we have transferred its name to the One, the Author of all good, but fatherhood is not the only duty of humanity. We reverence the Roman father who sacrificed his son at the bidding of the public law which he had sworn to support. Woman is a mother; but she is more than a mother. She is a living, immortal soul. She is a child of God and she is bound to fulfil all life and all righteousness as much as man is. Her life, her duty as wife and mother is great and holy. But she has righteousness, to the Infinite Whole. God is a very jealous God, and will accept no human relation as before the high allegiance to His truth. You remember, in Scott's beautiful story, the sore trial of the noble Jeanie Deans, who will not save her sister's life at the cost of truth; and the same courage which enabled her to hold true to right in spite of the entreaties of the poor girl, and most of all of her own loving heart, gives her the strength for the great effort which can redeem her sister and keep God's law unbroken.

There is an old legend, well told by Chaucer, of the wife Griselda, a poor peasant maiden beloved and wedded by a rich lord. After she had become the mother of his children he took the fancy to try her virtue (for he and she deemed absolute submission and self-sacrifice to be the sum of all virtue for a woman) by driving her from her home and children back to the peasant's hut from which he took her. She yields uncomplainingly, and separated from her home spends long years in poverty and exile, only to be restored to her children when the tyrant's greed of power was satisfied.

Womanhood

James Russell Lowell well says: "No woman approves Griselda, and I would not wish a woman for my wife who did. She sacrificed all duties to one she had taken a fancy to."

So woman has too often accepted a fancied duty, a romantic virtue, instead of recognizing her whole relation to God and humanity, which demands of her the full development of her nature, and the employment of every God-given faculty. And as "he who loseth his life for my sake shall find it," so the seeming sacrifice of the partial duty to the higher will give her back to the nobler fulfillment of the nearest and tenderest ties. "I could not love thee, dear, so much, loved I not honor more." With the exclusive acceptance of special function has grown the idea of woman as an accident of creation, an adjunct to the masculine type of humanity, created for his enjoyment and help, and having no right to seek her own fullness of life and action. Every great error is related to some great truth so closely that it is often very hard to separate them. So this false idea which has engendered all woman's wretchedness and fatal wrong to herself and others is nearly related to the great truth that the idea of womanhood always suggests that of relation. Symbolizing as she does the attractive forces of existence, beauty winning to union, the part never complete without its complement, in one all-comprehensive word, love.

Woman is constantly tending towards relation, and her happiness is not complete, her life is not fulfilled except in recognition of the life of others, in perpetual receiving from and giving out to others.

You will tell me and tell me correctly that this is also true of man, and that the highest man is no more self-dependent than the most loving woman.

But this truth of relation which has been emphasized and developed, though often in the poorest way, as regards woman, has been obscured in man, as he has so largely taken the material aggressive part of the life of the world, and as woman, in so far truly his worst enemy, has yielded to his exactions and fostered his pride of authority and self-love.

But woman's ideal of man is as truly that of a nobly, grandly, unselfish self-forgetfulness as his of her. Philip Sydney, passing the water from his own fevered lips to those of his dying fellow-soldier, is dearer to her memory than the conqueror of a battle-field, and Charles Lamb, giving up his own dearest hopes in life to shelter his unfortunate sister, is beloved and reverenced in spite of many a failing.

You may smile at the trifling anecdote I tell you, but the thought of it has remained with me nearly sixty years. On my first long journey to the mountains, as we stopped at a hotel, and the elders were making arrangements for rooms, I overheard a bright young fellow say, "Oh, put me anywhere, it does not matter what I have." In my girlish innocence I thought, "What a blessed privilege of manhood which does not ask to be guarded and sheltered and pleased, but can have the higher part of serving others and renouncing his comfort for their good." This chance word gave me an ideal of manhood, which, thank God, I have never lost, and have seen realized in many a noble, many an humble soul. True manhood and true womanhood are ever appearing in various forms, for the two are one. I know not whether Coleridge is right in asserting, or Theodore Parker was wrong in denying, that there is sex in souls. I fear we shall have to wait until we know more about souls and more about sex before we can settle that question; but I do know that the outward form, even the distinctive functions of sex, do not always secure the special characteristics which we suppose to belong to them; or rather, I believe that, as we rise higher and higher in the scale of spiritual being, the differing qualities which we find expressed in sex are blended into a more perfect harmony, and that out of the differentiation, out of the duality which is necessary for creation and life, we come ever and ever nearer to a restored harmony and unity of being.

So when we consider the highest representatives of masculine humanity, Philip Sydney, Fenelon, St. Francis, Channing, and above all the great founders of religions, Buddha and our own blessed Jesus, we cannot but recognize in them the perfect blending of the finest womanly traits with the strength and power which we attribute to man. And so in woman, Joan of Arc, the girl warrior; Elizabeth of Hungary; Catherine of Sienna; Louise of Prussia; Florence Nightingale,,--hold our reverence by their firm, manly courage and endurance, as much as they win our hearts by their feminine beauty and tenderness.

Womanhood

Dr. Bartol says: "The ever womanly leadeth us on, but the ever manly, too." Attractions must become equal for harmony and peace.

I have said that this is the era of womanhood. He who runs may read the prophecy of the future in the signs of the present. From Japan to Australia, in India, Russia, Finland, as well as in the foremost countries of Europe and America, we hear the echoes of her onward tread, and those who fear its victory are helping it on by the interest and discussion they excite. Everywhere there is new recognition of her rights and her duties. The Mohammedan woman of India rides in her palanquin to the polls to vote, and the woman on her bicycle is no more a wonder on the streets than a baby in its go-cart. The young woman no longer prides herself on the delicacy of her constitution and the nervous weakness which screams at the sight of a spider, but guards her health as a precious possession, not to preserve her personal beauty, but to give her strength to do her work.

Everywhere there is fresh inquiry in woman's essential nature. Science seeks to discover it by the analogies of the zoophyte and the trilobite and the loves of plants; and poetry finds it in the instincts of her heart. The great problem of the mutual relations between man and woman is the constant theme of discussion, and its solution varies from the old view, which gives all the rights to man and all the duties to women, to the sentimental dream which puts woman on a pedestal to be worshipped, instead of into the great school of life to be nourished and taught.

The scale has dipped pretty heavily on one side, until it becomes very evident that something must be done to restore the balance, or civilization will fall of its own false position. There may be not a little jarring before it is rightly adjusted. Already there are those who fear that man may have become so sure of his intellectual equality, and that the highest offices of life, the spiritual guiding of the child, the religious influence on the community, the aspiration for the highest purity are in danger of passing from his grasp, and he is likely to be left powerless and be obliged to give up the scepter to man. Was it not sadly significant when the great lawyer had to say," I don't understand Emerson; my gals do"? It is said that, great lawyer as Jeremiah Mason was, this recognition that it required the feminine intuition to understand the highest mind of his time is the only thing likely to be remembered of him.

Womanhood

Still sadder, still more alarming is the fact that man's grasp on moral truth has been in danger of loosening, and that in the selfish struggles of his lower nature for power and enjoyment he has sold his birthright of integrity and purity for the miserable pottage of sensual and worldly pleasure. A late speaker on Evolution finds this the danger of the hour, and asserts that woman is now in the van of the world's progress of evolution, but that until she can draw man up to her standard of truth and purity the onward march of the world will be stayed.

In the intellectual world the advance of woman is so rapid in comparison with that of the average man that educators are considering it as a serious problem which may disturb the right equilibrium. The finer faculties of the brain in man are so much injured by indulgence in intoxicating liquor, in the use of tobacco from an early age, and from still more dangerous and sinful sensual indulgences, that the danger is serious that they may not be able to do their rightful share of the thinking and the best working of the world. My heart leaped with joy when I heard the other day of two young men who said: "No; I cannot afford to drink; I cannot consent to smoke; it will hinder my power to do my work." And when I bethought myself that the mother of that family was one of the most celebrated intellectual women of the country I felt how this noble spirit was born in them, and that "the eternally womanly was leading them on."

While pessimism has been rampant in our day and the degeneration of society has been the theme of philosophers and the despairing question, "Is life worth living?" is answered by a jest, there are gleams of hope and promise which show us that "the eternally womanly is still leading us on," and that man's noblest nature is asserting itself and struggling up to the same high aims.

In our own day we are blessed with the reign of womanhood (long may it continue), which is enough to cheer our hearts and confirm our faith in its ultimate power in the kingdom of man.

England was wise indeed when she repudiated the salique law and recognized the right of the daughters of kings to their fathers' throne, even while her laws still held the common woman in abject servitude to her husband. By this means she has preserved an ideal of womanhood, an acknowledgment of her right in the universe, which, however partial and obscured, has kept an image for loyal devotion in the hearts of men, and has thus, by preserving for her a legitimate power, saved the nation from the basest influences. Michelet says: "France, which established the salique law, has always been ruled by the distaff." And the distaff has not been in the hands of the honest working-woman, but France has too often been ruled by the imperious false favorites of her kings, who, receiving nothing from their country, have given her nothing but treachery in return.

For sixty years a woman has sat upon the throne of the foremost nation of Europe. Her name is known, beloved, and honored all around the earth, for the sun does not set upon the world that owns her sway. We do not claim her as an exceptional woman, but as a true woman. Not gifted with the dangerously fascinating beauty of Mary of Scotland, the genius of Elizabeth of England, or the daring of Catherine of Russia; she is a typical woman, clear in her perceptions of right, entire in her devotion to duty, loving and tender in her heart, holy and pure in her life. She has accepted the high position to which she was called by inheritance, with its heavy responsibilities, but has done so, not that the nation might be governed by her personal will, but that the whole wisdom of the past, as embodied in law and the best intelligence of the whole people, might find expression in her action.

She has not, in gaining the kingdom of the world, lost her own soul; she has preserved her personality untouched, the Queen in all public relations; she has never forgotten her personal responsibility to her God in her private duties.

She has fulfilled every function of human life with simple fidelity. Blessed. thrice blessed among queens, her marriage was consecrated by deep and lasting affection, and in the partner of her life she found a fitting mate, a true and noble man whom she could value and respect for his own worth, and whom she did not consider as the first of her subjects, but as her equal and life helper. To his independent thought and life England is largely indebted for many a Queen. The royal home was as sweet and sacred as the peasant's cot. She has been the mother, not of future kings and queens alone, but of immortal human souls, and she felt that only greater responsibility rested upon her to guide them aright, since on their fidelity might rest the welfare of millions of her fellow-men.

Womanhood

What an influence has such a life, known and seen of all men, not exercised throughout the regions which have acknowledged her sway! It seems as if it were indeed a shining light set upon a hill to show that the truest womanliness is in union with the broadest usefulness, the widest relations of influence and responsibility.

The last sixty years have not been a period of millennial peace. It has been a time of wars and revolutions upon the earth, teeming with the most burning questions of capital and labor, of races and religions of systems of thought of material changes. England has had her full share in all these movements. Far different is the England of today and that overwhich the young maiden was called to preside, but under the leading of the ever womanly it has gone upward and onward. It has known progress through struggles, alterations of misery and hope, bitter passions seeking vent in violent action, cruel indifference to other's wrongs, and selfish quarrels for personal rights.

But through it all we can look back and see a marked progress in moral as well as material growth, and it has come through reform and not through revolution. Can we not feel thorugh all these years a calm sweet influence which has made itself quietly felt through the turmoil, and held many a turbulent spirit under the mild check of a loyalty which was of love rather than enforced obedience? I am a born and bred Republican, yet I have long felt that the gracious influence of England's Queen has brooded like a benediction over all her people, and has done more to hold closer the ties of country in the far-off homes of many an Englishman than any other influence. "I cannot forwear my allegiance to Queen Victoria" is the thought which fills the heart of many an immigrant and still holds it true to its native land.

Thus in many different ways the "eternaly feminie leadeth us on;" thus it will more and more find its full expression in all departments of the life of the world.

Last week when I listened to the gorious celebration of our young martyr to liberty for the Negro, Robert Shaw, the "Battle Hymn of the Republic" was sung. A chorus of male vioices began the strain with a quick, sharp, rhythm, which sounded like the quick tred of armed men or a volley of musketry. It left something wanting to the ear and the mind, of the magestic flow of a great nations's life; but one by one the voices of the people began to mingle with the strain and soon their came a sweet, harmonizing tone which seemed to float down from heaven, as the women's voices mingled with the music; and the rattle of the guns appeared to cease and the step to become more glad and free, and the watchword of the mystical chorus as they sang, "As He died to make men holy, let us die to make them free," recalled the beautiful voice and life of the young leader, and we felt the eternally feminine leadeth them on. So will that feminine voice mingle more and more in the world's life and complete the full harmony.

We are thankful to-day for the noble life of the Queen of these realms; we are thankful for it as a history of human progress towards more and better national life; but more than all do we prize it and thank God for it, as a prophecy of the finer, broader development of womanhood, and of the time when all the strength of manhood and all the love of womanhood shall be so blended in life that they shall bring us nearer to the kingdom of God the reign of truth and peace.

Bibliography
Ednah Dow Cheney

Primary Sources:

Books: Because this list encompasses a wide range of subjects, it is partially annotated.

Handbook for American Citizens. 1866. (For Freedman's Schools)

Faithful to the Light: And Other Tales. Boston: American Unitarian
Association, 1871. (Story founded on adventures of Mrs.Bray) 1884.

Social Games. 1871. (written for hospital patients) 1899.

Sally Williams: The Mountain Girl, Boston:Lee & Shepard, 1872.
(Story for young people)

Patience. Boston: Lee & Shepard, 1872. (Solitaire games for invalids)

The Child of the Tide. Boston: Lee & Shepard, 1874.(1890,1902).

Life of Susan Dimmock. Boston: New England Hospital for Women,1875. (First
surgeon at hospital)

Memoir of Seth W. Cheney, Artist. Boston: Lee & Shepard, 1881.
(1810-1856, biography and account of artisticaccomplishments, with
portraits and illustrations.)

Gleanings in the Fields of Art. Boston: Lee & Shepard, 1881.
(Collection of first lectures given at Concord School of Philosophy. An
aesthetics; periods: Greek, early Christian, Byzantine, contemporary;
nations: Italian, Spanish French, German, English, American;
artists: Michelangelo, Albrecht Durer, David Scott.)

Selected Poems from Michelangelo Buonarroti. Boston: Lee & Shepard,
1885.(Guasti and her own translations of Michelangelo's epigrams,
epitaphs, madrigals, sonnets, canzonets and triplets. Thesis is that
Michelangelo's subjects are metaphysical.)

Poems by David Atwood Wasson. Boston: Lee & Shepard, 1888.

320

(Edited by Cheney, includes complete sonnets and three long poems.)

Louisa May Alcott, The Children's Friend. Boston: L.Prang, 1888. (Illustrated by Lizbetly B. Comins, text dedicated to the children of America reveals Louisa's life and stories as exemplary.)

Harriet Sewell: Poems. With memoir by Ednah D. Cheney. Cambridge, Mass.: Riverside Press, 1889.

Memoir of Margaret S. Cheney. Boston: Lee and Shepard, 1889.

Memoirs of John Cheney, Engraver. Boston: Lee & Shepard, 1889. (Early life in Manchester, CT (1801-85), letters, engraving examples, notes by S.R. Koehler, C.H. Hart.)

Stories of the Olden Time. Boston: Lee and Shepard, 1890. (For the New England Society.)

Norah's Return: Sequel to Ibsen's `Doll House'. Boston: Lee & Shepard, 1890.

Care of the Sick, Hospitals and Training Schools for Nurses Managed Wholly or in Part by Women. New England Hospital, 1891.

Life of Christian Daniel Rauch of Berlin. Boston: Lee & Shepard,1893.(Rauch (1777-1857) German sculptor of monuments of Queen Louise, Frederick the Great, Albert Durer amid 378 works. Biography, chronological listing of works, influence.)

Memoirs of Lucretia Crocker and Abby May. 1893. (Women who worked for education, women's issues. Printed for private circulation.)

Louisa May Alcott Her Life, Letters and Journals (1889). Boston: Little,Brown, 1899.(From genealogy and parentage through authorship with Cheney's portrait of her. Lists 25 vols. of Alcott's stories.)

The Story of the Alcotts. Boston: Little, Brown, 1900.(Condensed from **Louisa May Alcott Her Life,...**) 189?,1900?,1932.

Reminiscences of Ednah Dow Cheney. (born Littlehale). Lee & Shepard:

Boston, 1902.(First four chapters-birth to after marriage, next seven on School of Design, Anti-slavery, Transcendentalism, Concord School of Philosophy, Art, Reforms. Appendix: three lectures--Transcendentalism, Margaret Fuller, Women; two poems dedicated to her, six psychometric readings on John Q. Adams, A. Bronson Alcott, Margaret Fuller, Jane Cheney, and letters of Seth W.Cheney.)

Essays in Books:

"Women of Boston." **Memorial History of Boston.** Boston:James R. Osgood, 1881:331-356.
"Emerson and Boston." **The Genius and Character of Emerson.** F.B. Sanborn, ed. Port Washington, N.Y.:Kennikat Press, 1885:1-35.
"Das Ewig-Weibliche." **The Life and Genius of Goethe: Lectures at the Concord School of Philosophy** ed. F.B. Sanborn, New York: Ticknor, 1886:218-250.
"Care of the Sick." **Woman's Work in America**. ed. Annie Nathan Meyer. New York: Henry Holt, 1891:346-58.
"Lucretia Mott." **Prophets of Liberalism**. Boston: James H. West, 1900:29-43. (Free Religious Association of America)

Periodicals:

Atlantic
"Life and Work of Ary Scheffer." 4:265.
Chatauquan
"Shall They Work For Pay?" 13:(1887)1131-42.

The Christian Examiner
"Springer's Period of Revolutions" 83 (Sept.1867):157-75
"Vittoria Colonna" 84 (Jan.1868):22-39.
"The Hope of the South" 87 (1869):24.

Commonwealth
"Allston as a Writer" (18 Feb. 1866)

The Index (over 100 articles 1872-1882).
"Mr. Morse's Bust of Theodore Parker" (9 March 1876) 114-15.

The North American Review
"Lesties' Handbook of Art" 83 (July 1856):422.
"The Life and Poems of Michael Angelo" 89 (July 1859):1.

Open Court

"The Radical."1(April) 117.

"Conversations of A. Bronson Alcott." 2 (August 2, 9,1888):
1131-33, 1142-44.

"The Mohonk Conference and the Education of Negroes." 4(July 3
1890):2370-71.

"Dramatic Poem by Ibsen." 4 (October 9, 23 1890):2557-59, 2579-82.

"Religious Prospects of Italy." 5(July 23, 1891):2885.

"Association for Advancement of Women." 9(January 10, 1895):4356-58.

"Sketch of Dr. Zakrzewska's Life" 16(July 1902) 391-93.

The Radical

"Art and Religion" 4 (July 1868):1-14.

"Jean Francoise Millet, The Peasant Painter." 8:24.

"Value of Individuality to Church and State" 8(February 1871):24-45.

"The Next Step in Popular Education:Labor Schools" 9(August 1871:1-19.

Unitarian Review

"Relations of the Child to the Home" 1(June 1874):336-46.

The Woman's Journal

"The Crown of Thorns" (4 March 1876):164.

"Miss Whitney's Samuel Adams" (8 July 1876):217.

"Fair Harvard to Fair Women" (22 March 1876):92.

"Art Exhibit by Women" (18 February 1888):58.

"In Memoriam:Mary Ann Haliburton" (19 May 1888):159.

"Marine Zoological Laboratory"(1 September 1888):282.

"A Valuable Discussion" (15 December 1885):392.

(and more articles in addition to these)

Pamphlet:

"Municipal Suffrage for Women," No. 2. Boston:1889.

Poems:

"Margaret" **The Woman's Journal** (18 January 1879):18.

"The Mayflower" **Open Court** 5(March 19,1891):2744-50.

Prayers:

"The Larger Prayer" or "The Prayer Answer" in James Gilchrist Lawson
comp. **Best Loved Religious Poems**, New York:Fleming H. Revell, 1933,
and in Caroline Miles Hill ed. **World's Great Religious Poetry**.
N.Y.:Macmillan, 1934, and Croft M. Pentz comp. **The Speaker's
Treasure of 400 Quotable Poems.** New York: Zondervan, 1963.

Lectures:

Horticultural Hall
      "The Function of Art in Life" 20 March 1870
International Council of Women: Washington D.C.
      "Hospitals Managed By And For Women" 27 March 1888

The Concord School of Philosophy
In part recorded in **Scrapbook**-Concord Memorial Library
      "Art" (10 lecture series) 1879
      "Color," "Early American Art" 1880
      "The Relations of Poetry to Science" 1881
      "Nature" 1882
      "Emerson and Boston" 1884
      "Dante and Michelangelo" 1887
      "Philip Massinger and John Ford" 1887

Congress of American Advancement of Women, New Orleans
      "Margaret Fuller" 1895 in **Reminiscences**

Mechanics Institute
      "The Reign of Womanhood" 1897 in **Reminiscences**

The New England Woman's Club, 1868-93
      Unpublished
      "Color"
      "Home"
      "Play"
      "Horticulture for Women"
      "Women's Capability for Higher Education"
      "Older Children in Home Relations"
      "Manners"
      "Spanish Art"
      "Women of Boston"
      "Dante and Michelangelo"
      "Names"
      "Civil Marriage"
      "Queen Louisa and her Statue by Rauch"

Secondary Sources:

Adams, Oscar Fay. **A Dictionary of American Authors**, Boston: Houghton
    Mifflin, 1901.

Blackwell, Alice Stone. "Ednah Dow Cheney" obit. **Women's Journal**. Nov.26,
    1904:First page and 389.

Bridgman, Raymond L. ed. **Concord Lectures on Philosophy**. Cambridge,
    Mass." Moses King, 1882.

Cameron, Kenneth Walter, ed. **Sixty Years of Concord: 1855-1915,**
    Franklin Benjamin Sanborn. Hartford: Transcendental Books,1976.

Chadwick, John White. **Theodore Parker Preacher and Reformer**. Boston:
    Houghton Mifflin, 1900.

Commager, Henry Steele, **Theodore Parker.** Boston: Beacon,1947.

Croce, Beneddeto. **Guide to Aesthetics** (1913) New York: Bobbs-Merrill, 1965.

"Ednah D. Cheney's Speech on the Horticultural School,"[delivered 17 Feb.]
    The Woman's Journal (5 March 1870):66.

Emerson, R.W. **Nature, Addresses, and Lectures.** Boston: Houghton Mifflin,
    1883.

Foster, Charles H. ed. **Beyond Concord: Selected Writings of David Atwood
    Wasson.** Bloomington: Indiana UP, 1965.

Hanaford, Phebe. **Daughters of America**. Jersey City Heights, N.J.: 1803.

Howe, Julia Ward. **Reminiscences 1819-1899**. Boston: Houghton Mifflin, 1899.

----- **Sex and Education: A Reply to Dr. E.H. Clarke's "Sex in Education"**
    (1874). New York: Arno Press, 1972.

Jameson, Anna B. **Memoirs and Essays Illustrative of Art, Literature and
    Social Morals**. New York: Wiley and Putnam, 1846.

Kunitz, Stanley J. and Howard Haycraft eds. **American Authors 1600-1900.**

New York: H.W. Wilson, 1960.

Leidecker, Kurt F. **Yankee Teacher: The Life of William Torrey Harris**.New York: The Philosophical Library,1946.

Mainiero, Lina. ed. **American Women Writers**. New York:Frederick Unger, 1979.

McFadden, Margaret. "Boston Teenagers Debate the Woman Question, 1837-1838." **Signs** (Summer 1990):832-47.

Memorial Meeting New England's Club. Boston: George H. Ellis, 1905.

Memoirs of Margaret Fuller Ossoli. R.W. Emerson, W.H. Channing & J. Clarke (1884) New York: Bart Franklin, 1972.

Miller, Perry. **Margaret Fuller: American Romantic**. New York: Doubleday, 1963.

Pearson, Norman Holmes. **Hawthorne's Two `Engagements'**. New Haven, CT: Yale UP, 1963.

Sanborn, F.B. **Recollections of Seventy Years** vols 1,2. Boston: Richard G. Badger, 1909.

Schneider, Herbert. **History of American Philosophy.** New York: Columbia UP, 1963.

Scrapbook of the Concord School of Philosophy. Concord Public Library Archives.

"Selected Poems by Michelangelo Buonaroti." **The Literary World**. (July 11, 1885):239.

Shakir, Evelyn. "Ednah Dow Cheney: Jack of All Trades'." **American Transcendental Quarterly** (Summer-Fall 1980) 47-48: 95-115.

Sprague, Julia A. comp. **History of New England Women's Club 1868-1893.** Boston: Lee and Shepard, 1894.

Stewart, Maria. **America's First Black Political Writer.** Editor Marilyn

Richardson, Bloomington: Indiana UP, 1987.

Tolmin, R.P. **Proceedings Mass. Hist. Soc.** Vol. LXIV New York: Chas.
Scribners, 1958:51-52.

Warren, Mercy Otis, **The Plays and Poems of Mercy Otis Warren**, New York:
Scholars Facsimiles, 1980.

Willard, Frances E. & Mary A. Livermore. **American Women**. vol.1. New
York: Mast, Crowell and Kirkpatrick, 1897.

Mary Whiton Calkins
In Memoriam, 1951

Chronology

Mary Whiton Calkins 1863-1930

1863	March 20 born to Walcott Calkins and Charlotte Whiton Calkins (first of five children, 2 daughters, 3 sons) in Hartford, Connecticut.
1865	Family moved to Buffalo N.Y. Taught German by parents & Frau Felt.
1880	Moved to Newton, Massachusetts. Attended Newton High School.
1882	Entered Smith College with advanced placement as a sophomore.
1883	Her sister Maud died, MWC left Smith. Took private lessons in Greek.
1884	Reentered Smith. Her Senior Essay won second honors.
1885	Awarded undergraduate and master degree from Smith. Tutored brothers for Harvard.
1886	Family trip to Europe for 18 months: Germany, France, Italy and Greece. Met Abby Leach, instructor in Greek from Vassar College.
1887	Began as classics tutor at Wellesley College.
1888	Published first book: **Sharing the Profits**.
1889	Appointed as instructor in Greek at Wellesley College.
1890	Asked to teach philosophy at Wellesley. Accepted by William James and Josiah Royce for attendance in their seminars and laboratory work at Harvard. Worked as a private student with Edmund Stanford on dreams at Clark College psychology laboratory.
1891	Made Instructor in Psychology in the Philosophy Department. Taught first psychology class at Wellesley. Established first psychology laboratory at a women's college.
1892	Allowed to study with Professor Munsterberg as guest at Harvard. Published first article in philosophy published by **Philosophical Review**.

1893   First article in psychology published by **American Journal of Psychology**.

1895   Her thesis accepted by Department of Philosophy at Harvard. Degree denied by Harvard Corporation. Promoted to Associate Professor of Psychology and Philosophy in fall.

1898   Promoted to Professor of Psychology and Philosophy.

1901   Published first edition of **Introduction to Psychology**.

1905   Published **A First Book in Psychology**. Published **Der Doppelete Standpunkt in der Pyschologie** in Germany. Elected President of the American Psychological Association.

1907   Published first edition of **The Persistent Problems of Philosophy**.

1909   Awarded Doctor of Laws degree by Columbia University. Offered position at Columbia.

1910   Awarded Doctor of Laws degree by Smith College. Offered a position at Smith.

1927   Invited to address British Psychological Society, elected honorary member. Thirteen prestigious graduates petition Harvard to grant Ph.D. to Calkins. Denied.

1929   After 42 years of teaching retired with title of Research Professor.

1930   Died of inoperable cancer, February 26.

7

Mary Whiton Calkins

1863 - 1930

Born March 30, 1863 in Hartford, Connecticut, Mary Whiton Calkins was the daughter of Charlotte Whiton Calkins and the Reverend Walcott Calkins. Her parents were both descendants of colonial families; her mother was of triple Mayflower descent; her father's American origins began with the immigration of a Welshman to Plymouth, Massachusetts in 1638.

Her father, Wolcott, did his undergraduate work at Yale University distinguishing himself in mathematics, composition and oratory. He then taught at Worcester Academy in Worcester Massachusetts. There he met, and later married Charlotte Whiton. Upon finishing graduate work at Union Theological Seminary in Syracruse, New York, Walcott traveled with his new wife in Europe and studied at the University of Halle, Germany. On their return, he became the Associate Minister of Center Congregational Church in Hartford, later moving to Philadelphia to be the minister of the Calvary Presbyterian Church, and then to North Presbyterian Church in Buffalo, where Mary Whiton Calkins spent most of her childhood. Here at a pre-school age Mary began to learn German from her parents and a tutor, Frau Felt. For the rest of her life she was a fluent German speaker and writer.

In 1880, her family moved to Newton, Massachusetts as her father had been appointed the minister of Eliot Church. The family bought a house a few blocks above the church at 22 Bellevue Street where Mary Whiton Calkins lived with her family for the fifty remaining years of her life, dying there on Feburary 26, 1930.

Mary Whiton Calkins' first philosophical interest is shown in her senior high school graduation essay: "The **Apology** that Plato Should Have Written," a vindication of Xanthippe, the maligned wife of Socrates. Mary began her undergraduate work at Smith College with advanced placement as a sophomore. After the death of her sister Maud at Easter of that academic year, Mary withdrew from school. She reentered Smith in the fall of 1884, distinguishing herself in the study of Greek and philosophy, and winning second honors for her senior essay, "The Old Testament Teaching of Immortality." Graduating in 1885, she spent the next year at home tutoring two of her brothers (both of whom were to enter Harvard with advanced standing due to this tutoring and the insistence of their father that they learn French in France). At this time Mary began a life long involvment with social questions: viz. profit sharing, woman's suffrage, labor unions, and the economic and industrial problems emerging at the end of the nineteenth century.

In May, 1886 her entire family sailed for Europe, her mother and herself spending the winter in Leipzig, her father and brothers staying mostly in Paris. While in Europe, Mary visited and made a study of French, German and Italian industrial experiments in profit sharing. This research produced the material for her first book, **Sharing the Profits** published in 1888. In Paris, Mary met a Vassar College instructor, Miss Abby Leach, and the two traveled to Italy and then spent some months in Greece. While there, Mary Whiton Calkins increased her skill in modern Greek, visited the great historical centers of philosophy and broadened her knowledge of the Greek classics.

When they came home in September, 1887, with the help of her father, she became a tutor in classics at Wellesley College. In 1889, Mary Whiton Calkins became an instructor in Greek. Then in 1890, because of the needs of the College, she was asked to study and teach metaphysics and psychology. At first she thought of returning to Europe for her philosophical studies, but because of her excellent command of both French and German and because of the opportunity to study with some of America's most outstanding philosophers and pyschologists at

Harvard and with the outstanding psychologist Edmund C. Stanford at Clark University, she remained in the Boston area.

Her studies in dream psychology, made under Dr. Stanford, were what first brought her into intellectual prominence.

Her studies in philosophy with Josiah Royce, Hugo Munsterberg and William James, caused these great philosophers to praise her as one of their most brilliant pupils. In 1895 she took the examination for a Harvard Ph.D. William James ranked her oral examination above any that he had ever heard. The Philosophy Department passed her with distinction, and recommended her for the doctoral degree. The Harvard Cooperation, however, refused her the degree because Harvard University did not award degrees to women. Years later when Radcliffe College offered her the doctor's degree, she declined maintaining all her work had been done at Harvard and none at Radcliffe.

In the fall of 1895 Mary Whiton Calkins was appointed an Associate Professor of Psychology and Philosophy. With the help of Professor Stanford, she established one of the first laboratories of psychology in America, and the very first to be founded in any college for women. By this time she had written one book and eight articles. Her primary interests were in the foundations, the methods and point of view of psychology. Her fundamental enthusiasm was for philosophy, and she began to move closer and closer to the philosophy and psychology of the self, which she eventually named Absolute Personalism.

Her teachings are clearly embodied in four important books: **An Introduction to Psychology** (1901), **The Persistent Problems of Philosophy** (1907), **A First Book in Psychology** (1909) and **The Good Man and The Good** (1918). Her last published book, a selection of texts of **Berkeley** (1929) begins with a brilliant forty-three page introduction portraying the personalism of George Berkeley as the forerunner of her own Absolute Personalism. She wrote over one-hundred articles and papers, equally divided between psychology and philosophy.

Mary Whiton Calkins was the only women ever elected to the presidency of both the American Philosophical Society and the American Psychological Association. In the history of the American scholarship only two others have ever been the president of both these associations; they were her teachers, William James and Hugo Munsterberg.

335

Mary Whiton Calkins was lionized at Wellesley College and in her contemporary academic community of America. She had been awarded honorary degrees by Columbia university in 1909 and Smith College in 1910. When offered positions at both of these institutions, she chose to remain at Wellesley. In 1927 the British Psychology Society invited her to become an honorary member and to address their annual meeting. That same year fifteen prestigious Harvard alumni, many college professors and administrators petitioned Harvard to award the Ph.D. to Calkins. For the third time, it was denied her.

At her death, Edger S. Brightman portrayed her as the Great American Personalist, and the American Philosophy Association, even as its was then turning to positivism and rejecting idealism, saw her as a continuing presence in the history of American philosophy and psychology. Her principal book, **The Persistent Problems of Philosophy** went through five revised editions and many many reissues from 1907 through 1930. The edition of her introduction and the selected texts of George Berkeley remained in print from 1928 until 1957.

Yet as a scholar, philosopher and as an influential women, Mary Whiton Calkins immediately fell into obscurity, where she unjustly remains. Despite her brilliant career and her important contributions to American philosophy and psychology she is not mentioned in the multivolumed bibliography **American Women Writers**. Listed as M.W. Calkins in the list of the presidents of the American Philosophical Association, she is almost forgotten in American philosophy. One of the intentions of this anthology is to display her power and her breadth as a women of philosophical and psychological perspicuity and depth.

Introduction to "The Just Man"

Mary Whiton Calkins published her book on ethics, **The Good Man and The Good**, in 1918, near the end of the First World War. This book reflects the social and the political troubles of those times, and it does so in the philosophical tradition of American liberalism. Calkins espoused this view all her adult life: her first book was on profit-sharing. An active member of the Fellowship of Reconciliation and the Civil Liberties Union, she often voted the Socialist ticket. In an article entitled "Enemies of the Republic, Are the 'Reds' Stalking our College Women?" Calvin Coolidge, then Vice-President of the United States wrote in the June 1921 issue of **The Delineator**, "She is said to have voted for [Eugene] Debs for President in the recent election" (66). Calkins was an uncompromising pacifist. Nevertheless, her liberal political perspective never took away her abilities as a rigorous and careful philosopher.

Mary Whiton Calkins' view of justice is traditional in its allegiance to the 18th century idea of approval and disapproval, yet it is original in its interpretation of what kind of personal approval that is and how the judgment of that approval is to be gained. Her attachment of the basic characteristics of justice to the community of selves shows the metaphysical influence of her teacher Josiah Royce, as surely as it reflects the results of her psychological research. The centrality of justice as constitutive of every other virtue on the one hand and particular to property on the other is traditional Aristotle as she asserts, but it is also peculiar to her unique analysis of the qualities of subject as distinguished from object. The forms of property--viz. property gained effortlessly versus that gained through personal effort--extend John Locke's ideas to the pragmatism of her friend and teacher William James.

At the conclusion of this excerpted chapter, Mary Whiton Calkins discusses the relation of justice to law and to social order, manifesting her own commitment to the Great Society envisioned by the turn of the century liberal politics of her day. At the same time, and with the same deliberation she leaves open the question of whether socialism or a modified individualism is the best way to gain such a society, referencing various studies that argue the question.

This respect for the social and political views of her students and her readers was especially noted by both students and the professional philosophical community. Many of her students and friends came away from her works with a philosophy very much different from her own, and she truly took this as a tribute to her eager and sincere interest in encouraging independent thought. Mary Whiton Calkins brought philosophers of opposing views to lecture in her courses. Her desire was that the intellectual life should encompass rather than restrict. She is both exponent and example.

Rosemarie Tong's **Feminine and Feminist Ethics**, 1993, continues the dialogue begun in Calkins' philosophy of justice. Calkins made the point clearly that "justice regards sympathy." Tong disagrees with current arguments which make justice and caring opposing issues. The philosophy of justice was also considered by predecessors of Calkins: justice informed and was informed by the feminist philosophy in the work of Judith Sargent Murray (**GI** vol.1 xxiii); justice is ingegral to the epistemology of Frances Wright who considered knowledge as "just knowledge."

For the careful reader Mary Whiton Calkins' remarks on justice, presented here, typify her metaphysics and reflect her epistemology as well as set forth her moral and intellectual purpose.

338

THE JUST MAN

The Nature and the Basal Forms of Justice

I.

Since the golden day when Socrates, stopping on his way from the Piraeus at the house of Cephalus, discussed with Glaucon and Adeimantus and Thrasymachus the nature of the just man, this problem -- which is even older than Socrates -- has pressed for solution. The problem arises because men are called just in so many situations and for so many reasons -- for their estimates of themselves and of their fellows, for their award of prizes and penalties, for their apportionment of treasure and gifts and time. There can be little question, however, that the basal form of justice is appraising justice, the virtuous estimate, or valuation, of oneself or of another self. Next to truthfulness, justice, as will appear, is the fundamental virtue; and, little as many of us suspect it, injustice is the most hotly resented of the vices not merely unjust apportionment of money and favors, but unjust estimates and valuations. A man's demand for justice is, in truth, far from satisfied when he has had all that is justly "coming to him" in goods or in positions. Quite as insistently he claims that he be justly estimated. He may indeed resent an unjust prejudiced judgment of himself or of his acts more than he resents an unjust apportionment of goods. No injury rankles and stings more sharply than undeserved blame, unjust perversion of one's meaning, unjust interpretation of one's motives.

The just man may be described as the man who holds his instinctive, personal likes and dislikes under moral control. Obviously, liking and disliking are very fundamental sorts of feeling, lying at the core of all emotional experiences. One likes, or is pleased with, things and qualities and persons of the most diverse types; and conversely one dislikes, or is displeased with all sorts of people or things. Where the object of like or dislike is relatively permanent and when the affective experience is overlaid with thought, like and dislike are transformed into approval and disapproval. Justice is a form of personal approval or disapproval; it

339

is the estimation of persons, or of personal activities or qualities, in their relation to the universal community of selves. The extremes which it modifies are extremes of prejudice undue liking, excessive dislike. The end which it holds before itself is - the end of moral loyalty: the fullest life of the universal community of selves.

It will be profitable to suggest at the outset some of the forms of prejudiced liking and prejudiced dislike, between which, as between Scylla and Charybdis, the just man must steer his way. The just man is governed in his moral appraisals neither by odd temperamental congenialities and incompatibilities; nor by conventional and traditional prejudices; nor finally, by likes and dislikes founded on agreeing or disagreeing interests. To illustrate: the just man does not take the position of the author of the famous couplet:

I do not like you, Dr. Fell;

The reason why I can not tell;

he is uninfluenced by racial prejudice in his estimate of "dago," negro, or oriental; his estimate of an I. W. W. leader is not weighted by the sense of the danger, to his own property interests, of the syndicalist propaganda.

We have next to study more closely the just man's estimation of his personal object -- that is, the discriminating appraisal either of man or of act as related to the Great Society. And we shall find that this just estimate of person or of deed, presupposes three fundamental characters of justice. (1) In the first place, justice involves sympathy, and the just man is one who comprehends. It is obviously essential to know the man whom one is justly to appraise; and one may not know a man save by taking his point of view, sharing his feelings and purposes, immersing oneself in his problems -- in a word, by sympathizing with him, taking on, as it were, his personality. The old opposition between justice and sympathy is evidently, therefore, founded on the misapprehension of both. The truly sympathetic critic will accuse no less often than he will excuse. He will feel, as no unsympathetic critic is capable of feeling, the undertow of inherited dispositions, the lure of primitive passions to which the tempted man has succumbed, but he will also sensitively apprehend his stifled aspirations, and his violated insights. "To understand all" will mean to the just man, who must needs sympathize, neither wholly to excoriate nor wholly to exculpate. It follows, as we may note in passing, that popular ethics is certainly in error when it sets down love as always blind. Of course no man can claim that he fully knows another, but certainly none know us so adequately as those who love us, for to no others can we show what really is in us. There is, therefore, no judge so inexorable as the just lover, who knows the highest reaches of the beloved's purpose and ability.

(2) The second of these fundamental characters of the just man is already implied in the first. For sympathy, like all the emotions, individualizes its object and the just man, accordingly, individualizes the man whom he estimates. Indeed it is clearly impossible really to know a conscious being except as an individual. "Probably," as William James says, "a crab would be filled with a sense of personal outrage if it could hear us call it without ado or apology a crustacean. 'I am no such thing,' it would say, 'I am MYSELF, MYSELF.'" Whatever is true of him in other situations, the man who is justly judged or appraised must be known for what he is, himself. The just man accordingly values a man not superficially for what he is said to be, nor for what he appears to be, but for what he really is as seen against the background of his opportunity and his environment.

This is indeed the reason why we make such sorry work of our attempts to estimate great groups of men in a wholesale fashion. We are too apt to judge a man by relegating him to a class say, of criminals or defectives, to be executed or segregated for the good of other people. It is the glaring fault of deterrent theories of punishment that they ignore the individuality of the criminal, treating him rather as the undistinguished kernel of a heap than as a unique individual, a person, a being with a life of his own. Evidently a punishment falls short of justice if it concerns itself exclusively for "society" — if, for example, it favors prison labor for the money it brings in, or criticizes it for breeding trouble with free labor, but never considers it from the standpoint of the prisoner's need for work. The unique advantage of the educative theory of punishment is that it sees the criminal in his relation to society, as himself suffering from his own attack on the community and that it seeks to train the criminal to control his own social impulses and to subordinate his skill to community interests.

(3) Justice, finally, involves thinking, not merely as every virtue requires thought in its control of instincts, but in a more special way. For thinking is of the very essence of justice. In approving or disapproving any one I ordinarily break up the *ensemble* of his character into constituent parts, dwelling on one or other of them; and I always compare him with some standard, explicitly or implicitly adopted. The rate of thinking in justice is accordingly of crucial importance. There is no such thing as unthinking justice. For example: to make a just promotion means thoughtful estimate of service given; to render a just decision means scrupulous analyzing and weighing of all evidence. In a word, the just man must of necessity be a thinker. And this is the reason why, admittedly, justice is a rather rare primitive virtue. For the habit of thinking is relatively late in experience, and little children like early races are notoriously deficient in the essentially intellectual virtue of justice. In truth, countless men and women, possessed of other graces and virtues, people who are scrupulously truthful, splendidly brave, and lavishly generous -- seem to be utterly incapable of being just. The fact that justice demands thought accounts also for the slow growth of political and industrial justice. For custom and tradition, which are the strong support of governments and institutions, are essentially unthinking imitations of past and present modes. Thus, the struggle for social justice is already half won when men are induced to discuss the problems of the short ballot, the minimum wage, or the old age pension instead of following on unthinkingly in the paths "their fathers trod."

It is of some importance to stress, in conclusion, what the preceding paragraphs have distinctly implied, that the great handicaps to justice, so conceived, are exaggerated egoism and undue altruism. If I am utterly immersed in myself I simply can not see myself as I truly am, one member only of a great living, pulsing organism of myriad selves whose life is my life; nor can I rightly value these other selves -- their reality, their claims and their needs -- if I am vividly conscious only of myself. In utter egoism and self-absorption I am, in a word, incapable of adequately estimating either myself or other people. And somewhat similarly I may make unjust moral estimates through absorption not in myself but in some one for whom I passionately care, whom therefore I constantly overvalue. This favored being or group is flawless in my eyes, can do no wrong; and every other person or group pales in significance. If opinions or estimates clash, the object of my love is always to be justified. Thus, Boswell found no fault in Johnson, - and Hume wrote a history in which, as Macaulay said, "all the high lights were Tory and all the shades Whig." The just man, on the contrary, appraises people neither from his own point of view nor from theirs; his horizon is not narrowed by his sympathy; rather he estimates men as unique, constituent members of the great human society.

II.

Like the non-moral forms of personal appraisal justice may be classified in two ways. Whether moral or non-moral, personal approval and disapproval are, in the first place, egocentric when directed toward myself, as in remorse and in pride, or aliocentric when concerned with some one else, as when I condemn the German government or approve of Arthur Henderson. In the second place, personal approval-disapproval, whether egocentric or aliocentric, may be concrete or abstract. That is to say, it may have regard, as in the illustration last given, to a man as a whole ar else to his specific qualities, decisions, or actions. So one may disapprove Clemenceau as a man or one may disapprove specifically his speech disavowing internationalist aims. It is important to note that one may approve either man or purpose while disapproving the other. So, for example, I may approve a man's work for civil service reform while I disapprove the man as one who neither seeks to achieve the good as he knows it nor acts in accordance with his consciousness of obligation. And conversely, I may abstractly disapprove of a specific choice or act while approving the man who makes it. In these latter cases, I am of course estimating decision and conduct according as it furthers or opposes the good as I conceive it; while, if I am truly just, I approve or disapprove the man who makes the choice on the basis of his own conception of the good and of the way to attain it. Thus, if I am a tolerant socialist, I may approve Mr. Carnegie as a conscientious and generous man, loyal to his own conception of the chief good,

343

while on the other hand I myself regard his philanthropies as subversive of the genuine co-operation of free men loyal to the Beloved Community. Or, if I am a large-minded militarist, I may approve the conscientiousness of the Quaker even while I reject his conception of the good on the ground (rightly or wrongly held) that it lacks the vital element of self-sacrifice. It must, however, be admitted that only the exceptionally just man can be trusted, in the case of another man, to make the complete divorce between actor and act and really to approve the conscientious seeker after political, religious, or social ends flatly in opposition to his own; or to exonerate the ignorant sinner while hotly resenting the sin. Jesus, indeed, said, "Neither do I condemn thee; go and sin no more;" but the human judge's sentence on the sinner is wont to be dyed by his disapproval of the deed. On the other hand, it is comparatively easy for a man to exculpate himself from the guilt of a choice which he later condemns and even easier to approve his own rectitude of purpose and his conscientiousness when he has grown to disapprove the former object of his moral will. So Paul records the sincerity of his youthful belief that he verily served God in consenting to the death of Stephen.

In conclusion it should once more be explicitly stated that approval and disapproval are not inevitably moral. All our aesthetic and intellectual appraisals of impersonal objects and a great number of our personal approvals and disapprovals are in truth either non-moral or even immoral in character. Especially is this true of egocentric self-appraisal. For I ordinarily make little effort to modify my self-satisfaction and remorse. Rather, I yield myself to their power; in my self-content I am too completely lapped about with pleasure, and in my remorse I am too bitterly or too hotly ashamed, to be capable of dispassionate analysis and balancing of motives and of that wide concern for all members of the Great Society, which are essential to just appraisal. And, more than this, both in self-content and in remorse I am likely to be too exclusively concerned with myself, and with the other self or little group whom I have pleased or offended, to assign myself my rightful place in the whole universe of selves. When, on the other hand, I justly approve and disapprove myself then I modify self-content till it turns into self-respect, the proper valuation of my own capacity and service; and I purge remorse of its abnormal intensity and its utter self-absorption till it issues in the virtue of humility, the just appraisal of my moral defects.

Admiration, or praise, and blame, the aliocentric forms of approval-disapproval, are also either non-moral or moral. To approve people whom we instinctively like and to disapprove those who are uncongenial; to approve men when they agree with us and to disapprove them when they disagree; to admire or despise people according as they help or hinder us, abet or thwart our purposes — all this is obviously emotional and non-moral. In truth, personal appraisal is justice only when a man modifies his instinctive like and dislike so as dispassionately to view himself, or another, in true relation to that Great Society of which all are members.

Justice in Distribution

I.

The just valuation of all the persons implicated in a moral decision is a factor in every moral situation, an element in the effectively virtuous control of every instinct. In other words, a man is never adequately brave or prudent or obedient without being justly brave, justly prudent, or justly obedient. His control of conflicting instincts is never fully virtuous unless he justly appraises each of the selves, and justly coordinates the relations of all the selves, who are involved in the given situation. Traditional ethics has obscured this truth, that justice is a constituent factor of every virtue, by its one-sided emphasis on what is known as distributive justice. In our study, immediately to be undertaken, of distributive justice, we must be on our guard against the implication that we are herewith exhausting the consideration of the forms of justice. Distributive justice is virtuous control, on the one hand of the appropriating and on the other hand of the surrendering instincts, which involves the adequate appraisal and comparison of all the persons concerned. Distributive justice accordingly includes both thrift and generosity. For example, a hard-worked man who justly distributes his money may well give up his club but not his camping trip in order to write a large cheque for war-relief; and he will not make the cheque so large that he must cut out his customary contribution to the Floating Hospital or his membership fee in the Consumers' League.

The form of thought which especially characterizes distributive justice is comparison. Its problem is to decide the claims of different persons or groups; and this requires not only an analytic study of the persons concerned but a specific comparison of their different needs, different capacities, and different claims. The just appointment of an official, for example, demands not only an independent estimate of his capacity and merit but a comparison of his claim with that of all the others who are eligible to the vacant position; and the just disposition of a man's estate, by will, requires not only the consideration of each of his possible heirs but a comparison of their rival claims. Obviously distributive justice presupposes just valuation, or appraisal, for only by rightly estimating the different persons involved is it possible to compare their needs and claims.

The great and constant hindrances to distributive as to fundamental appraising justice are on the one hand egoism, a man's over-concern for himself, and on the other hand narrow altruism, his exclusive absorption in one other self, or in a little group of others. For the truth is that (again to quote the Platonic Socrates) "for a long time past we have been talking of justice and have failed to recognize her." Clearly justice was already involved in that moral experience which is constituted by loyalty to the universal community and is sharply opposed to self-assertion and to incomplete altruistic loyalty. When a man's horizon narrows to himself he is incapable of adjusting his position to that of all environing selves. And when a man's desire is concentrated on one object -- friend, wife or child --he sees this figure alone exaggerated, not in its just proportions as one among others in family, state, or society. Thus, there is no commoner form of injustice than that of the devoted mother snatching food or clothing or pleasure for her child, in utter disregard of any other children or, for that matter, of any other human beings. Mrs. Squeers who invariably found that all "articles of apparel" sent by absent parents to their pupils of Dotheboys Hall "were too large or too small and calculated for nobody but young Squeers," and Madame Thenardier who grudged Cosette the blissful minutes with the doll reserved exclusively for her own children, are mere types of a class of mothers of all times and societies who, for the health or pleasure or advantage of their children, are ready to sacrifice not merely themselves but everybody else. In truth, there is no greater test of a man's justice than that which comes with the call to surrender something which he holds or grasps for one whom he passionately loves.

II.

So far, the discussion of distributive justice has concerned itself with the just man's attitude toward the persons whose conflicting claims he must estimate and harmonize. It is time now to consider what may be called the secondary object of distributive justice, namely, the object to be distributed. This may be of any form, material or spiritual. A man is just "with respect to whatever he has to distribute to others and to receive from them.... He distributes his attention, regard, and attachment . . . according to the reasonable . . . claim of each factor."[1] But the most difficult problem of distributive justice certainly concerns the distribution of property. We shall discuss successively the instinctive basis of property-holding; the principles fundamental to the just distribution of property; and the specific problems involved.

By property is meant the "title to the exclusive use or possession of goods,"[2] or objects of desire. The psychic basis of property lies, as has been shown, in the deep lying instincts of appropriation. "Birds defend their nests, the dog fights for his kennel," the child jealously guards his own plate or fork or coat. But these instincts must be disciplined, mere impulsive acquisitiveness and tenacity must be guided and dominated by self-control and endurance, before accidentally gained and loosely held possessions become property; and the appropriating and seizing instincts must be profoundly modified before the virtue of justice emerges from the struggle of instinct with instinct, appropriation with surrender, rapacity with sacrifice. The basis of all forms of property holding is

---

[1] Dewey and Tufts, **Ethics**, p. 415.
[2] Dewey and Tufts, **Ethics**, p. 487.

what is technically called "occupation,"[3] one of the expressions of the appropriative instinct. But there are two radically different sources of occupation and it is important to our purpose to distinguish them. (1) On the one hand occupation may be involuntary or effortless, that is, it may be due either to the bounty of nature, or to accidental discovery, or -- finally -- to gift or to inheritance, without effort of the occupier. Thus, a nomad owns the spot where he has pitched his tent and an Australian marks as his own a bees' nest which he has found, and the Astor baby inherits his millions. (2) The contrasted type of property holding has demanded action and effort, either working or fighting, and not mere receptiveness and tenacity. The instincts involved are acquisitiveness, a form of the appropriative instinct, and imperiousness. For "to seize, master and possess are instincts inbred by the biological process."[4] There is no lack of examples. All about us we see men and women, working at desks and machines, in hayfields and at fishing nets, at pianos and at washtubs, for the food they eat and the clothes they wear. And, looking further afield, we see nations fighting on the battlefield and high financiers fighting in legislature, court, and stock exchange to enlarge their holdings. From this consideration of the instinctive basis of property-holding we turn to the discussion of the principles underlying the just distribution of property of these two types, -- the moral adjustment of the apparently conflicting claims of different people and of different social groups. Here, as elsewhere, we may not expect ethics to provide us with ready-made solutions of specific problems. The possession of a clear conception of justice "only leads us," in Sidgwick's words, "to view the problem in a new aspect."[5] The basal principle of justice, however, may and must be held firmly in mind. Justice to any self involves the realization of him in relation, not alone to me or to any other individual, and not merely to his family or to any limited group, but to the most inclusive group to which he belongs. For no adjustment of one person to others can be adequate while it is incomplete; and the bonds which tie a man to his fellows are innumerable and ramify in all directions. This explains the fact that a

---

[3] Westermarck, **The Origin and Development of the Moral Ideas**, Chapter XXIX, pp. 35 ff.

[4] Dewey and Tufts, **Ethics**, p. 490.

[5] **The Methods of Ethics**, p. 271.

man may have injustice done him even when he is treated "for his own good" if he is thereby conceived as out of relation to the society to which he belongs. It would be unjust, for example, to tell a man a lie even if it would benefit him; and it would be unjust to deprive a man forcibly of the millions which are ruining him. For the man is not a separated unit which can be treated in isolation but a member of a society whose stability and efficiency (alike a condition and a goal of his own moral life) would be disturbed by untruth and by arbitrary force, whatever their specific aim. But, as so often has been argued, there are no assignable limits to the society of which every self is a member; and the just man can no more treat any one community, whether family or nation or church, in separation from the others than he can isolate any one individual. Justice is literally, therefore, regard not for one self nor for any restricted group of selves nor even (after the utilitarian ideal) for all the selves, taken each for each, but regard for the great all-including community of all selves inextricably and vitally related to each other.

From this enunciation of the basal principle of all justice there follows with entire necessity the statement of a second fundamental principle of distributive justice: there is no inherent, individual right to property since "every right, legal or moral, derives from the social whole."[6]   Even an individualistic and an incompletely socialized ethics must admit this as a statement of empirical fact, for recognition by others is necessary to constitute property. So also some form of government is necessary to secure a man in the occupation of his property. And to us for whom an individual self is a member of the Great Community, subordinate though essential to it, the conclusion is inevitable that no person, as separate and unrelated unit can assert his individual *right*, or just claim, to any possession. The claim to property is justified only when the possession of it is essential to a man's highest contribution to the universal community.

But this denial of an individual's inherent right to the "exclusive possession of goods" is far from being a denial of the justice of property holding. For if it can be shown that property holding so enhances a man's effectiveness and vigor that it is essential to his highest service to the Great Society, then the right to private property seems to be justified.   And this is precisely the conclusion to which

---

[6] Dewey and Tufts, **Ethics**, p. 415.

observation leads most of us. It seems to me perfectly certain, for example, that my efficiency is increased by my exclusive property right, in my own marked copy of James's **Psychology**, in my fountain pen, and in my toothbrush. The complete abolition of private property is, therefore, in no sense an obvious principle of distributive justice. On the contrary it would probably hamper effectiveness and initiative, squander time, and make for social disorder.

The conclusions so far reached about the just distribution of property are, thus, the following: that an individual self has no inherent right to property and yet that his ownership of private property is likely to enlarge his capacity to serve the Great Society. The pressing concrete problem of distributive justice concerns the extent and limits and methods of the just ownership of private property. And, once more, in discussing this question, we can attempt no more than the formulation of underlying principles. Distributive justice, in the first place, certainly does not imply a mechanical equalization of private property. Such a conception is nothing more nor less than a return to the outlawed dogma of the inherent individual right to property. That theory, fused with the sentimental form of democratic doctrine, the undiscriminating conviction that "a mon's a mon for a' that," precipitates this mechanical conception of equalization of property. But to parcel out, if it were possible, the world's possessions in equal shares and to hand over one apiece to every man would bear no remote resemblance to a just distribution. A man's sole claim, it must be remembered to any private property whatever is simply its power to raise his capacity for "doing his bit" in the common cause. And it well may be that to render society most morally efficient one man should have more and another less of concrete possessions. This conclusion, it must be at once noted and will later be argued, does not at all commit us to an assertion that all present-day inequalities of fortune are just!

It has next to be observed that justice, the adjustment of selves with each other, of necessity involves social order. Anarchistic propaganda, in so far as it is an effort to abolish not only government but ordered society, is inherently unjust, just because it is arrantly individualistic, because it flatly denies the fundamental interrelatedness of men with each other. But, once more, the truth that justice involves order must not be perverted, as too often it is, into the flagrantly absurd assertion that the political, the social and the industrial order of our day and our civilization are ideally just. It seems impossible, for example, to maintain that the seven hundred odd Englishmen who, a few years ago, owned one-fourth of the soil of England [7] were enabled by their ownership of these estates to render to society service so eminent that it offset the incapacity, demonstrably due to land-poverty, of the small-farming class. And, similarly, when we compare the growing number of American incomes running well up into the millions not merely with the abject poverty of the "submerged" but with the ten-dollar-a-week earnings of countless hard-working families, the justice of such inequality assuredly is not self-evident. For justice though unquestionably it permits, and indeed involves, property laws and property regulations, does not stand for tenacious, uncritical adherence to existing laws and traditions. Indeed, respect for the laws which preserve the social order is compatible with justice only if it is supplemented by a tireless effort to appraise, to modify and to enlarge laws -- in a word to make laws just. It follows, of course, that there will emerge great social crises when the just man must break with law and social order. John Hampden, when he refused to pay the ship taxes; the Boston men who threw the tea overboard and defied the Stamp Act; the English Nonconformists who in 1902 refused to pay the school rates -- all these were law-breakers, but many of us believe that they were just.

We have still therefore to press for the solution of our concrete, present-day problem. Granting unequivocally that there must be property laws, and granting that arithmetical equality of resources, even if attainable, would really run counter to the ideal of social justice: what, more exactly, is a just distribution of private property? In particular: are the property conditions of our own age and of our modern society in principle just, and are they therefore to be accepted and carried to their highest efficiency; or does justice demand a radical reconstruction? One answer to these questions, offered by an increasing number of contemporary thinkers, stresses the distinction already made between property gained without effort and property achieved through toil or struggle. Dispassionate examination of the facts shows that almost every great fortune and many a small one is founded in large part on natural resource on oil-well or mine or water-power accidentally in

---

[7] *Cf.* J. Herder, **The Case for Land Nationalisation**, (*in press*, 1913), Chapter III, p. 40.

possession of one man or of a few -- or else is founded on social increment, the increase in value due to the growth of communities. That is to say, even the fortunes which men make by adding thereto toil of mind and body are in part due to effortless occupation; while inherited fortunes are wholly of the effortless type. Now, not merely moralists but many publicists of our day are asserting that there are strict limits to the claim of private ownership through accidental occupation or discovery or through inheritance.   Accordingly there is a growing tendency to restrict private property by making individuals and corporations pay for franchises and waterrights, by setting off public reserves and, finally, by taxes on bequests.

On the other hand, most people still believe, with Locke, that a man is entitled to a share in the property to which he has contributed by his labor. "He that is nourished," Locke says, "by the acorns he picked up under an oak or the apples he gathered under a tree, has certainly appropriated them to himself.... I ask then, when did they begin to be his? . . . and it is plain, if the first gathering made them not his nothing else could. That labour . . . added something to them more than nature, the common mother of all, had done; and so they became his private right."[8] But we must guard ourselves, at this point, with the utmost care, against the danger of relapsing into the old discredited but long-lived doctrine of the individual's absolute right to anything that he holds.   We are beginning to realize that a man has no inherent right to an unearned fortune. But most of us have still to learn that, from the standpoint of moral justice, a man has the right to any property -- even to that which he earns -- only if the possession of it makes him a greater contributor to the universal good. For since truly I am inherently a member of the Great Society I must work for myself only as integral part of it; and I must look upon myself, literally, as steward, not owner, of the property which expresses my own thrift. We therefore utterly and finally reject -- more easily doubtless in the case of unearned property but as unequivocally in the case of our earnings -- the old dogma of the individual's inalienable right to any possession for himself, and assert with perfect literalness that, from the standpoint of justice, the ultimate owner is and must be the universal community.   Two sharply contrasted sociological doctrines are based on this ethical teaching that

---

[8] **Of Civil Government**, Chapter V., Sec 28.

private property is held not absolutely but in trust. According to one of these -- socialism, in a technical sense of the term -- the effective acknowledgment of the Great Society as ultimate owner can only be made by entrusting to a political or an industrial group -- to state or municipality or industrial guild, the ownership or the control of a significant part (if not all) of the property now privately held. According to the rival theory, often known as individualism, socialism is practically untenable because under these conditions of social ownership or social control the incentives would vanish to individual initiative, industry, and thrift and so the Great Society would suffer loss in the deterioration of its members. In reply most socialists urge that social control or ownership, especially if limited to basal necessities, would affect only the subhuman struggle for the bare requisites of life, that it would, in truth, "free moral energy"[9] for healthful competition and for individual initiative in truly social enterprises. Whatever the outcome of the controversy between the socialist and his critic, it is certain that the just man must actually and concretely not theoretically and verbally -- hold any property which he possesses, as he holds his spiritual treasure, in trust for the Great Society that in this age of unearned privilege and inherited injustice he must not cease to work for a social order in which property will be gained and held and used in direct furtherance of a completely moral loyalty.

---

[9] Simmel, **Moralphilosophie**, pp. 325-36.

Introduction to the "Self and Soul"

This short article, "Self and Soul" is Mary Whiton Calkin's response to Ellen B. Talbot's review of her most famous book **The Persistent Problems of Philosophy: An Introduction to Metaphysics through the Study of Modern Systems**, 1907. The friendly but firm review condemned Calkins for not having made a proper distinction between the contemporary ideal of the self and the traditional treatment of soul in the philosophers of the past. As the last text in this book, it is the first text wherein one woman philosopher responds to another. Thus it represents the early interaction of women philosophers, an activity now coming of age in twentieth century America.

In this article, published in **The Philosophical Review** in 1908, Mary Whiton Calkins brings precision and insightfulness to an examination of Ellen B. Talbot's criticism. Presented in a plain declarative style, with great philosophical savoir-faire, this distinction is finely made and carefully overcome.

In the first section she outlines the essentials of every contemporary psychologist and philosopher with respect to the doctrine of self, specifying also the differences in the psychological and the philosophical treatment of the "self." In the second section she compares these characteristics with the conceptions of the soul presented in the philosophies of Descartes, Leibniz, Locke and Alexander Baumgarten. In the third section she inquires into the important differences, which lead her to discuss the philosophies of Christian Wolff, Immanuel Kant and David Hume, as well, and to conclude with a claim of a special power for philosophy, Modern Personalism.

This article, though brief and often technical and sophisticated, shows the scope and the sensitivity that Mary Whiton Calkins has for the history of modern philosophy and for the distinctions that are formative of our present philosophical understandings.

The subsequent editions of **The Persistent Problems of Philosopher**, which went through many successive printings and five revised editions between its initial publication in 1907 and its last in 1925, respond to this article and provide fuller evidence of her excellence as a philosopher of history and a historian of philosophy.

SELF AND SOUL.

The conception of the self has undeniable significance in contemporary philosophy. By many who call themselves pragmatists as well as by many rationalists, and by almost all idealistic thinkers of whatever type, the universe is conceived as ultimately personal. And even our present-day realists are --most of them -- qualitative dualists, that is to say, they admit that selves exist alongside of extra-mental realities and related to them. In view of this modern emphasis, laid by writers of diverse tendency on the conception of self, there is timeliness in a recent suggestion[1] that the contemporary conception of self should be more carefully compared with the 'traditional doctrine' of soul, or spiritual substance.[2] Such a comparison is here attempted.

I

It is necessary, in the first place, to consider the essentials of the conception of self. In offering the outline which follows, I am of course formulating what is primarily my own doctrine. So far, however, as I am aware, there is nothing in my account of the self which diverges essentially from that expressed or implied by modern personalists.

At the outset It must be insisted that any conception of the self is taken over, by philosophy, from psychology conceived as doctrine of conscious selves. This view of the relation of philosophy to the psychology of selves need not obscure the difference between the two methods of treatment. The psychologist as such accepts the self as object of introspection, raising no questions about its ultimate reality, whereas the philosopher must attempt to settle the question of the

---

[1] In a review by Professor Ellen B. Talbot (in this **REVIEW**, Vol XVII, p 81) of my book, **The Persistent Problems of Philosophy**.
[2] The expressions 'soul,' 'spirit,' 'mind,' and 'spiritual substance' are used throughout this paper as virtually synonymous.

place of the self in the whole scheme of things. If he is a materialistic philosopher, he regards the self of the psychologist as a fiction ultimately reducible to non-psychic reality; if, again, he is a dualist, he accords to the self a position more or less coordinate with that of things or external objects; if, finally, he is a personalist, he conceives the universe as ultimately consisting in self or selves. But to the end he must include in his concept of self essentially what the psychologist should mean by the term. It is true that the consideration of the relation of the self to the rest of reality may lead him to infer from the characters discovered by the psychologist other attributes -- for example, moral predicates -- of the self, but he can only supplement and modify, he can never obliterate any characters of the psychologist's self.

There are two reasons for insisting, thus, that the self of philosophy is an immediately known and then reflected-on reality, not a merely inferred being. For so one gains both the guarantee of the existence of the self and a clue to the description of its rich content. By self is meant (1) a reality which is basal to the many conscious experiences, -- whether these are named ideas, mental processes, psychic contents, conscious functions, or faculties, -- a reality which in some sense includes the experiences and to which they belong.[3] This self is also known, both immediately and on reflection, as (2) persistent, as (3) unique, and (4) as further related (either assertively or receptively, and either egoistically or altruistically) with other-than-itself. By the *persistence* of a self is meant the realized fact of being the same self now as at some other time, -- a consciousness which is emphasized in anticipation and in recognition, but which forms an unaccented part of every experience. The *uniqueness* of a self is that character which distinguishes it from every other self, -- from every other reality of any sort. Such uniqueness, or irreplaceableness, the character by virtue of which one realizes that a self is a this-not-to-be-replaced-by-another, is an emphasized part of emotion, will, and

---

[3] *Cf. The Journal of Philosophy,* Dec, 1907, Vol. IV, pp 676 ff, and authors there cited for proof, or argument, that those who treat psychology as science of idea or of function implicitly assume the existence of the self whose the idea is, or of the self which functions. On the conception of the self, *cf.* the later papers of the series just mentioned (*Journal of Philosophy,* Jan.and Feb. 1908), and my *The Persistent Problems of Philosophy,* especially pp.408 ff., 422 ff.

faith, but an unattended to factor of all consciousness. The *relatedness* of a self, finally, so sharply emphasized by students of social psychology, may be shown to be a character of all consciousness. Always in being conscious I am aware not only of myself but of an other-than-self (either personal or impersonal). I may emphasize myself, -- for example, in will or in desire, -- and then I am egoistically conscious; or I may emphasize the other-than-self, as in sympathy or in loyalty, and then I am altruistically conscious. And my consciousness, whether egoistic or altruistic, may be assertive or receptive: I may assert myself or some other self, as in will and in faith; or I may fail, as in perception or in aesthetic emotion, to react upon my environment.

II.

The conception of self, thus briefly outlined, has now to be compared with the doctrine of the soul; and the discussion will be limited to the consideration of the soul-doctrine in the systems of philosophers of the seventeenth and eighteenth centuries. It must be noted at the outset that there is no one fixed and accepted concept of the soul; but that, in spite of divergences, all these spiritualistic thinkers, from Descartes downward, (1) agree in the teaching that the soul (or mind or spiritual substance) is a reality fundamental to its acts or faculties, its ideas or operations or experiences. Thus by Descartes spirit[4] is defined as "the substance in which thought [later described as including will, understanding, and even perception[5]] immediately resides"; and by Locke as "substratum to those operations which we experiment to ourselves within."[6] And Berkeley declares that, "besides that endless variety of ideas . . . there is likewise something which knows or perceives them and exercises divers operations. This . . . being," he asserts, "is what I call mind, soul. . . ."[7] This teaching of the soul as fundamental

---

[4] *Meditations,* Replies to the Second Objections, Def. VI. Cf. Wolff, *Psychologia Rationalis,* Sec. 10; Baumgarten, *Metaphysica,* Sec. 505.
[5] *Principles of Philosophy,* Part I, prop. ix.
[6] Essay Concerning Human Understanding, Bk. II, Chapter xxiii;, Sec. 5.
[7] Principle of Human Understanding, Sec. 2.

to its operations readily (2 involves the implication or the affirmation of its persistence, or identity. Berkeley[8] implies and Locke[9] definitely teaches the identity of the soul; and Leibniz unequivocally asserts that a monad, or soul, is an identical unity of its own states. "My inner experience," he says, "convinces me *a posteriori* of this identity, but there must also be some reason *a priori*. It is not possible to find any other reason, excepting that my attributes of the preceding time and state, as well as the attributes of the succeeding time and state, are predicates of the same subject . . . the so-called I . . . which is the basis of the interconnection of all my different states."[10]

Most of these writers (3) imply also the uniqueness of the soul. Leibniz lays special stress on this character. The uniqueness of the soul becomes in his hands its complete independence of everything else excepting God.[11] On the other hand, these seventeenth and eighteenth century writers (4) do not explicitly consider the essential and inherent relatedness of the self.

It is thus evident that the contemporary conception of self is reaffirmation and amplification of certain central factors of the earlier concept of soul. It is most important to recognize this fundamental likeness of the two doctrines; for in the exuberance of the criticism which Hume made fashionable and which later philosophers have perpetuated, too little justice has been done to the `traditional doctrine' of spiritual substance, or soul. It is high time to insist on the truth involved in the older doctrine, and to avow boldly the partial identity of the concept of self with the Cartesian and the Berkeleian conception of spiritual substance. It should be noted also that most of the older thinkers more or less consciously use the terms `spirit' and `soul' as synonym for `self,' or `I.' Berkeley indeed says explicitly: "What I am myself, that which I denote by the term I, is the same with what is meant by soul or spiritual substance."[12] Only Locke, whose teaching will presently be discussed, distinguished the two.

---

[8] **Principles**, Secs. 27, 89, et al.; **Dialogues between Hylas and Philonous**, III, Open Court edition, p. 95.
[9] **Essay**, Book II, Chapter xxvii, especially Secs. 2 and 14.
[10] **Letters to Arnaud**.
[11] **Ibid.**,IX.
[12] **Principles of Human Understanding**, Sec 139; cf. **ibid.**, Sec 2; Cf. also Descartes, **Meditations**, II; and Leibniz, **Letter to Arnaud**, XIV, and **Systeme nouveau**, 11.

III.

This admission of the likeness of `self' to `soul' should not, however, obscure the important differences between the earlier and the later conception. These are of two main types: The conception of soul differs from that of self, first, in that it is, in one sense or another, subordinated to that of body; second, in that it is needlessly empty and abstract. The first of these distinctions is, primarily, a difference in origin. According to the most primitive belief, the soul is merely a shadowy sort of body, a sublimated and attenuated material substance. This conception, crude as it is, tends to persist as an unharmonized feature of doctrines with which it is inherently incompatible. The soul is in truth conceived, in terms which seem to be more or less covertly materialistic, as body deprived of certain inconvenient or undesirable characters. Thus, the conceptions of qualities as `inhering' in a `substratum' has, as Berkeley[13] suggested, a distinctly materialistic flavor. And Locke's admission, though only for the sake of argument, "thinking being may also be material,"[14] suggests the latent materialism of his conception. Even more obviously the theories of soul in its relation to the body show the taint of an unrealized materialism. This appears both in the efforts to indicate the seat of the soul and in the doctrines of the soul as moving the body. So Descartes holds that there is in the body an organ, the pineal gland, "in which more particularly the soul exercises its functions"[15]; Wolff teaches that "souls preexist in the preexisting organic particles from which the foetus is formed";[16] and Baumgarten discusses the `locomotive faculty'[17] by which the human soul moves the body. From the fact that the conception of soul is reached by way of that of body follows another difficulty. Instead of starting, like modern personalists, from

---

[13] **Principles**, Secs. 16 and 17.

[14] *Essay Concerning Human Understanding,* Book IV, Chapter x, Sec. 3. It will be remembered that Locke is contented when he has pointed out that "the notion of spirit involves no more difficulty in it than that of body" (*Ibid.*, Book II, Chapter xxiii, Secs. 5, 15).

[15] *Les passions de l' ame,* Premiere partie, art. 31; *cf.* art. 42 *et. al.*

[16] *Psychologia rationalis,* Sect. IV, Cap. II, Sec 704.

[17] **Metaphysica** (1779), Pt. III, Chapter ii, sect. i, sec 750. *Cf.* Locke, **Essay concerning Human Understanding**, Book III, Chapter, xxiii, Sec 20.

the introspective observation of the conscious self, these spiritualistic philosophers of the seventeenth and eighteenth centuries describe the soul from the standpoint of its relation to the body, that is, they attribute to the soul predicates which are mere negations of bodily characters. The soul is described, for example, as a simple being,[18] and this character is inferred from the opposition of soul to body. Because body is extended and divisible, therefore, it is argued, the soul is unextended, indivisible, simple. In its purely negative signification, this doctrine is unobjectionable; but it is also useless. Certainly the soul is not extended; but introspection and reasoning fail to disclose its `simplicity' in any other sense of the word, unless by simplicity be meant no more than by identity.

It should be noted that Kant's criticism, in his "Paralogisms of Pure Reason,"[19] is directed in great part against this doctrine of the soul as thing, this conception of the soul as analogous, though opposed, to body. Kant, following Hume, points out that simplicity, identity, and the other traditional characters of the soul-thing are not objects of sense consciousness.

A second crucially important difference between the conception of soul and that of self is the following: The conception of substance, as often held, is a very barren and empty abstraction and is therefore sharply contrasted with the modern concept of the self as possessed of concrete characters, in a word, as conscious. The abstractness of the soul-concept is explicit and avowed in the philosophy of Locke; and Locke's doctrine of substance must, accordingly, be considered at somewhat disproportionate length. The peculiarity of Locke's teaching is the following: He holds to the existence of a conscious self, but he assumes, in addition, the existence of a soul or spiritual substance. The `self' or `person'[20] is characterized, Locke teaches, by consciousness. "Consciousness" he declares, "is that which makes every one to be what he calls self; . . . as far as ever it can be extended, should it be to ages past, [it] unites existences and actions . . . into the

---

18 *Cf.* Wolff, **Psychologia rationalis**, Secs. 48,49; Berkeley, **Principles**, Secs. 27,141.

19 **Kritik d. r. Vernunst**, edition A, pp. 344ff.; edition B, pp. 402ff. Of course, the criticism of the Paralogisms is directed, also, against the conception of the transcendental unity of apperception (or self), as known object. Indeed, Kant does not, in this section, sharply distinguish the two concepts.

20 **Essay**, Book II, Chapter xxvii, Sec 26: "Person, I take it is the name for this self."

same person . . . so that whatever has the consciousness of present and past actions, is the same person to whom they both belong."[21] This suggests what Locke unequivocally teaches, the identity of the self. He describes the self as "a thinking, intelligent being, that has reason and reflection, and can consider itself as itself, the same thinking thing, in different times and places."[22] He emphasizes, also, the individuality, realized in the emotional experience, of the self. The "intelligent being," he says, "sensible of happiness or misery must grant that there is something that is himself that he is concerned for and would have happy."[23]

From these quotations it is clear that Locke has a vivid conception (in its essentials closely parallel with that outlined in this paper) of the conscious self. But instead of following the fashion of preceding spiritualistic philosophers by identifying the concept of self with that of spiritual substance, Locke teaches that, besides the conscious, identical, individualized self, there exists an immaterial substance, a soul. He even regards it as possible, although unlikely,[24] that the identity of the self may persist through a change of souls, --in other words, that "the same consciousness," instead of being " annexed solely to one individual substance . . . can be continued in a succession of several substances." A man's "immaterial spirit" may be, for example, " the same soul that was in Nestor or Thersites at the siege of Troy . . .; but he now having no consciousness of any of the actions of Nestor or Thersites [cannot] conceive himself the same person with either of them."[25]

Locke reaches this conclusion,-- that besides the self there exists a spiritual substance, or soul,-- by the keen observation of the fact that "consciousness being interrupted always by forgetfulness . . . doubts are raised whether we are the same thinking thing, i. e., the same substance or no."[26] An estimate of this reasoning

---

[21] Ibid., Secs 9 and 16.

[22] Ibid., Sec 9.

[23] Ibid., Sec 25.

[24] Ibid.

[25] Ibid., Secs 10 and 14.

[26] Loc. cit., Sec 10. The whole chapter is full of suggestion to the student of what is nowadays called the dissociation of personality. It should be added that Locke is not always true to his own distinction between self and soul. For example, he describes each, in the same terms, as `thinking thing.'

would lead us too far from the main topic of our study, the analysis of Locke's conception of soul thus distinguishcd from the self. "If anyone will examine himself," Locke says, "concerning his notion of pure substance in general, he will find he has no other idea of it at all but only a supposition of he knows not what support of . . . qualities." From this notion of `pure substance in general,' Locke proceeds to form that of spirtual substance by the mere addition of the negative predicate `immaterial.' For though he also calls spiritual substance `thinking thing,' he deprives this positive attribute of all its meaning by the repeated and unequivocal teaching that consciousness belongs not to soul but to self, or person.

This arbitrary distinction, drawn by Locke, between abstract soul and concrete self has had a most curious result in philosophy. The justified polemic of Hume and others against that empty nonentity, the spiritual I-know-not-what, has been interpreted as a successful criticism of the concept of self.[27] And so it happens,--in defiance of Locke's sharp distinction between soul and self, -- that the unhappy self has staggered along through these two hundred odd years burdened with the obloquy which, with some show of justice, is heaped upon the Lockian spiritual substance. Other philosophers have been guilty of over-abstractness in dealing with the self for example, the whole difficulty with the outlawed doctrine of the mental 'faculties' is simply this: that the soul, or mind, is first conceived abstractly, after Locke's fashion, as mere substratum or agent, and that then specific kinds of consciousness are referred back to this empty nothing as if explained by being called faculties of what is, by hypothesis, a mere `somewhat,' or $x$. The weakness of the doctrine lies not so much in the vagueness of the concept of `faculty' as in its total neglect of scientific introspection, and in its effort to explain `faculty' by `soul,' or `soul ' by `faculty,' without adequate observation of consciousness under either designation. Another significant example of the tendency to divorce spiritual substance is Berkeley's insistence that "spirits and ideas . . . [are] kinds [of being] entirely distinct and heterogeneous," [28] "natures

---

[27] It should be noted that Hume is not himself guilty of this confusion. He devotes one section of the **Treatise** to the doctrine of the `immateriality of the soul" and a different section armed with different arguments to the doctrine of self, or, in his words, `personal identity.' (*Cf.* **Treatise**, Book I, Part IV, sections 5 and 6.)

[28] **Principles**, Sec 89.

perfectly disagreeing and unlike."[29] Berkeley's whole `copy-theory' of knowledge, so prolific of results mischievous to later idealism, may be traced to his failure to recognize that the ideas are really what he himself calls operations of the mind, and that mind is never rightly conceived in abstraction from these very operations or ideas.

The result of this comparison of the concept of `self' with that of `soul' is in brief, then, the following. The affiliation, logical and historical, between the two has been freely acknowledged. It has been argued that Descartes and Leibniz, Locke and Berkeley, Wolff and Baumgarten, were right in so far as they taught that the occurrence of forms of consciousness implies the existence of a unique, persistent, and self-identical, conscious soul, or self. It has been pointed out, on the other hand, that the traditional doctrine of the soul suffers from two significant defects: that it conceives soul either after a material analogy or as endowed with mere negations of corporeal characters; and that it tends to rob the concept of soul of its concrete predicates. Modern personalism, on the contrary, --the doctrine of the self, -- starts from the introspective study of the immediately realized self and recognizes in this self all the rich content of actual experience.

---

[29] The inconsistency should be noted with Berkeley's equally emphasized teaching that spirits possess ideas; and that ideas inhere in spiritual substance.

Bibliography
Mary Whiton Calkins

Primary Sources:

Books:

Sharing The Profits. New York: Ginn, 1888.

Association: An Essay Analytic and Experimental. This is a monograph
supplement published by the **Psychological Review**, 56 pages, & 23
statistical tables. New York: Macmillan, February, 1896.

Introduction to Psychology. New York: Macmillan, 1901.

**The Persistent Problems of Philosophy: An Introduction to Metaphysics
through the Study of Modern Systems**. New York: Macmillan, 1907.

A First Book In Psychology. New York: Macmillan, 1905.

Der Doppelte Standardpunkt In Der Psychologie. Leipzig: Verlag von Veit,
1905.

The Metaphysical System of Hobbes: in Twelve Chapters from "Elements of

**Philosophy Concerning Body," and in briefer extracts from "Human
Nature," and "Leviathan,"** selected and ed. M.W.C. Chicago:
Open Court, 1905.

**Locke's Essay Concerning Human Understanding: Books II & IV with
Omissions**, selected   & ed. M.W.C. Chicago: Open Court, 1905.

Psychology: What Is It About? Reprinted from four articles published in **The
Journal of Philosophy, Psychology and Scientific Method**. New
York: Macmillan, 1908.   Printed with book pagination plus the
original pagination of the four individual articles.

The Poems of Sophie Jewett. Biographical preface, selected & ed. M.W.C. New
York: Crowell Press, 1910.

The Good Man and the Good: An Introduction to Ethics. New York: Macmillan, 1921.

Berkeley: Essays, Principles, Dialogues, selected and ed. M.W.C. New York: Scribner's, 1929 through 1957.

Articles:

"A Suggested Classification of the Cases of Association," **Philosophical Review** (1 July, 1892) 389 -402.

"Experimental Psychology at Wellesley College," **American Journal of Psychology** (5 November 1892) 260 - 271.

"Statistics of Dreams," **American Journal of Psychology** (5 April 1893) 311 - 343.

"A Statistical Study of Pseudo-chromesthesia and Mental Forms," **American Journal of Psychology** (5 July 1893) 439-464.

"Association (I)," **Psychological Review** (1 September 1894) 476-483.

"Notes on Fichte's **Grundlage der Wissenshaftslehre**," **Philosophical Review** (3 July 1894) 459-462.

"Synaethesia," **American Journal of Psychology** (7 October 1895) 86-107.

"Wellesley College Psychological Studies," **Pedagogical Review, Monograph Supplements 1,** 3 (1895) 319-341.

"Wellesley College Psychological Studies," **Psychological Review**, 3 (1896) 426-430.

"The Religious Consciousness of Children," **New World** 5 (1896) 705-718.

"Association (II)," **Psychological Review** (3 January 1896) 32-49.

"Community of Ideas of Men and Women," **Psychological Review** (3 July 1896) 426-430.

"Kant's Conception of the Leibniz Space and Time Doctrines," **Philosophical Review** (6 July 1897) 356 - 369.

"Short Studies in Memory and in Association from Wellesley College Laboratory," **Psychological Review** 5 (1898) 451-463.

"Attributes of Sensation," **Psychological Review** (6 September 1899) 506-514.

"Time as Related to Causality and Space," **Mind** 8 (1899) 216-232.

"Review of I Sogni, **Studi Psicologic e Clinici de un Alienista**, " **Science** 10 (1899) 334-335.

"Elements of Conscious Complexes." **Psychological Review** (7 July 1900) 377-389.

"Psychology as Science of Selves." **Philosophical Review** (9 September 1900) 490 - 501.

"An Attempted Experiment in Psychological Aesthetics," **Psychological Review** (7 November 1900) 580-591.

"Theorem uber die Empfindung farbiger und farbloser Lichter," **Archiv fur Anatomine und Physiologie Physiologische Abtheilung, Supplement**, (1902) 244-261.

"The Order of Hegelian Categories in the Hegelian Argument," **Mind** 12 (1903) 317-340.

With Eleanor A. McGamble. "Die reproduzierte Vorstellung bein Wiedererkennen und bein vergleichen," **Sonder-Abdruck aus Zietschrift fur Physiologie der Sinnesorgane** 32 (1903) 177-193.

"Review of J.M.E. McTaggert's **Hegelian Cosmology**," **Philosophical Review** 12 (1903) 187-193.

"The Life and Teachings of Herbert Spencer," **The Outlook** 75 (Dec. 1903) 951-955.

With Eleanor A. McGamble. "Uber die Bedeutung von Wortvorstellungen fur die Unterscheidung von Qualitaten sukzessiver Reize," Teil 2, **Sonder-**

Abruck aus **Zeitschrift fur Psychologie und Physiologie der Sinnesorgane** 33 (1903) 161-170.

"Review of Margaret F. Washburn, **Some Examples of the Use of Psychological Analysis in System-making,**" **Psychological Review** 10 (1903) 128-132.

"On the Attributes of Sensation," **Psychological Review** 10 (1904) 221-222.

"Voluntaristic Psychology, Review of Nikolaj Losskij's **Die Grundlehren der Psychologie vom Standpunkte des Voluntarismus, Psychological Bulletin** 1 (1904) 185-187.

"The Limits of Genetic and of Comparative Psychology, **British Journal of Psychology** 1 (Jan. 1905) 261-285.

"A Reconciliation between Structural and Functional Psychology," **Psychological Review** 13 (March 1906) 61-81.

"Psychology: What Is It About?" **Journal of Philosophy** 4 (1907) 673-683.

"Is the Self Body or Does It Have Body?" **Journal of Philosophy, Psychology, and Scientific Method** 5 (1908) 12-20.

"The Ego and Empirical Psychology," **Psychological Bulletin,** 5 (1908) 27-30.

"Psychology as the Science of Self," **Journal of Philosophy, Psychology, and Scientific Method** 5 (1908) 64-68; 113-122.

"The Relation of Feeling to Emotion," **Psychological Bulletin,** 5 (Oct. 1908) 340-344.

"Self and Soul." **Philosophical Review** 17 (Jan. 1908) 272-280.

"Ultimate Hypotheses in Psychology," **Journal of Philosophy, Psychology, and Scientific Method** 5 (Nov. 1908) 634-635.

"The Abandonment of Sensationalism in Psychology," **American Journal of Psychology** 20 (1908) 269-277.

"Professor Titchener on Thought Processes," **Psychological Bulletin** 7 (Sept. 1910) 293-297.

"The Teaching of Elementary Psychology in Colleges Supposed to Have No Laboratory," **Psychological Monographs** 12 (No. 51) (1910) 41-53.

"Review of K. Osterreich's **Phenomenologie des Ich**," **Philosophical Review** 20 (1911) 636-641.

"General Standpoints: Mind and Body," **Psychological Bulletin** 8 (1911) 14-19.

"The Religious and Character Values of the Curriculum," **Religious Education** 6 (1911) 390-394.

"The Idealist to the Realist," **Journal of Philosophy, Psychology, and Scientific Method** 8 (August 1911) 449-450.

"Defective Logic in the Discussion of Religious Experience," **Journal of Philosophy, Psychology, and Scientific Method** 4 (Oct. 1911) 606-608.

"The Nature of Prayer," **Harvard Theological Review** 4 (Oct. 1911) 489-500.

"The Religious and Character Values of the Curriculium," **Religious Education** 6 (Dec. 1911) 390-394.

"Mr. Muscio's Criticism of Miss Calkins' Reply to the Realist," **Journal of Philosophy, Psychology, and Scientific Method** 9 (1912) 603-606.

"Review of A. W. Moore's **Pragmatism and Its Critics, International Journal of Ethics** 22 (1912) 222-226.

"Henri Bergson, Personalist." **Philosophical Review** 21 (Nov. 1912) 666 - 675.

"The Self in Recent Psychology," **Psychological Bulletin** 9 (1912) 25-30.

"Unjustified Cases for Neo-Realism." **Philosophical Review** 22 (Jan. 1913) pp. 53 - 56.

"Psychology and the Behaviorist," **Psychological Bulletin** 10 (1913) 288-291.

"Idealist to Realist, Once More," **Journal of Philosophy, Psychology, and Scientific Method** 11 (May 1914) 297-298.

"Arthur Schopenhauer and His Philosophy," in **The German Classics of the Nineteenth and Twentieth Centuries**, Ed. Kuno Francke, 15, New York: The German Publication Society, 1914, 1-16.

"Bertrand Russell on Neo-Realism." **Philosophical Review** 24 (Sept. 1915) 533 - 537.

"The Self in Scientific Psychology," **American Journal of Psychology** 26 (Oct. 1915) 495-524.

"The Foundation of Royce's Philosophy for Christian Theism," **Philosophical Review** 25 (1916) 282-293.

"The Self in Recent Psychology." **Psychological Bulletin,** 13 (Jan. 1916) 20-27.

"Review of B. Varisco, **The Great Problems, Journal of Philosophy,** 13 (1916) 132-135.

"Purposing Self Versus Potent Soul: A Discussion of Professor Warren's **Study of Purpose,**" **Journal of Philosophy, Psychology, and Scientific Method** 14 (April 1917) 197-200.

"Militant Pacifism," **International Journal of Ethics** 28 (1917) 70-79.

"The Case of Self Against Soul," **Psychological Review** 24 (1917) 278-300.

"A Clue to Holt's Treatment of the Freudian Wish," **Journal of Philosophy, Psychology, and Scientific Method** 14 (1917) 441-442.

"Aplogia Pro Philosophia," **Nation** 105 (1917) 12-13.

"Review of DeWitt H. Parker's **The Self and Nature, Psychological Bulletin** 15 (1918) 123-124.

"The New Rationalism and Objective Idealism." **Philosophical Review** 28 (Nov. 1919) 598 - 605.

"The Personalistic Conception of Nature.: **Philosophical Review**, 28 (March 1919) 115 - 146.

"Spaulding's Relations and Subsistent Entities," **Journal of Philosophy, Psychology and Scientific Method** 16 (Nov. 1919) 635-640.

"Review of May Sinclair's **A Defence of Idealism**," **Harvard Theological Review** 12 (1919) 123-128.

"The Self in Recent Psychology: A Critical Summary," **Psychological Bulletin** 16 (1919) 111-118.

"The Equivocal Position of the Presentation in the Psychology of James Ward," **Psychological Bulletin** 17 (1920) 492-432.

"The Metaphysical Monist as a Sociological Pluralist," **Journal of Philosophy, Psychology, and Scientific Method** 17 (Dec. 1920) 681-685.

"Review of C.A. Richardson's **Spiritual Pluralism and Recent Philosophy**, **Philosophical Review** 30 (1921) 507-519.

"The Truly Psychological Behaviorism," **Psychological Review** (1921) 1-28.

"Fact and Inference in Raymond Wheeler's Doctrine of Will and Self-activity," **Psychological Review** 28 (1921) 356-373.

"The Ancient Landmarks: A Comment on Spiritualistic Materialism," **Journal of Philosophy** 19 (August 1922) 493-497.

"Professor Keyser on Russell's **Analysis of Mind**," **Science** 55 (1922) 44-45.

"The Divergent Results of Analysis," **Psychological Review** 30 (1923) 148-150.

"Philosophers in Council," **School and Society** 17 (March 1923) 316-320.

"The Dual Role of Mind in the Philosophy of S. Alexander," **Mind** 30 (1923) 197-210.

"The Foundations of Psychology," **Journal of Philosophy** 20 (1923) 5-15.

"MacDougall's Treatment of Experience," **British Journal   of Psychology** 13
(1923) 337-343.

"Review of Robert MacDougall **The General Problems of Psychology**,"
Philosophical Review 32 (1923) 536-543.

"Review of C.D. Burns, **The Contact Between Minds, Journal of Philosophy**
20 (Nov. 1923) 629-632.

"A Personal Idealist Concern for Psychology," **The Personalist** 5 (Jan. 1924) 7-
11.

"Kant's Doctrine of Knowledge."   In **Immanuel Kant 1724-1924**, Ed. E. C.
Wilm. New Haven. Yale, 1925, 17-22.

"Review of M.P. Follett's **Creative Experience**," **Philosophical Review** 33
(1924) 12-22.

"Converging Lines in Contemporary Philosophy," **British Journal of Psychology**
16 (Jan. 1926) 171-179.

"Critical comments on the **Gestalt-theorie**," **Psychological Review** 33 (March
1926) 135-158.

"On Certain Difficulties in the Modern Doctrine of Essence," **Journal of
Philosophy** 23 (Dec. 1926) 701-710.

"The Ambiguous Concept: Meaning," **American Journal of Psychology** 39
(Dec. 1927) 7-22.

"The Basis of Objective Judgment in Subjective Ethics," **Proceedings of the Sixth
International Congress of Philosophy** 1927, 408-414.

"Biological or Psychological? A Comment of Perry's Doctrine of Interest and
Value," **Journal of Philosophy** 24 (Oct. 1927) 577-581.

"Self-awareness And Meaning," **The American Journal of Psychology** 38 (July
1927) 441-448.

"The Self in Recent Psychology," **Psychological Bulletin** 24 (April 1927) 205-
215.

"Value - - Primarily a Psychological Conception," **Journal of Philosophical Studies** 3 (Oct. 1928) 413-426.

"Analysis: Chemical or Psychological," **Psychological Review** 36 (1929) 348-352.

With E. A. McGamble and M.I. Zigler, "Some Recent Books in the Field of Psychology," **Wellesley Alumnae Magazine** 14 (1929) 71-73.

"Sociology Is a Psychological Science," **Adult Bible Class Magazine** 23 (1929) 162-163.

"The Case Against Behaviorism," **Sewannee Review** 38 (1930) 199-209.

"Autobiography." In **History of Psychology in Autobiography**, Worcester: Macmillan, 1930, 31-62.

With Eleanor A. McGamble. "The Self-psychology of the Psychoanalysts," **Psychological Review** 32 (1930) 277-304.

"The Philosophical Credo of An Absolute Personalist." In **Contemporary American Philosophy: Personal Statements**, ed. G.P. Adams and W.P. Montaque. New York: Macmillan, 1930, I, 197-218.

General Bibliography

This bibliography is suggestive rather than comprehensive. It is a selection of books providing background for seventeenth, eighteenth and nineteenth century women and philosophy. Recent books listed present additional historical evidence, or they represent current twentieth century issues, some of which carry forward the philosophical traditions begun or added to by the philosophers of this text.

A Selected Bibliography of Books About Women in Philosophy

Alexander, William. **The History of Women from Earliest Antiquity to the Present Time**. London: C. Dilly, 1732.

Alic, Margaret, **Hypatia's Heritage:A history of women in science from antiquity through the Nineteenth Century.** Boston: Beacon,1986.

Allen, Prudence, R.S.M. **The Concept of Woman:The Aristotelian Revolution 750-1250.** Montreal, Canada: Eden Press, 1985.

Ballard, George. **Memoirs of Several Ladies of Great Britain**. Oxford: W. Jackson, 1752.

Barth, Else M. **Women Philosophers: A Bibliography of Books Through 1990.** Bowling Green: Philosophy Documentation Center, 1992.

Bell, Linda A. **Visions of Women.** Clifton, New Jersey: Humana Press, 1983.

Benson, Mary Summer. **Women in Eighteenth Century America.** New York: Columbia UP, 1935.

Berkin, Carol Ruth and Mary Beth Norton, eds. **The Women of America, A History.** Boston: Houghton Mifflin, 1979.

Birch, Una. **Anna Van Schurman: Artist, Scholar, Saint.** New York: Longmans Green, 1909.

Brink, Jean R. **Female Scholars: A Tradition of Learned Women Before 1800.** Montreal, Canada: Eden, 1980.

Child, Lydia Maria. **A Brief History of Women in Various Ages and Nations.** New York: C.S. Frances, 1845.

Cixous, Helene and Catherine Clement. **The Newly Born Woman.**tr. Betsy Wing, Minneapolis: Minnesota UP, 1986.

Code, Lorraine **What Can She Know**. Ithaca: Cornell UP, 1991.

Cott, Nancy F. **The Root of Bitterness**. New York: Dutton, 1972.

----- **The Bonds of Womanhood: "Woman's Sphere" in New England, 1780-1833.** New Haven: Yale UP. 1977.

Crocker, Hannah Mather. **Observations on the Real Rights of Women and Their Appropriate Duties Agreeable to Scripture, Reason, and Common Sense**. Boston: Author, 1818.

Cross, Barbara M. **The Educated Woman in America.** New York: Teachers College, 1965.

Daly, Mary. **Gyn/Ecology**. Boston: Beacon, 1978.

Dorland, William A. Newman. **The Sum of Feminine Achievement**. ? Stratford, 1977.

Drake, Judith. **An Essay in Defence of the Female Sex** (1696). New York: Source Book, 1970.

Fell, Margaret **"Women's Speaking Justified"** (1667) Los Angeles: University of Calif, 1979.

Eisenstein. Hester. **Contemporary Feminist Thought**, Boston: G.K.Hall, 1983.

Gallant, Corinne. **La Philosophie au Feminin**. Moncton, N.B.: Les Editions d'Acadie, 1984.

Gould, Carol C. **Beyond Domination: New Perspectives on Women and Philosophy.** Totowa, New Hersey: Rowman and Allanheld, 1984.

Griffiths, Morwenna, and Margaret Whitford, eds. **Feminist Perspectives in**

Philosophy. Bloomington: Indiana UP, 1988.

Grimke, Sarah. **Letters on the Equality of the Sexes and Other Essay** (1838). ed. Elizabeth Ann Bartlett. New Haven: Yale UP, 1988.

Grimshaw, Jean, **Philosophy and Feminist Thinking.** University of Minnesota Press: Minneapolis, 1986.

Griswald, Rufus Wilmot. **The Female Poets of America.** New York: James Miller, 1873.

Hale, Sarah Josepha. **Biography of Distinguished Women;or Woman's Record.** New York: Harper, 1876.

Harding, Sandra and Merrill B. Hintikka, eds. **Discovering Reality**, Boston: D. Reidel, 1983.

Hays, Mary. **Female Biography.** 3 vols., 1807.

Heywood, Thomas. **The General History of Women.** London: W.H., 1657.

Hill, Bridget. **The First English Feminist.** Aldershot, England: Gower, 1986.

Holland, Nancy J. **Is Women's Philosophy Possible?** Savage, MD: Rowman and Littlefield, 1990.

Ilsley, Marjorie Henry. **A Daughter of the Renaissance: Marie le Jars de Gournay, Her Life and Works.** The Hague: Mouton, 1963.

Ireland, Norma Olin. **Index to Women of the World from Ancient to Modern Times.** Westwood, Mass.: F.W. Faxon, 1970.

Jagger, Alison and Paul Rothenberg Struhl, eds. **Feminist Frameworks**. McGraw-Hill Book Company, 1978.

James, Edward et.al.**Notable American Women**. Cambridge, Mass: Belknap, 1971.

Jordan, Constance. **Renaissance Feminism.** Ithaca, N.Y.:Cornell UP, 1990.

Keohane, Nannerl O., Michelle Z. Rosaldo, and Barbara C. Gelpi, eds.
Feminist Theory: A Critique of Ideology. Sussex, England: Harvester,
1982.

Kersey, Ethel. **Women Philosophers**. New York: Greenwood, 1989.

Mahowold, Mary, **Philosophy of Woman: Classical to Current Concepts,**
Hackett: Indianapolis, 1983.

Mason, Mary Grimley and Carol Hurd Green, eds. **Journeys:
Autobiographical Writings by Women**. Boston: G.K. Hall, 1979.

Mènage, Gilles, **The History of Women Philosophers,** tr. Beatrice
H. Zedler.Lanham, MD: University of America, 1984.

Millman, Marcia and Rosabeth Moss Kantor, eds. **Another Voice**.
New York: Anchor, 1975.

Nye, Andrea, **Feminist Theory and the Philosophies of Man**. Croom Helm:
London, 1988.

-----. **Words of Power: A History of Logic.** New York: Routledge, 1990.

O'Barr, Jean F. **Women and a New Academy**. Madison: University of
Wisconsin, 1989.

Okin, Susan Moller, **Women in Western Political Thought,** Princeton
University Press, Princeton, N.J., 1979.

Ostriker, Alician Suskin. **Stealing the Language**. Boston: Beacon, 1986.

Our Famous Women. Hartford: A.D. Worthington, 1884.

Peden, Margaret Sayers. **A Woman of Genius,** Salisbury, CT: Lime Rock, 1982.

Perry, Ruth. **The Celebrated Mary Astell:An Early English Feminist.** Chicago,
University of Chicago P, 1986.

Poulain de la Barre, Francois. **The Equality of the Sexes** tr. Desmond M. Clarke,
England:Manchester UP, 1990.

Reynolds, Myra. **The Learned lady in England 1650-1760.** Gloucester,
Mass.: Peter Smith, 1964. (Published in honor of Vassar 50th 1865-1915),
1920.

Richards, S.A. **Feminist Writers of the Seventeenth Century.** London: David
Nutt, 1914.

Riley, Glenda. **Inventing the American Woman (1607-1877).**
Arlington Hieghts, Ill.:Harland Davidson, 1986.

Schiebinger, Londa. **The Mind Has No Sex? Women in the Origins of
Modern Science.** Cambridge: Harvard UP, 1989.

Seigfried, Charlene Haddock, **William James's Radical Reconstruction of
Philosophy.** Ithica: State University of New York, 1990.

Shirley, John. **The Illustrious History of Women or a Compendium of the
Many Virtues That Adorn the Sex.** London: John Harris, 1686.

Smith, Hilda L. **Reason's Disciples: Seventeenth-Century English
Feminists.** Urbana: University of Illinois P, 1982.

Spender, Dale. **Women of Ideas and What Men Have Done to Them: From
Aphra Behn to Adrienne Rich.** London: Routledge & Kegan Paul, 1982.

A Sor Juana Anthology. trans. Alan S. Trueblood. Cambridge, Mass.:
Harvard UP, 1988.

Stewart, Maria W., **America's First Black Political Writer.** Editor, Marilyn
Richardson. Bloomington: Indiana UP, 1987.

Tuana, Nancy. **Woman and the History of Philosophy.** New York:
Paragon, 1992

Vetterling-Braggain,Mary, Frederick A. Elliston and Jane English, Editors.
Feminism and Philosophy, New Jersey: Littlefield, Adams, 1977.

Waithe, Mary Ellen, **A History of Women Philosophers,** v.l/600 B.C.-500 A.D.,
v.2/500-1600 A.D., v. 3/1600-1900. Dordrecht, The Netherlands: Martinus
Nijhoff Pub.1987, 1989, 1990.

Whitbeck, Caroline. **A Directory of Women in Philosophy**. Bowling Green, Ohio:Philosophy Document Center, 1980.

Wilson, Katherina M. and Frank J. Warnke, eds. **Women Writers of the Seventeenth Century**. Athens: University of Georgia Press, 1989.

Wister, O.J. and Agnes Irwin, Editors. **Worthy Women of Our First Century** (1877). Plainview, N.Y.: Books for Libraries, 1975.

Wollstonecraft, Mary. **Vindication of the Rights of Woman: With Strictures on Political and Moral Subjects**. London: J. Johnson, 1792.

Index

G

Gabrielle, 170
Gage, Matilda J., 202
Galileo, 7
Gallant, Corinne, 374
Gerry, Elbridge, 72, 73, 79
Gethin, Grace, 172
Gilbert, Sandra M., 22
Gilligan Carol, 27
God, 5, 30, 33, 34, 39, 41, 43, 44,
    45, 46, 47, 48, 50, 51, 52, 53,
    54, 56, 57, 66, 67, 124, 126,
    136, 140, 141, 142, 146, 149,
    154, 161, 232, 276, 277, 281,
    282, 295, 301, 302, 303, 305-
    314, 317, 319, 344, 358
Goddard, Lucy, 269
Godwin, William, 207, 208
Goethe, Johann, 8, 265, 268, 275,
    278, 282, 294, 296, 303, 306,
    307, 309, 322
good, 2, 30, 32, 33, 34, 38, 43, 44,
    49, 51, 52, 54, 55, 56, 69, 73,
    85, 96, 132, 145, 150, 171,
    176, 178, 207, 211, 214, 227,
    228, 237, 239, 245, 248, 250,
    252, 269, 272, 276, 278, 283,
    286-289, 291, 292, 293, 307,
    309, 310, 312, 314, 335, 337,
    341, 343, 344, 349, 352, 365
de Gournay, Marie 1,8,301
government, 5, 24, 65, 69, 70, 71,
    75, 76, 77, 78, 79, 83-93, 95,
    98- 101, 129-131, 157,167,
    193, 197, 242, 244, 255, 343,
    349, 350
Grey, Lady Jane, 160
Griffiths, Morwena, 374
Grimke, Sarah, 256
Grimshaw, Jean, 375
Guyon, 170

H

Hadewych of Antwerp, 11
Hale, Sarah H., 375
happiness, 83, 86, 100, 128, 143,
    146, 170, 178, 206, 207, 211,
    214, 217, 218, 220, 238, 244,
    245, 248, 253, 283, 284, 313,
    361
Harris, William Torrey, viii, 271, 326
Harding, Sandra, 375
Hartsock, Nancy, 2
Hays, Mary, 375
Hegel, G.W.F., 8, 275, 278
Hegelian, 366
Heilbrun, Carolyn, 11, 13
Hildegard of Bingen, 11
Hill, Bridget, 375
history, viii, 1- 4, 7, 9, 13, 14,
    20, 24, 25, 29- 31, 34, 59,
    64, 65- 67, 73, 75-79, 103,
    104, 112-114, 116, 117, 129,
    131, 149, 165-167, 171, 172,
    180, 182, 183-186, 193, 195,
    201, 203, 209, 213, 219, 224-
    226, 255, 259, 264, 268, 272,
    275, 278, 282, 286, 288, 293-
    296, 299, 302, 305, 310, 319,
    322, 326, 335, 336, 343, 354,
    372- 377
Hobbes, Thomas, 7
Holbach, Dietrich, van 207
Holland, Nancy, 11,13
Hortensia, 165
Howe, Julia Ward, 263, 271, 272,
    302
human, 5, 6, 22, 33, 59, 76, 78-80,
    83-86, 90, 95, 96, 101, 102,
    131, 138, 150, 154, 173, 195,
    196, 201, 209, 211, 213-217,
    221- 226, 228, 230-232, 239,

382

L

Langer, Suzanne K. 11, 13, 376
law, 65, 77, 80, 84, 89, 90, 91, 129,
    153, 170, 199, 203, 208, 219,
    230, 234, 251, 259, 282, 284,
    286, 291, 299, 306, 312, 316,
    317, 337, 351
Leibniz, Gottfried, 354, 358, 363,
    366
Lerner, Gerda, 201,258
liberal, 86, 113, 149, 183, 196, 198,
    208, 268, 337
liberty, 5, 65, 68, 73, 77, 83, 84, 86,
    89, 90, 91, 97, 98, 100, 103,
    123, 138, 140, 186, 201, 202,
    208, 209, 213, 233-235, 238-
    244, 246, 250, 251, 256, 318
Lincoln, Abraham, vii
Locke, John, 7, 68, 114, 337
logic, 14, 25, 368, 376
Longinus, 168
Louise of Prussia, 314
love, 24, 32, 33, 39, 76, 85, 98, 112,
    127, 136, 137, 145, 150, 158,
    199, 211, 234, 272, 284, 285,
    287-289, 294, 297, 300, 306-
    308, 310, 311, 313, 318, 319,
    341, 343
Lucretia, 24, 266, 321

M

Macauley, Catherine, 8, 78, 172
Machiavelli, Nicolo, 268
Mahowold, Mary, 376
Makin, Bathsua, 28
Mammaea, Julia, 167
Margaret of Anjou, 162
Martineau, Helen, 203
Mary Stuart, 169
Masham, Lady Damaris, 172

Mason, Mary, 376
materialism, 7, 359, 370
matter, 6, 31, 32, 34, 35, 51, 121,
    124, 129, 130, 131, 182, 193,
    206, 207, 214, 215, 218, 220,
    223, 226, 229, 232, 240, 246,
    249, 252, 255, 276-278, 281,
    282, 284, 291, 302,309, 314,
    346
Mechtild of Magdeburg, 11
memory, 18, 26, 84, 92, 98, 125,
    131, 138, 139, 150, 156, 158,
    167, 173, 175, 213, 214, 221,
    313, 366
metaphysics, 4, 124, 172,
    302, 306, 334, 338, 354, 364
method, 6, 121, 122, 129, 131, 211,
    225, 226, 269, 271, 276, 277,
    278, 296, 364, 367, 368, 369,
    370
Mill, John Stuart, 31, 196, 206, 208,
    209, 235
Millman, Marcia, 376
mind, 2, 21, 22, 29, 32, 34, 44, 46,
    55, 66, 83, 84, 86, 89-91,
    98, 101, 111, 117, 118, 123,
    124-126, 128-130, 136-145,
    147-150, 155, 156, 158, 159,
    161, 163, 168, 169, 171, 173,
    175, 177, 178, 186, 192, 196,
    201, 206, 207, 209, 214-216,
    222, 223, 225, 226, 233, 234,
    240-249, 251, 252, 254, 272,
    277, 283, 285, 287, 290, 295,
    296, 302, 306, 315, 319, 348,
    352, 357, 362, 363, 366, 368,
    370, 377
Minerva, 25, 26, 206
Montague, Mary Wortley, 172, 202
Moore, 172
morality, 25, 27, 31, 33, 34, 51, 150,
    252, 286

transcendentalism, viii, 3, 209, 268, 272, 278, 322
Trinity, 198, 302, 306, 307
Trollope, Frances, 192, 257
truth, 7, 83, 86, 89, 91, 96, 100, 101, 122, 124, 136, 138, 140, 144, 152, 155, 161, 169, 208, 209, 210, 211, 214, 215, 216, 217, 220, 222, 224, 227, 228, 230, 232, 234, 239, 248, 249, 250, 273, 277, 282, 283, 285, 297, 298, 303, 307, 309, 311-313, 316, 319, 339, 342, 344- 347, 350, 353, 358, 359
Tuana, Nancy, 377
Tubman, Harriet, 270

U

understanding, viii, 4, 6, 9, 10, 23, 26, 32, 77, 78, 92, 99, 150, 157, 159, 164, 168, 172, 175, 215, 223, 238, 297, 357, 364
unity, 22, 186, 276, 278, 291, 293, 294, 305, 306, 314, 358
utilitarianism vii, viii, 10, 206, 211

V

Valdemer, Margaret, 130
values, 13, 30, 31, 34, 70, 71, 73, 341, 368
Vetterling-Braggain, Mary, 375
Veturia, 164
virtue, 32, 33, 65, 67, 75, 83, 84, 86, 88, 92, 97, 98, 100, 126, 128, 132, 146, 149, 152, 153, 159, 165, 166, 167, 169, 172, 178, 182, 228, 230, 245, 247, 251, 252, 312, 313, 337, 339, 342, 345, 347, 356

volition, 224
Volumnia, 164

W

Waithe, Mary Ellen, 117
Washington, Martha, 109, 114, 115
wealth, 26, 27, 45, 54, 56, 67, 70, 71, 76, 77, 78, 79, 99, 243, 245, 286, 300
Wharton, Anna, 172
Whitbeck, Caroline, 14, 377
White, Elizabeth Wade, 19, 20, 21, 22, 25, 26, 27, 30, 60, 67, 105, 199, 206, 325
will, 34, 46, 77, 78
Williams, Anna M., 174
Wilson, Katherina, M. 377
Winchelsea, Anne, 172
Wittgenstein, Ludwig, 31, 34
Wolff, Christian, 354, 359, 363
Wollstonecraft, Mary, 8, 112, 115- 117, 192, 207, 256, 258, 301
women, vii, viii, ix, 1-10, 13, 14, 21-26, 31, 58, 59, 66, 68, 69, 70, 104, 111-113, 115-118, 121-132, 148, 149, 151-157, 161-164, 166, 170, 173-175, 178, 179, 182, 183-187, 196, 197, 199, 202, 206-211, 214, 227, 232-235, 239, 241, 247, 248, 256-260, 263, 264, 265, 269, 270, 271, 272, 275, 289, 301, 302, 308, 309, 315, 316, 319, 320-327, 331, 335, 336, 375-378
words, vii, 14, 39, 46, 47, 65, 69, 127, 132, 144, 164, 197, 202, 203, 206, 213, 215, 220-223, 226, 234, 243, 249, 250, 252, 270, 272, 291, 292, 295, 303, 308, 311, 345, 348, 361, 376